Praise for

THE WISDOM OF THE ENNEAGRAM

"*The Wisdom of the Enneagram* is a very important book. By combining the horizontal types of the Enneagram with a system of vertical levels of awareness, Riso and Hudson have produced one of the first truly integrated models of the human psyche. In addition to the importance of this pioneering work itself, it goes to point up the utter inadequacy of anything less than a full-spectrum model of human growth and development. Highly recommended."

—Ken Wilber, author of *The Marriage of Sense and Soul*

"I highly recommend this book, not only to anyone on the path of personal transformation, but to anyone who wants to understand the complex inner world of others, whether a spouse, family member, co-worker, or friend. The questionnaires were fun and illuminating. I received some very helpful information about myself, felt challenged to grow, and experienced a deepening of compassion. Perhaps the most profound contribution of *The Wisdom of the Enneagram* is reflected in the word 'wisdom.' The authors clearly communicate the complexity of human nature, the spiritual yearning resonant in all of us, and the ascending levels of our possibility. But they do not leave us there. They offer a clear path for personal and spiritual evolution."

—Harville Hendrix, Ph.D., author of *Getting the Love You Want*

"Don Riso and Russ Hudson thoughtfully engage the richness and depth of the Enneagram, and conjure with its power as a tool of transformation. *The Wisdom of the Enneagram* is filled with its own wisdom and depth. You'll find yourself returning to it over and over again and discovering new treasures."

—Tony Schwartz, author of *What Really Matters*

"*The Wisdom of the Enneagram* is not only a clear and comprehensive description and discussion of this ancient personality typology, but also a major and original contribution to its use and further development. Don Riso and Russ Hudson have designed simple, practical guidelines and tests that make it possible to determine one's own personality type and use this knowledge for healing and psychospiritual transformation."

—Stanislav Grof, M.D., author of *The Adventure of Self-Discovery*

▼

The Complete Guide to
Psychological and Spiritual
Growth for the
Nine Personality Types

THE
WISDOM
OF THE
ENNEAGRAM

DON RICHARD RISO
AND RUSS HUDSON

▲

BANTAM BOOKS   New York   Toronto   London   Sydney   Auckland

THE WISDOM OF THE ENNEAGRAM
A Bantam Book / June 1999

Library of Congress Cataloging-in-Publication Data
Riso, Don Richard.
The wisdom of the enneagram : the complete guide to
psychological and spiritual growth for the nine personality
types / Don Richard Riso and Russ Hudson.
p.   cm.
Includes bibliographical references.
ISBN 978-0-553-37820-7
1. Spiritual life.   2. Enneagram.   I. Hudson, Russ.   II. Title.
BL624.R57   1999
155.2'6—dc21   98-50577
CIP
Published simultaneously in the United States and Canada

PRINTED IN THE UNITED STATES OF AMERICA

24   23   22   21

*We dedicate this book to
the Ground of all Being,
the One from Whom we have come,
and to Whom we shall return,
the Font of wisdom and Light of lights,
the Maker, Renewer, and Keeper of all things.
May this book which comes from our hearts,
speak to the hearts of all who read it.*

CONTENTS

PREFACE

Beings of Light

WE ARE ALL DRIVEN by a deep inner restlessness. We may feel this restlessness as a sense that something is missing in us, although it is usually difficult to define exactly what it is. We have all sorts of notions about what we think we need or want—a better relationship, a better job, a better physique, a better car, and on and on. We believe that if we acquire that perfect relationship or job or new "toy," the restlessness will go away, and we will feel satisfied and complete. But experience teaches us that the new car makes us feel better for only a short time. The new relationship may be wonderful, but it never quite fulfills us in the way we thought it would. So what are we *really* looking for?

If we reflect for a moment, we may realize that what our hearts yearn for is *to know who we are* and *why we are here*. But little in our culture encourages us to look for answers to these important questions. We have been taught that the quality of our life will improve primarily if our external fortunes improve. Sooner or later, however, we realize that external things, while valuable in themselves, cannot address the deep restlessness of our soul.

So where can we look for answers?

Many of the currently available books on personal transformation speak movingly about the kind of person that we would all like to be. They recognize the vital importance of compassion, community, communication, and creativity. But as beautiful and attractive as these (and other) qualities are, we find it extremely difficult to maintain them or to put them into practice in our daily lives. Our hearts yearn to soar, yet we almost always come crashing down painfully on the rocks of fear, self-defeating habits, and ignorance. All too often our good intentions and noble hopes simply become new sources of disappointment. We give up on ourselves, return to familiar distractions, and try to forget about the whole matter.

> "There's a part of every living thing that wants to become itself, the tadpole into the frog, the chrysalis into the butterfly, a damaged human being into a whole one. That is spirituality."
>
> ELLEN BASS

"It seems to me that before we set out on a journey to find reality, to find God, before we can act, before we can have any relationship with another . . . it is essential that we begin to understand ourselves first."

KRISHNAMURTI

Are the vast majority of popular psychology books misguided or wrong? Are human beings really incapable of living more complete and fulfilling lives? The great spiritual and moral teachers throughout history have always insisted that we have the potential to achieve greatness—that we are, in fact, divine creatures in some real sense. So why do we find this state so hard to recognize and live up to?

We believe that most self-help books are not necessarily wrong, *but merely incomplete.* For example, even with a basic topic like weight loss, there are many possible reasons why a person might have a weight problem or issues with food—a sugar sensitivity, or excessive fat in the diet, or nervous eating to repress anxiety, or any number of other emotional issues. Without identifying the specific core issues that are causing the problem, no solution is likely, no matter how great the effort.

The self-help author's prescriptions are usually based on methods that have worked for him or her personally and reflect his or her own psychological makeup and personal process. If a reader happens to have a similar psychological makeup, the author's method may be effective. But if there is little "match," the reader may be misled rather than helped.

Any effective approach to growth must therefore take into account the fact that there are different kinds of people—*different personality types.* Historically many psychological and spiritual systems have attempted to address this key insight: astrology, numerology, the four classic temperaments (phlegmatic, choleric, melancholic, and sanguine), Jung's system of psychological types (extrovert and introvert orientations times sensation, intuition, feeling, and thinking functions), and many others. Furthermore, recent studies in infant development and in brain science have indicated that fundamental differences in temperament between different types of people have a biological basis.

This diversity explains why what is good advice for one person can be disastrous for another. Telling some types that they need to focus more on their feelings is like throwing water on a drowning man. Telling other types that they need to assert themselves more is as foolish as putting an anorexic person on a diet. In understanding ourselves, our relationships, our spiritual growth, and many other important issues, we will see that type—not gender, not culture, and not generational differences—is the crucial factor.

"Whatever your age, your upbringing, or your education, what you are made of is mostly unused potential."

GEORGE LEONARD

We believe that awareness of personality types is needed in many areas—in education, the sciences, business, the humanities, and therapy—and, above all, in spirituality and transformational work. While our restless yearnings may be universal, how they are expressed is much more particular and is, in fact, a function of the "filter" with which we approach all of life. The main filter that we use to understand ourselves and the world around us, to express ourselves, to defend ourselves, to deal with our past and anticipate our future, to learn with, to rejoice with, and to fall in love with, is our personality type.

What if there were a system that could enable us to have more insight into ourselves and others? What if it could help us discern our filters more clearly and take them into proper account? What if this system could show us our core psychological issues as well as our interpersonal strengths and weaknesses? What if this system did not depend on the pronouncements of experts or gurus, or on our birth date, or our birth order, but on our personality patterns and our willingness to honestly explore ourselves? What if this system showed us not only our core issues, but also pointed out effective ways of dealing with them? What if this system also directed us toward the depths of our soul? Such a system exists, and it is called the Enneagram.

BEINGS OF LIGHT

One of the most important incidents of my life happened to me, Don, several years ago when I was involved in a week-long spiritual retreat in upstate New York. About fifty of us were staying in a turn-of-the-century hotel that our teacher owned. Since the grounds and interior of the old house perpetually needed upkeep, it was a perfect place for us to do some grueling manual labor—and an occasion to observe our resistances and reactions while we worked. The summer heat was intense, the showers few, the lines to the common bathrooms long, and there were almost no rest periods. As we were aware, all of these physical and communal conditions were engineered by our teacher to bring out our personality "features" so that we could observe ourselves more clearly in the intensity of this living laboratory.

One afternoon we were given a rare opportunity to have a forty-five-minute nap between chores. I had been assigned to scrape paint off the outside of the old hotel, and was soon covered from head to toe with tiny weathered chips. By the end of our work session, I was so tired and sweaty that I did not care how grubby I felt—I needed a nap, and as soon as we were dismissed from our chores, I was the first one upstairs and into bed. Most of the other guys who shared the dorm room with me dragged themselves in shortly after, and within five minutes we were all settling down to sleep.

Just then, our one remaining roommate, Alan, banged his way into the room. He had been assigned to look after the children of group members, and it was clear from the way he was flinging things around that he was mad that he could not get off duty earlier for a nap himself. He did, however, have time to make enough noise so that no one else could rest, either.

"Spiritually speaking, everything that one wants, aspires to, and needs is ever-present, accessible here and now—for those with eyes to see."

SURYA DAS

"Spirit is an invisible force
made visible in all life."

MAYA ANGELOU

But shortly after Alan came crashing through the door, something amazing happened to me: I saw my negative reactions to him rising in my body like a train pulling into a station, and *I did not get on the train.* In a moment of simple clarity, I saw Alan with his anger and frustration—I saw his behavior for what it was without further elaboration—and I saw my anger "loading up" to let him have it—and I did not react to any of it.

When I simply observed my reactions of anger and self-justification rather than acting on them, it was as if a veil were suddenly pulled from my eyes, and *I opened up.* Something that normally blocked my perception dissolved in an instant, and the world became completely alive. Alan was suddenly lovable, and the other guys were perfect in their reactions, whatever they were. Just as astonishingly, as I turned my head and looked out the window, I saw that everything around me was glowing from within. The sunlight on the trees, the swaying of the leaves in the wind, the slight rattle of the panes of glass in the old window frame, were too beautiful for words. I was enthralled at how miraculous everything was. Absolutely everything was beautiful.

I was still in this state of amazed ecstasy when I joined the rest of the group for a late-afternoon meditation. As the meditation deepened, I opened my eyes and looked around the room—and fell into what I can only describe as an inner vision, the impression of which has stayed with me for years.

What I saw was that everyone there was a "being of light." I saw clearly that everyone is made of light—that we are like forms of light— but that a crust has formed over it. The crust is black and rubbery like tar and has obscured the inner light that is everyone's real, inner self. Some blotches of tar are very thick; other areas are thinner and more transparent. Those who have worked on themselves for longer have less tar and they radiate more of their inner light. Because of their personal history, others are covered with more tar and need a great deal of work to get free of it.

After about an hour the vision grew dim and eventually shut down. When the meditation was over, we had more work to do, and I rushed to take one of the most frequently avoided tasks, washing dishes in the steamy kitchen. But because the residue of ecstasy was still palpable, that chore, too, was a moment of bliss.

I share this story not only because of its significance for me personally but because it graphically showed me that the things we are talking about in this book are real. If we observe ourselves truthfully and non-judgmentally, seeing the mechanisms of our personality in action, *we can wake up, and our lives can be a miraculous unfolding of beauty and joy.*

USING THIS BOOK

The Enneagram can help us only if we are honest with ourselves. Thus, the elements of the system—and this book—are best used as a guide to self-observation and self-inquiry. We have designed this book with many practical features to help you use it this way, including:

▶ Each type's healing attitudes, gifts, and specific transformational process

▶ How to "observe and let go" of troublesome habits and reactions

▶ How to work with the motivations of each type

▶ Unconscious childhood messages

▶ Therapeutic strategies for each type

▶ "Spiritual jump starts," Wake-up Calls, and Red Flags for each type

▶ How to cultivate awareness in your daily life

▶ Inner Work sessions and practices for each type

▶ How to use the system for continuing spiritual growth

Since it is helpful to do the exercises in this book in a journal of some kind, you might want to dedicate a notebook or loose-leaf binder for this purpose. We suggest that you use your Inner Work Journal to record the insights that will come to you as you read about your personality type as well as the other eight types. Most people find that this information also brings up all kinds of related issues, memories, and creative inspirations.

As a first exercise in your Inner Work Journal, we suggest you write a biography of yourself—not an autobiography. Write about yourself in the third person—that is, as "he" or "she" rather than "I." Tell your life story, beginning from your earliest years (or earlier, from what you know of your family history) up to the present time as if you were describing someone else. You may also wish to dedicate a page in your Inner Work Journal to each decade, leaving room to add relevant thoughts and observations as you recall more. Do not worry about being literary or "correct." The important thing is to see your life as a whole, as if told by someone else.

What have been the defining moments of your life—your traumas and triumphs—those times when you knew that, for better or worse, your life would never be the same? Who have been the most significant people in your life—those who have acted as "witnesses" to your struggles and growth, those who have hurt you, and those who have been your understanding mentors and friends? Be as detailed as possible.

Come back to your biography whenever you wish to add something and as you move through this book and gain more insight into yourself. Your story will become richer and more meaningful as you understand yourself more deeply.

PART I

▼

The
Inward
Journey

▲

CHAPTER 1

▼

IDENTIFYING YOUR PERSONALITY TYPE

▲

THE ENNEAGRAM (pronounced "ANY-a-gram") is a geometric figure that maps out the nine fundamental personality types of human nature and their complex interrelationships. It is a development of modern psychology that has roots in spiritual wisdom from many different ancient traditions. The word *Enneagram* comes from the Greek for "nine"—*ennea*—and "figure"—*grammos;* thus, it is a "nine-pointed figure."

The modern Enneagram of personality type has been synthesized from many different spiritual and religious traditions. Much of it is a condensation of universal wisdom, the perennial philosophy accumulated by Christians, Buddhists, Muslims (especially the Sufis), and Jews (in the Kabbalah) for thousands of years. The heart of the Enneagram is the universal insight that human beings are spiritual presences incarnated in the material world and yet mysteriously embodying the same life and Spirit as the Creator. Beneath surface differences and appearances, behind the veils of illusion, the light of Divinity shines in every individual. Various forces obscure that light, however, and each spiritual tradition has myths and doctrines to explain how mankind has lost its connection with the Divine.

One of the great strengths of the Enneagram is that it steps aside from all doctrinal differences. It has helped individuals from virtually every major religious faith to rediscover their fundamental unity as spiritual beings. The Enneagram can therefore be enormously valuable in today's world to show white and black, male and female, Catholic and Protestant, Arab and Jew, straight and gay, rich and poor that if they search beneath the surface differences that separate them, they will find an entirely new level of common humanity. With the help of the Enneagram, we will discover that Sixes are like all other Sixes—and

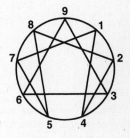

THE ENNEAGRAM

"The great metaphors from all spiritual traditions—grace, liberation, being born again, awakening from illusion—testify that it is possible to transcend the conditioning of my past and do a new thing."

SAM KEEN

"Do not weep; do not wax indignant. Understand."

SPINOZA

that they share the same values as others of their type. Ones who are black are much more like Ones who are white than they could have imagined, and so forth. A new level of community and compassion emerges that obliterates old ignorance and fear.

The Enneagram is not a religion, however; nor does it interfere with a person's religious orientation. It does not pretend to be a complete spiritual path. Nevertheless, it concerns itself with one element that is fundamental to all spiritual paths: *self-knowledge*.

Without self-knowledge, we will not get very far on our spiritual journey, nor will we be able to sustain whatever progress we have made. One of the great dangers of transformational work is that the ego attempts to sidestep deep psychological work by leaping into the transcendent too soon. This is because the ego always fancies itself much more "advanced" than it actually is. How many first-year novices have persuaded themselves that they are just about ready for sainthood? How many meditation students have been certain that they attained enlightenment in record-breaking time?

Real self-knowledge is an invaluable guardian against such self-deception. The Enneagram takes us places (and makes real progress possible) because it starts working from where we actually are. As much as it reveals the spiritual heights that we are capable of attaining, it also sheds light clearly and nonjudgmentally on the aspects of our lives that are dark and unfree. If we are going to live as spiritual beings in the material world, then these are the areas we most need to explore.

Presence (awareness, mindfulness), *the practice of self-observation* (gained from self-knowledge), and *understanding what one's experiences mean* (an accurate interpretation provided by a larger context such as a community or spiritual system) are the three basic elements needed for transformational work. *Being* supplies the first, *you* supply the second, and *the Enneagram* supplies the third. When these three come together, things can happen quickly.

"What can we gain by sailing to the moon if we are not able to cross the abyss that separates us from ourselves?"

THOMAS MERTON

INTRODUCING THE NINE TYPES

Work with the Enneagram starts when you identify your type and begin to understand its dominant issues.

While we will recognize in ourselves behaviors of all nine types, our most defining characteristics are rooted in one of these types. On page 13 you will find a questionnaire, the Riso-Hudson QUEST, that can help you narrow down your basic type, and at the beginning of each type chapter there is a second independent test, the Riso-Hudson TAS or Type Attitude Sorter, to help you check your findings. Between these two tests and the descriptions and exercises in the type chapters, you should be able to discover your type with a high degree of certainty.

For now, read the following type names and brief descriptions to see which two or three strike you as being most typical of yourself. Keep in mind that the characteristics listed here are merely a few highlights and do not represent the full spectrum of each personality type.

Type One: The Reformer. The principled, idealistic type. Ones are ethical and conscientious, with a strong sense of right and wrong. They are teachers and crusaders, always striving to improve things but afraid of making a mistake. Well-organized, orderly, and fastidious, they try to maintain high standards but can slip into being critical and perfectionistic. They typically have problems with repressed anger and impatience. *At their best,* healthy Ones are wise, discerning, realistic, and noble, as well as morally heroic.

Type Two: The Helper. The caring, interpersonal type. Twos are empathetic, sincere, and warm-hearted. They are friendly, generous, and self-sacrificing, but they can also be sentimental, flattering, and people-pleasing. They are driven to be close to others, and they often do things for others in order to be needed. They typically have problems taking care of themselves and acknowledging their own needs. *At their best,* healthy Twos are unselfish and altruistic and have unconditional love for themselves and others.

Type Three: The Achiever. The adaptable, success-oriented type. Threes are self-assured, attractive, and charming. Ambitious, competent, and energetic, they can also be status-conscious and highly driven for personal advancement. Threes are often concerned about their image and what others think of them. They typically have problems with workaholism and competitiveness. *At their best,* healthy Threes are self-accepting, authentic, and everything they seem to be—role models who inspire others.

Type Four: The Individualist. The romantic, introspective type. Fours are self-aware, sensitive, reserved, and quiet. They are self-revealing, emotionally honest, and personal, but they can also be moody and self-conscious. Withholding themselves from others due to feeling vulnerable and defective, they can also feel disdainful and exempt from ordinary ways of living. They typically have problems with self-indulgence and self-pity. *At their best,* healthy Fours are inspired and highly creative, able to renew themselves and transform their experiences.

Type Five: The Investigator. The intense, cerebral type. Fives are alert, insightful, and curious. They are able to concentrate and focus on developing complex ideas and skills. Independent and innovative, they can become

"If men knew themselves, God would heal and pardon them."

PASCAL

THE ENNEAGRAM WITH RISO-HUDSON
TYPE NAMES

preoccupied with their thoughts and imaginary constructs. They become detached, yet high-strung and intense. They typically have problems with isolation, eccentricity, and nihilism. *At their best,* healthy Fives are visionary pioneers, often ahead of their time and able to see the world in an entirely new way.

Type Six: The Loyalist. The committed, security-oriented type. Sixes are reliable, hardworking, and responsible, but they can also be defensive, evasive, and highly anxious—running on stress while complaining about it. They are often cautious and indecisive but can also be reactive, defiant, and rebellious. They typically have problems with self-doubt and suspicion. *At their best,* healthy Sixes are internally stable, self-confident, and self-reliant, courageously supporting the weak and powerless.

Type Seven: The Enthusiast. The busy, productive type. Sevens are versatile, optimistic, and spontaneous. Playful, high-spirited, and practical, they can also be overextended, scattered, and undisciplined. They constantly seek new and exciting experiences, but they can become distracted and exhausted by staying on the go. They typically have problems with superficiality and impulsiveness. *At their best,* healthy Sevens focus their talents on worthwhile goals, becoming joyous, highly accomplished, and full of gratitude.

Type Eight: The Challenger. The powerful, dominating type. Eights are self-confident, strong, and assertive. Protective, resourceful, and decisive, they can also be proud and domineering. Eights feel that they must control their environment, often becoming confrontational and intimidating. They typically have problems with allowing themselves to be close to others. *At their best,* healthy Eights are self-mastering—they use their strength to improve others' lives, becoming heroic, magnanimous, and sometimes historically great.

Type Nine: The Peacemaker. The easygoing, self-effacing type. Nines are accepting, trusting, and stable. They are good-natured, kindhearted, easygoing, and supportive but can also be too willing to go along with others to keep the peace. They want everything to be without conflict but can tend to be complacent and minimize anything upsetting. They typically have problems with passivity and stubbornness. *At their best,* healthy Nines are indomitable and all-embracing; they are able to bring people together and heal conflicts.

THE QUESTIONNAIRES

The first questionnaire, which follows on pages 14-15, is the Riso-Hudson QUEST, the *QUick Enneagram Sorting Test*. This test will help you narrow down the possibilities for your type in less than five minutes with about 70 percent accuracy. At the least you will be able to identify the top two or three possibilities for your type.

The second set of questionnaires is the Riso-Hudson TAS, or Type Attitude Sorter. At the beginning of each of the nine type chapters is a set of fifteen statements that are highly characteristic of the type under consideration. If you are interested in taking a self-scoring, computerized Enneagram Test, you can do so at our website, *www.EnneagramInstitute.com*. This test, the RHETI (*Riso-Hudson Enneagram Type Indicator*, Version 2.5), involves choosing between 144 paired statements and is about 80 percent accurate. Beyond indicating the main type, it also produces a profile showing the relative strengths of each of the nine types in your personality. The RHETI usually takes about forty-five minutes to complete.

If you are new to the Enneagram, take the QUEST and then the TAS to see if there is a match. For instance, the QUEST might indicate that you are a Type Six. You could then go immediately to the fifteen statements of the TAS for Type Six (in Chapter 12) to see if you score high on those statements as well. If so, you are probably on the right track.

We urge you, however, to continue to keep an open mind and to read the full chapter of Type Six (to continue the example) until more pieces fall into place. If the description and exercises have a strong impact on you, then you are almost certainly a Six.

We are qualifying these statements slightly because it is always possible to be wrong in one's self-diagnosis—just as, unfortunately, it is easy to be wrongly diagnosed by an "Enneagram expert" of some sort. Therefore, take your time identifying your type. Read this book carefully, and more important, *live with the information for a while* and talk about it with those who know you well. Remember that self-discovery is a process, and that the process does not end with discovering your type—in fact, that is only the beginning.

When you do discover your type, you will know it. Waves of relief and embarrassment, of elation and chagrin, are likely to sweep over you. Things that you have always known unconsciously about yourself will suddenly become clear, and life patterns will emerge. You can be certain that when this happens, you have identified your personality type correctly.

THE RISO-HUDSON QUEST℠

The Quick Enneagram Sorting Test

INSTRUCTIONS:

For the QUEST to yield a correct result, it is important that you read and follow these few simple instructions.

▶ Select *one* paragraph in each of the following two groups of statements that best reflects your general attitudes and behaviors, as you have been most of your life.

▶ You do not have to agree completely with every word or statement in the paragraph you select! You may agree with only 80 to 90 percent of a particular paragraph and still select that paragraph over the other two in the group. However, you should agree with the general tone and overall "philosophy" of the paragraph you select. You will probably disagree with some part of each of the paragraphs. Do not reject a paragraph because of a single word or phrase! Again, look at the overall picture.

▶ Do not overanalyze your choices. Select the paragraph that your "gut feeling" says is the right one for you, even though you may not agree with 100 percent of it. The general thrust and feeling of the paragraph as a whole is more important than individual elements of it. Go with your intuition.

▶ If you cannot decide which paragraph best fits you in one of the groups, *you may make two choices,* but *only in one group;* for example, C in group I, and X and Y in group II.

▶ Enter the letter you have selected for that group in the appropriate box.

GROUP I

A. I have tended to be fairly independent and assertive: I've felt that life works best when you meet it head-on. I set my own goals, get involved, and want to make things happen. I don't like sitting around—I want to achieve something big and have an impact. I don't necessarily seek confrontations, but I don't let people push me around, either. Most of the time I know what I want, and I go for it. I tend to work hard and to play hard.

GROUP I CHOICE

B. I have tended to be quiet and am used to being on my own. I usually don't draw much attention to myself socially, and it's generally unusual for me to assert myself all that forcefully. I don't feel comfortable taking the lead or being as competitive as others. Many would probably say that I'm something of a dreamer—a lot of my excitement goes on in my imagination. I can be quite content without feeling I have to be active all the time.

C. I have tended to be extremely responsible and dedicated. I feel terrible if I don't keep my commitments and do what's expected of me. I want people to know that I'm there for them and that I'll do what I believe is best for them. I've often made great personal sacrifices for the sake of others, whether they know it or not. I often don't take adequate care of myself—I do the work that needs to be done and relax (and do what I really want) if there's time left.

GROUP II

X. I am a person who usually maintains a positive outlook and feels that things will work out for the best. I can usually find something to be enthusiastic about and different ways to occupy myself. I like being around people and helping others to be happy—I enjoy sharing my own well-being with them. (I don't always feel great, but I try not to show it to anyone!) However, staying positive has sometimes meant that I've put off dealing with my own problems for too long.

Y. I am a person who has strong feelings about things—most people can tell when I'm unhappy about something. I can be guarded with people, but I'm more sensitive than I let on. I want to know where I stand with others and who and what I can count on—it's pretty clear to most people where they stand with me. When I'm upset about something, I want others to respond and to get as worked up as I am. I know the rules, but I don't want people telling me what to do. I want to decide for myself.

Z. I tend to be self-controlled and logical—I am uncomfortable dealing with feelings. I am efficient—even perfectionistic—and prefer working on my own. When there are problems or personal conflicts, I try not to bring my feelings into the situation. Some say I'm too cool and detached, but I don't want my emotional reactions to distract me from what's really important to me. I usually don't show my reactions when others "get to me."

GROUP II CHOICE

To interpret your answer, see p. 18.

THINGS TO KEEP IN MIND ABOUT TYPE

▶ While everyone has a certain mix of types in their overall personality, one particular pattern or style is our "home base," and we return to it over and over. Our basic type stays the same throughout life. While people change and develop in numerous ways, they do not change from one basic personality type to another.

▶ The descriptions of the personality types are universal and apply equally to males and females. Of course, males and females will express the same attitudes, traits, and tendencies somewhat differently, but the basic issues of the type remain the same.

▶ Not everything in the description of your basic type will apply to you *all the time*. This is because we fluctuate constantly among the healthy, average, and unhealthy traits that make up our personality type, as we will see in our discussion of the Levels of Development (Chapter 6). We will also see that increasing maturation or increasing stress have a significant influence on how we are expressing our type.

▶ Although we have given each type a descriptive title (such as the Reformer, the Helper, and so forth), in practice we prefer to use its Enneagram number. Numbers are value neutral—they provide an unbiased, shorthand way of referring to the type. Furthermore, the numerical ranking of the types is not significant: being a type with a higher number is not better than being a type with a lower number. (For example, it is not better to be a Nine than a One.)

▶ None of the personality types is better or worse than any other—all types have unique assets and liabilities, strengths and weaknesses. Some types can be more valued than others in a given culture or group, however. As you learn more about all of the types, you will see that just as each has unique capacities, each has different limitations.

▶ No matter what type you are, *you have all nine types in you, to some degree.* To explore them all and see them all operating in you is to see the full spectrum of human nature. This awareness will give you far more understanding of and compassion for others, because you will recognize many aspects of their particular habits and reactions in yourself. It is much more difficult to condemn the aggressiveness of Eights or the disguised neediness of Twos, for instance, if we are aware of aggressiveness and neediness in ourselves. If you investigate all nine types in yourself, you will see how interdependent they are—just as the Enneagram symbol represents them.

TYPING OTHERS

We feel strongly that it is always more problematic to use the Enneagram to type others than it is to use it on ourselves. Everyone has blind spots, and there are so many possible variations among the types that it is inevitable that we simply will not be familiar with all of them. Because of our own personal prejudices, it is also very likely that we have an outright aversion to some types. Remember the Enneagram is to be used primarily for self-discovery and self-understanding.

Furthermore, knowing our type or that of someone else can provide us with many valuable insights, but it cannot begin to tell us everything about the person, any more than knowing a person's race or nationality does. In itself, type tells us nothing about the person's particular history, intelligence, talent, honesty, integrity, character, or many other factors. On the other hand, type does tell us a great deal about how we view the world, the kinds of choices we are likely to make, the values we hold, what motivates us, how we react to people, how we respond to stress, and many other important things. As we become familiar with the personality patterns revealed by this system, we more easily appreciate perspectives that are different from our own.

THE DEEPER PURPOSE OF THE ENNEAGRAM

Identifying oneself as one of nine personality types can be revolutionary. For the first time in our lives, we may see the pattern and overall rationale for the way we have lived and behaved. At a certain point, however, "knowing our type" becomes incorporated into our self-image and may actually begin to get in the way of our continued growth.

Indeed, some students of the Enneagram have become attached to their personality type—"Of course I get paranoid! After all, I'm a Six," or "You know how we Sevens are! We just have to stay on the go!" Justifying questionable behavior or adopting a more rigid identity are misuses of the Enneagram.

But by helping us see how trapped we are in our trances and how estranged we are from our Essential nature, *the Enneagram invites us to look deeply into the mystery of our true identity.* It is meant to initiate a process of inquiry that can lead us to a more profound truth about ourselves and our place in the world. If, however, we use the Enneagram simply to arrive at a better self-image, we will stop the process of uncovering (or, actually, recovering) our true nature. While knowing our type gives us important information, that information is merely an embarkation point for a much greater journey. In short, *knowing our type is not the final destination.*

"He who knows others is learned. He who knows himself is wise."

LAO TZU

The aim of this Work is to stop the automatic reactions of the personality by bringing awareness to it. Only by bringing insight and clarity to the mechanisms of personality can we awaken—which is why we have written this book. The more we see the mechanical reactions of our personality, the less identified with them we become and the more freedom we have. That is what the Enneagram is all about.

INTERPRETING THE QUEST *(from page 14-15)*

Together the two letters you have selected form a two-letter code. For example, choosing paragraph C in group I, and paragraph Y in group II, produces the two-letter code CY.

To find out which basic personality type the QUEST indicates you are, see the QUEST codes to the right:

2-Digit Code	Type	Type Name and Key Characteristics
AX	7	**The Enthusiast:** Upbeat, accomplished, impulsive
AY	8	**The Challenger:** Self-confident, decisive, domineering
AZ	3	**The Achiever:** Adaptable, ambitious, image-conscious
BX	9	**The Peacemaker:** Receptive, reassuring, complacent
BY	4	**The Individualist:** Intuitive, aesthetic, self-absorbed
BZ	5	**The Investigator:** Perceptive, innovative, detached
CX	2	**The Helper:** Caring, generous, possessive
CY	6	**The Loyalist:** Engaging, responsible, defensive
CZ	1	**The Reformer:** Rational, principled, self-controlled

CHAPTER 2

▼

ANCIENT ROOTS,
MODERN INSIGHTS

▲

THE MODERN ENNEAGRAM of personality types does not come from any single source. It is a hybrid, a modern amalgam, from a number of ancient wisdom traditions combined with modern psychology. Various authors have speculated about its origins, and Enneagram enthusiasts have created a good deal of folklore about its history and development, but much of the information being passed around is unfortunately misleading. Many early authors, for example, attributed the entire system to Sufi masters, which we now know is not the case.

To understand the Enneagram's history, it is necessary to distinguish between the Enneagram *symbol* and *the nine personality types*. It is true that the Enneagram symbol is ancient, dating back some 2,500 years or more. Likewise, the roots of the ideas that eventually led to the development of the psychology of the nine types go back at least as far as the fourth century A.D. and perhaps further. It was not until the last few decades, however, that these two sources of insight came together.

The exact origins of the Enneagram *symbol* have been lost to history; we do not know where it came from, any more than we know who discovered the wheel or how to write. It is said to have originated in Babylon around 2500 B.C., but there is little direct evidence that this is so. Many of the abstract ideas connected with the Enneagram, not to mention its geometry and mathematical derivation, suggest that it may well have roots in classical Greek thought. The theories underlying the diagram can be found in the ideas of Pythagoras, Plato, and some of the Neoplatonic philosophers. In any case, it is clearly a part of the Western tradition that gave rise to Judaism, Christianity, and Islam, as well as Hermetic and Gnostic philosophy, aspects of which can be found in all three of these great prophetic religions.

> "Learn what you are and be such."
>
> PINDAR

"Take the understanding of the East and the knowledge of the West—and then seek."

GURDJIEFF

There is no question, however, that the person responsible for bringing the Enneagram *symbol* to the modern world was George Ivanovich Gurdjieff. Gurdjieff was a Greek-Armenian born around 1875; as a young man, he became interested in esoteric knowledge and was convinced that a complete science for transforming the human psyche had been developed by the ancients but that this knowledge had subsequently been lost. Along with a handful of friends who shared his passion for recovering this lost science of human transformation, Gurdjieff spent the early part of his life attempting to piece together whatever ancient wisdom he could find. Together these friends formed a group called the Seekers After Truth (SAT) and decided that they would each explore different teachings and systems of thought independently and then regroup periodically to share what they had learned. They traveled widely, visiting Egypt, Afghanistan, Greece, Persia, India, and Tibet, spending time in monasteries and remote sanctuaries, learning everything they could about ancient wisdom traditions.

Somewhere in his travels, possibly in Afghanistan or Turkey, Gurdjieff encountered the symbol of the Enneagram. Thereafter he developed his own synthesis of what he and other SAT members had discovered. He ended his many years of searching just before World War I and began teaching in St. Petersburg and Moscow, immediately attracting an enthusiastic audience.

"Remember yourself always and everywhere."

GURDJIEFF

The system that Gurdjieff taught was a vast and complex study of psychology, spirituality, and cosmology that aimed at helping students understand their place in the universe and their objective purpose in life. Gurdjieff also taught that the Enneagram was the central and most important symbol in his philosophy. He stated that a person did not understand anything completely until he or she understood it in terms of the Enneagram, that is, until he or she could correctly place the elements of a process at the correct points on the Enneagram, thereby seeing the interdependent and mutually sustaining parts of the whole. The Enneagram taught by Gurdjieff was therefore primarily a *model of natural processes,* not a psychological typology.

Gurdjieff explained that the Enneagram symbol has three parts that represent three Divine laws, which govern all of existence. The first of these is the *circle,* a universal mandala, used in almost every culture. The circle refers to unity, wholeness, and oneness and symbolizes the idea that *God Is One,* the distinguishing feature of the major Western religions, Judaism, Christianity, and Islam.

Within the circle we find the next symbol, the *triangle.* Traditionally, in Christianity, this refers to the Trinity of Father, Son, and Holy Spirit. Similarly, the Kabbalah, an esoteric teaching of Judaism, teaches that God initially manifests Himself in the universe as three emanations or "spheres," the *Sefirot* (Kether, Binah, and Hokmah) named in the Kabbalah's principal symbol, the Tree of Life. We can also see reflections of the trinitarian idea in other religions: the Buddhists talk about Buddha, Dharma, and Sangha, the Hindus talk about Vishnu, Brahma, and Shiva, and the Taoists talk about Heaven, Earth, and Man.

Quite strikingly almost all of the major world religions teach that the universe is a manifestation not of duality, as much of Western logic teaches, but of trinity. Our usual way of looking at reality is based on pairs of opposites such as good and bad, black and white, male and female, introvert and extrovert, and so forth. The ancient traditions, however, do not see man and woman, but man, woman, and child. Things are not black or white, but black, white, and gray.

Gurdjieff called this phenomenon "the Law of Three" and said that everything that exists is the result of the interaction of three forces (whatever they may be in a given situation or dimension). Even the discoveries of modern physics seem to support the idea of the Law of Three. On the subatomic scale, atoms are made of protons, electrons, and neutrons, and rather than there being four fundamental forces of nature as was once thought, physics has now discovered that there are really only three—the strong force, the weak force, and electromagnetism.

The third part of this triple symbol is the *hexad* (the figure tracing the numbers 1-4-2-8-5-7). This figure symbolizes what Gurdjieff called "the Law of Seven," which has to do with process and development over time. It states that nothing is static; everything is moving and becoming something else. Even rocks and stars eventually become transformed. Everything is changing, recycling and evolving or devolving—although in lawful and predictable ways according to their own nature and the forces that are acting on them. The days of the week, the Periodic Table, and the Western musical octave are all based on the Law of Seven.

When we put these three elements together (the circle, the triangle, and the hexad), we get the Enneagram. It is a symbol that shows the

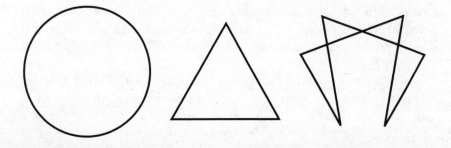

THE THREE PARTS OF THE ENNEAGRAM SYMBOL

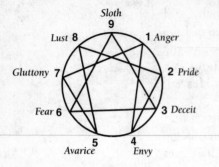

OSCAR ICHAZO'S ENNEAGRAM
OF THE PASSIONS (DEADLY SINS)

wholeness of a thing (the circle), how its identity is the result of the interaction of three forces (the triangle), and how it evolves or changes over time (the hexad).

Gurdjieff taught the Enneagram through a series of sacred dances, explaining that it should be thought of as a *living symbol* that was moving and dynamic, not as static. However, nowhere in the published writings of Gurdjieff and his students did he teach the Enneagram of personality types. The origins of that Enneagram are more recent and are based on two principal modern sources.

The first is Oscar Ichazo. Like Gurdjieff, as a young man, Ichazo was fascinated with uncovering lost knowledge. In his childhood he used his remarkable intelligence to absorb information from his uncle's vast library of philosophical and metaphysical texts. When Ichazo was still fairly young, he traveled from his home in Bolivia to Buenos Aires, Argentina, and later to other parts of the world in search of ancient wisdom. After traveling in the Middle East and elsewhere, he returned to South America and began to distill what he had learned.

Ichazo researched and synthesized the many elements of the Enneagram until, beginning in the 1950s, he discovered the connection between the symbol and the personality types. The nine types that he linked with the Enneagram symbol come from an ancient tradition of *remembering nine Divine attributes as they are reflected in human nature.* These ideas began with the Neoplatonists, if not earlier, and appeared in Plotinus' *The Enneads* in the third century A.D. They found their way into the Christian tradition as their opposites: the distortion of the Divine attributes became the Seven Deadly Sins (or "Capital Sins" or "Passions") plus two others (fear and deceit).

Common to both the Enneagram and the Seven Deadly Sins is the idea that while we have all of them in us, *one* in particular crops up over and over again. It is the root of our imbalance and the way we become trapped in ego. Ichazo traced early ideas about the nine Divine attributes from Greece to the desert fathers of the fourth century who first developed the concept of the Seven Deadly Sins, and from there into medieval literature, including *The Canterbury Tales* by Chaucer and Dante's *Purgatorio*.

Ichazo also explored the ancient Jewish tradition of the Kabbalah. This mystical teaching was developed in Jewish communities in France and Spain in the twelfth to fourteenth centuries of our era, although it had antecedents in ancient Jewish mystical traditions, as well as in Gnosticism and Neoplatonic philosophy. Central to Kabbalistic philosophy is a symbol called the Tree of Life (*Etz Hayim*) which, like the

THE NINE PASSIONS

The idea of the Deadly Sins (also called the "Passions") is best understood if we think of the word *sin* not as something bad or evil, but as the tendency to "miss the mark" in some way. The Passions represent the nine main ways that we lose our center and become distorted in our thinking, feeling, and doing.

1	ANGER	This Passion might be more accurately described as *Resentment*. Anger in itself is not the problem, but in Ones the anger is repressed, leading to continual frustration and dissatisfaction with themselves and with the world.
2	PRIDE	Pride refers to an inability or unwillingness to acknowledge one's own suffering. Twos deny many of their own needs while attempting to "help" others. This Passion could also be described as *Vainglory*—pride in one's own virtue.
3	DECEIT	Deceit means deceiving ourselves into believing that we are only the ego self. When we believe this, we put our efforts into developing our egos instead of our true nature. We could also call this passion *Vanity*, our attempt to make the ego feel valuable without turning to our spiritual source.
4	ENVY	Envy is based on the feeling that something fundamental is missing. Envy leads Fours to feel that others possess qualities that they lack. Fours long for what is absent but often fail to notice the many blessings in their lives.
5	AVARICE	Fives feel that they lack inner resources and that too much interaction with others will lead to catastrophic depletion. This Passion leads Fives to withhold themselves from contact with the world. Thus they hold on to their resources and minimize their needs.
6	FEAR	This Passion might be more accurately described as *Anxiety* because anxiety leads us to be afraid of things that are not actually happening now. Sixes walk around in a constant state of apprehension and worry about possible future events.
7	GLUTTONY	Gluttony refers to the insatiable desire to "fill oneself up" with experiences. Sevens attempt to overcome feelings of inner emptiness by pursuing a variety of positive, stimulating ideas and activities, but they never feel that they have enough.
8	LUST	Lust does not only refer to sexual lust; Eights are "lusty" in that they are driven by a constant need for intensity, control, and self-extension. Lust causes Eights to try to push everything in their lives—to assert themselves willfully.
9	SLOTH	Sloth does not simply mean laziness, since Nines can be quite active and accomplished. Rather, it refers to a desire to be unaffected by life. It is an unwillingness to arise with the fullness of one's vitality to fully engage with life.

Enneagram, contains the ideas of unity, trinity, and a process of development involving seven parts.

In a flash of genius, Ichazo was able to place all of this material properly, in the right sequence, on the Enneagram symbol for the first time in the mid-1950s. It was only then that the different streams of transmission came together to form the basic template of the Enneagram as we know it today.

In 1970 noted psychiatrist Claudio Naranjo, who was developing a program of gestalt therapy at the Esalen Institute in Big Sur, California, and a number of other thinkers in the human potential movement traveled to Arica, Chile, to study with Ichazo. Ichazo was directing an intensive forty-day program that he had designed to lead students to self-realization. One of the first things he taught was the Enneagram, together with the nine types or, as he called them, "ego fixations."

The Enneagram immediately captivated a number of people in the group, particularly Naranjo, who returned to California and began to teach it in conjunction with other psychological systems that he had studied. Naranjo became interested in correlating the Enneagram types with the psychiatric categories he was familiar with, and he began to expand Ichazo's brief sketches of the types. One way he demonstrated the validity of the system was by gathering together panels of people who identified with a particular type, or whose psychiatric categories were known, interviewing them to highlight their similarities and to elicit further information. For instance, he would gather together all the people in his group who had obsessive-compulsive personalities and observe how their responses fit with the descriptions of personality type One, and so forth.

Naranjo's method of using panels to understand types is not an ancient oral tradition as is sometimes claimed; nor does the Enneagram of personality come from a body of knowledge that has been passed down to us from an oral source. The use of panels began with Naranjo in the early 1970s, and is but one way of teaching and illuminating the Enneagram.

Naranjo began teaching an early version of the system to private groups in Berkeley, California, and it spread rapidly from there. The Enneagram was taught by enthusiasts in the San Francisco Bay Area as well as in Jesuit retreat houses across North America, where one of us, Don, then a Jesuit seminarian, learned the early material. Since the fundamental work of Ichazo and Naranjo, a number of others, including the authors, have been developing the Enneagram and discovering many new facets of it.

Our work has primarily involved developing the psychological basis of the types by filling out the original very brief descriptions and by showing how the Enneagram relates to other psychological and

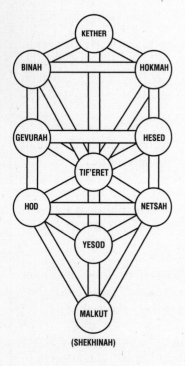

THE TREE OF LIFE
(ETZ HAYIM)

spiritual systems. Don's conviction has always been that until the descriptions of the types were fully and accurately worked out, the Enneagram would be of little real use to anyone—and would, in fact, become a source of misinformation and misguided attempts at growth.

A major breakthrough came in 1977 when he discovered the Levels of Development. The Levels revealed the gradations of growth and deterioration that people actually move through in their lives. They showed which traits and motivations went with which types, and why. Most profoundly, they indicated the degrees of our identification with our personality and our consequent lack of freedom. He also emphasized the psychological motivations of the types, as distinct from the impressionistic descriptions which were prevalent when he began working. He developed these and other ideas, such as the correlations with other psychological typologies, and presented his findings in *Personality Types* (1987) and in *Understanding the Enneagram* (1990).

Russ joined Don in 1991, initially to assist in developing an Enneagram type questionnaire, which ultimately became the Riso-Hudson Enneagram Type Indicator (RHETI), and later worked on the revisions to *Personality Types* (1996). Russ has brought his understanding and experience of the traditions and practices underlying Enneagram theory to this work. Subsequently, he further developed the ideas Don had pioneered, uncovering many of the deeper structures of the types as well as many of the system's implications for personal growth. Since 1991, both of us have been teaching workshops and seminars around the world, and many of the insights in this book have come from our experience of working with our students. We have had the privilege of working with people from every inhabited continent and from every major religious background. We continue to be amazed and impressed by the universality and practicality of the Enneagram.

▼   ▼   ▼

THE STORY OF THE LOCKSMITH: A SUFI TALE

Once there lived a metalworker, a locksmith, who was unjustly accused of crimes and was sentenced to a deep, dark prison. After he had been there awhile, his wife who loved him very much went to the King and beseeched him that she might at least give him a prayer rug so he could observe his five prostrations every day. The King considered that a lawful request, so he let the woman bring her husband a prayer rug. The prisoner was thankful to get the rug from his wife, and every day he faithfully did his prostrations on the rug.

Much later, the man escaped from prison, and when people asked him how he got out, he explained that after years of doing his prostrations and praying for deliverance from the prison, he began to see what was right in front of his nose. One day he suddenly saw that his wife had woven into the prayer rug the pattern of the lock that imprisoned him. Once he realized this and understood that all the information he needed to escape was already in his possession, he began to make friends with his guards. He also persuaded the guards that they all would have a better life if they cooperated and escaped the prison together. They agreed since, although they were guards, they realized that they were in prison, too. They also wished to escape, but they had no means to do so.

So the locksmith and his guards decided on the following plan: they would bring him pieces of metal, and he would fashion useful items from them to sell in the marketplace. Together they would amass resources for their escape, and from the strongest piece of metal they could acquire, the locksmith would fashion a key.

One night, when everything had been prepared, the locksmith and his guards unlocked the prison and walked out into the cool night where his beloved wife was waiting for him. He left the prayer rug behind so that any other prisoner who was clever enough to read the pattern of the rug could also make his escape. Thus, the locksmith was reunited with his loving wife, his former guards became his friends, and everyone lived in harmony. Love and skillfulness prevailed.

This traditional Sufi teaching story, from Idries Shah, can symbolize our study of the Enneagram: The lock is our personality, the prayer rug is the Enneagram, and the key is the Work. Note that although the wife brings the rug, in order to get the tools, the locksmith has to create something useful for his guards. He cannot get out alone, or for nothing. Furthermore, during the whole time he was praying for deliverance, the means of his liberation was literally "right under his nose," although he never saw the pattern or understood its meaning. One day, however, he woke up, saw the pattern, and then had the means to escape.

The heart of the story is clear: *each of us is in prison*. We have only to awaken to "read" the pattern of the lock that will allow us to escape.

▲   ▲   ▲

CHAPTER 3

▼

ESSENCE AND
PERSONALITY

▲

THE CORE TRUTH that the Enneagram conveys to us is that *we are much more than our personality.* Our personalities are no more than the familiar, conditioned parts of a much wider range of potentials that we all possess. Beyond the limitations of our personalities, each of us exists as a vast, largely unrecognized quality of Being or Presence—what is called our *Essence.* In spiritual language we could say that within each person is an individual spark of the Divine, although we have forgotten this fundamental truth because *we have fallen asleep to our true nature.* We do not experience our own Divine nature; nor do we experience others as manifestations of the Divine. Instead, we often become hard, even cynical, treating others as objects to be defended against or used for our own gratification.

Most of us have some notion about what personality is, but the idea of Essence is probably foreign to us. When we talk about Essence, we mean it in the literal sense of the word—what we fundamentally are, our *Essential self,* the ground of Being in us. (*Spirit* is another appropriate word.)

It is also important to distinguish Essence, or spirit, from "soul." The fundamental ground of our Being is Essence or Spirit, but it takes a dynamic form we call "the soul." Our personality is a particular aspect of our soul. Our soul is "made of" Essence or Spirit. If Spirit were water, soul would be a particular lake or river, and personality would be waves on its surface—or frozen chunks of ice in the river.

Generally, we do not experience our Essence and its many aspects because our awareness is so dominated by our personality. But as we learn to bring awareness to our personality, it becomes more transparent, and we are able to experience our Essence more directly. We still function in the world but with a growing realization of our connection with Divinity. We become aware that we are part of a Divine Presence all around us and in us that is constantly and miraculously unfolding.

"The spirit is the true self, not that physical figure which can be pointed out by your finger."

CICERO

"Spiritual development is a long and arduous journey, an adventure through strange lands full of surprises, joy, beauty, difficulties, and even dangers."

ROBERTO ASSAGIOLI

The Enneagram can help us see what prevents us from remembering this deep truth about who we really are, the truth of our spiritual nature. It does this by providing highly specific insights into our psychological and spiritual makeup. The Enneagram also helps us by giving us a direction in which to work, but only as long as we remember that it is not telling us who we are, but how we have limited who we are. *Remember, the Enneagram does not put us in a box, it shows us the box we are already in—and the way out.*

SACRED PSYCHOLOGY

One of the profound lessons of the Enneagram is that psychological integration and spiritual realization are not separate processes. Without spirituality, psychology cannot really free us or lead us to the deepest truths about ourselves, and without psychology, spirituality can lead to grandiosity, delusion, and an attempt to escape from reality. The Enneagram is neither dry psychology nor fuzzy mysticism but a tool for transformation that uses the clarity and insight of psychology as a point of entry into a profound and universal spirituality. Thus, in a literal sense, the Enneagram is "the bridge between psychology and spirituality.™"

The core of this sacred psychology is that *our basic type reveals the psychological mechanisms by which we forget our true nature—our Divine Essence—the way in which we abandon ourselves.* Our personalities draw upon the capacities of our inborn temperament to develop defenses and compensations for where we have been hurt in childhood. In order to survive whatever difficulties we encountered at that time, we unwittingly mastered a limited repertoire of strategies, self-images, and behaviors that allowed us to cope with and survive in our early environment. Each of us therefore has become an "expert" at a particular form of coping which, if used excessively, also becomes the core of the dysfunctional area of our personality.

"Man wishes to be happy even when he so lives as to make happiness impossible."

ST. AUGUSTINE

As the defenses and strategies of our personality become more structured, they cause us to lose contact with our direct experience of ourselves, our Essence. The personality becomes the source of our identity rather than contact with our Being. Our sense of ourselves is based increasingly on internal images, memories, and learned behaviors rather than on the spontaneous expression of our true nature. This loss of contact with our Essence causes deep anxiety, taking the form of one of the nine Passions. Once in place, these Passions, which are usually unconscious and invisible to us, begin to drive the personality.

Understanding our personality type and its dynamics, therefore, offers an especially potent approach to the unconscious, to our wounds and compensations, and ultimately, to our healing and transformation.

The Enneagram shows us where our personality most "trips us up." It highlights both what is possible for us, as well as how self-defeating and unnecessary many of our old reactions and behaviors are. This is why, when we identify with the personality, we are settling on being much less than who we really are. It is as though we were given a mansion to live in, with rich furnishings and beautifully kept grounds, but have confined ourselves to a small dark closet in the basement. Most of us have even forgotten that the rest of the mansion exists, or that we are really its owner.

As spiritual teachers through the ages have pointed out, *we have fallen asleep to ourselves and to our own lives.* Most of the day we walk around preoccupied by ideas, anxieties, worries, and mental pictures. Seldom are we present to ourselves and to our immediate experience. As we begin to work on ourselves, however, we begin to see that our attention has been taken or "magnetized" by the preoccupations and features of our personality, and that we are actually sleepwalking through much of life. This view of things is contrary to common sense and often feels insulting to the way we see ourselves—as self-determining, conscious, and in control.

At the same time, our personality is not "bad." Our personality is an important part of our development and is necessary for the refinement of our Essential nature. The problem is that we become stuck in personality and do not know how to move on to the next phase. This is not the result of any inherent flaw in ourselves, rather it is an arrested development that occurs because almost no one in our formative years was aware that any more was possible. Our parents and teachers may have had some glimmers of their true nature, but like us, they generally did not recognize them, much less live as expressions of them.

Thus one of the most transformational insights that the Enneagram can provide is the realization that *we are not our personality.* To begin to grasp this is to undergo a transformation of our sense of self. When we begin to understand that we are not our personality, we also begin to realize that we are spiritual beings who *have* a personality and who are manifesting themselves through that personality. When we stop identifying with our personality and stop defending it, a miracle happens: our Essential nature spontaneously arises and transforms us.

PERSONALITY DOES NOT GO AWAY

The purpose of the Enneagram is not to help us get rid of our personality. Even if we could, it would not be very helpful. This is reassuring to those of us who fear that if we let go of our personality, we will lose our identity or become less capable or effective.

In fact, exactly the opposite is true. When we get in touch with our Essence, we do not lose our personality. It becomes more transparent

> ". . . the neurotic process . . . is a problem of the self. It is a process of abandoning the real self for an idealized one; of trying to actualize this pseudoself instead of our given human potentials."
>
> KAREN HORNEY

> "The greatest happiness is to know the source of unhappiness."
>
> DOSTOYEVSKY

and flexible, something that helps us live rather than something that takes over our lives. Moments of "flow" and "peak performance" arise when we are most present and aware—qualities of Essence—whereas the manifestations of our personality often cause us to overlook things, make mistakes, and create problems of all kinds. For example, if we are particularly anxious about a trip, we will likely pack the wrong clothes or forget important articles. Learning how to stay relaxed and present under everyday pressures can make our lives easier.

As we become less identified with our personality, it becomes a smaller part of the totality of who we are. The personality still exists, but there is a more active intelligence, a sensitivity, and a Presence underlying it that uses the personality as a vehicle rather than being driven by it. As we identify more with our Essence, we see that we do not lose our identity—we actually find it.

It would be misleading, however, to suggest that one experience of awakening, or even a few of them, will free us from identification with our personality. While each moment of self-realization transforms us to some degree, it usually takes many such experiences before we can live and function with an expanded awareness. But as these experiences accumulate, our identity gradually opens up to include more and more of our Essential nature. A capacity for deeper experiences is created and the vessel expands to become a more constant carrier of the Divine. Our inner light becomes brighter and shines more warmly into the world.

THE BASIC FEAR AND BASIC DESIRE

The mechanism of the personality is set in motion by what we call the *Basic Fear* of each type. The Basic Fear arises because of the inevitable loss of contact with our Essential nature in early childhood. This loss occurs for a number of reasons.

As newborn babies, we arrived in the world with natural, innate needs that had to be met for us to develop into mature human beings. However, even in the best circumstances, our parents inevitably could not meet all of our developmental needs perfectly. No matter how well intentioned they were, at certain times they had difficulty coping with our needs, especially those that had not been adequately met in themselves. As babies, it is our nature to express a wide range of emotions and states of being. If these qualities are blocked in our parents, they will feel anxious and uncomfortable whenever those qualities arise in us. This made our infant selves anxious and unhappy.

If, for example, a baby is expressing her joyfulness and delight in being alive, but her mother is depressed, it is unlikely that the mother will feel comfortable with the baby's joy. As a result, the baby learns to

"Whenever a man awakes, he awakes from the false assumption that he has always been awake, and therefore the master of his thoughts, feelings, and actions."

HENRI TRACOL

"The very things we wish to avoid, neglect, and flee from turn out to be the 'prima materia' from which all real growth comes."

ANDREW HARVEY

suppress her joy to keep the mother from getting more upset. Another baby with a different temperament might cry or make stronger attempts to get a reaction from the mother, but no matter what response the baby uses, her own joy is not mirrored. It is important to realize that these reactions did not occur because our parents were "bad" but because they could only mirror the qualities that were not blocked in themselves. This limited—and often dysfunctional—range of behaviors and attitudes become imprinted on the child's receptive soul as the psychic backdrop that the child brings into life and all future relationships.

As a result of unmet infant needs and subsequent blockages, we begin to feel very early in life that certain key elements in us are missing. Naturally, this feeling creates deep anxiety. It is likely that our innate temperament determines how we may respond to that anxiety, but no matter what our later personality type, we eventually come to the conclusion that there is something fundamentally wrong with us. Even if we cannot express it in words, we feel the tug of a powerful, unconscious anxiety—our Basic Fear.

Each type has its own characteristic Basic Fear, although the Basic Fears are also universal. (From a more subtle perspective, each Basic Fear is a reaction to the universal fear of death and annihilation—our personality's fear of nothingness.) We will recognize the Basic Fears of all nine types in ourselves, although our own type's Basic Fear motivates our behavior much more than the others.

"All men should strive to learn before they die what they are running from, and to, and why."

JAMES THURBER

UNCONSCIOUS CHILDHOOD MESSAGES

We all received many different unconscious messages from our mother and father (as well as from other significant figures) during childhood. Those messages had a profound effect on our growing identity and on how much we were allowed to fully be ourselves. Unless our parents were highly developed, conscious human beings themselves, the expansive brilliance of our soul was forced to shut down to varying degrees.

Although some of us received many of the following messages, one message tends to be central to each type. Which messages particularly affect you?

Type One: "It's not okay to make mistakes."
Type Two: "It's not okay to have your own needs."
Type Three: "It's not okay to have your own feelings and identity."
Type Four: "It's not okay to be too functional or too happy."
Type Five: "It's not okay to be comfortable in the world."
Type Six: "It's not okay to trust yourself."
Type Seven: "It's not okay to depend on anyone for anything."
Type Eight: "It's not okay to be vulnerable or to trust anyone."
Type Nine: "It's not okay to assert yourself."

THE BASIC FEARS OF THE TYPES

1	Fear of being bad, corrupt, evil, or defective
2	Fear of being unworthy of being loved
3	Fear of being worthless or without inherent value
4	Fear of being without identity or personal significance
5	Fear of being useless, incapable, or incompetent
6	Fear of being without support or guidance
7	Fear of being deprived or trapped in pain
8	Fear of being harmed or controlled by others
9	Fear of loss of connection, of fragmentation

"We do not succeed in changing things according to our desire, but gradually our desire changes."

PROUST

To compensate for the Basic Fear, a Basic Desire arises. The Basic Desire is the way that we defend against our Basic Fear in order to continue to function. The Basic Desire is what we believe will make us okay; it is as if we said to ourselves, "If I had X (love, security, peace, and so forth), everything would be great." We might also call the Basic Desire the *ego agenda*, because it tells us what the ego self is always striving after.

The Basic Desires represent legitimate universal human needs, although each type idealizes and grasps after its Basic Desire so much that other legitimate human needs begin to suffer. It is important to understand, however, that there is nothing wrong with our Basic Desire. The problem is that we try to fulfill it in misguided ways that lead us down paths that are ultimately self-defeating.

For example, the Basic Desire of the Six is to find security. As we will see, Sixes can seek security until they ultimately ruin everything in their lives, including, ironically, their security. In a similar way, every type is capable of becoming self-destructive by misguidedly and excessively pursuing its Basic Desire. We keep chasing after the same thing, using the same strategies, even though they are not giving us the results that we want.

Our Basic Desire also unwittingly blocks our Essential nature because the personality will not relinquish its control until it believes that the Basic

Desire has been obtained. For instance, a Six will not allow himself to relax and be present until he feels that his world is completely secure. Similarly, a One will not want to relax and become more present until everything in her world is perfect. Of course, these things will never happen.

Understanding the Basic Fear and Basic Desire gives particular insight into the ancient and universal teaching that human nature is driven by fear and desire. Thus, we might say that the whole of our personality structure is composed of our flight from our Basic Fear and our single-minded pursuit of our Basic Desire. The entire feeling-tone of our personality emerges out of this dynamic, and it becomes the foundation for our sense of self.

ESSENCE HAS BEEN CONSTRICTED BY PERSONALITY

Psychology suggests that much of our ability to function as well-integrated, mature adults is determined by how well our specific developmental needs were met in our early childhoods. Those needs that

BASIC DESIRES AND THEIR DISTORTIONS	
1	The desire to have integrity (deteriorates into critical perfectionism)
2	The desire to be loved (deteriorates into the need to be needed)
3	The desire to be valuable (deteriorates into chasing after success)
4	The desire to be oneself (deteriorates into self-indulgence)
5	The desire to be competent (deteriorates into useless specialization)
6	The desire to be secure (deteriorates into an attachment to beliefs)
7	The desire to be happy (deteriorates into frenetic escapism)
8	The desire to protect oneself (deteriorates into constant fighting)
9	The desire to be at peace (deteriorates into stubborn neglectfulness)

were not adequately met can be thought of as "gaps" that interfere with our ability to experience our Essential wholeness. Spiritual tradition further suggests that our personality has been formed to compensate for these gaps in our development. Our personality is like a cast that protects a broken arm or leg. The more extreme the original injuries, the more extensive the cast has to be. Of course, the cast is necessary so that the limb can heal and regain its full functioning. But if we never take the cast off, it severely limits the use of the limb and makes further growth impossible. Some people have had to develop the personality equivalent of a full body cast. None of us has gotten out of childhood without some need to hide, or to shut down and protect ourselves from any further hurt.

Seen as a temporary cast, the personality is a highly useful, utterly necessary aid because it has developed most powerfully around the areas of our soul's greatest wounding. It has become strongest where we are weakest. Thus, not only has personality helped us to survive psychologically, it can also now direct us to where we most need to do our transformational work.

But because most of our personality is no more than a collection of

LOST CHILDHOOD MESSAGES

While we receive many messages from childhood that limit us, there are also messages that every child needs to hear. We may have heard at least a few of them, but almost certainly not all. The Lost Message, the message that has not been heard (even if it has been sent), often becomes the central issue for the child and the core of his or her Basic Fear. Thus, for each type, the adult personality structure does whatever it can to have others give us the Lost Message we never adequately received.

Read the following Lost Messages and observe their impact on you. What message did you most need to hear? How does acknowledging that need affect you now?

Type One: "You are good."

Type Two: "You are wanted."

Type Three: "You are loved for yourself."

Type Four: "You are seen for who you are."

Type Five: "Your needs are not a problem."

Type Six: "You are safe."

Type Seven: "You will be taken care of."

Type Eight: "You will not be betrayed."

Type Nine: "Your presence matters."

conditioned reactions, fears, and beliefs and is not our true Self, our identification with it results in *a profound self-abandonment.* The experience of our identity has shifted from our true nature to the shell of defenses that we have had to develop. As long as we believe that "My personality is me," we will stay identified with our personality. One of the main reasons that we resist changing is that the movement back to our Essence always entails feeling the pain of our self-abandonment. When we are willing to say, "I want to be who I really am, and I want to live in the truth," the process of recovering ourselves has already begun.

For these reasons, in working with this material, we may be exposed to truths about ourselves that we have never known before, or we may reexperience old hurt, fear, or anger. That is why it is important to cultivate *compassion for ourselves:* we have to love ourselves enough to know that we are worth the effort to get to know ourselves *as we really are.* We have to love ourselves enough to know that even if we become anxious or depressed, we will not abandon ourselves again. When we are willing to experience the truth of how we have been and how we are now, and when we are willing to let ourselves be healed, our true nature emerges. The outcome is guaranteed: all we have to do is to show up.

Essence Cannot Be Lost or Harmed

No matter what our past, we can take heart that *even the most traumatic childhood experiences cannot damage or destroy our Essence.* Our Essence is still pure and untarnished, although it is constricted and obscured by the structures of our personality. If we come from a highly dysfunctional family, this structure will be extremely rigid and restricting. If we come from a more functional family, the personality structure will be lighter and more flexible.

Those who have come from highly dysfunctional families can take heart in knowing that the Essential self within us is completely intact and always looking for ways to manifest itself. Initially, we may have to spend a great deal of time and effort working on the gaps in our development, but the core of our Being is always there to support us. *Again, no matter how painful our early experiences were, our Essence cannot be harmed.* Our Essence is waiting for the opportunity to reveal itself. In a very true sense, *we* are waiting for the opportunity to become ourselves. Our spirit is yearning to break free, to express itself, to come back to life, to be in the world in the way that it was meant to be.

And yet, ironically, we always fear and resist opening to that which is most real in us. When we trust in the process and give ourselves over to it, however, our true nature comes forth. The result is real integrity, love, authenticity, creativity, understanding, guidance, joy, power, and serenity—all of the qualities we are forever demanding that personality supply.

"We are all serving a life-sentence in the dungeon of self."

CYRIL CONNOLLY

CHAPTER 4

CULTIVATING
AWARENESS

▲

HOW CAN WE get in touch with our true nature—the spark of divinity that lives within each of us? How can we peel away the layers of defenses and identifications that we have taken to be ourselves and learn to trust our Essence to give us sustenance and guidance? How do we do so not just in a workshop or in a peaceful mountainside retreat but in our daily lives? How can we move from an intellectual recognition of what is true, to *living* our truth from moment to moment? How can we make life our practice?

The Enneagram helps us let go of the limiting mechanisms of our personality so that we can more deeply experience who and what we really are. But this does not happen automatically. Understanding the personality types clearly and deeply is the prerequisite, although information alone is not enough to free us. We cannot will, or think, or "technique" our way into transformation. Yet without our participation it cannot happen. So what part do we play in our own transformation?

"CATCHING OURSELVES IN THE ACT"

Sacred traditions from around the world are united in stressing the importance of our being witnesses to our transformation. We are called on to be vigilant, to observe ourselves, and to bring mindfulness to ourselves and our activities. If we want to benefit from this map of the soul, we must cultivate the art of awareness, learning to be more awake to our lives in each moment without judgment and without excuse. We must learn to "catch ourselves in the act" of behaving according to the dictates of our personality, seeing how we are manifesting mechanically and unfreely from moment to moment. When we are able to notice what we are doing now, to experience our current state completely and without judgment, the old patterns will begin to fall away.

Awareness is vitally important in the work of transformation because the habits of our personality let go most completely when we see them *as they are occurring*. Analyzing past behavior is helpful, but it is not as powerful as observing ourselves as we are in the present moment. For example, it is certainly worthwhile to understand why we had a terrible argument with our spouse, or were irritable with an associate or a child. But if, while we are having an argument or are being irritable, we suddenly "catch ourselves in the act," something extraordinary can occur. In that moment of awareness, we may realize that we do not really want to do the questionable behavior that only seconds before we were so invested in. We may also see a deeper truth about our situation—for instance, that the "important point" we were so eager to make was really only an attempt to justify ourselves, or worse, a covert attempt to get back at someone. Or that the "witty remarks" we were having such fun with were really an attempt to avoid feeling sad or lonely.

If we are able to stay with these impressions, our awareness will continue to expand. We may initially feel embarrassed or ashamed; we may feel the urge to shut down or to distract ourselves in various ways. But if we stay present to our discomfort, we will also feel something else arising, something more real, capable, sensitive, and exquisitely aware of ourselves and our surroundings. This "something" feels compassionate and strong, patient and wise, indomitable, and of great value. This something is who we actually are. It is the "I" beyond name, without personality—our true nature.

WAKING UP

Awareness can not only change your life, it can save your life. Several years ago a major bridge on an interstate highway collapsed during the night of a heavy storm. Several sections in the middle of the bridge fell into the river, leaving unsuspecting motorists exposed to a life-threatening situation in the driving rain and confusion of the storm.

One alert driver saw what had happened and was able to bring his car to a stop only a few feet from the edge before he would have plunged to certain death in the river some forty feet below. He risked his life by running toward the oncoming traffic, frantically attempting to alert other drivers to the danger. Almost immediately a carload of five young men came along. They saw the man's frantic attempts to stop them but apparently thought that he was only trying to get help with his own stalled car. Laughing, they made a crude gesture at him and pushed the accelerator to the floor. A few seconds later they plunged off the edge of the bridge into the river below and were all killed.

From our perspective, it could be said that their personality killed them. Contemptuousness, hostility, bravado, unwillingness to listen, a lack of compassion, or showing off—any one of a number of related impulses—could have been the cause of the driver's decision not to stop. Some habit, some feature of his personality, had the upper hand at a critical moment, with tragic results.

It is a major breakthrough when we fully appreciate the extent to which we entrust our lives to the mechanisms of our personalities and what peril we are in when we do so. Many times it is as if a three-year-old were making many crucial life decisions for us. Once we understand the nature of our personality's mechanisms, we begin to have a choice about identifying with them or not. If we are not aware of them, clearly no choice is possible. As we see our Fiveness, or our Twoness, or our Eightness, however, the opportunity to "not do" our type appears.

Gurdjieff and other spiritual teachers have often asserted that our normal state of consciousness is a kind of "sleep." This may sound strange, but relative to the level of awareness that is possible for us, our ordinary state of consciousness is as far from a direct experience of reality as sleep is from waking consciousness. Nevertheless, we know that when we are asleep, our dreams can seem very real at the time. When we awaken and realize that we have been dreaming, our connection with reality shifts. Our sense of who and what we are comes into another focus.

Waking up from the trance of personality occurs in much the same way. We do a kind of double take, asking ourselves, "What was that all about? Where was I a moment ago?" We can be surprised at how lost we were, although in those previous states we did not feel lost. If someone had asked us if we were fully present and awake, we would have said yes, but from this new perspective we can see that we were not. We may realize that entire sections of our lives have actually been spent in "sleep."

"The Bible says that a deep sleep fell upon Adam, and nowhere is there a reference to his waking up."

A COURSE IN MIRACLES

CONSCIOUS LOOKING

Take a moment to look around the room that you are in right now. What have you not noticed about it before? Are there aspects of it that you have never seen? Really look. Don't take it for granted that you know everything in it. As you are looking, can you feel your body? Can you notice your posture while you are looking? As you attempt to do this, do you notice anything different between your current sense of yourself and the way you usually experience yourself?

What Is Awareness?

We use the term *awareness* a great deal, and it is an important term in many different approaches to psychological and spiritual growth. Yet finding an adequate definition for this word is difficult. It may be easier to define awareness by what it *is not* than by what it *is*. For instance, we can say that awareness is not thinking, not feeling, not moving, not intuition, and not instinct—even though it can contain any one or all of these things.

Even the most active, focused thinking is not the same thing as awareness. For example, we might be thinking intensely about what to write in this chapter, and we can also simultaneously be aware of our thinking processes. At another time we might notice that we are thinking about an upcoming business meeting—or rehearsing a possible conversation with someone in our head—while we are taking a walk. Usually our awareness is so completely taken up with our inner talk that we do not experience ourselves as separate from it. With more awareness, however, we are able to step back from our imaginary conversation and observe it.

In the same way we can become more aware of our feelings. We may catch ourselves getting caught up in irritation, or boredom, or loneliness. When we are less aware, we are identified with a feeling—*I* am frustrated, *I* am depressed—and we do not see its temporary nature: *we believe it is how we are.* After the storm has passed, we realize that the feeling actually was temporary, even though when we were in the middle of it, it was our whole reality. By contrast, when we are aware of our feelings, we clearly observe their arising, their impact on us, and their passing away.

We can also become more aware of what we are doing—of the actual sensations of our body in action or at rest. For both better or worse, our bodies have learned to do many things on automatic pilot. For instance, we are capable of driving a car and of having a conversation at the same time. We might be thinking about what we are going to say next while also feeling worried about getting to our destination, while our body is doing all the complicated things it needs to do to drive the car. All of this can occur automatically and without much awareness, or with awareness of any part of it, or with awareness of all of it.

Each moment presents us with the possibility of expanding our awareness—with many benefits to ourselves:

▶ When we relax and allow awareness to expand, we become less caught up in whatever has magnetized our attention. If we have been fearful or anxious or lost in daydreams and fantasies, we will gain objectivity and perspective about what we are doing. As a result, we will suffer less.

"Each thought, each action in the sunlight of awareness, becomes sacred."

THICH NHAT HANH

▶ Our expanded awareness enables us to bring more of ourselves and thus more resources to bear on whatever problems or difficulties we may be facing. We will see fresh solutions instead of reacting habitually, according to the mechanisms of our personality.

▶ Expanded awareness opens us to a real relationship with others and with the world around us. We are nourished and enriched by the pleasure and wonder of each moment. Even what we would ordinarily regard as unpleasant experiences have a very different quality when we experience them with awareness.

We also often use the word *see,* as in the expression "it is important for us to *see* the mechanisms of our personality." However, as with awareness, we need to be clear about what we mean by this word. More specifically, *it is vital that we understand what in us is doing the "seeing."* We are all well practiced at commenting on ourselves, or evaluating our experiences. In such cases, one part of our personality is criticizing or commenting on another part, as if to say, "I don't like that part of me" or "That was a great comment I just made," and so forth. This inner commentary usually leads to nothing more than an increasingly inflated, empty, and impoverished ego structure—and eventual inner warfare. This is not the kind of "seeing" we wish to cultivate.

"Seeing" is not a purely intellectual understanding, either. Our intellect certainly has a part to play, and we do not want to suggest that we do not need our minds in the process of transformation. But the part of us that sees is something more omnipresent yet elusive. It is sometimes called the *inner observer* or the *witness.* It is our total awareness, alive, here and now, and able to take in experience at many different levels.

LEARNING TO "OBSERVE AND LET GO"

One of the most important skills we must acquire as we embark on the inward journey is the ability to "observe and let go" of the habits and mechanisms of our personality that have trapped us.

Our maxim is deceptively simple. What it means is that we must learn to observe ourselves, seeing what arises in us from moment to moment, as well as seeing what calls us away from the here and now. Whatever we find, whether pleasant or unpleasant, we simply observe it. We do not try to change it, nor do we criticize ourselves for what we uncover. To the extent that we are fully present to whatever we find in ourselves, the constrictions of our personality begin to relax, and our Essence begins to manifest more fully.

Unlike what our ego may believe, it is not our role to repair or transform ourselves. Indeed, one of the major obstacles to transformation is the idea that we can "fix" ourselves. This notion, of course, raises some interesting questions. What in us do we believe needs fixing, and what part of us is claiming the authority to be able to fix another part? What parts are the judge, the jury, and the defendant in the dock? What are the tools of punishment or rehabilitation, and what parts of us will wield them on what other parts?

We are programmed from early childhood to believe that we need to be better, to try harder, and to discount parts of ourselves that other parts do not approve of. The whole of our culture and education constantly reminds us of how we can be more successful, desirable, secure, or spiritual if we were only to change in some way or other. In short, we have learned that we need to be different from how we actually are according to some formula the mind has received. The idea that we simply need to discover and accept who we actually are is contrary to almost everything we have been taught.

Clearly, if we are doing things that harm ourselves—such as abusing drugs or alcohol, or engaging in destructive relationships or criminal activities—then stopping that behavior is necessary before we can do meaningful transformational work. But what usually enables us to change is neither haranguing nor punishing ourselves but cultivating a quiet, centered awareness so that we can see what is compelling us to harm ourselves. When we bring awareness both to our bad habits as well as to the parts of ourselves that would like to rid us of them, something entirely new enters the picture.

As we learn to be present to our lives and open to the moment, miracles begin to happen. One of the greatest miracles is that we can drop a habit that has plagued us for many years in a minute. When we are fully present, the old habit lets go, and we are no longer the same. To experience the healing of our oldest and deepest wounds through the action of awareness is *the miracle we can all count on*. If we follow this map of the soul into the depths of our hearts, hatred will turn into compassion, rejection into acceptance, and fear into wonder.

Always remember that it is your birthright and natural state to be wise and noble, loving and generous, to esteem yourself and others, to be creative and constantly renewing yourself, to be engaged in the world in awe and in depth, to have courage and to rely on yourself, to be joyous and effortlessly accomplished, to be strong and effective, to enjoy peace of mind and to be present to the unfolding mystery of your life.

"We do not have to improve ourselves; we just have to let go of what blocks our heart."

JACK KORNFIELD

"Through our senses the world appears. Through our reactions we create delusions. Without reactions the world becomes clear."

BUDDHA

SPIRITUAL JUMP STARTS

No matter what type you are, there are specific things you can do to "jump start" your spiritual and personal growth. All of the following are type-specific problem areas, but everyone gets caught up in them from time to time. So, if you want to move forward in your inner work, bring your awareness, as fully as possible, to the following patterns:

▶ Value-judging, condemning yourself and others (One)

▶ Giving your value away to others (Two)

▶ Trying to be other than you authentically are (Three)

▶ Making negative comparisons (Four)

▶ Overinterpreting your experience (Five)

▶ Becoming dependent on something outside yourself for support (Six)

▶ Anticipating what you are going to do next (Seven)

▶ Trying to force or control your life (Eight)

▶ Resisting being affected by your experiences (Nine)

IDENTIFICATION AND THE INNER OBSERVER

As we gain experience with being present and observing ourselves, we begin to notice the development of a seemingly new aspect of our awareness—a profound ability to "witness" our experience more objectively. As we have noted, this quality of awareness has been called the *inner observer*. The inner observer allows us to observe what is going on in and around us simultaneously, without commentary or judgment.

The inner observer is necessary for transformation because of a psychological mechanism Gurdjieff called "identification," which is one of the primary ways our personalities create and sustain their reality.

The personality can identify with just about anything—an idea, our body, an itch, a sunset, a child, or a song. That is, at any moment in which we are not fully awake in the present moment, our sense of identity comes from whatever we are paying attention to. For instance, if we are fretting, focusing our attention on an upcoming meeting, it is as if we were experiencing the meeting (although an imaginary one) instead of what is actually happening right now. Or, if we are identified with an emotional reaction—for instance, an attraction to another person—it is as if we *become* that attraction. Or if we feel berated by a critical voice in our heads, we cannot separate ourselves from that voice.

If we quiet our minds even a little, we notice how our states fluctu-

"Identification . . . is a form of escape from the self."

KRISHNAMURTI

ate from one moment to the next. One instant we are thinking about our job, in the next we notice someone crossing the street who reminds us of a date we had some years ago. An instant later we are recalling a song from our school days until we are splashed by a car driving through a puddle. Instantly we are filled with rage at the idiot driving the car and can think of nothing else until we realize that we want a candy bar to make ourselves feel better. And on it goes. The only thing that is consistent is our personality's tendency to identify with each successive state.

Awareness expands and contracts like a balloon, but identification always causes it to become smaller. We might notice that when we are identified with something, our awareness of our immediate surroundings is greatly diminished. We are less aware of other people, of our environment, and of our own inner state. Simply put, the more identified we are, the more contracted our awareness is—and the more out of touch with reality we are.

> "Very few men, properly speaking, live at present, but are providing to live another time."
>
> JONATHAN SWIFT

CONTINUUM OF AWARENESS

For this exercise you will need a watch or a clock and, if possible, a tape recorder. Find a place where you can sit comfortably and observe the room or location you are in. For five minutes, follow your attention as best you can, naming whatever you are paying attention to. For example, you might say, "I am noticing the way the light hits that wall. I am noticing that I am wondering why I looked at the wall. I am noticing that I am tensing my right shoulder. I am noticing that I feel nervous," and so forth.

You may wish to record your observations, or you may wish to do this exercise with a partner. Even if you do the exercise without a recording or a partner, see if you can discern any patterns in the movement of your awareness. Do you focus more on your thoughts? On the environment? On your sensations? On your feelings and reactions? Do certain themes emerge?

Over time our identification with a certain set of qualities (such as strength, empathy, peacefulness, or spontaneity, to name just a few) becomes fixed, and our type's characteristic sense of self is established. The feelings and states that comprise our sense of self are those we think are necessary for achieving our Basic Desire. The more we identify with our sense of self, the more we become locked into it, and the more we forget that other choices and other modes of being are available to us. We start to believe that we *are* this pattern. We focus on only certain qualities from the total range of our human potentials as if saying, "These qualities are me, but those are not. I am this way, but not that way." Thus we develop a self-image, a self-definition—a predictable personality type.

For example, the Basic Fear of Eights is of being harmed or controlled by other people or by life, and their Basic Desire is to protect and defend themselves. Self-protection and self-reliance are universal human

CORE IDENTIFICATIONS OF THE TYPES

Type	Identifies powerfully with:	To sustain the self-image of being:		
1	The superego, with the capacity to evaluate, compare, measure, and discern experiences or things. Resists recognizing anger-based tension.	reasonable sensible objective	moderate prudent moral	"good" rational
2	Feelings for and about others and feelings about others' responses to them. Resists recognizing own feelings about self and needs.	loving caring selfless	thoughtful warm-hearted concerned	kind compassionate
3	A self-image developed in response to what they perceive as admiration by others. Resists recognizing feelings of emptiness, own self-rejection.	admirable desirable attractive	outstanding well-adjusted effective	having "unlimited potential"
4	Feelings of "otherness," of being flawed, and with emotional reactions. Resists recognizing authentic positive qualities in self and being like others.	sensitive different unique	self-aware gentle intuitive	quiet, deep honest with self
5	Sense of being a detached, outside observer of the world—not part of it. Resists recognizing physical presence and state, feelings and needs.	perceptive "smart" curious	self-contained insightful unusual	alert objective
6	The need to respond and react to inner anxiety about perceived lack of support. Resists recognizing support and own inner guidance.	reliable dependable trustworthy	likable "regular" careful	having foresight questioning
7	Sense of excitement coming from anticipating future positive experiences. Resists recognizing personal pain and anxiety.	enthusiastic free-spirited spontaneous	cheerful eager outgoing	energetic positive
8	Sense of intensity coming from resisting or challenging others and environment. Resists recognizing own vulnerability and need for nurturing.	strong assertive direct	resourceful action-oriented tenacious	robust independent
9	Sense of inner stability coming from disengagement from intense impulses and feelings. Resists recognizing own strength and capacity.	peaceful relaxed steady	stable gentle natural	easygoing friendly

needs, and even if we are not Eights, we need to protect ourselves physically and emotionally. Young Eights, however, begin to focus on the qualities they find in themselves that will help them protect themselves. They discover their strength, willpower, perseverance, and self-assertion and start using these capacities to develop and reinforce their ego identity.

THE FEAR OF BEING PRESENT

Inevitably, when we stay open to ourselves for any period of time, we begin to feel anxious, intuiting that something uncomfortable may arise. This happens because we are "pushing the envelope" of our personality. We can take heart because experiencing some degree of anxiety during transformational work is a good sign. When we move beyond our old defenses, we also start to experience the very feelings that we have been defending ourselves from all of our lives.

This explains why we can have fulfilling spiritual experiences and then quickly find ourselves in a fearful, reactive, or negative state again. *The process of growth entails an ongoing cycling among letting go of old blockages, opening up to new possibilities in ourselves, and then encountering deeper levels of blockage.* Although we might wish that spiritual growth would be more linear and that it could be accomplished in one or two major breakthroughs, the reality is that it is a process that we must go through many times on many different fronts until our whole psyche is reorganized.

Spiritual growth is also a process that requires us to be gentle and patient with ourselves. Frustration, specific expectations about our growth, timetables for spiritual progress, and disparaging ourselves when we fall short of our expectations are all common reactions, but they do not help. It took many years to build up our ego defenses, so we cannot expect to dismantle them overnight. Our soul has its own wisdom, and it will not allow us to see anything about ourselves (much less release it) until we are truly ready to do so.

When we begin to do this kind of work, there is also a common fear that being present means sitting around "contemplating our navel" or staring at a wall. We have the notion that if we become more present, we will not be able to deal with the important problems in our lives—we will be "spacey," impractical, and ineffective. In fact, just the reverse is true: we are more alert and our judgments and insights are more accurate.

Likewise, many of us believe that if we become more present, we will lose all of our hard-won maturity or professional skills. Again, this is the reverse of what actually happens. When we are present, we are able to do things better and more consistently than ever before; we also acquire new skills far more easily because our concentration improves. When we are mindful, our intelligence operates in ways that will

"And if not now, when?"

THE TALMUD

"If you are irritated by every rub, how will your mirror be polished?"

RUMI

"In the final analysis, we count for something only because of the essential we embody, and if we do not embody that, life is wasted."

JUNG

surprise us, calling forth exactly the piece of information or skill required to solve the problem at hand.

On yet a deeper level, we are afraid to stay present and to really show up in our lives because we are terrified that we will relive all of our childhood wounds. If we dare to unveil our true nature, it might not be seen or loved. It might be rejected or humiliated; it might make us feel vulnerable or cause others to fear or betray us. We fear that others will abandon us. We fear that the preciousness of our souls will be disregarded or harmed again.

And yet when we actually show up more fully, we experience immense space, peace, and a quiet aliveness. We discover that we are solid, immensely alive, and connected with the world around us. There is no reason not to live this way, except for the reasons that our personality gives us—biased, self-interested reasons, to be sure.

AWARENESS LEADS TO PRESENCE

If we stay with this process, paying attention to what is real—to what is happening right now—we begin to experience a subtle *Presence* pervading our inner space and our surroundings. It feels light, exquisite, and pleasurable and can manifest many different qualities. Thus, by bringing our awareness to the actual experience of the present moment, we begin to be filled with Presence. Indeed, we may recognize that *this Presence is what we fundamentally are.*

"If you would only switch on the light of awareness and observe yourself and everything around you throughout the day, if you would see yourself reflected in the mirror of awareness the way you see your face reflected in a looking glass, that is, accurately, clearly, exactly as it is without the slightest distortion or addition, and if you observed this reflection without any judgment or condemnation, you would experience all sorts of marvelous changes coming about in you. Only you will not be in control of those changes, or be able to plan them in advance, or decide how and when they are to take place. It is this nonjudgmental awareness alone that heals and changes and makes one grow. But in its own way and at its own time."

ANTHONY DeMELLO,
THE WAY TO LOVE

What is remarkable is that *Presence always reveals what in us is blocking us from becoming more present.* The more we become present, the more we become aware of the parts of our selves that are not relaxed, the parts that we have not fully occupied. The more we are able to relax, the more we become aware of the subtle movement of Presence filling us and surrounding us. It may be helpful just to stay with that impression without labeling it or thinking about it too much. In time, what was subtle and vague will become clearer and more distinct as new layers of Being reveal themselves to us.

Presence breaks in on our daydreams and identifications all the time, and yet because of the structures of our personality, we cannot hold our ground to remain present. The further into the trance of our ego we go, the more "charged" our personality mechanisms become, as if they were electromagnets exerting a fierce and desperate energy. However, becoming attuned to the vibrant nature of Presence, and seeing the enormous investment of our life energy in the "projects" of the personality, provides a way out. At the same time, we cannot simply decide to be present; yet without the intention to be present, Presence is impossible. So how can a person in a trance break out of his own trance?

Clearly, such a heroic undertaking is almost impossible without adequate tools and support. In subsequent chapters we will look at how help in awakening can come from a profound system of understanding like the Enneagram and, most importantly, from a daily practice to cultivate awareness and Presence. In addition, we will suggest a number of tools and supports that can function as "alarm clocks" to awaken us from our trance. The more we heed these "wake-up calls," the more Presence we will have (and the more possible it will be *to wake ourselves up*). But this takes much practice.

Make no mistake—this is a lifelong work. The more moments of awakening we have, however, the more they collectively add momentum to the process of awakening: something is deposited in us—a kernel, the seed of a pearl—that does not go away when we return to our ordinary state. To help us know when we are awake, there are three characteristics we can look for:

1. *We fully experience our Presence as a living being, here and now.* We know that there is someone here; we feel our substantiality, our "is-ness," and, as a result, we are grounded in the moment. Moreover, this occurs not because we are picturing ourselves from some outside viewpoint, but because we are "inside" our experience, fully connected with the sensations of life in our bodies, from the top of our heads to the bottoms of our feet. There is no feeling of resistance to the reality of the moment.

2. We take in the impressions of our internal and external environments completely and *without judgment or emotional reaction.* We are able to observe the many thoughts and feelings that pass through our awareness without becoming attached to any of them. We interact with life from an inner quiet and stillness rather than from anxieties and inner franticness. Our attention is on what is occurring now, not dreaming of the past or anticipating the future or fantasizing about something else.

3. *We are fully participating in the moment,* allowing ourselves to be touched by the impressions around us and to fully taste and experience the richness and subtlety of our life. We are utterly sincere and without artifice or self-consciousness. In each moment, we experience our identity as something entirely new and fresh. We are always looking for a formula, a rule, or a prayer that will turn the trick for us. But *there is no substitute for Presence.* Without Presence, none of the prayers, meditations, teachers, and techniques in the world can transform us. This is why we can spend many years observing the practices of our religion and still not be able to consistently embody the beliefs that we hold. We can have extraordinary experiences and moments of being free from the shackles of our personality, but sooner or later—and usually much sooner than we would like—we return to our old ways. This is because we do not understand the vital importance of Presence: it is not, and cannot be, part of our personality or its agenda.

"Spirit is *always* present, just as the sun is always shining above the clouds."

DAN MILLMAN

The good news is that Presence is already here, even though our awareness of it has become limited by our preoccupation with the narrow concerns of personality. As we begin to value awareness and to cultivate it and engage in practices to strengthen it, the deeper qualities of our Essential nature manifest themselves more and more clearly.

AN INVITATION TO ABUNDANCE

The Enneagram reminds us of the different elements or qualities that constitute a complete human being. Each of the following invitations is based on the strengths symbolized by the nine types; no matter what type we are, we can respond to all of them.

Invitation **1**	*To live for a Higher Purpose.* Remember that it is your true nature to be wise and discerning.
Invitation **2**	*To nurture yourself and others.* Remember that it is your true nature to be good to yourself and to have goodwill and compassion for others.
Invitation **3**	*To develop yourself and set an example for others.* Remember that it is your true nature to take pleasure in your existence and to esteem and value others.
Invitation **4**	*To let go of the past and be renewed by your experiences.* Remember that it is your true nature to be forgiving and to use everything in life for your growth and renewal.
Invitation **5**	*To observe yourself and others without judgment or expectations.* Remember that it is your true nature to be engaged with reality, contemplating the infinite riches of the world.
Invitation **6**	*To have faith in yourself and trust in the goodness of life.* Remember that it is your true nature to be courageous and capable of dealing with life under all conditions.
Invitation **7**	*To joyously celebrate existence and share your happiness.* Remember that it is your true nature to be happy and to add to the richness of experience for everyone.
Invitation **8**	*To stand up for yourself and to speak out for what you believe.* Remember that it is your true nature to be strong and capable of affecting the world in many different positive ways.
Invitation **9**	*To bring peace and healing into your world.* Remember that it is your true nature to be an inexhaustible font of serenity, acceptance, and kindness in the world.

▼

CHAPTER 5

THE TRIADIC
SELF

▲

IF HUMAN BEINGS were able to stay centered in their Essential unity, there would be no need for the Enneagram. But without working on ourselves, we cannot become centered. It is a universal perception of the great spiritual traditions that human nature is divided—against itself, and against the Divine. Our *lack* of unity is, in fact, more characteristic of our "normal" reality than our Essential unity.

Amazingly, the Enneagram symbol accounts for both aspects of human nature in its unity (the circle) and in the way it is divided (the triangle and the hexad). Every part of the Enneagram reveals psychological and spiritual truths about who we are, deepening our understanding of our predicament while simultaneously suggesting solutions to that predicament.

In this chapter, we will examine the major ways in which the original unity of the human psyche has been divided—into Triads, different groups of three. The nine types are not isolated categories but are interrelated in extremely rich and profound ways that have meanings beyond individual psychological types.

THE TRIADS

The Triads are important for transformational work because they specify where our chief imbalance lies. The Triads represent the three main clusters of issues and defenses of the ego self, and they reveal the principal ways in which we contract our awareness and limit ourselves.

This first grouping of the types refers to the three basic components of the human psyche: instinct, feeling, and thinking. According

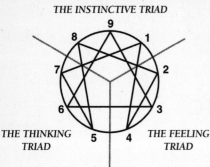

THE INSTINCTIVE TRIAD

THE THINKING
TRIAD

THE FEELING
TRIAD

to Enneagram theory, these three functions are related to subtle "Centers" in the human body, and the personality fixation is associated primarily in one of these Centers. Types Eight, Nine, and One comprise the Instinctive Triad; types Two, Three, and Four make up the Feeling Triad; and types Five, Six, and Seven are the Thinking Triad.

It is worth noting that modern medicine also divides the human brain into three basic components: the root brain, or instinctual brain; the limbic system, or emotional brain; and the cerebral cortex, or the thinking part of the brain. Some teachers of the Enneagram also refer to the three Centers as the head, heart, and gut, or as the thinking, feeling, and doing Centers respectively.

No matter what type we are, our personality contains all three components—instinct, feeling, and thinking. All three interact with each other, and we cannot work on one without affecting the others. But for most of us, caught in the world of personality as we usually are, it is difficult to distinguish these components of ourselves. Nothing in our modern education has taught us how to do so.

Each of these Triads represents a range of Essential capacities or functions that have become blocked or distorted. The personality then tries to fill in the gaps where our Essence has been blocked, and the Triad that our type is in indicates where the constrictions to our Essence and the artificial filler of our personality are most strongly operative. For example, if we are an Eight, we have been blocked in the Essential quality of strength; thus, our personality has stepped in and has attempted to *imitate* real strength by causing us to act tough and sometimes to assert ourselves in inappropriate ways. The false strength of our personality has taken over and concealed the blockage of real strength even from us. Until we understand this, we cannot recognize or recover our authentic, Essential strength.

In a similar way, each personality type replaces other Essential qualities with imitations that we identify with and try to make the most of.

Paradoxically, if someone's type is in the Feeling Triad, this does not mean that they have more feelings than other people. Similarly, if someone is in the Thinking Triad, this does not mean that they are more intelligent than others are. In fact, in each Triad, the function in question (instinct, feeling, or thinking) is the function that the ego has most strongly formed around, and it is therefore *the component of the psyche that is least able to function freely.*

THE MAJOR THEMES OF THE THREE TRIADS

The Instinctive Triad

Types Eight, Nine, and One are concerned with maintaining resistance to reality (creating boundaries for the self that are based on physical tensions). These types tend to have problems with aggression and repression. Underneath their ego defenses they carry a great deal of *rage*.

The Feeling Triad

Types Two, Three, and Four are concerned with self-image (attachment to the false or assumed self of personality). They believe that the stories about themselves and their assumed qualities are their actual identity. Underneath their ego defenses these types carry a great deal of *shame*.

The Thinking Triad

Types Five, Six, and Seven are concerned with anxiety (they experience a lack of support and guidance). They engage in behaviors that they believe will enhance their safety and security. Underneath their ego defenses these types carry a great deal of *fear*.

IN THE INSTINCTIVE TRIAD

Types Eight, Nine, and One have formed around distortions in their instincts, the root of our life-force and vitality. The Instinctive Triad is concerned with the intelligence of the body, with basic life functioning and survival.

The body plays a crucial role in all forms of genuine spiritual work, because bringing awareness back to the body anchors the quality of Presence. The reason is fairly obvious: while our minds and feelings can wander to the past or the future, *our body can only exist here and now, in the present moment.* This is one of the fundamental reasons why virtually all meaningful spiritual work begins with coming back to the body and becoming more grounded in it.

Moreover, the instincts of the body are the most powerful energies that we have to work with. Any real transformation must involve them, and any work that ignores them is almost certain to create problems.

▶ CONCERNED WITH: Resistance & Control of the Environment

▶ HAVE ISSUES WITH: Aggression & Repression

▶ SEEKS: Autonomy

▶ UNDERLYING FEELING: RAGE

"All spiritual interests are supported by animal life."

GEORGE SANTAYANA

The body has an amazing intelligence and sensitivity, and it also has its own language and its own way of knowing. In indigenous societies, such as the aboriginal tribes of Australia, people have maintained a more open relationship with the intelligence of the body. There have been documented cases in which aborigines knew in their bodies that one of their relatives had been injured many miles away. This body-knowledge enabled them to walk directly toward the injured person to help them.

Most of us in modern societies are almost entirely estranged from the wisdom of our bodies. The psychological term for this is *dissociation,* in everyday language we call this *checking out.* In a busy, stress-filled day, it is likely we sense our body only if it is in pain. For instance, we do not usually notice that we have feet unless our shoes are too tight. Even though our back is highly sensitive, we are usually unaware of it unless we are getting a massage, or have a sunburn or a back injury—and sometimes not even then.

BEING PRESENT IN THE BODY

At this moment, as you are reading the words on this page, can you feel your body? How much of it? Where is your body positioned right now? How deeply are you experiencing it? What helps you experience it more deeply?

When we truly inhabit our Instinctive Center—fully occupying our body—it gives us a profound sense of fullness, stability, and autonomy or independence. When we lose contact with our Essence, the personality attempts to "fill in" by providing a false sense of autonomy.

To give us this false sense of autonomy, the personality creates what psychology calls *ego boundaries.* With ego boundaries, we are able to say, "This is me and that is not me. That out there is not me, but this sensation (or thought, or feeling) here is me." We usually believe that these boundaries correspond with our skin and therefore with the dimensions of our real bodies, but this is not always true.

This is because we are usually sensing habitual tensions, *not* necessarily the actual contours of our bodies. We may also notice that we have almost no sensation in some parts of our bodies: they feel blank or empty. The truth is that we are always carrying around a felt sense of self that has little to do with how our body actually is, where it is positioned, or what we are doing. The set of *internal tensions* that create our unconscious sense of self is the foundation of the personality, the first layer.

While all of the types employ ego boundaries, the Eight, Nine, and One do so for a particular reason—*they are attempting to use their will to affect the world without being affected by it.* They try to influence their environment, to remake it, control it, hold it back, without having their sense of self influenced by it. To put this differently, all three of these types *resist being influenced by reality in different ways.* They try to create a sense of wholeness and autonomy by building a "wall" between what they consider self and not self, although where these walls are varies from type to type and from person to person.

Our ego boundaries fall into two categories. The first boundary is directed *outward.* It usually corresponds to our physical body, although not always. When we cut our fingernails or hair, or have a tooth extracted, we no longer regard them as part of ourselves. Conversely, we may subconsciously regard certain people or possessions as part of ourselves—our home, our spouse, or children—although, of course, they are not.

The second boundary is directed *inward.* For example, we say that we "had a dream," but we do not think that we *are* the dream. Some of our thoughts or feelings will also be seen as separate from our identity, while we definitely identify with others. Of course, different people will identify with different feelings and thoughts. One person may experience anger as part of the self while another will view anger as something alien. In all cases, however, it is important to remember that these divisions are arbitrary and are the results of habits of the mind.

In Type Eight the ego boundary is primarily focused outward, against the environment. The focus of attention is also outward. The result is an expansiveness and an outpouring of the Eight's vitality into the world. Eights are constantly putting out energy so that nothing can get too close and hurt them. Their whole approach to life is as if they were saying, "Nothing's going to get the upper hand on me. No one is going to get through my defenses and hurt me. I'm going to keep my guard up." The more wounded an Eight is from childhood, the thicker their ego boundary, and the tougher they are going to make it for others to get through to them.

Type One individuals also hold a boundary against the outside world, but *they are far more invested in maintaining their internal boundary.* All of us have aspects of ourselves that we do not trust or approve of that make us feel anxious and that we want to defend ourselves from. Ones expend enormous energy trying to hold back certain unconscious impulses, trying to keep them from getting into consciousness. It is as if Ones were saying to themselves, "I don't want that feeling! I don't want to have that reaction or that impulse!" They create a great deal of physical tension to maintain their inner boundaries and hold aspects of their own inner nature at bay.

Type Nine, the central type in the Triad (the type positioned on the

"When you are describing or explaining or even just inwardly feeling your 'self,' what you are actually doing, whether you know it or not, is drawing a mental line or boundary across the whole field of your experience, and everything on the *inside* of that boundary you are feeling or calling your 'self' while everything *outside* that boundary you feel to be 'not-self.' Your self-identity, in other words, depends entirely upon where you draw that boundary line. . . ."

KEN WILBER

DIRECTIONS OF EGO BOUNDARIES IN THE INSTINCTIVE TRIAD

EIGHTS: ENERGY DIRECTED OUTWARD AGAINST THE ENVIRONMENT

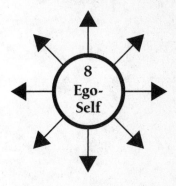

ONES: ENERGY DIRECTED INWARD AGAINST THEIR INTERNAL IMPULSES

equilateral triangle), tries *to hold their ego boundaries in both areas, internal and external.* In the internal realm, Nines do not want certain feelings and states to disturb their equilibrium. They put up a wall against parts of themselves just as Ones do, suppressing powerful instinctive drives and emotions. At the same time, Nines maintain a strong ego boundary against the outside world so that they will not be hurt, like Eights. They often engage in passive-aggressive behaviors and turn a blind eye to whatever threatens their peace. It is no wonder that Nines report that they often feel fatigued, because it takes a tremendous amount of energy to resist reality on both "fronts." If Nines use most of their vitality to maintain these boundaries, it is not available for living and engaging more fully in the world.

Each of these three types has problems with *aggression.* (While all nine personality types are aggressive in different ways, the energy of aggression is a key component in the Instinctive types' ego structures.) Sometimes the aggression is directed toward the self, sometimes at others. In the course of psychological or spiritual work, this aggressive energy often emerges as a powerful sense of *rage.* Rage is the instinctive reaction to feeling the need to suppress ourselves—the need to close down and constrict our aliveness. *Eights tend to act out rage, Nines tend to deny it,* and *Ones tend to repress it.*

We can understand the function of rage more clearly in the experience of a child. All of us, either consciously or unconsciously, feel that as children we did not have the space that we needed to fully develop. When we start exploring this realm of experience, we will discover that beneath our grown-up veneer, we are suppressing (or even more so, repressing) an intense anger that has resulted from this insult to our Essential integrity. (On the positive side, anger is also a way of telling others "Stay away from me so that I can have my own space! I want and need to be whole and independent.") The problem is that if we carry these issues from our childhood, we will continue to feel as though we need to protect our "personal space" even when there is no actual threat to it. Once these issues have been worked through, the energy that drives our rage—as well as the energy that keeps it suppressed—can be released and redirected toward other, more fulfilling goals, including our transformation.

IN THE FEELING TRIAD

In the Instinctive Triad, we saw how seldom we really occupy our bodies and are really present with our full vitality. In the same way, we seldom dare to be fully in our hearts. When we are, it is often overwhelming. We therefore substitute all kinds of reactions for the power of real feelings. This is the core dilemma of the Feeling Triad: types Two, Three, and Four.

At the deepest level, *your heart qualities are the source of your identity.* When your heart opens, you know who you are, and that "who you are" has nothing to do with what people think of you and nothing to do with your past history. You have a particular quality, a flavor, something that is unique and intimately *you.* It is through the heart that we recognize and appreciate our true nature.

When we are in contact with the heart, we feel loved and valued. Moreover, as the great spiritual traditions teach, the heart reveals that *we are love and value.* Our share in the Divine nature means not only that we are loved by God, but that the presence of love resides in us— we are the conduit through which love comes into the world. When our hearts are closed off and blocked, however, not only do we lose contact with our true identity, but we do not feel valued or loved. This loss is intolerable, so the personality steps in to create a substitute identity and to find other things to give us a sense of value, usually by seeking attention and external affirmation from others.

▶ CONCERNED WITH: Love of False Self & Self-Image

▶ HAVE ISSUES WITH: Identity & Hostility

▶ SEEKS: Attention

▶ UNDERLYING FEELING: SHAME

THE FEELING CENTER

Right now, as you are reading these words on this page, turn your attention to the area of your heart. Take some deep, easy breaths, and actually sense into your chest. What sensations do you experience in this area? Allow yourself to relax and breathe deeply and see what you are feeling in the area of your heart. Does it feel sharp? Tender? Numb? Aching? What is the exact feeling you are experiencing? If this feeling had a color or shape or taste, what would it be? What effect does this exercise have on your sense of yourself?

Thus, the three types of the Feeling Triad are primarily concerned with the development of a self-image. They compensate for a lack of deeper connection with the Essential qualities of the heart by erecting a false identity and becoming identified with it. They then present this image to others (as well as to themselves) in the hope that it will attract love, attention, approval, and a sense of value.

In psychological terms, Twos, Threes, and Fours are the types most concerned with their "narcissistic wounding," that is, with not being valued for who they really were as children. Because no one graduates from childhood without some degree of narcissistic damage, as adults, we have a lot of difficulty being authentic with one another. There is always the fear that, when all is said and done, we are really empty and worthless. The tragic result is that we almost never actually see each other or allow ourselves to be seen, no matter what type we are. We

"All we need to do is to give up our habit of regarding as real that which is unreal. All religious practices are meant solely to help us do this. When we stop regarding the unreal as real, then reality alone will remain, and we will be that."

RAMANA MAHARSHI

substitute an image instead, as if we were saying to the world, "This is who I am—isn't it? You like it—don't you?" People may affirm us (that is, our image), but as long as we identify with our personality, something deeper always goes unaffirmed.

The types of the Feeling Triad present us with three different solutions to this dilemma: going out to please others so that they will like you (Type Two); achieving things and becoming outstanding in some way so that people will admire and affirm you (Type Three); or having an elaborate story about yourself and attaching tremendous significance to all of your personal characteristics (Type Four).

Two major themes in this Triad involve *identity issues* ("Who am I?") and *problems with hostility* ("I hate you for not loving me in the way I want!"). Because Twos, Threes, and Fours unconsciously know that their identity is not an expression of who they really are, they respond with hostility whenever their personality-identity is not validated. Hostility serves both to deflect people who might question or devalue this identity, and to defend these types against deeper feelings of shame and humiliation.

Type Two is looking for value in the good regard of others. Twos want to be wanted; they try to obtain favorable reactions by giving people their energy and attention. Twos look for positive responses to their overtures of friendliness, help, and goodness in order to build up their own self-esteem. The focus of their feelings is outward, on others, but as a result, they often have difficulty knowing what their own feelings are telling them. They also frequently feel unappreciated, although, as much as possible, they must conceal the hostile feelings that this generates.

Type Four is the opposite: their energy and attention go inward to maintain a self-image based on feelings, fantasies, and stories from the past. Their personality-identity centers on being "different," being unlike anyone else, and as a result, they often feel estranged from people. Fours tend to create and sustain moods rather than allow whatever feelings are actually present to arise. Less healthy Fours often see themselves as victims and prisoners of their pasts. They believe that there is no hope of being another way because of all the tragedies and abuses that have befallen them. This is also their way of eliciting attention and pity from others and, hence, some degree of validation.

Type Three, the central type of this Triad (the type positioned on the equilateral triangle), directs attention and energy both inward and outward. Like Twos, Threes need the positive feedback and affirmation of others. Threes primarily seek value through accomplishment; they develop notions about what a valuable person would be like, then try to become that person. But Threes also engage in a great deal of internal "self-talk," attempting to create and sustain a consistent internal picture of themselves, like Fours. They are always in danger of "believing their own press releases" more than the truth.

FOCUS OF SELF-IMAGE IN THE FEELING TRIAD

TWOS: SELF-IMAGE PRESENTED OUTWARDLY TO OTHERS

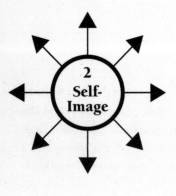

FOURS: SELF-IMAGE PRESENTED INWARDLY TO THEMSELVES

Despite the various images presented by these types, at root they feel valueless, and many of their personality's agendas are attempts to disguise this from themselves and others. Twos attempt to get a sense of value by saying, "I know I am valuable because others love and value me. I do good things for people, and they appreciate me." Twos are *rescuers*. On the opposite side of the spectrum, Fours are *rescuees*. Fours tell themselves, "I know I am valuable because I am unique and unlike anyone else. I am special because someone took the trouble to rescue me. Someone is taking the trouble to attend to my distress, so I must be worthwhile." Threes are paragons who *do not need rescuing,* as if to say, "I know I am valuable because I've got my act together—there's nothing wrong with me. I am valuable because of my accomplishments." Despite their individual methods for "building self-esteem," all three of these types lack a proper love of self.

If the types of the Instinctive Triad are trying to manage feelings of rage, in the Feeling Triad Twos, Threes, and Fours are trying to deal with feelings of *shame*. When our authentic, Essential qualities are not mirrored in early childhood, we come to the conclusion that something is wrong with us. The resulting feeling is shame. By attempting to feel valuable by means of their self-image, these types hope to escape feelings of shame. Twos become ultragood, trying to be caring and of service to others so that they will not feel shame. Threes become perfect in their performance and outstanding in their achievements so they will be able to resist feeling shame. Fours avoid deeper feelings of shame by dramatizing their losses and hurts and by seeing themselves as victims.

IN THE THINKING TRIAD

If the Instinctive Triad is about *maintaining a felt sense of self* and the Feeling Triad is about *maintaining a personal identity,* the Thinking Triad is about *finding a sense of inner guidance and support.* The dominant feelings in types Five, Six, and Seven are *anxiety* and *insecurity.* To put it another way, the Instinctive Triad types are concerned with resisting aspects of the present. The Feeling Triad types are all past-oriented because our self-image is built up out of memories and interpretations of the past. The Thinking Triad types are more concerned about the future, as if to ask, "What's going to happen to me? How am I going to survive? How can I prepare myself to keep bad things from happening? How do I move forward in life? How do I cope?"

The Thinking Triad has lost touch with the aspect of our true nature that in some spiritual traditions is called the *quiet mind.* The quiet mind is the source of inner guidance that gives us the ability to perceive

THREES: SELF-IMAGE
PRESENTED BOTH TO SELF
AND TO OTHERS

▶ CONCERNED WITH: Strategies & Beliefs

▶ HAVE ISSUES WITH: Insecurity & Anxiety

▶ SEEKS: Security

▶ UNDERLYING FEELING: FEAR

"We must be willing to get rid of the life we've planned, so as to have the life that's waiting for us."

JOSEPH CAMPBELL

reality exactly as it is. It allows us to be receptive to an inner knowing that can guide our actions. But just as we are seldom fully in our bodies or in our hearts, we seldom have access to the quiet, spacious quality of the mind. Quite the contrary, for most of us, the mind an inner chatterbox, which is why people spend years in monasteries or in retreats trying to quiet their restless minds. In personality, the mind is not quiet and not naturally "knowing"—it is forever trying to come up with a strategy or a formula so that it can do whatever it thinks will allow us to function in the world.

THE THINKING CENTER

Right now, allow yourself to relax and get in greater contact with the sensations and impressions you are having. Actually sense what it feels like to be alive in your body at this time. Don't visualize—let yourself experience whatever is here. As you become more grounded and calm, you may begin to notice your mind becoming less "noisy." Continue this process for a few minutes. Stay in contact with your immediate sensations and impressions, and see what effect this has on your thinking. As your mind becomes quieter, are your perceptions clearer or fuzzier? Does your mind seem sharper or duller?

Fives, Sixes, and Sevens cannot get their minds to simmer down. This is a problem because the quiet mind allows us to feel profoundly supported; inner knowing and guidance arise in the quiet mind and give us confidence to act in the world. When these qualities are blocked, we feel fear. Their reactions to fear distinguish the three types of the Thinking Triad.

Type Five responds by retreating from life and reducing their personal needs. Fives believe that they are too frail and insubstantial to safely survive in the world. The only safe place is in their minds, so they stockpile whatever they believe will help them survive until they are ready to rejoin the world. Fives also feel that they do not have enough to "bring to the table" to meet the demands of practical life. They retreat until they can learn something or master some skill that would allow them to feel safe enough to come out of hiding.

Type Seven, by contrast, charges into life and appears to be afraid of nothing. It at first seems strange that Sevens are in a Triad whose types are afflicted by fear since they are so outwardly adventurous. Despite appearances, however, Sevens are full of fear, but not of the outside world: they are afraid of their inner world—of being trapped in emotional pain, grief, and especially feelings of anxiety. So they escape into activity and anticipation of activity. Sevens unconsciously attempt to keep their minds occupied so that their underlying anxieties and hurts will not surface.

DIRECTIONS OF "FLIGHT" FOR THE THINKING TRIAD

FIVES: FLEE INWARD DUE TO FEAR OF ASPECTS OF THE OUTSIDE WORLD

In Type Six, the central type of this Triad (the type positioned on the equilateral triangle), attention and energy are directed both inward and outward. Sixes feel anxious inside, and so launch into external action and anticipation of the future like Sevens. But having done so, they eventually become afraid that they will make mistakes and be punished or overwhelmed by demands on them, so like Fives, they "jump back inside." They get scared by their feelings again, and the reactive cycle continues, with anxiety causing their attention to bounce around like a Ping-Pong ball.

The types of the Thinking Triad tend to have issues related to what psychologists call the "separation phase" of ego development. This is the stage, around two to four years old, when toddlers begin to wonder, "How do I move away from the safety and nurturance of Mommy? What is safe and what is dangerous?" Under ideal circumstances, the father-figure becomes the support and the guide, the person who helps the child develop skills and independence.

The types of this Triad represent the three ways children might attempt to negotiate the separation phase and overcome dependency. *Sixes* look for somebody like a father-figure, someone who is strong, trustworthy, and authoritative. Thus, Sixes deal with the loss of inner guidance by seeking guidance from others. They are looking for support to become independent, although ironically they tend to become dependent on the very person or system they use to find independence. *Fives* are convinced that support is unavailable or not reliable, so they attempt to compensate for the loss of inner guidance by mentally figuring everything out on their own. But because they are "going it alone," they believe they must reduce their need for and attachment to anyone if they are going to break away and be independent. *Sevens* try to break away by pursuing substitutes for their mother's nurturing. They go after whatever they believe will make them feel more satisfied and secure. At the same time, they respond to the lack of guidance by trying everything—as if by the process of elimination, they could discover the source of nurturance they are secretly looking for.

The Hornevian Groups indicate the social style of each type and also how each type tries to get its primary needs met (as indicated by its Triadic Center). Bringing awareness to the ways in which we unconsciously pursue our desires can help us disengage from powerful identifications and wake up.

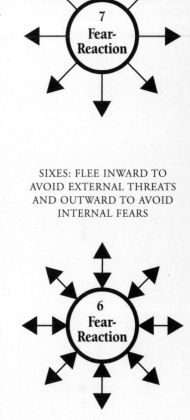

SEVENS: FLEE OUTWARD DUE TO FEAR OF ASPECTS OF THEIR INNER WORLD

SIXES: FLEE INWARD TO AVOID EXTERNAL THREATS AND OUTWARD TO AVOID INTERNAL FEARS

SOCIAL STYLE— THE HORNEVIAN GROUPS

PERSONALITY AND ESSENCE: CONTRASTING QUALITIES

Personality (Asleep)	*Essence* (Awake)
THINKING CENTER	
Mental chatter	Quiet mind
Figuring it out	Inner guidance
Strategies, doubt	Knowing, clarity
Anxiety and fear	Support and steadiness
Anticipation	Open to present moment
(Future orientation)	*(Here and now)*
FEELING CENTER	
Self-image	Authenticity
Stories	Truthfulness
Emotionality	Compassion
Holding on to moods	Forgiveness and flow
Adapting to affect others	Inner-directed
(Past orientation)	*(Here and now)*
INSTINCTIVE CENTER	
Boundaries	Connected with life
Tension, numbness	Relaxed, open, sensing
Defending	Inner strength
Dissociating	Grounded
Irritation	Acceptance
(Resistant to present)	*(Here and now)*

Besides the three Triads, there is another important three-times-three grouping of the types, the Hornevian Groups, which we named in honor of Karen Horney, a psychiatrist who developed Freud's work by identifying three fundamental ways in which people attempt to solve inner conflicts. We could also say that the Hornevian Groups indicate the "social style" of each type: there is an assertive style, a withdrawn style, and a compliant (to the superego, that is, "dutiful") style. All nine types fall into these three major styles.

The *assertives* (Horney's "moving against people") include the Threes, Sevens, and Eights. The assertive types are ego-oriented and ego-expansive. They respond to stress or difficulty by building up, reinforcing, or inflating their ego. They expand their ego in the face of difficulty rather than back down, withdraw, or seek protection from others. All three of these types have issues with processing their feelings.

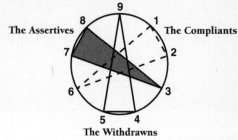

THE HORNEVIAN GROUPS

Each of the Hornevian Groups has an intrinsic sense of self in relation to other people. Recognizing and understanding the untruth of this "sense of self" can be extremely valuable for seeing through some of the major features of our ego. A simple example will make this clear: if you were to walk into a room full of people, you would automatically experience yourself in a certain way. If you are in the assertive group, your first automatic response would be, "I am the center. I am what is important here. Now that I am here, something is going to happen." Assertives automatically feel that everything meaningful happening is in relation to them.

Sevens and Eights naturally feel this way. Sevens come into a room and subconsciously think, "Here I am, everybody! Things are going to be more lively now!" Eights subconsciously think, "Okay, I'm here. Deal with me." These types "take over" the space and expect others to react to them. Threes, however, do not easily or naturally feel like the center because, as we have seen, they are covertly dependent on the attention of others to feel valuable. As much as possible, Threes will find subtle ways to get positive regard from others so they will feel like the center, as if to say, "Look at what I have achieved. Look at me and affirm my value."

The *compliants* (Horney's "moving toward people") include types One, Two, and Six. These three types share a need to be of service to other people. They are the advocates, crusaders, public servants, and committed workers. All three respond to difficulty and stress by consulting with their superego to find out what is the right thing to do, asking themselves, "How can I meet the demands of what others expect of me? How can I be a responsible person?"

It is important to understand that the compliant types are not necessarily compliant to other people; they are, however, highly compliant to the demands of their superegos. These three types try to obey the internalized rules, principles, and dictates that they have learned from childhood. As a result, they often become authority figures themselves—especially Sixes and Ones. (Twos can sometimes also be authority figures, although more often by trying to be the "good parent" or a trusted adviser to others.)

When a person whose type is in the compliant group enters a room, their automatic sense of self is that of being "better than" others, although how this is expressed is usually subtle. Ones may come into the room and subconsciously think, "This is so sloppy and disorganized. If I were in charge, things would not be such a mess."

Twos enter a room and subconsciously think, "These poor people! I wish I had time to give everyone my attention. They look troubled—they need my help!" By approaching others from the position of the "loving person" who gives their concern and service to others, Twos automatically put themselves in the superior role of being "better than" others.

Sixes are more troubled by inferiority feelings than Ones or Twos, but they get a sense of "better than" through their affiliations and social identifications. ("I'm a Democrat, and we are better than Republicans!" "I live in New York, which is a better city than Los Angeles." "Nobody's better than my team, the 49ers!")

The *withdrawns* (Horney's "moving away from people") include types Four, Five, and Nine. These types do not have much differentiation between their conscious self and their unconscious, unprocessed feelings, thoughts, and impulses. Their unconscious is always welling up into consciousness through daydreams and fantasies.

All three types respond to stress by moving away from engagement with the world and into an "inner space" in their imagination. Nines withdraw into a safe and carefree Inner Sanctum, Fours withdraw into a romantic and idealized Fantasy Self, and Fives withdraw into a complex and cerebral Inner Tinker Toy. In common language, they all can "zone out" and go into their imaginations very easily. These types have problems with staying in their physicality and with getting out of their imaginations and into action.

The automatic sense of self that arises when they come into a room is, "I am not part of what is going on. I am not like these other people. I don't fit in." The Four and the Five most clearly feel separate from others. They reinforce their sense of self by staying apart and being different. In a room full of people, Fours would typically be standoffish and aloof and would act in some kind of "mysterious" fashion. On the other hand, if they were not in the proper mood, they might simply leave, especially since their sense of social obligation is tenuous ("It is too much for me. I'm just not up to it right now. . . .").

Fives might not mind being there, but they would be just as happy at home reading a book or pursuing their own interests. If they stayed, Fives would probably sit on the sidelines and watch everybody else. They would be more likely to socialize if they could have a context, like photographing the proceedings with a camcorder.

Nines might well enjoy the gathering and even participate, but they would remain disengaged. They might nod and smile while thinking about a fishing trip, or they might "tune out" almost entirely and simply "tag along" with someone, allowing the other person to do most of the social interacting while the Nine remains benignly silent, or good-humoredly unresponsive.

Earlier in this chapter, we saw that the Triads tell us what each type most wanted in childhood. The types in the Instinctive Triad most wanted *autonomy:* they sought independence, the ability to assert their own will and direct their own life. The types in the Feeling Triad most wanted *attention:* to be seen and validated by their parents. Lastly, the types in the Thinking Triad most wanted *security:* to know that their environment was safe and stable.

The Hornevian Groups tell us the strategy each type employs to get its needs met. The assertive types (Three, Seven, and Eight) insist or *demand* that they get what they want. Their approach is active and direct as they go after what they believe they need. The compliant types (One, Two, and Six) all attempt to *earn* something by placating their superego to get what they want. They do their best to be "good boys and girls" to get their needs met. The withdrawn types (Four, Five, and Nine) all *withdraw* to get what they want. They disengage from others to deal with their needs.

If we go around the Enneagram, we can put these three groups together in a way that succinctly characterizes each type's core motivation and style. Beginning with the types in the Instinctive Triad we can see that the Eight demands autonomy, the Nine withdraws to gain autonomy (to have their own space), and the One attempts to earn autonomy (feeling that if they are perfect, others will not interfere with them).

Moving into the Feeling Triad, we see that the Two, a compliant type, tries to earn attention (serving and doing thoughtful things for others). The Three, being an assertive type, demands attention (doing whatever wins recognition and attention), and the Four, a withdrawn type, withdraws for attention (in the hope that someone will come and discover them).

In the Thinking Triad, the Five withdraws for security ("I will be safe if I stay away from others"), the Six tries to earn security ("I will be safe if I do what is expected of me"), and the Seven demands security ("I am going after whatever I need to feel secure").

THE HORNEVIAN GROUPS WITH THE MOTIVATIONAL AIMS OF THE TRIADS

COPING STYLE— THE HARMONIC GROUPS

The Harmonic Groups are useful for transformational work because they indicate how each person copes when they do not get what they want (as indicated by the Triad they are in). Thus they reveal the fundamental way that our personality defends against loss and disappointment.

We have also discovered a third significant way to group the nine types that we have named *the Harmonic Groups.* For each primary type (those located on the equilateral triangle, the Three, Six, and Nine), there are two secondary types that seem very much like it in numerous ways—and people repeatedly misidentify themselves as a result of the similarities between these types. For example, Nines often misidentify themselves as Twos or Sevens; Threes misidentify themselves as Ones or Fives, and Sixes are almost notorious in misidentifying themselves as either Fours or Eights.

Even though there are no lines that connect them in the Enneagram symbol, common themes and issues unite these types. The Harmonic Groups tell us what attitude the type adopts if it fails to meet its dominant need. In other words, *the Harmonic Groups tell us how we cope with conflict and difficulty: how we respond when we do not get what we want.*

The Positive Outlook Group is composed of types Nine, Two, and Seven. All three respond to conflict and difficulty by adopting, as much as possible, a "positive attitude," reframing disappointment in some positive way. They want to emphasize the uplifting aspects of life and to look at the bright side of things. These types are morale-builders who enjoy helping other people feel good because they want to stay feeling good themselves ("I don't have a problem").

These types have difficulty facing the dark side of themselves; they do not want to look at anything painful or negative in themselves. Also, depending on the type, each has trouble balancing their own needs with the needs of others. Twos focus primarily on the needs of others, Sevens focus primarily on their own needs, and Nines try to focus on both, although often with the result that they have trouble adequately fulfilling either.

The Competency Group is composed of types Three, One, and Five. These people have learned to deal with difficulty by putting aside their personal feelings and striving to be objective, effective, and competent. They put their subjective needs and feelings on the back burner; they try to solve problems *logically* and expect others to do the same.

These three types also have issues related to working within the confines of a structure or a system. ("How do I

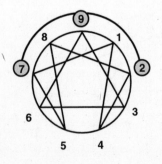

THE 9-2-7 HARMONIC PATTERN:
THE POSITIVE OUTLOOK GROUP

function within a system? Can I use it to my advantage? Will it hamper me from doing what I want to do?") The types' attitude toward systems evolved from their relationship with their families. These types are not sure how much they want to give themselves over to the values of the system, and how much they want to withhold themselves from it. Ones operate inside the rules, following them so well that no one would dare question their integrity. By contrast, Fives tend to operate outside of the rules. Threes want to play it both ways, having the benefit of the rules and structures while not having the restrictions.

The Reactive Group is composed of types Six, Four, and Eight. These types react emotionally to conflicts and problems and have difficulties knowing how much to trust other people: "I need you to know how I feel about this." When problems arise, these types look for an *emotional* response from others that mirrors their concern. In conflicts, the reactive types want the other person to match their emotional state. "This is really bothering me! It should bother you, too!" The types

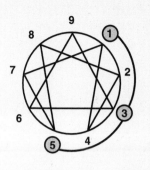

THE 1-3-5 HARMONIC PATTERN:
THE COMPETENCY GROUP

MAIN THEMES OF THE POSITIVE OUTLOOK GROUP

	Emphasizes:	*Avoids seeing:*	*Problems with needs:*
2	Positive self-image: "I am a caring, loving person." They focus on their good intentions.	Their own neediness, disappointment, and anger.	Overemphasis on the needs of others; neglect of their own needs.
7	Positive experiences, enjoyment, activity, excitement, and fun.	Their pain and emptiness; their role in creating suffering for self and others.	Overemphasis on their own needs. They easily feel burdened by the needs of others.
9	The positive qualities of others and of their environment. They idealize their world.	Problems with their loved ones or their environment as well as their own lack of development.	Feeling overwhelmed by their own needs and needs of others. They do not want to deal with either.

in this group have strong likes and dislikes. If there is a problem, others are going to hear about it. In conflicts, they need to deal with their feelings first, and usually once they are able to do so, things can blow over fairly quickly and permanently. If they are not able to vent their feelings, however, these types can become increasingly resentful and vindictive.

The Reactive Group types also have difficulty balancing their need for independence and self-determination with their need to be nurtured and supported by others. They simultaneously trust and distrust others: to accept the support and affection of others is a deep desire for

MAIN THEMES OF THE COMPETENCY GROUP

	Emphasizes:	Manages feelings:	Relation to systems:
1	Being correct, organized, and sensible. They focus on standards, improving themselves, and knowing the rules.	By repression and denial. Feelings are channeled into activity, getting things done perfectly. Feelings are also held as physical rigidity in the body.	Ones want to work with the system. They try to be a "good boy or girl" and are irritated with people who disregard the rules.
3	Being efficient, capable, and outstanding. They focus on goals, being pragmatic, and knowing how to present self.	By repression and keeping attention on tasks, staying active. Achievement offsets painful feelings. They look to others for feeling cues.	Threes want to work with the system. But they also like being outside of it— bending rules and finding shortcuts.
5	Being the expert and having deep information. They focus on the process, objective facts, and maintaining clarity and detachment.	By splitting off and abstracting feelings, they stay preoccupied and cerebral, as if their feelings were happening to someone else.	Fives reject the system and want to work on their own, outside of it. They have little patience with rules or procedures.

MAIN THEMES OF THE REACTIVE GROUP

	Seeks:	Fears:	Deals with others by:
4	A rescuer, someone to understand them and support their life and dreams. They want to be seen.	Abandonment—that no one will care for them; that they will not have enough support to find and become themselves.	Keeping others interested by limiting access, playing "hard to get," and holding on to supporters.
6	Both independence and support. They want someone to rely on, but they also need to be "the strong one."	Being abandoned and without support, but also becoming too dependent on others.	Being committed and reliable while trying to maintain their independence; they are engaging but also defensive.
8	Independence and self-reliance. They want to need others as little as possible, to be their own person.	Being controlled or dominated by others. Thus, they fear intimacy and becoming vulnerable by trusting or caring too much.	Keeping their guard up, not letting others get too close, and toughening themselves against hurt and their need for others.

these types, but to do so feels like losing control of themselves and of their circumstances. They fear being betrayed and need feedback from people in order to know where others stand toward them. They are either looking for advice and direction ("parenting") or defying it (rebelling). Subconsciously, Fours want to be parented, whereas Eights want to play the role of parent and provider. Sixes want it both ways, sometimes being the parent, sometimes being parented by someone else.

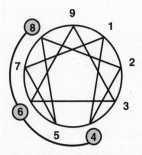

THE 4-6-8 HARMONIC PATTERN:
THE REACTIVE GROUP

HARMONIC GROUPS AT A GLANCE

The Positive Outlook Group: *Deny that they have any problems*

Nine: "What problem? I don't think there is a problem."
Two: "You have a problem. I am here to help *you*."
Seven: "There may be a problem, but *I'm* fine."

The Competency Group: *Cut off feelings and solve problems logically*

Three: "There's an efficient solution to this—we just need to get
         to work."
One: "I'm sure we can solve this like sensible, mature adults."
Five: "There are a number of hidden issues here: let me think
         about this."

The Reactive Group: *React strongly and need response from others*

Six: "I feel really pressured, and I've got to let off some steam!"
Four: "I feel really hurt, and I need to express myself."
Eight: "I'm angry about this and you're going to hear about it!"

▼

CHAPTER 6

DYNAMICS AND VARIATIONS

▲

THE ENNEAGRAM IS not vague. It can help us pinpoint and personalize our understanding through a finer set of distinctions than the nine basic types. Each type has two *Wings* and three *Instinctual Variants*. These two "lenses" help us zero in on our personality traits with greater accuracy and specificity. But the Enneagram is also unique among personality typologies in that it shows us ways to develop. It precisely maps out the patterns of our growth as well as those which get us into trouble. Through the *Levels of Development* and the Directions of *Integration and Disintegration,* we can understand the dynamics of our personality—the ways in which we change over time.

THE WINGS

The wings help us to individualize the nine (more general) types of the Enneagram. Each wing is a subtype of the general type. Knowing the wing enables us to narrow down the issues that we must face on the spiritual path.

Because the nine types are arranged around a circle, no matter what your basic type, you will have a type on each side of it. One of these two types will be your *wing*. The wing modifies and blends with the basic type and highlights certain tendencies in it. For example, if your basic type is Nine, you will have either an Eight-wing or a One-wing.

Nine with an Eight-wing   *Nine with a One-wing*

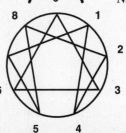

THE WINGS OF TYPE NINE

9w8: The Referee 9w1: The Dreamer
8w9: The Bear
8w7: The Independent
7w8: The Realist
7w6: The Entertainer
6w7: The Buddy
6w5: The Defender
5w6: The Problem-Solver
5w4: The Iconoclast

1w9: The Idealist
1w2: The Advocate
2w1: The Servant
2w3: The Host/Hostess
3w2: The Charmer
3w4: The Professional
4w3: The Aristocrat
4w5: The Bohemian

THE 18 RISO-HUDSON WING SUBTYPE NAMES

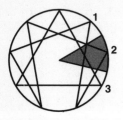

**THE RANGE OF
"TWONESS"**

No one is a pure type, and in some cases, we also find Nines with both wings. Most people, however, have one dominant wing.

Taking the dominant wing into consideration produces a unique subtype that is recognizable in daily life. For instance, when we look at Sevens in the real world, we see that there are Sevens with an Eight-wing and Sevens with a Six-wing. Each of these two different wing subtypes has a very different flavor. All of the type and wing combinations yield eighteen wing subtypes, with two for each type. They are each described in their respective type chapters.

It may help you to think of individual differences by picturing the circumference of the Enneagram as a color wheel that gives the full range of available colors.

The types can therefore be thought of as a family of related shades. Indicating that someone is a Six, for example, would be the equivalent of saying that they are in the "blue family." While we might not have a precise notion about what exact shade of blue is being referred to (teal, navy blue, sky blue, indigo, powder blue, and so forth), we certainly know the difference between blue and red, or between blue and orange, for instance.

This way of looking at the types shows us that there is a continuum of human expression, just as there is a continuum on the color spectrum. There are no real divisions between the varieties of personality types, just as there are none between the colors of the rainbow. Individual differences are as unique as different shades, hues, and intensities of color. The nine points on the Enneagram are simply "family names" that we use to speak meaningfully about differences in personality, ways of speaking about main features without getting lost in details.

THE INSTINCTUAL VARIANTS

The Instinctual Variants indicate which of our three basic instincts have been most distorted in childhood, resulting in characteristic preoccupations and behaviors throughout the entire range of the personality type.

In addition to the two wing subtypes for each point of the Enneagram, there are three *Instinctual Variants* for each type, indicating the different areas of life in which each type's particular concerns will be focused. A person's dominant Instinctual Variant represents the arena in which the issues of their type will be most often played out.

Just as all nine Enneagram types operate in us, so do all three

Variants, although as with type, one of these Variants will predominate. The three instincts can be ranked like the layers of a cake with the most dominant instinct on the top layer, another in the middle, and the least powerful instinct on the bottom. Further, this can be done without knowing the person's Enneagram type; the instincts are clearly defined and observable in their own right and are a variable that functions independently of type and are not therefore a true "subtype."

The Instinctual Variants are based on three primary instincts that motivate human behavior: *the Self-Preservation Instinct, the Social Instinct,* and *the Sexual Instinct.* Thus, each Enneagram type has three variations based on the three possible dominant instincts. For example, a Six could be a Self-Preservation Six, a Social Six, or a Sexual Six, and each of these Sixes would have a noticeably different set of concerns.

A person can therefore be described as a combination of a basic type, a wing, and a dominant Instinctual Variant—for example, a Self-Preservation One with a Two-wing, or a Sexual Eight with a Nine-wing. Since Instinctual Variants and wings are not directly related, it is usually easier to look at a type either through the "lens" of the wing or through the "lens" of the dominant Instinctual Variant. However, combining these two separate frames of reference produces *six variations for each type,* with a total of fifty-four major variations in the entire Enneagram.

Taking this dimension of personality into account may be a finer degree of detail than most people require, but for transformational work the Instinctual Variants are important. The Instinctual Variants are also noteworthy because they play a pivotal role in relationships. People of the same Variant tend to share values and to understand each other, whereas couples of different Variants (for example, Self-Preservation and Sexual types) will tend to have more conflicts because their fundamental values are so different.

THE SELF-PRESERVATION VARIANT

Most people can easily identify this Instinctual Variant. Self-Preservation types are *preoccupied with getting and maintaining physical safety and comfort,* which often translates into concerns about food, clothing, money, housing, and physical health. These issues are their main priority, and in pursuing them, other areas of their lives may suffer.

For example, we might identify this Instinctual Variant in ourselves or others by observing what a person would first notice on entering a room. Self-Preservation types tend to focus on the comfort of the environment. Does the environment support their sense of well-being? They are quick to notice and respond to poor lighting, or uncomfortable chairs, or to be dissatisfied with the room temperature, and they are constantly adjusting these things. They may wonder when their next meal or coffee break will come, worry if there will be enough food, or if it will be the kind they like, or if it will meet their dietary requirements.

When this instinct is functioning harmoniously with the personality type, these people can be earthy and practical. They apply their energies to taking care of basic life necessities—creating a secure environment, shopping, maintaining the home and workplace, paying bills, and acquiring useful skills so that the orderly flow of life will not be interrupted. When the personality becomes unhealthy, however, it distorts the instinct, causing these people to take poor care of themselves, possibly developing eating and sleeping disorders. They may stock up on too many things, overbuy, overeat, and overpurge themselves of unnecessary "baggage" of all sorts.

Less healthy Self-Preservation types let themselves go physically, or they become obsessive about health and food matters, or both. Further, their normal practicality and financial sense may become distorted, resulting in problems with money and organizing their affairs. If the Self-Preservation instinct becomes completely overwhelmed by personality issues, individuals may engage in deliberately self-destructive behavior, in which the instinct has the effect of turning against itself.

When the other two instincts dominate in an individual and the Self-Preservation instinct is the *least developed*, attending to the basics of life does not come naturally. It will not always occur to such individuals that they need to eat or sleep properly. Environmental factors will be relatively insignificant, and they will tend to lack the drive to accumulate wealth or property—or even to care about such matters. Time and resource management will typically be neglected, often with seriously detrimental effects to their own careers, social life, and material well-being.

THE SOCIAL VARIANT

Most of us are aware that we have a social component, but we tend to see it as our desire to socialize, to attend parties, meetings, belong to groups, and so forth. The Social instinct, however, is actually something much more fundamental. It is a powerful desire, found in all human beings, to be liked, approved of, and to feel safe with others. On our own, we are rather weak and vulnerable and can easily fall prey to a hostile environment. We lack the claws, fangs, and fur of other animals, and if we did not band together and cooperate with each other, it is unlikely that our species—or we as individuals—would be able to survive. Being able to adjust ourselves to others and be acceptable is a fundamental, survival-based human instinct.

People who have a dominant Social instinct are preoccupied with being accepted and necessary in their world. They are concerned with maintaining the sense of value they get from participating in activities with others, be they family, group, community, national, or global activities. Social types like to feel involved, and they enjoy interacting with others for common purposes.

On entering a room, Social types would be immediately aware of the power structures and subtle "politics" between the different people and groups. They are subconsciously focused on others' reactions to them—particularly on whether they are being accepted or not. They are attuned to the notion of "place" within a hierarchical social structure, in regard both to themselves and to others. This can manifest in many ways, such as the pursuit of attention, success, fame, recognition, honor, leadership, and appreciation, as well as the security of being part of something larger than themselves. Of all the Instinctual Variants, Social types like to know what is going on in their world; they need to "touch base" with others to feel safe, alive, and energized. This can range from an interest in office politics or neighborhood gossip to world news and international diplomacy. We could say that the Social instinct is a kind of contextual intelligence: it gives us the ability to see our efforts and their effects in a broader context.

In general, Social types enjoy interacting with people, although ironically, they tend to avoid intimacy. As with all of the instincts, if the person becomes unhealthy, the instinct manifests as its opposite. Unhealthy Social types can become extremely *antisocial,* detesting people and resenting society, and as a result, they may have poorly developed social skills. They fear and distrust others and cannot get along with people, while at the same time they are unable to disengage from their social connections. In brief, Social types focus on interacting with people in ways that will build their personal value, their sense of accomplishment, and their security of place with others.

When the other two instincts dominate in an individual and the Social instinct is *least developed,* attending to social endeavors and commitments does not come naturally. Such individuals have difficulty seeing the point of creating and sustaining social connections, often disregarding the impact of the opinions of others. Their sense of involvement with their community, at any scale, may be minimal. They often have little connection with people, feeling that they do not need others and that others do not need them. Thus, there may be frequent misunderstandings with allies and supporters as well as friends and family members.

THE SEXUAL VARIANT

Many people initially want to identify themselves as this Variant, perhaps because they believe that this would mean that they are sexy or because they enjoy sex. Of course, sexiness is highly subjective, and there are "sexy" people in all three of the Instinctual Variants. If we wish to be one Variant rather than another, it is good to remember that *the personality tends to interfere with and distort the dominant instinct.* Thus, people of the Sexual Variant tend to have recurrent problems in the areas of intimate relationships. As with the other Variants, we need to see the way that the instinct plays out more broadly.

In the Sexual types, there is a constant search for connection and an attraction to intense experiences—not only sexual experiences but any situation that promises a similar charge. In all things, Sexual types seek intense contact. They may find intensity in a ski jump, a deep conversation, or an exciting movie. They are the "intimacy junkies" of the Instinctual Variants. On the positive side, Sexual types possess a wide-ranging, exploratory approach to life; on the negative side, they have difficulty focusing on their own real needs and priorities.

On entering a room, Sexual types quickly focus on finding where the most interesting people are. They tend to follow their attractions. (By contrast, Social types notice who is talking with the host, who has power, prestige, or who might be able to help them. Self-Preservation types will note the temperature of the room, where the refreshments are, and what might be a comfortable place to sit.) Sexual types gravitate toward people they feel magnetized by, regardless of the person's potential for helping them or their social standing. It is as if they were asking, "Where is the juice in this room? Whose energy is most intense?"

Sexual types tend to have difficulty pursuing their own projects or taking adequate care of themselves, because on a subconscious level, they are always looking outside themselves for the person or situation that will complete them. They are like a plug looking for a socket and can become obsessed with another if they feel they have found the right person for them. They may neglect important obligations, or even their own basic necessities, if they are swept up in someone or something that has captivated them.

When they are unhealthy, Sexual types can experience a scattering of their attention and a profound lack of focus. They may act out in sexual promiscuity or become trapped in a fearful, dysfunctional attitude toward sex and intimacy. When the latter becomes their orientation, they will be equally intense about their avoidances.

When the other two instincts dominate in an individual and the Sexual instinct is *least developed,* attending to matters of intimacy and stimulation—mental or emotional—does not come naturally. They know what they like, but often find it difficult to get deeply excited or enthusiastic about anything. Such individuals also tend to have difficulty being intimate with others and may even avoid it altogether. They also tend to fall into routines, feeling uncomfortable if there is too much that is unfamiliar in their lives. They may feel socially involved with people but strangely disconnected even from spouses, friends, and family members.

The Levels of Development offer a way of observing and measuring our degree of identification with our personality structures. Further, they make crucial distinctions between the types possible, and within each type, they add the "vertical" dimension to an otherwise "horizontal" categorical system.

THE LEVELS OF DEVELOPMENT

Clearly, some people are high-functioning, open, balanced, stable, and able to handle stress well, while others are more troubled, reactive, emotionally stuck, and cannot handle stress effectively. Further, most of us have experienced a wide range of states over the course of our lives, from free, life-affirming ones, to painful, dark, neurotic ones.

The nine personality types alone are merely a set of "horizontal" categories, however subtle they may be. But if the system is to mirror human nature accurately and reflect the ever-changing states within our type, there also needs to be a way to account for "vertical" movement and development within each type. The Levels of Development and the Directions of Integration and Disintegration answer this need.

Ken Wilber, a pioneer in developing models of human consciousness, has pointed out that any complete psychological system needs to account for both horizontal and vertical dimensions. The horizontal dimension alone describes only the characteristics of the types; for a system to be complete, however, the vertical element must be taken into account, which is what the Levels of Development do.

As obvious as it now seems, and as widely used as the distinction now has become, it had not been done until Don began to develop the vertical dimension of the Enneagram types (by distinguishing the healthy, average, and unhealthy ranges). When he accounted for the even finer nine Levels of Development, the Enneagram became a fully developed, two-dimensional model, vastly more capable of representing the complexity of human nature. These two dimensions can be represented somewhat like a cake with nine layers.

The Levels of Development have many profound practical and therapeutic implications, as we will see throughout this book. They are a framework that makes movement, growth, and deterioration within each type clear; they help predict behavior, and at their simplest, they are a yardstick of a person's mental and emotional health.

The Levels within each type are distinct and yet interrelated; they give us a way of thinking about "where" in the range of healthy, average,

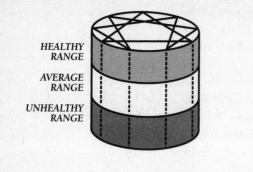

HEALTHY
RANGE

AVERAGE
RANGE

UNHEALTHY
RANGE

**THE HORIZONTAL AND VERTICAL DIMENSIONS
OF THE ENNEAGRAM**

and unhealthy traits a person is within each type and the "direction" in which they are moving. They are important for therapy and self-help as a way of specifying which issues are uppermost in a person's transformational work at any given time. They are also helpful for understanding which traits and motivations properly go with each type and, as a result, for understanding the causes of mistyping and other confusions. For example, Eights are often characterized as "aggressive" and Twos as "seductive," although all types can be aggressive and seductive in their own ways. The Levels help us see how and when an Eight might be aggressive, for instance, and more importantly, *why.* Perhaps most profoundly, the Levels give us a measure of a person's degree of identification with his or her personality—that is, how defended and shut down or how liberated and open the person is.

It is almost impossible to make generalizations about the types without taking the Levels into consideration, because as each type deteriorates down the Levels, many of its characteristics become their opposite. For instance, healthy Eights are the most big-hearted and constructive of the types. They provide the circumstances in which others can flourish and be strong. But the opposite is true of unhealthy Eights: full of rage and feeling that the world is against them, they are extremely destructive and hard-hearted. Healthy and unhealthy Eights will seem so different from each other that they may seem to be two different types. Furthermore, because people range within the Levels of their type, *no single trait will always be true of a type.* It is therefore unwise to type anyone on the basis of a handful of traits, since all of the behaviors associated with each type change at different Levels of Development.

While our type seems to be mainly inborn, the result of hereditary and prenatal factors including genetic patterning, our early childhood environment is the major factor in determining at which Level of Development we function. Interviewing people on panels in our workshops and professional trainings has confirmed the commonsense observation that the quality of parenting and other related environmental factors (such as health, education, nutrition, and the availability of other resources) all have a tremendous impact on a child's subsequent level of functioning.

This is because each Level represents an increasing layer of fear and defense. It is important to remember, however, that all of these fears and defenses arose in childhood and are carried into our adult life by automatic habits and unexamined belief systems. We can also see how the degree of dysfunction that we had to cope with in our early life determined how many layers of these defenses we had to adopt. The more toxic our childhood environment, the greater the fear that has been instilled in us, and the more limited and rigid are the ways we employ to deal with our situation.

The Levels encourage us to think of the development of the types not as a simple on/off switch, but as a continuum of growth. They provide us with early warnings of when we are becoming enmeshed in dysfunctional behaviors before it is too late and bad habits have become entrenched. In the type chapters, we will indicate specific "Wake-up Calls," "Social Roles," "Red Flags," and other features that will help you become more aware of your progress or deterioration along the Levels of your type. As you get to know them and see them functioning in yourself and others, they will become a tool for awareness second in importance only to the Enneagram itself.

THE STRUCTURE OF THE LEVELS

Each type has three main ranges: *healthy, average,* and *unhealthy,* with three Levels within each of those ranges. The healthy range (Levels 1–3) represents the high-functioning aspects of the type. The average range (Levels 4–6) represents the "normal" behaviors of the type. This is where we most often find ourselves and where most people operate. The unhealthy range (Levels 7–9) represents the deeply dysfunctional manifestations of the type.

We can also understand the Levels as a measure of our degree of freedom and awareness. In the healthy range, we are increasingly free from the constraints of our personality structures, as well as the habits and mechanisms of our ego. We are free to be in the moment, to choose, and to act with spontaneous wisdom, strength, and compassion, among other positive qualities.

As we spiral down the Levels, however, our freedom is increasingly constricted. We become so identified with our personality mechanisms that we are entirely driven by them, resulting in more suffering for ourselves and others. We become more and more out of touch with reality, with our capacity to make balanced assessments of our situation, and with our ability to stop the avalanche of our ego compulsions. And if we should deteriorate into the unhealthy range, we have almost no freedom of choice whatsoever. Perhaps the only freedom we have in the lower Levels is the ability to choose to go on in the same destructive patterns or to reach out for help—to say either no or yes to life.

The Bandwidth

While our basic type does not change, the Level at which we are operating changes all the time. We may move up and down several

Levels of our type in a single day within a certain "bandwidth" or range of habitual behaviors. We may wake up in a balanced, healthy state, but have a bad argument with a colleague and fall two or three Levels. Even though our state can radically change in a short time, we are not a different personality type—we are simply manifesting different behaviors at different Levels of our type.

It may be helpful to visualize the nine Levels of our type as a wooden pegboard with nine holes drilled in it, with one hole for each Level. We have a wooden peg sitting in one of the nine holes. The placement of our peg represents the "center of gravity" of our personality. At the same time, we also have a rubber band attached to the wooden peg, and it stretches up when we are more relaxed and centered, or it stretches down in times of stress. All things being equal, we will tend to return to the Level of our peg, wherever our center of gravity is. The important thing to understand is that real transformation is denoted not by the movement of the rubber band but *by the movement of the peg*. When our center of gravity shifts, it marks a profound change in our entire state of being.

Our mood or state changes all the time, whereas our center of gravity changes much more slowly—usually only as the result of major life crises, or of doing long-term transformational work. When our center of gravity shifts upward even a single Level, we often look back at our former states and wonder how we could have lived that way. We can see our former lower-Level behaviors and attitudes for the constrictions and compensations that they actually were, but which we could not see when we were identified with them.

The illustration may make these ideas more clear. Person A has a bandwidth from Levels 2 to 5, whereas Person B has one from Levels 5 to 8. Even though they are the same type, these two individuals would still be noticeably different in their motivations, attitudes, and behaviors, as well as their emotional stability and the quality of their relationships. The arrows indicate at which Level each person has his or her "peg" or center of gravity. As we can see, Person A's center of gravity is at Level 3, whereas Person B's is at Level 6, again accounting for vast differences in the expression of their personality structure.

If our inner work is to be effective, it is important to recognize an unsettling truth: no matter what Level we are actually functioning at (that is, no matter where our center of gravity is), we tend to see our motivations as coming from the healthy

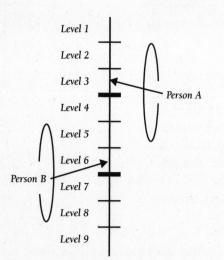

**THE BANDWIDTH AND
THE CENTER OF GRAVITY**

range. The defenses of our ego are such that we always see ourselves as our idealized self-image, even when we are only average or even pathological. For example, our actual behavior might be at Level 6 or 7, but we will tend to see ourselves at a much healthier Level (generally, Level 2). Therefore, perhaps the first real step we can take on our inner journey is to accurately identify not only our type, but the range of Levels we normally traverse and, importantly, where our center of gravity currently is. The Enneagram will do us no good if we delude ourselves into thinking we are healthier than we actually are.

Mood Versus Level

It is also worth noting that a shift up the Levels is not the same as a shift in our mood. Being in a better mood is not necessarily a marker of being at a higher Level of Development. Our Level is really a function of freedom and awareness, not of mood. Thus, being at a higher Level does not mean that we will always be in a good mood, just as being at a lower Level does not mean that we always will be in a bad mood. An individual could be solidly entrenched at Level 6, completely identified with his personality and highly reactive. He may have just smashed someone in a business deal and be feeling great about it. This kind of gleeful reaction is not the same thing as having internal freedom or real joy. When something goes wrong, the person becomes reactive and negative again—and is once again at the mercy of externals.

On the other hand, having serenity and vitality and engagement with the real world—as opposed to our illusions and delusions—in the midst of difficulties are signs of spiritual growth. When we are centered and grounded, connected with ourselves and our Essential Being, we experience a quiet joy that is palpably different from being in a good mood. Thus, at their most profound, the Levels are really a measure of how connected or disconnected we are with our true nature.

We will now examine some of the major features of the average, unhealthy, and healthy ranges of the Levels of Development— and their relevance for inner work. We follow this sequence because the type chapters are structured this way, and because most people will find themselves in the average range as they begin their inner work.

THE AVERAGE RANGE

In this range, people are functional and act in ways that others would consider normal, but they are increasingly identified with their ego identity. As a result, they are aware of and able to actualize only a relatively narrow range of their full human potential. Indeed, as individuals spiral down the Levels within the average range, each type manifests increasing degrees of ego-centricity since the maintenance of the ego becomes the personality's main agenda. Moreover, life and relationships present many situations that do not support their self-image, so manipulation of self and others is always involved and interpersonal conflicts inevitably occur.

The Wake-up Call

The *Wake-up Call* serves as an indicator that we are moving from the healthy range of our type to the more fixated average range. This is a clue that we are becoming more identified with our ego and that conflicts and other problems are sure to arise. For example, the Wake-up Call for Nines is the tendency to avoid conflicts by going along with people. As Nines become more identified with their particular ego structure, they say yes to things that they do not want to do, repressing themselves and their legitimate needs and desires until conflicts inevitably occur.

THE WAKE-UP CALLS

1	Feeling a sense of personal obligation to fix everything themselves
2	Believing that they must go out to others to win them over
3	Beginning to drive themselves for status and attention
4	Holding on to and intensifying feelings through the imagination
5	Withdrawing from reality into concepts and mental worlds
6	Becoming dependent on something outside the self for guidance
7	Feeling that something better is available somewhere else
8	Feeling that they must push and struggle to make things happen
9	Outwardly accommodating themselves to others

We will discuss the Wake-up Calls for the nine types at more length in each of the type chapters. Observing yourself doing these is one of the most powerful ways to use the Enneagram in your daily life.

The Social Role

Once we enter the average range, we increasingly feel that we need to be a certain way and we need other people to respond to us as being that way. We are much more dependent on the particular coping mechanisms of our type, and we are much more fixated on achieving our Basic Desire through those mechanisms. Although we are still functional and pleasant enough, a certain sameness or repetitiveness enters the picture. In family systems theory, this is where the child starts playing a particular role, such as the Family Hero, the Lost Child, or the Scapegoat. We will discuss the Social Role of each type in the individual type chapters. Observing yourself as you slip in and out of your own Social Role is an extremely practical and powerful way to make life your arena for transformational practice.

HOW EACH TYPE MANIPULATES OTHERS

1	By correcting others—by insisting that others share their standards
2	By finding out others' needs and desires—thus creating dependencies
3	By charming others—and by adopting whatever image will "work"
4	By being temperamental—and making others "walk on eggshells"
5	By staying preoccupied—and by detaching emotionally from others
6	By complaining—and by testing others' commitment to them
7	By distracting others—and by insisting that others meet their demands
8	By dominating others—and by demanding that others do as they say
9	By "checking out"—and by passive-aggressively resisting others

"He who cannot change the very fabric of his thought will never be able to change reality."

ANWAR SADAT

The Social Role and Relationships

When we become locked into our Social Roles, we try to get the environment—mainly other people—to support our ego and its agendas, usually resulting in conflicts. When this occurs, we know that we are becoming more identified with our personality's agenda. We require others to interact with us only in ways that support our self-image. Conflicts arise because each type uses other people to get what it needs for its ego payoffs. People identified with their Social Role can get locked into a frustrating dance with each other, rewarding and rejecting each other just enough to keep the other person in the dance. In relationships of this kind, one person's neurosis dovetails with the other person's neurosis, creating a static balance that can be difficult to break.

We may also attempt to manipulate others into meeting our Basic Desire in various ways through inappropriate strategies that backfire in the long run. Many of our failed or troubled relationships are a testa-

THE LEADEN RULE FOR THE TYPES

1	Fearing that they may be evil, corrupt, or defective in some way, Ones point out evil, corruption, and defectiveness in others.
2	Fearing that they are unwanted and unloved, Twos make others feel unworthy of their love, generosity, or attention.
3	Fearing that they are worthless and without value in themselves, Threes make others feel valueless by treating them arrogantly or with contempt.
4	Fearing that they do not have an identity or any personal significance of their own, Fours treat people disdainfully, as if others were "nobodies" and had no value or significance.
5	Fearing that they are helpless, incapable, and incompetent, Fives make others feel helpless, incompetent, stupid, and incapable.
6	Fearing that they are without support or guidance, Sixes undermine the support systems of others, trying to isolate them in some fashion.
7	Fearing that they are trapped in pain and deprivation of some sort, Sevens cause pain and make others feel deprived in various ways.
8	Fearing that they will be harmed or controlled by others, Eights make others fear that they will be harmed or controlled by their belligerent and intimidating threats.
9	Fearing that they will suffer loss of connection with others, Nines make others feel that they have lost connection with the Nine by "tuning out" people in various ways.

ment to how frustrating these strategies can be. Once we are locked into a pattern of defending our self-image and manipulating others into supporting it, real relating becomes difficult if not impossible.

The Leaden Rule

If such manipulations fail to get our needs met, we may intensify our campaign. Rather than stopping our self-defeating behaviors, without awareness, we tend to employ them more aggressively. At this stage, we are not merely trying to get other people to support our ego agendas, we are forcing them on others. Ego inflation is at its maximum, and we act out our anxieties and aggressively pursue our Basic Desire, either overtly or covertly.

We have discovered a feature of the types that occurs at the bottom of the average range. We call this feature the *Leaden Rule*, the opposite of the more famous Golden Rule. If the Golden Rule tells us, "Do unto others as you would have them do unto you," the Leaden Rule states, "*Do unto others what you most fear having done unto you.*"

The Leaden Rule points out that each type has its own special way of aggressively undermining others to bolster its own ego. The false belief is that "If I put someone else down a notch, it will lift me up one." Thus, each type begins to inflict its own Basic Fear on others. For instance, if Eights fear being harmed or controlled by others, they start threatening people with harm and control. ("You better do it my way, or else I'm going to make you sorry. If I get angry, you know what's going to happen!") They become intimidating, belligerent, and extremely confrontational. If the Four's Basic Fear is of having no personal significance, they may aloofly dismiss others, treating them as if they had no personal significance. They may treat waiters or doormen rudely, or cut off friends from further contact as if they did not exist and had no feelings of their own.

The Red Flag

Before each type moves into the unhealthy range, each encounters what we call the *Red Flag fear*. If the Wake-up Call was an invitation to awaken before the person moved deeper into the average Levels and into fixation and increasing "sleep," the Red Flag is a far more serious alarm that signals an imminent crisis.

The Red Flag is a fear, although one that is realistic and needs to be heeded if the person is to resist the destructive forces that are threatening to sweep him or her down the Levels. If the person is shocked into awareness by his Red Flag fear, he may be able to stop acting out the behaviors and attitudes that have gotten him into his current perilous

THE RED FLAG FEARS

1	That their ideals are actually wrong and counterproductive
2	That they are driving friends and loved ones away
3	That they are failing, that their claims are empty and fraudulent
4	That they are ruining their lives and wasting their opportunities
5	That they are never going to find a place in the world or with people
6	That their own actions have harmed their security
7	That their activities are bringing them pain and unhappiness
8	That others are turning against them and will retaliate
9	That they will be forced by reality to deal with their problems

position. If, however, he is unable or unwilling to heed his Red Flag, he may persist in his self-defeating attitudes and behaviors, with the almost certain result that he will fall into increasingly destructive states.

THE UNHEALTHY RANGE

For any number of reasons, people can fall into the unhealthy range, but fortunately, it is not as easy to get really stuck there. We may temporarily resort to unhealthy behaviors, but it is rare for our center of gravity to move into the unhealthy range. This is because the demarcation or zone between the average and unhealthy ranges seems to act as a brake in the personality's deterioration. Thus, many people can function within the average range for years without becoming unhealthy. We call this demarcation in the Levels a *shock point*.

Because it takes an additional "shock" or input of energy to move into the unhealthy Levels, most people do not move there unless one of two things has occurred. The first is a major life crisis, such as the loss of a job or of a spouse through divorce or death, or a major medical or financial catastrophe. If we do not have the psychological and spiritual tools to deal with such crises, we can suddenly fall into the unhealthy range and be unable to get out. Fortunately, under these circumstances, many people realize that they are "going under" and need to see a therapist or become involved in a recovery program of some kind.

The second reason people move into the unhealthy range is that unhealthy patterns were established in childhood. People regress to earlier, more primitive behavior when conditions become too challenging for them. People who have been extremely abused and hurt (emotionally, mentally, sexually, or physically) as children have had to build huge defenses to protect themselves. Under these conditions, they were never able to learn healthy coping skills and are highly vulnerable to slipping back into destructive patterns.

When we become unhealthy, we lose touch with our true nature; to an increasing degree, we lose touch with reality. We become caught in a maze of reactions and illusions, out of control, and we cannot see solutions to our intensifying fears and conflicts—nor to any practical problems we face. We can only react more intensely and put more pressure on the environment to solve our problems for us. We become so completely identified with the limited mechanisms of our personality that other solutions do not occur to us; or even if they do, we realize that we cannot act on them without extraordinary help. Of course, we do not will ourselves to be unhealthy, but we collapse into these states through ignorance and because the earlier circumstances of our lives did not show us healthier ways of coping with our problems.

In the end, the unhealthy range represents a profound self-abandonment—although a self-abandonment that was forced on us by circumstances. While we cannot undo the history of our childhood and we cannot prevent catastrophes from occurring, we *can* develop our internal resources so that problems do not destroy us. We can also shorten our recovery time when troubles occur. Our transformational work can eventually produce great serenity, acceptance, nonreactiveness, compassion, and an expanded perspective about our lives.

THE HEALTHY RANGE

In this range, although the ego identity is in place, it is worn lightly, so to speak, and expresses itself beneficially in the world. Each type has a healthy way of embodying the personal qualities with which they have most identified. An individual operating in the healthy range would be seen by most people within their culture as extremely balanced, mature, and high-functioning; however, even at Levels 2 and 3,

"Look into the depths of your own soul and learn to know yourself, then you will understand why this illness was bound to come upon you and perhaps you will thenceforth avoid falling ill."

FREUD

the person is still operating from some degree of ego, compensating for his or her Basic Desire and Basic Fear.

For example, in response to their Basic Fear of being harmed or controlled by others, Eights define themselves as strong, capable, action-oriented, and assertive. They feel the need to prove these qualities to themselves and to others, so they take on challenges and engage in constructive activities that require strength and willpower. They become empowering, protective leaders, creating conditions in which others can flourish.

Twos define themselves as loving, caring, and selfless, but healthy Twos reinforce this self-image by actually going out in the world to perform loving, caring, generous acts. They become good friends and benefactors who share their gifts and resources with others because this behavior reinforces their self-definition.

If more people were operating in the healthy range, the world would be a much better place. Although most of us have experienced what it is like to function in this range at one time or another, our environment, culture, and perhaps our family generally do not support this kind of openness, so few of us are able to maintain this degree of freedom for long. All too often, fears arise, causing us to fall into the average range.

To stay healthy, however, requires the intention to be healthy—and this requires the intention to be present and awake. This means that we must use the tools and practices available to us to cultivate awareness. As our awareness strengthens, we can become conscious of another "shock point" between the healthy and average ranges (between Levels 3 and 4) that can be activated by the Wake-up Call that we have already seen. Just as there is a profound shift between the unhealthy and average ranges, there is another between the average and healthy ranges. We can pass through this "shock point" in either direction, falling into the average and unhealthy ranges through crises or life circumstances, or ascending the Levels by consciously working through the issues involved.

THE LEVEL OF LIBERATION

By the time we have worked through our issues (more or less Level by Level) and have arrived fully in the healthy range, our ego has achieved a noteworthy degree of balance and transparency, and we are poised to take the last step toward living out of our Essential nature. Simply stated, *liberation happens to the degree that we no longer identify with our ego.* Aspects of it may well still exist, but they are no longer the center of our identity. However, the ego must be restored to its natural balance and functioning before real and lasting liberation can be achieved. At this stage, the person has let go of a particular self-image and

"We have to become some-body before we can become no-body."

JACK ENGLER

worked through his or her Basic Fear and has expanded his or her awareness to act rightly on the Basic Desire. All of these processes take balance, wisdom, courage, fortitude, and enough psychological integrity to withstand the anxiety involved in the dissolution of the ego identity.

When we arrive at the Level of Liberation, it usually comes as a big surprise to find that we already have the very qualities that we have been looking for. We become aware that they were present all along, but that we were going about looking for them in the wrong way. Just like Dorothy at the end of *The Wizard of Oz,* we discover that we were closer to realizing our goal than we imagined. Everything we need for our transformation, everything we require to be complete human beings, is available to us in our Essential nature and always has been. In fact, at Level 1, we actually achieve our Basic Desire. Once we understand this, our most burning question becomes how we can sustain this more open, vibrant state—or really, how we can allow it to be sustained in us. How can we continue to open ourselves to the action of grace?

The Directions of Integration and Disintegration help us recognize whether we are progressing or regressing in our development. Integration gives us objective markers of our growth. Disintegration shows us how we act out under stress, what our unconscious motivations and behaviors are, and, paradoxically, what qualities we most need to integrate.

THE DIRECTIONS OF INTEGRATION AND DISINTEGRATION

If you look at the Enneagram, you will notice that each number around the circle has two inner lines attached to it. For example, the Eight has one line to Two and another to Five. The Nine has one line to Three and another to Six, and so forth for all the types.

One line represents the *Direction of Integration,* or the line of natural development toward wholeness for each type, while the other line represents the type's *Direction of Disintegration,* which shows what behaviors we manifest when we have pushed the behaviors of our type to the limit. The movements in both directions are naturally occurring processes because the Enneagram predicts what each type will be like as it becomes healthier (less constricted and fixated) or, conversely, as it becomes more identified, tense, and ultimately dysfunctional. (The movements in the Directions of Integration and Disintegration are distinct from, though related to, the movement up and down the Levels. We will have more to say on this later.)

Strictly speaking, we cannot say that one Direction is necessarily "all good" and the other is necessarily "all bad." Human nature has developed coping mechanisms in both Directions, and the Enneagram is

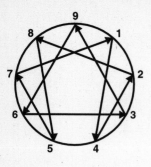

**THE DIRECTION OF
DISINTEGRATION**

able to track the shifts of these subtle mechanisms as no other system can. Understanding these movements and recognizing them in our daily lives can be extremely helpful in accelerating our development.

The arrows on the following Enneagram indicate the Directions of Disintegration for each type. For example, Type Eight represents the Two's Direction of Disintegration.

The arrows for the Direction of Integration move in the reverse order, so that the Direction of Integration for Type Eight is toward Two, and so forth, for all the types.

If the types are rightly defined, the Enneagram can predict future behavior. It tells us what each type is going to become like if it continues to deteriorate in its pattern of identifications, defenses, and self-defeating behaviors. It also predicts what healthy qualities will emerge as a person becomes less identified with the patterns, structures, and defenses of their type.

THE DIRECTION OF DISINTEGRATION

	The Basic Type	Direction of Disintegration	
	Level 1	X → X	
Healthy	Level 2	X → X	*Healthy*
	Level 3	X → X	
	Level 4	X → X	
Average	Level 5	X → X	*Average*
	Level 6	X → X	
	Level 7	X → X	
Unhealthy	Level 8	X → X	*Unhealthy*
	Level 9	X → X	

**THE DIRECTION OF
DISINTEGRATION**

The Direction of Disintegration usually manifests when we are in a period of increased stress or uncertainty. When we have pushed the strategy of our own type as far as it can go (without deteriorating to a lower Level entirely), and it is not improving our situation or getting us what we want, we will unconsciously start to behave like the type in our Direction of Disintegration. In psychological terms, this is called *acting out,* because these attitudes and behaviors tend to be unconscious and compulsive, although they are not necessarily immediately destructive.

We almost always will see ourselves (or someone else) act out *at more or less the same Level* that we are functioning at within our basic type. This helps to explain all sorts of puzzling "reversals" of behavior that we see in people. Furthermore, this also explains why we do not suddenly jump from the average behavior of our own type into pathological behavior in our Direction of Disintegration, and why we do not have to be in the unhealthy range of our type to go in the Direction of Disintegration.

Twos, for example, believe that they must always be kind and loving and that they need to take care of the needs of others rather than their own. But actually Twos also want *their needs* to be taken care of, and they hope that if they shower enough love on others, someone will reciprocate their generosity. If they keep giving endlessly, and no one seems to be responding to them—or not responding in ways that Twos recognize as loving—they will become more angry and more forceful about getting their own needs met. This is the meaning of the Twos' movement to Eight: they begin to act out their repressed anger aggres-

THE DIRECTION OF DISINTEGRATION (WITH REVERSAL)

1	Methodical Ones suddenly become moody and irrational at Four.
2	Needy Twos suddenly become aggressive and dominating at Eight.
3	Driven Threes suddenly become disengaged and apathetic at Nine.
4	Aloof Fours suddenly become overinvolved and clinging at Two.
5	Detached Fives suddenly become hyperactive and scattered at Seven.
6	Dutiful Sixes suddenly become competitive and arrogant at Three.
7	Scattered Sevens suddenly become perfectionistic and critical at One.
8	Self-confident Eights suddenly become secretive and fearful at Five.
9	Complacent Nines suddenly become anxious and worried at Six.

sively and impulsively. Instead of continuing to suppress their neediness and flattering others, they become direct and assertive. The more Twos deny their anger and their needs, the more explosive and destructive their acting out will be.

The following principle operates in all of the types: *whatever is repressed by a type is acted out under pressure in ways indicated by the type's Direction of Disintegration.* The following chart will hint at this process; the individual type chapters will describe it in more detail.

It is important to understand that, from a certain perspective, the movement in the Direction of Disintegration is just another survival mechanism. Nature has equipped us with a number of useful "escape

ACTING OUT

What is the difference between feeling an emotion and acting it out? If we feel angry, we can act it out by throwing a tantrum or we can resist the tendency and sit quietly with whatever we feel, noting the sensations that anger causes in our bodies. When we do this, we have the opportunity to see on a deeper level what our feelings are about. This does not mean that we are suppressing our feelings. On the contrary, it means that we will actually feel them instead of letting them lead us into compulsive behavior.

As an Inner Work task, when you next catch yourself acting out in your Direction of Disintegration, try to stop yourself from continuing to do so, even if you have already begun it. Stop in the middle of a sentence, if necessary, and sense your body. Check in with yourself to see how not acting out feels, and where the energy is in your body. See what happens to the energy as you experience it directly rather than discharging it. How long can you do so? Notice any "stories" you may be telling yourself about the situation. What happens if you continue to act out? Observe yourself without judging yourself, either for your success or for your failure to do the task.

hatches" for our psyches so that we cannot easily become pathological. The Direction of Disintegration is thus a way of allowing some pressure to ventilate. Acting out gives us temporary relief and slows down a potentially more devastating descent into the unhealthy range of our basic type, but of course it does not solve our problems. After we have acted out, we will have expended a great deal of energy and will still have to face the same issues. Acting out simply allows us to postpone dealing with our problems until a later time. When our personality is under stress for a long period of time, we may begin to shunt so habitually that we may appear *to be the type in the Direction of Disintegration.* For this reason, people who have been suffering from emotional difficulties or major crises in their lives will often misidentify themselves as the type in their Direction of Disintegration rather than their basic type.

For instance, Ones under great stress for long periods may mistake themselves for Fours because they will chronically act out many average to unhealthy Four characteristics. Similarly, Nines under extreme stress may appear more like average Sixes. Furthermore, this process accelerates as we go down the Levels, peaking in intensity in the lower average to unhealthy range.

We also have observed that people who have suffered from post-traumatic stress disorder (PTSD), or who have significant borderline features in their personality, tend to move in their Direction of Disintegration more often and more easily. Their personalities have more volatility and are less strongly grounded in the basic type, and they therefore intensely shunt to the Direction of Disintegration.

THE DIRECTION OF INTEGRATION

The Direction of Disintegration is unconscious and compulsive; it is the ego's way of automatically compensating for imbalances in our psyches. Transformation in the Direction of Integration is another matter, however, because moving in the Direction of Integration requires conscious choice. When we are on the path of integration, we are saying to ourselves, "I want to show up in my life more fully. I want to let go of my old stories and habits. I am willing to be with the truth of whatever I learn about myself. No matter what I feel, and no matter what I find, I want to be free and really alive."

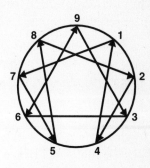

THE DIRECTION OF INTEGRATION

Thus, the Direction of Integration starts to be felt around Level 4, but it becomes more accessible at Level 3 and above.

When we start to let go of our personality's baggage, there will be growth and development in a certain "direction"—a healing of our core issues symbolized by the type in the Direction of Integration. The very qualities we need for our growth become more accessible to us, and the more we avail ourselves of them, the more they speed the progress of liberating ourselves from the limiting patterns of our personality. For example, when Eights start letting go of their issues around self-protection, armoring, and not letting down their guard, they automatically start getting in touch with their vulnerability and hurt. They begin to understand why they put on their armor in the first place. The more free of these defenses they become, the more they realize how good it feels to care about people, like healthy Twos. Eights know that they are on the right track when they start noticing that they really enjoy being connected with people and wanting to do good things for them.

As we learn to become more present, the positive qualities of the type in our Direction of Integration naturally begin to arise. When this happens, the limitations of the average range of our own type become painfully apparent. This gives us more incentive to stay with our practice and to recognize when we are slipping into the automatic compulsions of our type. Thus, we could say that the Direction of Integration represents the antidote to the fixated states of our type.

The Security Point

There are specific restricted circumstances in which we can exhibit behaviors from the *average* Levels of the type in our Direction of Integration. As a rule of thumb, we tend to act out the average behaviors in the Direction of Integration when we feel sure of where we stand in a situation. When we feel secure in the strength of our relationship with another person, we may try out behaviors that would be too risky

THE DIRECTION OF INTEGRATION

1	Angry, critical Ones become more spontaneous and joyful, like healthy Sevens.
2	Prideful, self-deceptive Twos become more self-nurturing and emotionally aware, like healthy Fours.
3	Vain, deceitful Threes become more cooperative and committed to others, like healthy Sixes.
4	Envious, emotionally turbulent Fours become more objective and principled, like healthy Ones.
5	Avaricious, detached Fives become more self-confident and decisive, like healthy Eights.
6	Fearful, pessimistic Sixes become more relaxed and optimistic, like healthy Nines.
7	Gluttonous, scattered Sevens become more focused and profound, like healthy Fives.
8	Lustful, controlling Eights become more open-hearted and caring, like healthy Twos.
9	Slothful, self-neglecting Nines become more self-developing and energetic, like healthy Threes.

with someone we did not know as well. For this reason, we call this phenomenon the *security point*.

For example, average Ones will sometimes behave like average Sevens, but not as often as they tend to act out the average to unhealthy issues of Type Four. Ones are not going to act like average Sevens unless they feel safe and secure to do so. Similarly, Fives may frequently act out average Seven behaviors, letting their minds go into overdrive and becoming scattered. But in more secure circumstances, Fives can also act like average Eights, forcefully asserting themselves and their wills, if they are very sure of their relationship with the other person.

The security point is thus not the same as moving in the Direction of Integration: it is another escape valve, like the Direction of Disintegration; it is another way of acting out, although one that requires special conditions. Persons functioning in the average to unhealthy Levels of their basic type may know that they need the qualities of the Direction of Integration, but when they are reacting compulsively and automatically, they are not capable of really integrating the healthier aspects of that type. Movement to the security point is not a real integrative process but an instance of one part of the personality being replaced or supplemented by another. This is not the same as becoming more free and aware. The movement toward the security point for each type is, by definition, within the average Levels.

The Real Meaning of Integration

Although the movement in the Direction of Integration requires *conscious choice,* it is not accomplished by imitating the attitudes and behaviors of the type in that direction, especially not the average characteristics. For instance, if you are an Eight, it does *not* mean that you should start "acting like a Two," baking cookies or opening doors for people. Imitating the behavior of the type in your Direction of Integration can actually make the personality "denser" since real transformation involves letting go of ego patterns and defenses, not adding new ones. This kind of behavior is doomed to failure.

We must always remember that *the personality cannot solve the problems of the personality,* and until our Essence is deeply felt and is guiding our activities, the personality can do little except to "not do" its old tricks.

The process of integration is not about what we "should" do—it is a process of consciously letting go of aspects of our type that block us. When we stop holding on to defenses, attitudes, and fears, we experience an organic unfolding and balancing as natural as the blossoming of a flower. A tree does not have to do anything to go from a bud to a flower to a fruit: it is an organic, natural process, and the soul wants to unfold in the same way. The Enneagram describes this organic process in each type. The type in the Direction of Integration gives us clues about when this is taking place and helps us understand and activate this process more easily.

Moving in the Direction of Integration deeply enriches the quality of all of our activities because the type in our Direction of Integration guides us to what really fulfills us and helps us realize the full potentials of our basic type. For instance, a Four who wants to express herself through music will be self-disciplined and will engage in regular practice like a healthy One, because this will help actualize her potential. "Going to One" is a Four's way of being the most effective Four that he or she can possibly be.

"Awareness is curative."

SURYA DAS

"There are only two ways to live your life. One is as though nothing is a miracle. The other is as though everything is a miracle."

ALBERT EINSTEIN

When we fully see, understand, and experience all the self-defeating blockages that have covered our Essential qualities, they fall away like dead leaves from a growing plant, and the fullness of our soul emerges naturally. Our soul, with all of the magnificent gifts that we see in the healthy range, is already here. Only our deeply ingrained belief in and attachment to the defenses of our personality—the resistance, self-image, and fear-based strategies of our type—prevent us from showing up and claiming our birthright.

PART II

▼

The
Nine Personality
Types

▲

CHAPTER 7

▼

TYPE ONE:
THE
REFORMER

▲

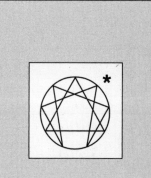

THE TEACHER

THE ACTIVIST

THE CRUSADER

THE MORALIST

THE PERFECTIONIST

THE ORGANIZER

"I have learned through bitter experience the one supreme lesson: to conserve my anger, and as heat conserved is transmuted into energy, even so our anger controlled can be transmuted into a power which can move the world."

—MOHANDAS K. GANDHI

"The unawakened mind tends to make war against the way things are."

—JACK KORNFIELD

"We shall never have friends, if we expect to find them without fault."

—THOMAS FULLER

"The real advantage which truth has, consists in this, that when an opinion is true, it may be extinguished once, twice, or many times, but in the course of ages there will generally be found persons to rediscover it."

—JOHN STUART MILL

THE RISO-HUDSON
T A S

Type Attitude Sorter

Score each of the following statements according to how true or applicable to you it is on the following scale:

1.......*Not at All True*

2.......*Seldom True*

3.......*Somewhat True*

4.......*Generally True*

5.......*Very True*

See page 124 for scoring key.

_____ 1. Most people see me as a serious, no-nonsense person—and when all is said and done, I suppose I am.

_____ 2. I have always tried to be honest and objective about myself—and I'm determined to follow my conscience no matter what the cost.

_____ 3. While there is some part of me that can be wild, generally speaking that just hasn't been my style.

_____ 4. It seems that I am living with a judge inside my head: sometimes the judge is wise and discerning, but often it is simply stern and harsh.

_____ 5. I feel that I have paid a great price for trying to be perfect.

_____ 6. I like to laugh as much as anyone—I should do it more often!

_____ 7. My principles and ideals inspire me toward greater achievement and make my life feel meaningful and worthwhile.

_____ 8. I do not understand why so many people have such lax standards.

_____ 9. So much depends on me getting things done that I have to be more organized and methodical than others.

_____ 10. I have a personal sense of mission, maybe even a calling to something higher, and I believe that there is something extraordinary that I may accomplish during my life.

_____ 11. I hate mistakes, and so I tend to be extremely thorough to make sure that things are being done properly.

_____ 12. Much of my life I have believed that right is right and wrong is wrong—and that's all there is to it.

_____ 13. I have a hard time leaving well enough alone.

_____ 14. Many responsibilities have fallen on my shoulders: if I hadn't risen to the occasion, God only knows what would have happened.

_____ 15. I am deeply moved by human nobility and grace under pressure.

PERSONALITY TYPE ONE: THE REFORMER

The Rational, Idealistic Type:
Principled, Purposeful, Self-Controlled, and Perfectionistic

We have named personality type One *the Reformer* because Ones have a sense of mission that leads them to want to improve the world in various ways, using whatever degree of influence they have. They strive to overcome adversity—particularly moral adversity—so that the human spirit can shine through and make a difference. They strive after higher values, even at the cost of great personal sacrifice.

History is full of Ones who have left comfortable lives to do something extraordinary because they felt that something higher was calling them. During the Second World War, Raoul Wallenberg left a comfortable middle-class life to work for the protection of thousands of European Jews from invading Nazis. In India, Gandhi left behind his wife and family and life as a successful lawyer to become an itinerant advocate of Indian independence and nonviolent social changes. Joan of Arc left her village in France to restore the throne to the dauphin and to expel the English from the country. The idealism of each of these Ones has inspired millions.

Ones are people of practical action—they wish to be *useful* in the best sense of the word. On some level of consciousness, they feel that they "have a mission" to fulfill in life, if only to try their best to reduce the disorder they see in their environment.

Although Ones have a strong sense of purpose, they also typically feel that they have to justify their actions to themselves and often to others as well. This orientation causes Ones to spend a lot of time thinking about the consequences of their actions, as well as about how to keep from acting contrary to their convictions. Because of this, Ones often persuade themselves that they are "head" types, rationalists who proceed only on logic and objective truth. But the real picture is somewhat different: *Ones are actually activists who are searching for an acceptable rationale for what they* feel *they must do.* They are people of instinct and passion who use convictions and judgments to control and direct themselves and their actions.

In the effort to stay true to their principles, Ones resist being affected by their instinctual drives, consciously not giving in to them or expressing them too freely. The result is a personality type that has problems with repression, resistance, and aggression. They are usually seen by others as highly self-controlled, even rigid, although this is not

▶ BASIC FEAR: Of being "bad," defective, evil, corrupt

▶ BASIC DESIRE: To be good, virtuous, in balance—to have integrity

▶ SUPEREGO MESSAGE: "You are good or okay if you do what is right."

"I have a mission in life."

how Ones experience themselves. It seems to them that they are sitting on a cauldron of passions and desires and that they had better "keep the lid on" lest they and everyone else around them regret it.

Cassandra, a therapist in private practice, recalls the difficulty this caused her in her youth.

> I remember in high school getting feedback that I had no feelings. Inside, I felt my feelings intensely and yet I just couldn't let them out as intensely as I felt them. Even now, if I have a conflict with a friend and need to address an issue, I rehearse ahead of time how to express clearly what I want, need, and observe, and yet not be harsh or blaming in my anger, which is often scathing.

Ones believe that being strict with themselves (and eventually becoming "perfect") will justify themselves in their own eyes and in the eyes of others. But by attempting to create their own brand of perfection, they often create their own personal hell. Instead of agreeing with the statement in Genesis that God saw what He had created "and it was good," Ones intensely feel, "It wasn't—there obviously have been some mistakes here!" This orientation makes it difficult for them to trust their inner guidance—indeed, to trust life—so Ones come to rely heavily on their superego, a learned voice from their childhood, to guide them toward the greater good that they so passionately seek. When Ones have gotten completely entranced in their personality, there is little distinction between them and this severe, unforgiving voice. Separating from it and seeing its genuine strengths and limitations is what growth for Ones is about.

THE CHILDHOOD PATTERN

Please note that the childhood pattern we are describing here does not cause the personality type. Rather, it describes tendencies that we observe in early childhood that have a major impact on the type's adult relationships.

Ones tried hard to be good kids: they often report feeling that, as children, they needed to justify their existence. Simply being a child was somehow not acceptable, and many young Ones developed a sense of seriousness and adult responsibility at an early age. They understood that their parents expected a lot from them, and like Threes, they often played the role of the Family Hero. Young Ones generally take on such expectations with great earnestness.

Jeanne, a spiritual director for women religious in Quebec, still remembers the pressure she felt to uphold her family's values.

> When I had frequent and serious nosebleeds, Dad would tell me I mustn't be praying enough. Knowing what was "enough" always eluded me, but I suspected that more had to be better. . . . Dad ex-

pected me to pray and intercede for him and the whole family. Needless to say, I made time to be at daily Mass. I had a serious mission for which to intercede; the family's well-being could be at stake.

For various reasons, Ones experience a sense of being "disconnected" from their protective-figure (who is usually, although not always, the biological father). Having another stable adult figure that the child can identify with and move toward gives the child the ability to separate from dependency on the mother and to increasingly sense his or her own individuality and autonomy. If, however, the protective-figure is not adequately fulfilling his role, young Ones sense a fundamental disconnection. They realize that their real or symbolic father does not adequately fit their temperament and needs. This does not necessarily mean that the protective-figure is bad or abusive, but that, for whatever reason, a certain effortless bonding simply does not take place.

The result is a feeling of frustration for the child and the sense that he must "father" himself. In some cases, young Ones respond to chaotic conditions around them by becoming hyperresponsible, the "voice of reason" in their families. In this way they are able to establish some sense of autonomy and boundaries—the key issues of their type.

Justine is a business consultant who was forced by her painful childhood to develop a vigilant and strict set of ego defenses.

> Since there was a lot of conflict in the family I grew up in, I felt I had to stop it or fix it in some way. That probably contributed to my very controlling nature. I had poor boundaries as the result of an imposing, aggressive mother, so I identified strongly with her less-than-healthy behaviors to protect myself. I grew up very critical, judgmental, and opinionated. I treated my younger sisters as she treated us, and was very bossy and demanding.

In effect, the child says, "I will give myself guidelines. I will become my own father-figure and be my own moral guide. I will police myself so no one else will police me; I will punish myself so no one else will punish me." Ones try to surpass what is expected of them by adhering to the rules so rigorously that no one will be able to catch them in error, thus earning independence.

Leo, a successful business consultant, recalls the difficult demands of his childhood adaptations.

> As a child I learned quickly that there was only one right way of doing things and only one—my father's way. His way would sometimes change—he was inconsistent. But his way was always the "right"

way. . . . So, in reaction to my father's inconsistencies, I developed a conscience that launched me into a quest for the "true" right way that I myself could subscribe to.

In a sense, Ones feel that they need to outdo the expectations of their protective-figure. They feel that they must come up with a better set of rules for themselves; *they* decide right or wrong. But in so doing, the child feels guilty for judging (and implicitly condemning) its own protective-figure. To escape the guilt of this situation, young Ones construct an identity that allows them to see themselves as good and responsible and others as lazy, sloppy, or at least less correct and "mature" than themselves. Such self-justification becomes the bedrock of the One's identity and the emotional pattern that will be reenacted throughout their lives.

THE WING SUBTYPES

▲

Examples

Plato
Gandhi
Sandra Day O'Connor
George Harrison
Henry David Thoreau
Martha Stewart
Katharine Hepburn
Al Gore
George F. Will
Noam Chomsky

THE ONE WITH A NINE-WING: THE IDEALIST

Healthy   People of this subtype are highly discerning, wise, and civilized. They can be scholarly and erudite, maintaining a dispassionate philosophical stance that focuses on long-range concerns—the "big" picture. They can have an introverted, reclusive quality about them, seeking relief from "the maddening crowd," often in quiet, natural settings. They are emotionally reserved but generous, kind, and considerate, generally loving nature, animals, and innocence wherever they find it. They wish to improve things but with a gentler, more detached touch than other Ones.

Average   Idealistic and less likely to engage in the politics and "dirty work" necessary to bring about the reforms they believe in, average people of this subtype would rather explain their ideals than personally persuade others of their correctness. The anger seen in Ones is harder to detect in this subtype than in the other, tending to express itself in stiffness, impatience, and sarcasm. People of this subtype prefer to be alone and look for situations where they can work by themselves in order to avoid dealing with the disappointing messiness of human relationships. They can be more remote, otherworldly, and impersonal than the other subtype, potentially disdainful, elitist, and condescending to their fellow humans.

THE ONE WITH A TWO-WING: THE ADVOCATE

Healthy   People of this subtype blend their quest for ideals and higher principles with empathy and compassion for others. Less purely idealistic than the other subtype, they are genuinely interested in improving the lot of mankind and more willing to get into the trenches to bring about the changes they advocate. They are also more overtly passionate and interpersonal, enjoying the give-and-take of "political" involvement. People of this subtype are persuasive and go out of their way to get others to care about the causes and beliefs they espouse.

Average   Highly active and outgoing, average people of this subtype can be fairly aggressive and forceful in the pursuit of the ideals and reforms they seek. While they are comfortable being alone and need a good deal of "down time" to recharge and think, they are also energized by engaging with others, particularly debating and refining their ideas. This makes them naturally good at politics on whatever scale they engage in it. The needs of others are the focus for their altruism, so long as they feel they are making a difference. They can become critical and irritable and highly vocal about their discontents when they are frustrated. They are also more fiery and action-oriented than the other subtype, and so the possibility of being frustrated by people and events is higher.

THE SELF-PRESERVATION INSTINCT IN THE ONE

Self-Control.   In the average range, Self-Preservation Ones tend to worry about their material well-being, both in terms of finances and health, and they often castigate themselves for not working hard enough (like average Sixes). The Self-Preservation instinct also gives them strong drives for gratification, but their Type One superego can be severe in countering those drives. The resulting inner conflict is the source of continual stress, physical tension, and an all-or-nothing attitude with regard to their pleasures and desires. They may either indulge themselves and their desires, or go through periods of asceticism, during which their desires are suppressed as much as possible.

As they become more identified with their superego dictates, they become very fearful about making mistakes that seem like catastrophes to them. They feel that any wrong action could result in the undoing of their well-being. They can be quite picky and fastidious about their environment. (Picture Felix Unger in *The Odd Couple.*) They value cleanliness, order, hygiene, and aesthetics, and they are often preoccupied with health and diet, religiously subscribing to beliefs about vitamins, macrobiotics, homeopathic remedies, and so forth. With others, they tend to be overprotective about the things that they worry about in themselves. If they are worried about getting sick, they scold others about not taking care of their health. If they have money concerns, they exhort others to save. In the lower Levels, the harshness of their superego causes them to feel undeserving of any kind of comfort or reward.

In the unhealthy range, Self-Preservation Ones begin to oscillate between periods of strict restraint of their appetites and periods of excess and debauch. They often become obsessed with health matters, especially

Examples

Jerry Brown
Hillary Clinton
Celine Dion
John Bradshaw
Emma Thompson
Jane Fonda
Joan Baez
Vanessa Redgrave
Ralph Nader
John Paul II

THE INSTINCTUAL VARIANTS

▲

with regard to food. They often attempt to justify or undo their violations of their own dietary or health requirements. They may binge on sweets, or drink excessively, then go on a crash diet. Milkshakes and fries are followed by handfuls of vitamins. Self-Preservation Ones are prone to eating disorders and extreme practices to curb their instinctual impulses, including asceticism, excessive fasting, bingeing and purging, and so forth.

THE SOCIAL INSTINCT IN THE ONE

The Crusader.   In the average range, Social Ones believe that they represent objective values, social standards, and that they speak for others. Teaching, advocating, and moralizing can be part of the picture, but mostly about social issues and about rules and procedures. They are often interested in politics, current affairs, and journalism and are adept at uncovering the "dirt," exposing wrongdoing and speaking out against injustices. On the other hand, they will work patiently to bring about the reforms they see as necessary—improving the local schools, getting their co-op involved with recycling, and so forth.

Social Ones derive a vivid sense of themselves by holding strong opinions and convictions and arguing for their perspective. They value these qualities in others as well, although when more fixated, they expect others always to agree with them. This can lead to rigidity both in their thinking and in their behavior. Their views can become a boundary, an armor against the world. And since Ones apply the rules most rigorously to themselves, they fear ever being caught contradicting their own stated beliefs and opinions.

Although Social Ones insist that others should not take their criticisms and views personally, *they* take things personally, often reacting to public policies as if they were personal affronts or triumphs.

In the unhealthy range, Social Ones hold unrealistic standards and expectations for themselves, others, and society at large. They may become involved in extreme political views or strict religious dogmas (libertarianism is the *only* solution to the country's ills; no sexual activity in marriage unless it can lead directly to conception). In the lower Levels, they can engage in rants and tirades, constantly feeling outrage at the imperfections of humanity.

THE SEXUAL INSTINCT IN THE ONE

Shared Standards.   In the average range, Sexual Ones want a flawless relationship with an idealized partner. They long for the perfect mate, an unwavering source of stability in their lives. In this respect, they can be mistaken for Fours. They have high expectations of their partner, their family, and their close friends and want to believe that the other person in the relationship holds the same standards. ("We share these ideals, don't we?") Sexual Ones fear that the other will fall short, thus destroying the harmony and perfection of the relationship. This can lead to feeling that they must push loved ones to meet their standards. They also may have trouble finding someone who meets their standards, trying one relationship after another but always feeling disappointed.

Sexual Ones place a great emphasis on fidelity. ("Love is forever.") Although they do not appear needy, they often suffer from well-hidden fears of abandonment and a chronic sense of loneliness. The mix of high expectations with abandonment issues can result in a critical, controlling attitude toward the partner. ("Don't ever let me down. Don't ever deceive me.") At lower Levels, they may constantly need to "check in" on the other's activities and whereabouts. Sexual Ones feel that they have earned a good relationship, earned their pleasure, and feel threatened at the possible loss of one of their few areas of reward. Criticism and control may be used to keep the other off balance, to undermine confidence, thus postponing potential abandonment.

In the unhealthy range, the Sexual variant endows them with strong desires and appetites, but this is difficult to justify to the One's superego. Sexual Ones may experience intense desire alternating with a need to reject that desire. This may lead to both sexual compulsivity and repression. ("I don't want to be attracted to him.") At the same time, they may believe that the other is the source of their obsessions and want to control the other so that the balance of the relationship can be restored. Less healthy Sexual Ones are prey to bouts of intense jealousy. Their fears are such that they constantly question and grill the other. In extreme cases, they may punish the self or others to purge themselves of their desires.

The following are issues most Ones will encounter at some point in their lives. Noticing these patterns, "catching ourselves in the act," and simply seeing our underlying habitual responses to life will do much to release us from the negative aspects of our type.

THE ONE'S CHALLENGES TO GROWTH

▲

THE WAKE-UP CALL FOR TYPE ONE: A SENSE OF INTENSE PERSONAL OBLIGATION

Ones can grow tremendously simply by recognizing and being aware of their particular Wake-up Call, a heavy and constant sense of *personal obligation.* They begin to think that it is up to them to fix whatever mess they encounter. ("If I do not do this, no one else will!") Further, they are convinced that even if others are willing to tackle

				TYPE I
H E A L T H Y	Level 1	*Key Terms:* *Accepting* *Wise*	Ones let go of the belief that they are in a position to judge anything objectively and are able to approach life without emotionally reacting to it. They also paradoxically achieve their Basic Desire—to have integrity and to be good. As a result of their self-actualization, they become wise, discerning, accepting, hopeful, and often noble.	**L E V E L S**
	Level 2	*Evaluating* *Reasonable*	Ones focus on the dictates of their superegos to guide them in life and defend them from the "disordered" parts of themselves. Self-image: "I am sensible, moderate, and objective."	
	Level 3	*Principled* *Responsible*	Ones reinforce their self-image by trying to live their lives in accordance with their consciences and with reason. They are highly ethical and self-disciplined and possess a strong sense of purpose and conviction. Truthful and articulate, they teach by example, putting aside personal desires for the greater good.	**O F**
A V E R A G E	Level 4	*Obligated* *Striving*	Ones begin to fear that others are indifferent to their principles, so they want to convince others of the rightness of their viewpoint. They become serious and driven, debating others and remedying problems, while evaluating their world and pointing out what is wrong with things.	**D E V E L O P M E N T**
	Level 5	*Self-* *Controlled* *Orderly*	Ones worry that others will condemn them for any deviation from their ideals. Having argued their point of view, Ones are now obliged to live up to it at all times, so they try to rigorously organize themselves and their world. They are punctual and methodical but also irritable and tense.	
	Level 6	*Judgmental* *Critical*	Ones are afraid that others will mess up the order and balance that they have achieved and they are angry that others do not take their ideals as seriously. They react by reproaching and correcting others for not living up to their own standards. They are perfectionistic, opinionated, and sarcastic.	
U N H E A L T H Y	Level 7	*Self-* *Righteous* *Inflexible*	Ones fear that their ideals may actually be wrong, which may be true. To save their self-image, they attempt to justify themselves and silence criticism. They are closed-minded and allow no compromises or negotiations in their positions. They are bitter, misanthropic, and highly self-righteous.	
	Level 8	*Obsessive* *Contradictory*	Ones are so desperate to defend themselves from their irrational desires and impulses that they become obsessed with the very parts of themselves they want to control. They begin to act out all of their repressed desires while publicly continuing to condemn them. They cannot stop themselves.	
	Level 9	*Condemnatory* *Punitive*	The realization that they have lost control of themselves and are doing the very things they cannot tolerate in others is too much for unhealthy Ones. They try to rid themselves of the apparent cause of their obsessions in themselves, others, or the environment, possibly resulting in self-mutilation, murder, or suicide.	

problems, they are not going to do as thorough a job as Ones themselves would. They therefore become increasingly fixated on correcting and organizing and controlling their environment. They also become tense and serious, automatically focusing on what is wrong with things.

When they start to feel as if the weight of the world is on their shoulders, it is a strong indication that average Ones are slipping into their characteristic trance.

Cassandra, the therapist we met earlier, reveals how difficult it has been for her to let go of this tendency in herself.

> Being a One is to feel burdened much of the time—burdened with the need to do the right thing in every situation, to monitor one's thoughts and feelings so they do not show or, if they do, to express them both appropriately and in the "right" amount. I still struggle with feeling resentful when people won't listen to me or, worse yet, when they come to the same conclusions as me after having made horrendous mistakes that are damaging to themselves and others. I still haven't found a balance in this area.

LONELY RESPONSIBILITY

Average Ones feel obligated not only to "do the right thing" but to make up for the carelessness and foolishness of others. Do you notice this pattern in yourself? What situations, specifically, are likely to bring this up? When this occurs, what opinions are you holding about others? How does this make you feel toward them? Toward yourself?

The Social Role: The Educator

In the average range, Ones begin to define themselves in the Social Role of the Educator or the Teacher, the person whose place it is to instill wisdom in the ignorant, uplift the fallen, and show others how to do something useful and productive with their lives. They feel compelled to instruct others on the best way to accomplish things, even something as simple as washing dishes or refolding a newspaper after reading it.*

Unconsciously, average Ones see themselves as mature, responsible adults surrounded by irrational, careless children, and this attitude is

"I know how things should be done."

---

* Fives also "teach" by focusing on their expertise. However, Ones are people of action, whereas cerebral Fives are generally less interested in the practical application of their ideas.

often communicated to others in subtle and not-so-subtle ways. This patronizing stance usually makes others resist the One's help and views—even if others might agree with them in principle. Such resistance often frustrates Ones even more.

The role of Teacher can also cause Ones to become impatient with the responses of others. Ones may recognize that others are making efforts, but they question whether those efforts are *sufficient*. They are irritated that people are wasting valuable time by questioning their way of doing things. Ones feel that they must work overtime to make up for others' sloppiness or laziness, and so they often fail to take adequate care of themselves. Their irritation and impatience, however, make it extremely difficult for average Ones to communicate their suggestions to others in a nonthreatening way. Fortunately, this very quality is a tip-off that a One is getting into trouble.

Cassandra has learned to use her frustration as an indication that she is becoming more trapped by her personality.

> Irritability is a sure sign that I'm starting the downward slide. I've learned when I become irritable, some unmet need is present. It could be as simple as needing to eat, or as complex as needing to address an unrecognized conflict with a friend. I am learning not to "blame" myself for being irritable, but to take steps to intervene before it becomes harshness or depression.

As they become less healthy, Ones are much more easily annoyed by others' different—and to their minds, lax—standards. ("Why aren't the other people in this office as organized as I am?" "It's a simple matter for the children to keep their rooms tidy.") What average Ones do not seem to understand is that while their own habits and methods might be very effective *for themselves,* they may not be appropriate for other people. They do not seem to grasp that others might want to devote their time and energy to different projects and pursuits. (Not everyone cares if the spice rack is organized alphabetically.)

PARENTING GROWN-UPS

Four largely unconscious ways of communicating with others have been identified by a field of psychology called *transactional analysis*. We can communicate as adult-to-adult, as child-to-adult, as child-to-child, or as adult-to-child. Ones often create problems in their relationships by choosing the last of these: adult-to-child. Psychologists have found that this is the *least* effective way of communicating with others. Notice when you unconsciously fall into this pattern. What response does it get from others? How does it make you feel? What payoff are you getting for communicating to others this way?

Anger, Resentment, and Frustration

The anger of Ones is directed both at themselves for failing to live up to their ideals, and at others for what Ones see as their laziness and irresponsibility. As Ones become more unhealthy, they displace more of their anger onto others as they make themselves the sole judge of who and what is right and wrong. They also become more irritable with others because others seem to them to be getting off the hook. They feel that others are not taking an equal share of the responsibility—and seem to be having all the fun. ("Why am I doing all the work and being so responsible while everyone else is out fooling around?")

Anger, in itself, is not a bad thing. It is what arises naturally when there is something around us that we do not like or want in our lives. Anger is a way of resisting an attack on our integrity, whether physical, moral, or spiritual. Anger, when fully experienced (and not acted out, repressed, or "swallowed"), is instantaneous and short-lived. When we allow our anger without resisting it, it usually arises like a wave and passes through us within a minute. When we resist anger or hang on to it (for other strategic reasons of our ego), it perpetuates itself in increasing obsessive thinking, emotional constriction, and physical tension. Even when these thinking patterns have run their course, the anger remains stored in the body, locked in muscular tension and habitual behaviors such as pacing, nail biting, and teeth grinding. Ones can grow enormously by learning to feel their anger without attempting to suppress it or justify it. Talking openly about their anger with significant others can be very healing for Ones and a positive step in learning to process their resentments.

Ironically, though, Ones are not always aware of their anger. They seldom experience anger *as* anger because their superego generally prohibits them from being "too emotional." To be angry is to be out of control, to be less than perfect, so Ones often deny their anger through clenched teeth—"I'm not angry! I'm just trying to get it right!"

"Everyone is so lazy and irresponsible."

Striving After the Ideal

Average Ones strive after their ideals since doing so makes them feel worthwhile and provides a way to suppress negative superego voices. But the more they want the ideal, the more frustrated they become by the real, and it becomes difficult for them to see the good in things right before their eyes, whether in a relationship, a coworker's performance, or a child's behavior. The specter of the ideal also begins to overshadow their own performance and the satisfaction they take in their own work. Everything from working at the office, to doing homework with the kids, to writing a letter becomes more burdensome since it must be done as perfectly as possible.

Like all the types, Ones have an inherent contradiction at the center of their personality structure. They wish to find integrity and a sense of wholeness—and yet by constantly sitting in judgment, their superego splits them into "good" and "bad" parts. They thereby lose the integrity and sense of wholeness they seek. An internal war rages between the various factions of themselves, between themselves and others, and between themselves and the world.

Even if Ones come within range of meeting their own standards, the standards are raised by their active superego. (By definition, an ideal cannot be attained, and so the One must redefine the ideal and try harder.) Continually striving for perfection means being very hard on oneself, inevitably leading to a constant state of tension and frustration.

DISAPPOINTMENT

Notice how many times a day you are disappointed with yourself or others. Use your Inner Work Journal to keep track of this for a few days. What standards are you measuring everything against? Question and examine the nature of these standards and their effect on you and the people in your life.

Being Purposeful and Making Progress

"There's a sensible way of handling everything."

The high-minded seriousness and sense of purpose of healthy Ones becomes more compulsive if they feel they must constantly work to justify their existence. If this happens, healthy, balanced self-discipline deteriorates into grim determination, even workaholism, and it becomes increasingly difficult for Ones to take a break: relaxation or play must be constantly earned. They feel that there is little time for frivolity or lightness; even vacations can take on the aura of responsibility and of not frittering around too much (less time at the beach, more time in museums!), guilt forbids "idling" ("An idle mind is the Devil's playground."), and Ones feel that they are wasting time if they are not improving themselves and their environment in some way.

Anne describes some of the anxiety her "purposefulness" has caused her.

I probably wouldn't take any extended vacations if it weren't for my husband. It's only when I'm away that I realize how badly I need the rest and change of scene. But I wouldn't dream of going anywhere without at least one serious and instructive book.

Because progress is so important to Ones, efficiency and working according to methods, systems, and timetables are as well. They are constantly developing and refining procedures, seeking the most effective way to do things in the least amount of time. Ones are like Sixes in that both approach problems with protocols: flow charts, formulae, or rules (using *Robert's Rules of Order* to conduct meetings, for example). Sixes prefer working within established parameters and often resent surprises or disruptions of the "system" as they have understood it. Ones, on the other hand, are guided by their own sense of judgment and may balk at agreed-upon guidelines, feeling that their own method would be more effective. They care less about who agrees with them or whether or not they had precedent and social convention on their side.

UNATTAINABLE STANDARDS

When you find yourself becoming frantic about some goal you have set, stop and ask yourself what is really at stake. Is the level of frustration you are experiencing commensurate with the problem you are dealing with? Especially notice your own self-talk. What are you saying to yourself? Whom are you trying to appease?

Being Right and Pointing Out Problems

Ones have learned that to be loved they must be good, and to be good they must be right. This behavior manifests as a continual need to point out errors or a better way of doing things. Average Ones feel compelled to debate others about any number of things, from political and religious views, to optimal study habits, to the most exalted examples of music and art.

Despite the fact that they may have good points to make, others may sense that Ones are unconsciously bolstering their egos through these actions—thereby justifying themselves in subtle ways. It is as if they were constantly demonstrating their own worthiness to their superegos. ("See how hard I'm working? See how I just noticed that problem? I was more effective than those other people, wasn't I?") A further problem is that while average Ones may make a point worth listening to, they begin to express themselves in such a forceful (even abrasive) way that others cannot take in their message.

Being right is another effort to get on the good side of the superego—to identify oneself with it, thus lessening its attacks and the suffering it creates. The cost of this strategy is high, however: it creates alienation, tension, and a profound lack of relatedness to the environment, both inner and outer. A simplistic view of right and wrong is a

"Right is right and wrong is wrong and there are no exceptions."

dualism that seldom results in any satisfying conclusion or lasting solutions to disagreements.

BROADENING YOUR VIEW

As an exercise, take up a position that is the opposite of your usual view and find a way to argue it convincingly. For instance, if you find most network television programming appalling, see if you can come up with a convincing thesis declaring the virtues of network television. After you can do this, you may try more challenging topics about which you have stronger views: morality, sexuality, religion, and so forth. At the very least, you will understand the other person's point of view better, leading to more compassion and tolerance. It may be difficult at first, but you will eventually find it extremely enjoyable, and this little game can do much to free you from your superego.

Order, Consistency, and Punctuality

Some Ones are compulsively neat; others need to schedule their time meticulously; and still others need to monitor their health and diet carefully. Others care little for being neat but are extremely particular about procedures in the workplace. Concern about external order seems to escalate in proportion to the average One's deeper concern about some *internal disorder* they feel in themselves.

Average Ones are particularly troubled by perceived inconsistency, either in themselves or others, and therefore they attempt to make all their behavior consistent, sensible, and justifiable. (It is as if the One child, by modeling a high level of consistency, were seeking to elicit the same from a parent.) This further cements their attachments to methods and procedures that have worked in the past—and blinds them to other possible solutions or viewpoints.

Justine is quite familiar with this problem.

> I feel like I am so tense and serious. I can't seem to lighten up! There is such a driving need that everything be right and in its place, whether it be an event, situation, conversation, or the arrangement of a room, trip, or workshop. I can be tough on a trainer or speaker if I think the information is not all there or is incomplete. The saying "Let go and let God" is a tough one to submit to. Everything has to be done right, with little regard to importance or priority. It is easy not to have or to lose perspective on what is important enough to warrant attention and what isn't.

Ones typically feel that there is only so much time in the day, or in their lives, for that matter, and that they need all of it to accomplish their "missions." Of course, as in other areas, they may have some useful ideas about time management, but if Ones deteriorate, obsessions about punctuality can become a constant source of tension and stress. Ones readily berate themselves for being even slightly late for work or an appointment, while giving no weight to their willingness to stay extra hours to complete a task.

Anne confronted her rigid punctuality during the course of group therapy.

> I get a headache whenever I'm late, even when I'm meeting someone who is never on time. In group therapy years ago, the therapist who basically wanted people to be on time gave me the task of coming ten to fifteen minutes late. He knew I couldn't do it. Every day there is a schedule—in my head. I'll find myself anxiety ridden if I'm not running according to that schedule, until I suddenly realize that most of the things can be done tomorrow, or perhaps, heaven forbid, I could ask someone else to do them. I get really resentful when I think, "I have to do everything around here"—then I realize that the only person who is demanding that is me.

COMPULSIVE ORGANIZING

In your Inner Work Journal, spend fifteen minutes making a list of the areas in your life in which you demand and expect order and control and those in which you do not. Be honest with yourself, as there may be more in either group than you might expect. Do you expect order from people or things, situations at home or at the office? What kinds of disorder make you most annoyed? How does your annoyance show itself?

At the end of the exercise, make a two-column list of the benefits and drawbacks of attempting to be orderly and organized in areas you have identified. Is order and predictability more important to you than people and relationships? Some kinds of relationships? Do you unconsciously and unintentionally treat yourself or others impersonally, as objects or machines?

Self-Control and Self-Restraint

In order to be internally consistent and unaffected by the environment, Ones believe that they must be scrupulously self-controlled. Increasingly, then, Ones must struggle not only against the resistance they meet in others but against the resistance they meet in themselves. They sense that there are parts of themselves that are not at all interested in their self-improvement projects. And yet failing to live up to their own professed standards would leave them prey to intense feelings of guilt.

"I've got to get control of myself."

On a subconscious level, average Ones often have issues (guilt, shame, anxiety) about their bodies and bodily functions. They have been taught that they and their needs are messy, and that their body and its natural instincts are dirty, something to be ashamed of. They have to be ultraclean, ultracareful, and ultrascrupulous. In many Ones, this manifests as an exaggerated modesty, or in a nervousness about matters of eating, elimination, or sex.

In reaction to their superego demand for self-control, Ones start giving themselves secret "outs," or what we call *escape hatches.* They develop secret behaviors and indulgences, giving themselves permission to do as they please in a way that feels safe and that they can rationalize. Their escape hatches represent a partial rebellion against the superego, a way of letting off steam without throwing off the superego altogether. Thus, the proper workaholic office manager takes secret weekend trips to Las Vegas; the minister, decrying godless humanism, develops a secret enthusiasm for pornography; and the human rights activist secretly abuses his girlfriend.

IDENTIFYING ESCAPE HATCHES

Do you have some escape hatches? What are they? What are they an escape from? What do they tell you about your own superego's prohibitions?

Being Critical and Judgmental

"A day spent judging another is a painful day. A day spent judging yourself is a painful day."

BUDDHA

As they become more strict with themselves and unforgiving of their errors, average Ones cannot help but dwell on their shortcomings. Some of their "defects" are too painful to face and are quickly repressed. They become preoccupied with other, smaller infractions and seldom get a break from their critical inner judge on these matters. All they can do is to strive even harder to be "good." They may also become more judgmental and critical of others.

If we examine the function of judgment in personality, we see that it serves to reinforce our sense of self by separating us from that which we are judging. Judgment is one of the most powerful ways that human beings draw boundaries and cut themselves off from direct contact with their experience. When we judge ourselves, we create a state of internal war. Like war, judging is very expensive in the energy, time, and effort it consumes. Rather than expand us or liberate us, our judgments exhaust us and limit us.

The Essential self exercises discernment, notes differences, and makes decisions about what to do; by contrast, ego-based judgment always carries a certain negative emotional charge. Its primary function is not to discern but to create distance (or a boundary). *The hallmark of judgment (rather than Essential knowing) is that it is divisive.*

Ego judgment also contains an element of being "better than" that which is being judged. Even when we are judging some aspect of ourselves, some part of us is saying about another part, "Well, I'm better than that!" Such a position is paradoxical and conflicted since, in a single human being, who is judging whom?

Ted is a carpenter who prides himself on fine craftsmanship, but he is aware of the cost of his exacting standards.

> I know that when I'm getting caught up in my stuff, I can be pretty severe with people sometimes. The worst of it is that no matter how tough I am on others, I'm always ten times harder on myself. When I actually stop and listen to what I'm saying to myself, I can't believe it. I wouldn't talk like that to my worst enemy!

THE RUNNING COMMENTARY

In your Inner Work Journal, write down all of the judgments (good or bad) that you have made about other people in the last three hours or so. If you have just gotten up in the morning, write down all of the judgments you have made about others since arising. Did you make judgments about people you heard on the radio, or on television, or saw in your home, apartment building, or on the street going to work?

Now do the same about yourself. How have you judged yourself in the last three hours? Is there a common theme to your judgments?

The Inner Critic and Perfectionism

Average Ones are highly sensitive to criticism. This is not particularly surprising given their background of constant *self*-criticism: any further negative feedback from others can be extremely threatening. Ones feel as though they need all of their strength and concentration to meet the ruthless standards of their own Inner Critic, so they possess few resources for handling even the slightest hint of criticism from others.

The only way that Ones can escape self-criticism is by being *perfect.* Of course, this is virtually impossible, although average Ones give it their best effort since they feel that nothing less than perfection will be acceptable either to them or to others (who would be disappointed with them with less) or to their own standards. They therefore feel that they can never afford to take a day off, so to speak, lest they come under attack from their harsh inner judge.

> "Perfectionism is self-abuse of the highest order."
>
> ANN WILSON SCHAEF

Morton, a successful architect, relates to this experience.

Several years ago I won a prestigious architectural prize from an international jury. But the problem was that it was only second prize. It wasn't so much that I didn't win first because I wanted "first prize" but more the fact that I berated myself for the mistakes in my design. I tossed and turned for days, redrawing the plans in my head. I was so critical and negative and down on myself that I couldn't enjoy the fact that I actually won second prize! Not bad for someone barely out of school—but not good enough for my superego, I guess.

No matter how critical, destructive, and erosive of their self-confidence their Inner Critic is, average Ones are convinced that their Critic is the sole voice of reason—their guiding star that will lead them to salvation. They would be greatly helped by recognizing that their superego voices are actually destroying their integrity and harming them and their relationships. But once they become identified with their Inner Critic, it gives them a real (but shaky) sense of self-confidence that is difficult for Ones to question or to change—that is, until they see how destructive it can be.

REACTING TO STRESS: ONE GOES TO FOUR

▲

Under conditions of increased stress, average Ones long to be free of their burdens and obligations and may find themselves spending time in daydreams and fantasies of romance or escapes to exotic locales much like average Fours. They may also feel romantic and harbor forbidden longings for people they have encountered. As Ones, however, they are generally too self-inhibiting to inform the object of their desire of their true feelings, much less act on these feelings. If Ones do risk hinting at their interest in their fantasy "lover," any rebuff or ridicule results in profound feelings of shame and a deeper resolve to hold their impulses at bay. Ones feel guilty for being irresponsible and become even stricter with themselves.

The move to Four can be seen as an indication of Ones' growing disenchantment and alienation. They feel that no one understands them or how hard they are working, and they can suddenly become moody, melancholy, and withdrawn. Their discipline and self-control collapse into stormy feelings of envy and resentment. ("Everyone else is having a better life than me.") Usually steady Ones may engage in unexpected displays of drama or pouting or in a highly affected way of behaving that seems out of character with their background. Emotional outbursts, moodiness, hostility, and social withdrawal can all be part of the picture. Should they be questioned about any of this, Ones will become even more painfully self-conscious and self-controlled.

In the lower Levels, the move to Four can lead Ones into growing self-indulgence and a willingness to give themselves a few exceptions to their own rules. After all, no one has been working as hard as they have. Who would fault them for having a few drinks or a steamy, illicit romance? In and of themselves, these behaviors might not be particularly harmful, but because these activities run counter to Ones' superegos' dictates, they become the source of even more pressure and anxiety. Further, Ones' choices of distractions tend to be self-indulgent rather than truly nurturing, so they have little effect in actually relieving Ones' tension and frustration. As they become more unhealthy, their superego becomes so severe that they may unconsciously seek more destructive escapes to counteract it.

THE RED FLAG: THE ONE IN TROUBLE

▲

If Ones have suffered a serious crisis without adequate support or coping skills, or if they have suffered from chronic abuse in childhood, they may cross the shock point into the unhealthy aspects of their type. This may lead them to a fearful recognition that their views, positions, and methods may actually be wrong, or at least limited, flawed, and overstated. Ones may also fear that because they have been so strident in expressing their standards, others will hold them mercilessly accountable for their errors. Some of these fears may be based on fact.

These realizations can be a turning point in a One's life. If Ones can recognize the truth in these fears, they may begin to move toward health and liberation. On the other hand, they may become even more self-righteous and inflexible. ("Right is right, and wrong is wrong, and there are no exceptions." "They disagree with me because they are corrupt.") If Ones persist in this attitude, they may cross into the unhealthy levels. If you or someone you know is exhibiting the below warning signs for

---

WARNING SIGNS

POTENTIAL PATHOLOGY: Obsessive-Compulsive Disorder, Depressive Personality Disorder, eating disorders, crippling guilt, and self-destructive behaviors.

▶ Taking rigidly inflexible positions

▶ Extremely self-righteous and very judgmental

▶ Rationalizing and justifying their own actions

▶ Intense feelings of disillusion and depression

▶ Outbursts of rage, intolerance, and condemnation

▶ Obsessive thinking and compulsive behaviors

▶ Periods of masochistic self-punishment

an extended period of time—more than a few weeks—getting counseling, therapy, or other support is highly advisable.

PRACTICES THAT HELP ONES DEVELOP

▲

▶ First and foremost, become acquainted with your superego—your inner judge. Learn to distinguish it from your self, to recognize its "voice" and its effects on you. Pay attention to the ways in which it affects your sense of well-being and your connectedness with your environment. Begin to think of that commanding voice as "it," not as "I." Remember it only *sounds* like the voice of God.

▶ Be aware of your tendency to push yourself beyond your limits of endurance. No doubt the projects you are working on are important, but you cannot remain as effective if you fail to take breaks or refresh yourself. Your work will not suffer from these "breathers"; in fact, the fresh perspectives they may give you can provide better ways of approaching your task. Leave time for play. Many of your greatest inspirations will come from your sense of playfulness.

▶ You tend to believe that everything falls on your shoulders, and this can be extremely stressful. Let others help you, and understand that while their approach may not be as well considered as yours, their contributions may even enhance your own perspective. You can also create a space for more serenity in your life by accentuating the positive in what others do. If you are a One, it is likely that others in your life know that you are capable of constructive criticism, and they may well seek you out for honest input. Don't be afraid, however, to express your appreciation of others and their efforts, as well. They will not think less of you, and since you are probably known for your honesty and forthrightness, a compliment from you will mean a lot.

▶ It sometimes takes time for you to notice that you need something, especially in the area of emotional needs. But when you do realize it, by all means let others know. Your integrity will not be lost if others see that you are upset or troubled. On the contrary, being open and honest about your vulnerabilities is a key element to developing greater integrity. At the same time, be aware of the tendency to talk *at* others rather than *to* them. When you are frustrated or annoyed, be sure to make eye contact when communicating with people so that they do not become abstractions to you.

▶ Realize that you are not going to be able to get rid of the parts of yourself that you do not like. At best, you can repress them for a while, but this only postpones and magnifies your problems. As long as you hold that there is some way that you are *supposed* to be, you cannot really be with who and what you are right now. Try becoming more aware of these parts of yourself, understanding them more intimately instead of trying to change them. *You cannot transform yourself—none of us can.* Stop your self-improvement projects and learn to be with yourself. That will be far more challenging than straining to conform to an idealized notion of what a good person is like.

▶ Learn to recognize and *process* your anger. While you do not act out your anger or pretend it is not there, you hold a lot of it in your body, so any kind of therapeutic massage or energy work can be extremely beneficial for you. Similarly, yoga or simple stretching exercises can do wonders for your physical and emotional well-being. You can also become aware of ways that you unconsciously hold your body in certain postures, or how you may use more tension than necessary when performing even simple tasks. Anything from writing a letter to driving a car can be done with relaxation and attention or with tightness and resistance.

BUILDING ON THE ONE'S STRENGTHS

▲

Although all of us face difficult issues, regardless of our type, we also possess many strengths, although we do not always recognize them. It is important to remember that these positive qualities do not need to be acquired or added—they already exist and can be called upon at any time.

THE ONE'S GIFTS

While no healthy type is comfortable with untruth, Ones in particular are powerfully motivated to be honest in all of their affairs. Further, merely speaking honestly is not enough. As much as possible, Ones want their word and deed to be consistent—to "walk the walk." Deceiving someone or claiming abilities they do not possess is inconceivable to them. They say what they mean and do what they say. This kind of integrity is deeply moving and inspiring to others. It is a call to excellence that leaves few unaffected.

Jeanne, the spiritual director we met early in this chapter, describes the pleasure she derives from maintaining her integrity.

> As a school principal, it was my duty to see to it that the children were primary in our focus. Nothing else could supersede that moral duty. There was always satisfaction in being able to transcend my own needs for the sake of the whole. Being your best meant never cutting corners or taking the easy way out of a situation.

Healthy Ones reinforce their sense of integrity by developing a set of clear principles that they live by. Central among their principles is a sense of evenhandedness, of wanting other people to be treated fairly. These principles, for Ones, are the objective yardstick by which they hope to evaluate their experiences and choose wise courses of action. But healthy Ones utilize *flexible* standards and are always open to improving them.

Further, healthy Ones are not motivated by personal advantage or gain. They can put aside their personal comfort and agenda for something that is the long-range good for everyone involved. For instance, acknowledging the deterioration of their local school systems, Ones might vote to support tax levies for the schools. Needless to say, Ones do not like paying taxes any more than anyone else, but they are willing to tighten their belts if it means a long-range benefit to their community. Further, it is likely that the healthy One will have done his homework and will try to convince others of the problems that will be faced if the schools are not improved. (Also, since healthy Ones are more flexible in their positions, they are able to communicate their views to others in ways that others are able to hear.) Without such foresight and sacrifice, the world would certainly be a much poorer place. Indeed, in the current "throwaway culture" of mass consumption, sound bites, and profit and loss measured in weeks or even days, the Ones' gift is more important than ever.

Although healthy Ones care passionately about specific issues and feel that they have rational approaches to the problems they encounter, their principles, methods, and ethical standards are *for their own guidance.* They are not necessarily trying to fix anyone else, and they appeal to others by setting an extraordinary example, not by preaching or proselytizing. Even so, others are willing, even eager, to hear their views. Further, because they accept most of their own humanity and are understanding of the foibles of others, they can be quite eloquent and effective at conveying the truth and wisdom of their perspective.

Healthy Ones are able to accomplish many of their objectives because they maintain a balanced self-discipline. They work very hard and make good use of their time, but they also know when "enough is enough" and it is time to rest or play. They understand that an important part of their effectiveness comes from taking good care of themselves, getting sufficient rest, and not working themselves into the ground. Even with their pleasures, however, they tend to be selective, seeking out vacations, diversions, or leisure activities that will be enriching as well as enjoyable. (Healthy Ones, in contrast to average Ones, are also quite capable of levity and even occasional silliness.) One might say that their self-discipline is based on the notion of "moderation in all things."

Cassandra came to the realization that *balance* rather than perfection is what is needed.

Finally I have found an activity I really love: dancing. I dance frequently now and have found that I can lose myself completely in that activity.

A playful, sensuous, flirtatious side of me comes out when I dance, and I love it! It gives permission for me to express myself more fully and in healthy ways. I feel that dancing has created a wonderful counterbalance to my overserious One-ness.

In a nutshell, Ones care deeply about being good people and are moved into action by wanting to do something about the problems they see around them. They would like to show others that they do not need to settle for many of the horrific and unjust conditions in the world. Like healthy Eights, Ones firmly believe they can make a difference and find it difficult to turn away from challenges. Whether they are dealing with homelessness, corruption in their profession, problems in the educational system, matters of health and diet, or lapses of ethical behavior in their own immediate environment, Ones feel strongly that change is possible and that they want to be part of the solution.

Thus, high-functioning Ones are a source of wisdom and discernment in an ambiguous world. They have an extraordinary ability to know how to do the right thing, particularly regarding moral values. Because of their great realism and objectivity, they can set aside their own passions and preferences—even their own past experiences and education—in order to discern the best choice in a given situation.

Ones actualize themselves and remain healthy by allowing the spontaneous arising of their instinctive response to life, as in healthy Sevens. Ones discover that they can permit themselves to be affected by reality without needing to tense themselves against it. This is particularly true of their inner reality—they gradually learn to relax their guard and feel more comfortable with whatever state they find themselves in.

Also like healthy Sevens, integrating Ones become less opinionated and more open to a wider variety of possibilities for themselves. They become more curious, more optimistic, more interested in learning, and especially more interested in learning about views differing from their own. Rather than harming their integrity, Ones discover that this approach to life brings depth and breadth to their own views. They are more able to relate to others' perspectives.

In the process of integrating the qualities of the healthy Seven, Ones may encounter fears of losing control of themselves. Their superego will launch a fierce attack, telling them that if they relax and allow themselves to feel more free and positive or even to accept themselves, all hell will break loose. This attack often manifests as a fear of their own anger. Ones are terrified of feeling the full extent of their anger, believing that to do so would lead them to perform horrible acts. But if Ones are

THE PATH OF INTEGRATION: ONE GOES TO SEVEN

▲

healthy enough to be conscious of their impulses, it is highly unlikely that they will be driven to act them out. Indeed, *it is the lack of awareness and lack of self-acceptance that leads to uncontrolled acting out.*

Of course, Ones cannot integrate by imitating the qualities of the average Seven. There is no point in their becoming more hyperactive and hedonistic. Ones need rather to recognize the repression and sorrow inherent in their own personality structure. As Ones become more aware of the stringent rules of their superegos and learn to distinguish themselves from these internal "voices," they begin to naturally unfold the qualities of the healthy Seven—joy, enthusiasm, curiosity, and open-mindedness.

TRANSFORMING PERSONALITY INTO ESSENCE

▲

"Wisdom is not just about moral behavior, but about the 'center,' the place from which moral perception and moral behavior flow."

MARCUS BORG

The challenge for Ones is to make peace in their internal war, and they can do that only by accepting all parts of themselves as they are without judgment. Whatever is part of human nature is there for a purpose (presumably for a Divine purpose). If humans come with sexual urges, desires for pleasure, feelings, irrational impulses, and the ability to perceive and judge (rightly or wrongly), it makes little sense to condemn them—because that is the way human beings are equipped. We can either complain to the manufacturer, as it were, and attempt to get another model—or learn to go places with the one we have.

What Ones are actually seeking is not judgment but the quality of *discernment.* Discernment is noticing that things have different qualities. Judgment, however, includes an emotional reaction that actually interferes with discernment. It is one thing to say that the carpet is a different color from the wall. It is another thing to say that one is better, more important, or more righteous than the other. In other words, a witness and a judge are not the same thing. Discernment requires us to be a witness.

Note that we are not talking about situation ethics or ethical relativism but about the ability to see that as situations and facts change, so does what can be expected as a best outcome from them. Wisdom allows us to see reality exactly as it is, not as we wish it to be. Wisdom does not ignore right or wrong or deny that there are better or worse choices that a person might have made. Rather, wisdom looks at the choices that *have been made,* at the situation in which we find ourselves *now,* and considers the best possible thing to do. Wisdom always sees what is truly necessary and for the best—although it can only arise in the present moment and spring forth from an absence of preconceived values, opinions, and judgments. Even if we have created some kind of hell for ourselves, wisdom can show us a way out—if we are willing to suspend judgment about what we "should" do, or how we "must" respond. Only if we are not obsessed with being right will we be able to find true righteousness—which is, after all, finding true balance.

The key word Ones need in order to heal is *acceptance*. This does not mean permissiveness; it means that if I really want to be in the service of good, I have to work with what is. For Ones to accept reality is also to *accept themselves* by learning the quality of *allowing*—allowing people to be, including themselves. They allow everyone to learn the truth on their own, at their own time, and in their own way. Acceptance does not reduce our capacity to discern or to choose wise actions; rather, it increases that capacity infinitely.

Acceptance opens doors, both inner and outer. People instinctively respond to healthy Ones precisely because Ones make them feel that their concerns are understood and that they are accepted. Many twelve-step meetings end with what is called the *Serenity Prayer*. Ones who seek inner growth would do well to reflect on it.

> *God grant me the serenity to accept*
> *the things I cannot change,*
> *the courage to change the things I can,*
> *and the wisdom to know the difference.*

> "The curious paradox is that when I accept myself just as I am, then I can change."
>
> CARL ROGERS

THE EMERGENCE OF ESSENCE

Deep down, Ones remember the essential quality of *perfection*. They know that, at a profound level, the universe is unfolding exactly as it must. (As in Julian of Norwich's famous dictum, "All will be well. Every manner of thing will be well.") This sense of perfection is related to the sense of wholeness and completeness that we saw in Types Eight and Nine. Ones experience this perfect oneness as *integrity*.

In the state of integrity, all the parts of the whole have seamlessly come together to create something more than the sum of the parts. We feel a deep peace and acceptance of life that gives us the ability to know exactly what is required in each situation and in each moment. We know exactly how much energy is required to accomplish a task, whether it is cleaning a window or sharing an insight. We move and act in life with a certain effortlessness—while accomplishing far more than we can with our bodies locked in tension. We are empowered by the direct knowledge that we are part of the perfect unfolding of something far beyond anything in our ego consciousness.

Staying with awareness releases a profoundly wise and discerning intelligence that illuminates all that we attend to. When Ones, through patient self-acceptance and open-mindedness, are able to relax enough to recognize that this quality is, and always has been, available to them, they become the true instruments of the Divine will that they have longed to be.

Add your scores for the fifteen statements for Type One. Your result will be between 15 and 75. The following guidelines may help you discover or confirm your personality type.

▶ 15   You are probably not a compliant type (not a One, Two, or Six).

▶ 15–30   You are probably not a Type One.

▶ 30–45   You most probably have One-issues, or a Type One parent.

▶ 45–60   You most likely have a One-component.

▶ 60–75   You are most likely a One (but could still be another type if you are thinking too narrowly about the One).

Ones are most likely to misidentify themselves as Fives, Fours, and Sixes. Threes, Sixes, and Sevens are most likely to misidentify themselves as Ones.

CHAPTER 8

▼

TYPE TWO:
THE
HELPER

▲

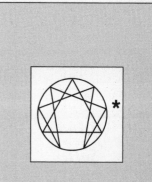

THE ALTRUIST

THE LOVER

THE CARETAKER

THE PLEASER

THE ENABLER

THE SPECIAL FRIEND

"Love is the admiration and cherishing of the amiable qualities of the beloved person, upon the condition of yourself being the object of their action."

—SAMUEL TAYLOR COLERIDGE

"We cannot love ourselves unless we love others, and we cannot love others unless we love ourselves. But a selfish love of ourselves makes us incapable of loving others."

—THOMAS MERTON

"For one human being to love another: that is perhaps the most difficult of all our tasks, the ultimate, the last test and proof, the work for which all other work is but preparation."

—RAINER MARIA RILKE

"To love a thing means wanting it to live."

—CONFUCIUS

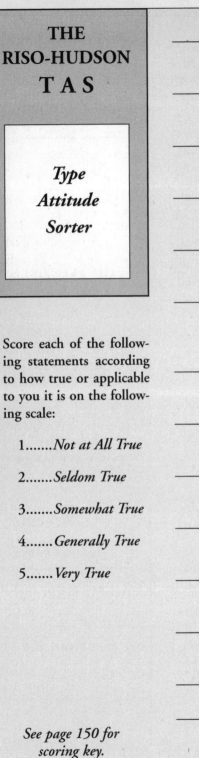

THE RISO-HUDSON
T A S

*Type
Attitude
Sorter*

Score each of the following statements according to how true or applicable to you it is on the following scale:

1.......*Not at All True*

2.......*Seldom True*

3.......*Somewhat True*

4.......*Generally True*

5.......*Very True*

*See page 150 for
scoring key.*

_____ 1. My genuine concern for others makes me become deeply involved with them—with their hopes, dreams, and needs.

_____ 2. It feels natural to be friendly: I strike up conversations easily and am on a first-name basis with everyone.

_____ 3. I have found that people respond warmly to me when I give them some attention and encouragement.

_____ 4. I cannot see a stray dog in the street without wanting to bring it home.

_____ 5. I feel good about the fact that I am a thoughtful, generous person.

_____ 6. It's hard for me to take credit for the many things I've done for people, but it bothers me a lot when they don't seem to notice or care.

_____ 7. It is true that I often do more for others than I should—I give away too much and do not think of myself enough.

_____ 8. I often find myself trying to win people over—especially if they initially seem indifferent to me.

_____ 9. I take special joy in entertaining and hosting my friends and "extended family."

_____ 10. I can be warm and supportive, but there is more steel in me than others might think.

_____ 11. I am able to express my feelings for people more openly than most.

_____ 12. I make special efforts to know what's going on with the people I care about.

_____ 13. I see myself as something of a "healer of broken hearts."

_____ 14. My health and finances have frequently suffered because I have put other people's needs and interests before my own.

_____ 15. I love to knock myself out to make people feel welcomed and appreciated.

PERSONALITY TYPE TWO: THE HELPER

The Caring, Interpersonal Type:
Generous, Demonstrative, People-Pleasing, and Possessive

We have named personality type Two *the Helper* because people of this type are either the most genuinely helpful to other people or, when they are less healthy, the most highly invested in *seeing themselves* as helpful. Being generous and going out of their way for others makes Twos feel that theirs is the richest, most meaningful way to live. The love and concern they feel—and the genuine good they do—warms their hearts and makes them feel worthwhile. Twos are most interested in what they feel to be the really, really good things in life—love, closeness, sharing, family, and friendship.

Louise is a minister who shares the joy she finds in being a Two.

> I cannot imagine being another type and I would not want to be another type. I like being involved in people's lives. I like feeling compassionate, caring, nurturing. I like cooking and homemaking. I like having the confidence that anyone can tell me anything about themselves and I will be able to love them.... I am really proud of myself and love myself for being able to be with people where they are. I really can, and do, love people, pets, and things. And I am a great cook!

When Twos are healthy and in balance, they really are loving, helpful, generous, and considerate. People are drawn to them like bees to honey. Healthy Twos warm others in the glow of their hearts. They enliven others with their appreciation and attention, helping people to see positive qualities in themselves that they had not previously recognized. In short, healthy Twos are the embodiment of the good parent that everyone wishes they had: Someone who sees them as they are, understands them with immense compassion, helps and encourages with infinite patience, and is always willing to lend a hand—while knowing precisely how and when to let go. Healthy Twos open our hearts because theirs are already so open. They show us the way to be more deeply and richly human.

Louise continues:

> All of my jobs revolved around helping people. I was a teacher who wanted to be sensitive to children and help them get off to a good start. I was a religious education director in a number of parishes. I thought that if people learned about the spiritual life, they'd be

▶ **BASIC FEAR:** Of being unloved and unwanted for themselves alone

▶ **BASIC DESIRE:** To feel loved

▶ **SUPEREGO MESSAGE:** "You are good or okay if you are loved by others and are close to them."

happier. . . . The most important part of my life is my spiritual life. I was in a religious community for ten years. I married a former priest, and we both have our spirituality as the basis of our life together.

"I care about people."

However, Twos' inner development may be limited by their shadow side—pride, self-deception, the tendency to become over-involved in the lives of others, and the tendency to manipulate others to get their own emotional needs met. Transformational work entails going into dark places in ourselves, and this very much goes against the grain of the Two's personality structure, which prefers to see itself in only the most positive, glowing terms.

Perhaps the biggest obstacle facing Twos, Threes, and Fours in their inner work is having to face their underlying Triad fear of *worthlessness*. Beneath the surface, all three types fear that they are without value in themselves, and so they must be or do something extraordinary in order to win love and acceptance from others. In the average-to-unhealthy Levels, Twos present a false image of being completely generous and un-selfish and of not wanting any kind of payoff for themselves, when in fact they can have enormous expectations and unacknowledged emotional needs.

Average-to-unhealthy Twos *seek validation of their worth by obeying their superego's demands to sacrifice themselves for others.* They believe they must always put others first and be loving and unselfish if they want to get love. The problem is that putting others first makes Twos secretly angry and resentful—feelings they work hard to repress or deny. Nevertheless, the feelings eventually erupt in various ways, disrupting Twos' relationships and revealing the inauthenticity of many of the average-to-unhealthy Twos' claims about themselves and the depth of their love.

But in the healthy range, the picture is completely different. My own (Don's) maternal grandmother was an archetypal Two. During World War II, she was "Moms" to what seemed like half of Keisler Air Force Base in Biloxi, Mississippi, feeding the boys, allowing her home to be used as a home away from home, giving advice and consolation to anyone lonely or fearful about going to war. Although she and her husband were not wealthy and had two teenage children of their own, she cooked extra meals for the servicemen, put them up at night, and saw to it that their uniforms had all of their buttons and were well pressed. She lived until her eighties, remembering those years as the happiest and most fulfilling of her life—probably because her healthy Two capacities were so fully and richly engaged.

THE CHILDHOOD PATTERN

During their childhood, Twos come to believe three things. First, that they must put other people's needs ahead of their own; second, that they must give in order to get; and third, that they must *earn* a place in the affections of others because love will not simply be given to them. They felt that the way to be loved was to repress their own needs and to attend to the needs of others, lavishing attention on everyone else in an effort to be liked and wanted. To the degree that their childhood environment was dysfunctional, they also learned that to acknowledge their own needs was a form of selfishness and was strictly forbidden by their superego. ("Good people do not have needs. Taking too much time for yourself is selfish.")

Thus, Twos learned to function within the family system—*and in all subsequent relationships*—by being the helper, the selfless friend, the pleaser, and the giver of attention and nurturance to everyone else. Young Twos may have established a place for themselves in the family by looking after siblings, or by doing housework, or by taking care of their parents in a variety of ways. They are deeply conditioned to believe that by sacrificing themselves, they will be rewarded with whatever is called *love* in their family system.

Lois, an expert educator and administrator, shares some of the sense of burden Two children feel.

> For as long as I can remember, I felt that it was my job to take care of others in my family. I felt I needed to help my mother and father to alleviate their stress. I am the second oldest of six children. I took care of my twin sisters who are eleven years younger than me. I recall many times when I felt all depended on me. I spent the biggest share of my childhood cooking, cleaning, and washing clothes to help my mother who always seemed to be overwhelmed with her lot in life.

This orientation creates a major problem for Twos, however. To fully identify with the role of nurturer and to maintain the positive feelings that this role creates for them, Twos must deeply repress their own needs, hurts, and self-doubt. Once this repression occurs, Twos have increasing difficulty acknowledging their own needs and pain and are drawn automatically to the needs and pain they see in others. On a deep psychological level, Twos are trying to fix in others the hurts they are unable to fully acknowledge in themselves.

Maggie is a gifted therapist who has devoted her life to helping her clients heal their childhood wounds. Here she speaks vividly about her early self-abandonment.

> *Please note that the childhood pattern we are describing here does not cause the personality type. Rather, it describes tendencies that we observe in early childhood that have a major impact on the type's adult relationships.*

On the first day I went to school for first grade, I saw many children playing at the playground. They were yelling, screaming, pushing, and running. I felt like I had fallen into hell since I was not used to being around children, and these children appeared to me to be very "out of control." What to do? Across the play yard I saw a little girl. She was crying very hard. She looked disheveled, and her hair was messy. Her shoes weren't tied. She needed help! Bingo, I made a beeline for her, put my arms around her, and told her not to worry, I'd take care of her. It was instant codependency. I felt confident and needed. It would be many years before I ever realized how frightened I was and how that other child was my mirror.

Given this inner dynamic, Twos learn to deal with their negative feelings by focusing on others, trying hard to please and help them. However, the more dysfunctional their background, the more they will expect rejection, and the more desperate they will be to elicit a positive response. Ultimately, they will do almost anything to get some sign, some token, that they are loved.

THE WING SUBTYPES

▲

Examples

Mother Teresa
Eleanor Roosevelt
Desmond Tutu
Danny Thomas
Ann Landers
Barbara Bush
Lewis Carroll
Florence Nightingale
Albert Schweitzer

THE TWO WITH A ONE-WING: THE SERVANT

Healthy   People of this subtype combine warmth with seriousness of purpose, as they strive after personal goodness and selfless service. The combination of the morality of the One and the empathy of the Two lead to a strong desire to relieve human suffering. These people are often Good Samaritans, willing to take on thankless and unglamorous tasks that others generally avoid. They are more serious-minded than the other subtype, more overt caretakers, often found in teaching, public service, healing professions, the ministry, and working with the disenfranchised or the physically or mentally challenged.

Average   People of this subtype feel obligated to struggle against their "selfish" attitudes and feelings: they feel responsible for others' welfare and are typically dutiful, proper, and severe with themselves. They are emotional but tend to be strained in their emotional expressions because they feel awkward about drawing attention to themselves. They prefer working in the background, yet they want to feel significant in others' lives. Twos with a One-wing feel conflicts between their emotional needs and their principles, often leading them to get involved in moral or religious teachings. They can become extremely self-critical and neglectful of their health, denying their personal needs and tending to play the martyr.

THE TWO WITH A THREE-WING: THE HOST/HOSTESS

Healthy   People of this subtype are more outgoing: they seek love through the creation of personal connection and making others feel good. The self-esteem of a Two with a Three-wing is tied to personal qualities rather than the quality of service to others. They are sociable and talkative, charming and adaptable, with much "personality" in evidence. They enjoy bestowing whatever talents and resources they possess on friends and family—cooking, entertaining, singing, and listening—all as ways of sharing their inner bounty.

Average   People of this subtype are friendly and good-humored, although focused and ambitious. They are not typically into overt caretaking; more often they consider their friendship and the quality of their attention to be a sufficient gift to others. There can be a seductive aspect to people of this subtype, as well as more of a focus on relationships, excessive friendliness, exaggerated sentimentality, and histrionic displays, the result of the Three's desire for acceptance blending with the Two's drive for intimacy. Less serious and more task-driven than Twos with a One-wing, they are also less likely to engage in self-questioning and self-criticism. People of this subtype are direct about what they want, drawing attention to the services they provide. They can be self-important, high-handed, and sometimes arrogant.

THE SELF-PRESERVATION INSTINCT IN THE TWO

Entitlement.   In the average range, Self-Preservation Twos repress their own Self-Preservation instincts while focusing on taking care of the needs of others. They are the Instinctual Variant most likely to wear themselves out for people while ignoring their own needs, often failing to get adequate rest or time for themselves. They often enjoy cooking or entertaining, but they may not eat well themselves or allow themselves to enjoy the events they host. Subconsciously, however, they expect others to take care of the Two's own Self-Preservation needs, but seldom are able to ask for help directly. Thus they are especially prone to feelings of martyrdom. They feel that others "owe" them for their services, as if to say, "I'm entitled to whatever I need because of how much I've done for everyone else."

As their anxiety increases, Self-Preservation Twos have to find more indirect ways of meeting their needs. At the same time, their Self-Preservation instincts become distorted by a tendency to repress their feelings and impulses. Further, Self-Preservation Twos feel self-important, taking pride in their sacrifices and increasingly feeling entitled to indulge themselves in whatever they feel will compensate for their

Examples

Luciano Pavarotti
Sammy Davis, Jr.
Sally Jesse Raphael
Arsenio Hall
Anne Meara
Jack Paar
Anne Jackson
Delta Burke
Merv Griffin
John Denver

THE INSTINCTUAL VARIANTS

▲

suffering. Demands for special privileges and repayment for their sacrifices coexist with overeating and medicating to suppress aggressive feelings. Denials of their problems alternate with complaints. Either "*I* don't need help" or "Nobody notices *my* needs." They increasingly rely on emotional manipulation of others—guilt trips—to get their needs met.

In the unhealthy range, Self-Preservation Twos become trapped in delusional self-importance and gross neglect or abuse of their own physical well-being. Obsessions with food and with medical symptoms and syndromes are common, as are somatic disorders and hypochondria. Suppression of emotional needs or aggressive feelings, however, can create real health problems.

THE SOCIAL INSTINCT IN THE TWO

Everybody's Friend.   In the average range, the Social instinct expresses itself in Twos as a powerful desire to be liked and approved by everyone in their social sphere. They (like Sevens) usually maintain a busy social calendar and enjoy introducing people, networking, and hosting get-togethers. Others are amazed that they seem to be on a first-name basis with almost everyone. They like being the hub, the center of their social arena. Social Twos have a strong need to be noticed, to be remembered by people, and are driven by fears of being left out or overlooked.

As their need for love and attention increases, they start to seek validation through popularity or by having closer contact with people who are successful or especially valued in their group. Social Twos may well have ambitions of their own, but these are mostly unconscious and indirect. Thus, they often maneuver to become the indispensable supporters of those they see as successful: "You scratch my back and I'll scratch yours." If they are insecure about their social desirability, they may cultivate talents to enhance their value and have more to offer (for example, being psychic). They attempt to impress people by dispensing advice—be it spiritual, financial, or medical—but also by name-dropping. The latter often gets them into trouble, because their desire to let others know that they are friends with important people often leads them to be indiscreet and to reveal confidences. Lower-average Twos can also create frustration for their significant others because they tend to scatter themselves among a wide range of social contacts, while not giving much real attention to any one of them. They may pursue anyone who offers even a hint of approval and attention.

In the unhealthy range, Social Twos can be highly patronizing, constantly drawing attention to "good deeds" and calling in their favors: "Where would you be without me?" In a similar vein, they may become classic enablers, covering up the misdeeds or dysfunction of their valued others in order to keep them around and in their debt.

THE SEXUAL INSTINCT IN THE TWO

Craving Intimacy. In the average range, Sexual Twos are the true intimacy junkies of the Enneagram. They are driven to get closer to others, both emotionally and physically. Sexual Twos like to win over people who are attractive to them, especially if these people present a challenge or seem initially uninterested. If Social Twos want to be everybody's friend, Sexual Twos want to be one person's best friend: they focus on a few individuals and like to see themselves as their friends' number-one intimate, their closest confidante. Sexual Twos enjoy private time with the other, sharing secrets and talking about "the relationship." They like to learn about whatever subjects are valued by their partner, and they may even do research into them in order to be closer. ("Wow—I've been listening to Sinatra recordings from the forties, too!")

The word *seductive* has often been associated with Twos in general, but it would mostly apply to the Sexual Two. All nine types can be seductive in their way. Sexual Twos seduce primarily by giving the other lots of attention. They offer to talk about the other's problems in order to draw them closer. Overt sexual activity can also be part of the picture, though this is not always conscious.

As Sexual Twos' anxieties about their desirability escalate, they begin to *pursue* the other. They fall prey to fears that others would not spend time with them if they did not make extra efforts to go after them. Lower-average Sexual Twos become increasingly pushy and demanding and cannot take no for an answer. Even if they have the affections of the other, they feel that they cannot get close enough. While Social Twos like to network and introduce people to one another, Sexual Twos want to keep their friends apart, lest they discover one another and cut the Two out of the relationship.

In the unhealthy range, Sexual Twos become extremely jealous, possessive, and hovering, fearing to let the desired other out of sight or telephone reach. They may begin to obsess about the other, compulsively "checking in," unable to accept rejection or even inadequate responses from the object of their desire. They may stalk the person they are romantically obsessed with or prey on those who cannot refuse their overtures.

		Key Terms:	
H **E** **A** **L** **T** **H** **Y**	Level 1	*Self-Nurturing* *Unconditionally* *Loving*	Twos let go of the belief that they are not allowed to care for themselves. Thus they can own their feelings and needs and are free to love others without expectations. They also achieve their Basic Desire, and liberated Twos experience unconditional love for self and others. They are joyous, gracious, and humble.
	Level 2	*Empathetic* *Caring*	Twos focus on the feelings of others with loving concern as a defense against their Basic Fear. Self-image: "I am loving, thoughtful, and selfless."
	Level 3	*Supportive* *Giving*	Twos reinforce their self-image by doing good things for others. They are generous with their time and energy and are appreciative, encouraging, and supportive of others. They are also emotionally expressive and enjoy sharing their talents with others.
A **V** **E** **R** **A** **G** **E**	Level 4	*Well-Intentioned* *People-Pleasing*	Twos begin to fear that whatever they have been doing is not enough—others do not really want them around. They want to be closer to others and to be reassured that others like them. Twos try to cultivate friendships and win people over by pleasing, flattering, and supporting them.
	Level 5	*Possessive* *Intrusive*	Twos worry that the people they love will love someone else more than them, so they want to be needed. They attempt to have a claim on people by putting the needs of others before their own. Proud, but needy, they do not want to let the others out of their sight.
	Level 6	*Self-Important* *Overbearing*	Twos are angry that others are taking them for granted but are unable to freely express their hurt. Instead, they complain about their health, draw attention to their good deeds, and remind others of how much they owe them. Repressed feelings begin to cause physical problems.
U **N** **H** **E** **A** **L** **T** **H** **Y**	Level 7	*Self-Justifying* *Manipulative*	Twos fear that they are driving people away, and this may be true. To save their self-image, they rationalize their behavior by seeing others as "selfish ingrates." They try to elicit pity as a substitute for love and keep others dependent on them to prevent them from leaving.
	Level 8	*Entitled* *Coercive*	Twos have become so desperate for love that they begin to pursue it obsessively. They feel they are entitled to whatever they want because they have suffered so much, and they may act out their need for affection recklessly and inappropriately.
	Level 9	*Feel Victimized* *Burdensome*	The realization that they may have been "selfish" or even have harmed others is too much for unhealthy Twos. They fall to pieces, physically and emotionally, playing out the role of victim and martyr. Others are then obliged to step in and take care of them.

T Y P E   2

L E V E L S   O F   D E V E L O P M E N T

▲

Most Twos will encounter the following issues at some point in their lives. Noticing these patterns, "catching ourselves in the act," and simply seeing our underlying habitual responses to life will do much to release us from the negative aspects of our type.

THE WAKE-UP CALL FOR TYPE TWO: "PEOPLE-PLEASING"

As we have seen, Twos tend to be very generous, but they also tend to fall prey to insecurities about others' affections for them. If they begin to fear that whatever good they have been doing for others is not enough, they can begin to get caught up in "people-pleasing"—looking for things to say and do that will make people like them. It is very difficult for Twos operating this way to resist approaching people or to let others have their own feelings and experiences. They tend to rush forward and virtually engulf the other person.

People-pleasing can take many forms, from a forced friendliness, to being overly solicitous of others' welfare, to being too generous, to flattering others shamelessly. Further, Twos feel compelled to connect with people indiscriminately, becoming the best friend of the mailman and practically adopting all of the kids in the neighborhood because their self-esteem depends on being close to others. Twos are trying to fill a hole in their own hearts with positive feelings from someone else. Like most ego projects, this strategy is doomed to failure.

Deep down, Twos are unsure whether others would be close to them if they stopped being so generous and supportive. Thus, while people may acknowledge their kind actions, Twos' hearts remain untouched. Appreciation does not heal their underlying feelings of worthlessness. Also, on some level others know that there is a hidden agenda to the average Two's "generosity." This can, in time, cause others to distance themselves and ultimately to reject the Two's overtures.

Rich, a married writer in his forties, recalls a childhood event that illustrates the pain behind this behavior.

> I was four or five years old and I wanted to be friends with a little girl who lived down the block from me although she wasn't having much to do with me. I had a little wind-up locomotive that was one of my favorite toys, and I thought of giving it to her as a gift so that she would like me. I brought the locomotive to her house one afternoon and found her playing on her porch. But when I was just about to give it to her, I realized (without knowing the word for it) that I was bribing her. Still, I recall that it was a real struggle for me since

"I can make anyone like me."

everything in me really wanted to give it to her so that she would like me and be my friend.

WINNING PEOPLE OVER

In your Inner Work Journal, devote a page to making notes about your own forms of people-pleasing. Do you tend to flatter others in order to attempt to get them to like you? Do you give money or do special favors? How do you call attention to what you do for others, no matter how subtle you think you are being? Do you find yourself denying, or justifying, your own degree of people-pleasing? Is it something you are proud of or ashamed of? How would you react if others called you on it? How do you feel as you consider these things? How do you feel when the tables are turned and others are flattering or attempting to please you?

The Social Role: The Special Friend

"Isn't it wonderful how close we are?"

Average Twos begin to define themselves as the Special Friend or the Confidante. They want others to regard them as their best friend and to seek them out for advice and to share special secrets and intimacies. Having a special place in the lives of their family and friends and knowing privileged information about them—the little things that no one else knows about—becomes "proof" of their closeness. Average Twos spend a considerable amount of time making new friends and staying in contact with old ones. They want to be kept informed about everything and consulted on all significant decisions.

Twos also want others outside the relationship to know how intimate they are with their friends, so they often gossip in order to tout their intimacy and may well begin to drop tidbits of privileged information. Gossiping can also demonstrate how concerned Twos are for others. ("Jack and Mary are having marital problems—again. And poor Jack isn't doing well at the office, either.")

Twos also put a lot of energy into finding ways *of having more to bring to others* by pursuing such interests as spirituality within their own religious tradition. Tarot card reading, massage, energetic healing, nutritional information, cooking, child care information, and crafts are all ways of being of service and of making people feel good about themselves—*and about the Two.* Twos feel that if they have some kind of spiritual power or gift (reading auras, or giving others the Sacraments, for instance), then others will always want them.

DO THEY REALLY LIKE ME?

Notice what you personally do to ensure your connections with others. Do you render extra services? Do you talk a great deal about the relationship? Do you need a lot of reassurance? If you catch yourself feeling the need to get closer to someone, stop and take three deep breaths. Note your posture. Then continue speaking to the person.

Pride, Flattery, and Self-Satisfaction

When the ego attempts to see itself as the source of love and value in others' lives, the result is *pride,* the Passion or "Capital Sin" of the Two. ("If it weren't for *me,* where would you be?") Genuine love and value are a part of our Essential nature and arise spontaneously when we are truly connected with our hearts. When we are not in touch with this aspect of our nature, we feel empty and worthless, and pride is an ego strategy to cover over these painful feelings.

Pride often expresses itself in forms of *flattery.* Twos in the sway of pride feel compelled to offer compliments to others, but with the unconscious desire that such positive attention will be returned to them. They hope that others will see how generous and loving they are being and acknowledge them in a similar way. The more insecure Twos are, the more they tend to flatter others with the hope that they will be thanked, appreciated, and flattered themselves.

For all types, pride is an expression of the unwillingness to acknowledge our own hurt and to ask for help; it is the unwillingness to admit to the severity of our own suffering, emptiness, and need. As a result of pride, Twos minister to everyone else's hurts but neglect their own. ("I don't need anything. I'm fine! I'm here to take care of *you.*") Pride betrays itself in the defensiveness that arises when someone has the audacity to suggest that Twos do indeed have needs and hurts.

Like the other types in the Feeling Triad, the loving self-image of Twos covers deep feelings of shame, grief, and hostility. As long as these are unprocessed, Twos cannot express all of their feelings. Thus, pride both prevents them from experiencing love and nurturance from others and diverts them from ever really healing the wounds that are disguised by their seemingly selfless actions.

> "Who knows his virtue's name or place, hath none."
>
> JOHN DONNE

Looking for Terms of Endearment

As Twos feel less lovable, they focus more on specific things that signify to them that they are loved. The tokens of love that they focus on can differ from Two to Two and can be anything from a hug, to a particular tone of voice, to receiving immediate thanks for a favor, to receiving a phone call or a sexual response.

We call these specific responses *terms of endearment*. Unless the other person says certain words such as "I love you"—and in a particular tone of voice, and with a certain look in their eyes—average Twos do not feel that they are loved. If the other person has chosen to express their love in a way other than the Two's term of endearment, *it does not count*. In effect, Twos unconsciously judge the responses of others, and only a few select actions get through their superego filter. ("Jeff said hello and asked me about my day, but if he *really* cared, he would have stopped and had coffee with me.") Of course, the more insecure Twos are, the more difficult it will be for them to accept even overt signs of affection as evidence of love.

To get their need for terms of endearment met, average Twos drop hints about what will make them feel loved. ("Your birthday is January sixteenth, isn't it? Mine is coming up soon.") If love means getting flowers, a Two will send the other person flowers on her birthday—hoping that she will remember and reciprocate. Unfortunately, a distinct element of "giving in order to get" has entered the picture.

To the degree that we are locked into needing terms of endearment, we can miss a lot of the love that is offered to us. And since the Two's terms of endearment are largely shaped by what they experienced as love during childhood, what passes for "love" can be extremely warped due to various forms of abuse. Further, the more rejected Twos feel as a result of childhood problems, the more difficult it will be for them to be convinced that anyone really does love them. Eventually, even genuinely loving responses from others will be seen as inadequate or even negative.

RECOGNIZING LOVE

In your Inner Work Journal, explore the question, "How do I know that I am loved?" What counts for love in your life? Whose love are you looking for? What are the signs that this person(s) is giving you love? How do you know, or how *would* you know that you are loved?

Intimacy and Loss of Boundaries

Bestowing approval, compliments, applause, and flattery can be seductive to others, and average Twos know it. They know the power of positive attention and how starved for it most people are. Their willingness to give attention and to express an interest in others can lead quickly to a degree of intimacy that is unexpected and unusual for most people. Often without warning, others find themselves "in a relationship" with a Two and are expected to respond. If the Two is healthy, the other is free to respond in any way; but as Twos become increasingly needy, they expect others to respond in particular ways.

Average Twos want to be physically close with those from whom they desire intimacy. They hug and kiss unself-consciously, putting an arm around a shoulder or giving an appreciative squeeze on the arm. They are often in danger of being too familiar in their body language, speech, and manner, something that can easily be misunderstood in the office or in other social settings.

The more intent they become on establishing a relationship, the more trouble Twos have recognizing boundaries. They may ask extremely personal questions about someone's finances, health, and sex life. They may also offer unsolicited advice and opinions. ("Mary is just not the right girl for you.") If others have no particular needs or difficulties, Twos may begin to create them, often in unnecessary and meddlesome ways. ("I'll come over Saturday and take you to the grocery, then we'll come back and we'll clean your house together, and then we'll go to a movie.") If others back off because they feel intruded on, Twos generally react by redoubling their solicitude.

"I won't take no for an answer."

Their intrusiveness can have sexual overtones. The Social and Sexual Instinctual Variants can make their emotional and sexual needs known rather clearly and forcefully, whether or not the other person wants that kind of interaction. A more innocent aspect of this, but one that still creates problems, is their tendency to "hover" and to follow others around, even into the bathroom or a dressing room. ("Why do you have the door closed?") Of course, these sorts of things usually have the unintended effect of actually driving others away.

MEETING NEEDS—FINDING A BALANCE

Remember to ask people that you care about what they need from you and *what they do not need from you.* Be willing to hear them and accept their boundaries. Also, notice when you are unable to do things for yourself because you have overextended your efforts for others. Compile a daily list of things you need to do *for yourself* and stick with it! Keep this list in a prominent place where you can see it.

Disguised Neediness

Twos have learned that they cannot express their needs and demands directly—they must do so indirectly, hoping that others will pick up the hints and repay them in various ways. Like Ones, Twos

"Come get a hug."

have a strong superego that is involved with judging what they must do to be loved, what "counts for love" from others, the quality of their self-sacrifice, and so forth. Having needs and going after them openly (as the assertive types do) seems to average Twos to be selfish.

Maria is an educator who has worked many years on her Type Two issues.

> I've had to practice being clear and direct with people, a remedial skill for me, at best. The real problem in this area occurs when I have to set limits, give a refusal, or ask a difficult favor of someone whose relationship I value. It takes tremendous courage for me to refuse someone or to ask a favor without offering justification, and it is *terrifying* to await an answer.

Most Twos are afraid that having problems and needs of their own will only drive people away. Indeed, Twos may actually persuade themselves that they do not have any needs of their own and that they exist only to be of service to others.

Despite the fact that Louise is a minister and has many people depending on her already, she still "needs to be needed."

> One of the things I am aware of is waking up in the morning and thinking about the people in my life in order to assess what they will need from me today. I did that with my children until they went away to college. I always told them where I was "in case they might need me."

"Let me do that for you."

Once these behaviors become habitual, there begins to be an element of compulsiveness in Twos' giving: they cannot *not* help. It becomes an obligation to step in and save others. This puts others in the role of the "needy child" and enshrines the Two in the place of a strong and capable parent. Rescuing people this way can rob them of the opportunity to solve their own problems and to build dignity and self-esteem. Unacknowledged and unresolved resentments can build on both sides. The person getting help becomes resentful for being treated like a child, and the Two starts to feel resentful for having put so much energy into the person without a payoff. Often, if the Two is successful in helping the person, once healed, the person is off to greener pastures and the Two is left with another heartbreak.

Less healthy Twos may attempt to meet their hidden needs by steering people to compromising or embarrassing positions. For example, Twos often have issues with money (and all forms of repayment) and may borrow $1,000 from a friend or family member. In time, they may pay back $800, mentioning that they will repay the balance later.

Time passes, and no payment comes. The other person is put in the position of having to either remind the Two of their debt or let it go. The Two's high-handedness puts the other in the position of feeling cheap or petty for bringing the issue up. But to not bring up the problem often puts a cloud on the relationship or could end it altogether. This is a big gamble, but Twos are often willing to take it for two reasons. First, if the other person does not speak up, it enables them to feel repaid in some way; second, if the other person does not speak up, they can persuade themselves that the other needs them so much that they dare not speak. They can feel that they are still wanted.

RECOGNIZING NEEDS

Whenever you find yourself *needing* to do something for someone, stop your activities, quiet yourself, and from your heart, ask what *you need* at this time.

Being a Rescuer and Collecting Needy People

On the positive side, Twos' emotional and empathetic connections with others make them genuinely want to do whatever they can to help someone in distress, while their generosity and energy enable them to follow through in tangible ways. But on the negative side, rescuing others prevents them from relating to people in more satisfying ways.

Assuming the position of rescuer leads Twos to begin focusing their attention and efforts on more needy people, even what might be called desperate cases. The appreciation they anticipate getting from successfully helping needy people promises to be a source of gratitude and self-esteem. Furthermore, the more needy the beneficiary, the more selfless the Two seems to be, at least to their own superego.

There are inherent problems with this situation, however. In extreme cases, the Two may be nursing someone literally in a coma. Since they cannot get an adequate response from the comatose person, they may turn to the person's family and start ministering to their needs as well, thereby overextending themselves even further. They may work professionally with very young children, old people, orphans, drug addicts, alcoholics, or terminally ill patients, all of whom need their services but who are unable to adequately return the Two's love and attention.

Going to deeply damaged, incapacitated people is self-defeating if one is looking for a mature emotional response from them. And yet this is what secretly emotionally needy Twos do. In their need to be needed, they give to people who cannot repay their gift. In the words of a popular saying from the twelve-step programs, Twos are "looking for an orange in a hardware store."

FINDING GOOD BOUNDARIES

When you involve yourself with someone, make explicit with the person what you want or expect from him or her. Notice when you get involved with people who you perceive as needing you in some way. Learn to avoid falling in love with fixer-uppers. ("He's really cute, and he's honest because he told me he's a drug addict who beat up his last girlfriend. But if I just love him enough . . .") It is good to help people, but only if we are doing so without expectations about what they may do for us in the future.

Possessiveness and Control

The more average Twos spend time and energy on others, the more they begin to feel that they have an investment in them—an investment that they want to protect. Others experience this as being possessive, and a related quality of jealousy can surface if these issues are not recognized.

"Where would you be without me?"

If an average Two becomes possessive, it is a sure sign that they are beginning to fear that others are losing interest in them or are about to leave them, possibly for a relationship with someone else. As a result, anxiety drives Twos to do things that can ultimately sabotage their relationship, although in the short term these tactics seem to them to be the way to save it and to further demonstrate their devotion. Possessiveness can be expressed in worrying about the other and in acting on all kinds of unacknowledged ulterior motives.

Control issues are also part of the picture. Instead of bringing out the other person's undeveloped qualities, average Twos may try to mold the other into someone who will meet their own emotional needs. Twos run the risk of becoming enablers, condoning—or worse, encouraging—behaviors in the other that will be debilitating in the long run but that will virtually ensure that the other person will not abandon the Two.

To compensate for feeling unappreciated, low-average Twos may also take a patronizing or condescending attitude toward others, complaining about how much they have done or the expenses they have incurred for them, or both. They may feel indispensable, convinced that people could not live without them. They cannot understand why others do not love them back immediately and wholeheartedly. They typically feel that they are being taken for granted—and perhaps they are being pushed away.

GIVING RELATIONSHIPS ROOM TO GROW

In your Inner Work Journal, explore the ways in which you have been possessive of your family and friends. In what ways have you found it difficult to let them go? How have you tried to hold on to people? Do you see the action of jealousy in your relationships? When in childhood did you begin to be aware of this emotion, and how did you deal with it then? Did someone in your childhood attempt to manipulate you through the use of jealousy or possessiveness? How does it make you feel when someone is being possessive of you?

Health and "Suffering"

If Twos continue to overextend themselves for others, they wear themselves out physically as well as emotionally and financially. Their health inevitably begins to suffer because they are also "stuffing their feelings" (somatizing), producing eating disorders, weight gain, psychosomatic illnesses, and/or substance abuses.

Their real (as well as their exaggerated) suffering allows them to feel like martyrs who are overburdened by their sacrifices for others, although they may well overrate their efforts on others' behalf. Healthy Twos do not talk much about their own problems; lower-average-to-unhealthy Twos talk about little else. Past operations, scars, traumatic experiences, and health scares of all sorts are paraded before others in an attempt to elicit signs of concern and love. Hypochondria can become part of the picture as a further bid for gratitude and sympathy. They may erupt in rashes, intestinal problems, or arthritis and other stress-related diseases.

For low-average Twos, health problems become "proof" that they have actually "worn themselves out for others," just as they have always claimed. In addition, being ill is often the only way they can get a vacation from their responsibilities and from the demands of their superegos.

Harold, an opera coach, recognizes this pattern in himself.

> I get resentful and emotionally unglued and histrionic. I cannot function. I cry when I am angry. I cannot speak without my lips quivering. I feel that I do everything for everyone else, and no one does anything for me. I cannot let things go. I cannot help thinking about things. I also have taken on too many obligations and when I cannot handle them, I get sick. This has been my way of reacting when I need a break or a vacation.

> ## TAKING CARE OF YOU, TOO
>
> Learn to listen to your body—especially around matters of rest. Notice when you are eating for emotional reasons rather than because you are hungry. Give yourself the kind of care you would insist on for someone you love.

REACTING TO STRESS: TWO GOES TO EIGHT

▲

When their anxieties and stress exceed their coping abilities, Twos go to Eight, becoming more blunt and forceful. Twos normally present an image of selfless kindness, but the move to Eight reveals that they are remarkably tough underneath—others discover that beneath the velvet glove is an iron fist. Their usual indirectness shifts into a more frontal approach in which average Twos confront people directly about their lack of response—complaining about not being given an expected term of endearment or sufficient appreciation. They can be surprisingly aggressive and argumentative, insisting quite strongly that they have been wronged in some way. Needless to say, these kinds of complaints can come as quite a surprise to others.

At the same time, like average Eights, Twos under stress become concerned about their survival needs and begin to work harder and more relentlessly. They do not want their efforts to go unrecognized, however, and like Eights, they put people on notice as to who is running things. ("I hope you're aware of how important I am in your life.") Under severe stress, Twos become more openly domineering and controlling. They make threats and undermine the confidence of the people who need them. The move to Eight can be seen as the acting out of feelings of rage and betrayal that, under ordinary circumstances, Twos feel unable to face.

THE RED FLAG: THE TWO IN TROUBLE

▲

If Twos have suffered a serious crisis without adequate support or coping skills, or if they have suffered from chronic abuse in childhood, they may cross the shock point into the unhealthy aspects of their type. This may lead them to a fearful recognition that their efforts to get closer to others are actually driving people away. Indeed, some of these fears may be based on fact.

If Twos can recognize the truth in these fears, they may begin to turn their lives around and move toward health and liberation. On the other hand, they may become even more self-deceptive and manipulative and desperately attempt to maintain the belief that they have not done anything wrong or selfish. They may try to hold on to others at any cost while justifying their actions. ("I'm doing this for your own good." "I understand if you want to go off and have a career, but what's going to happen to me?") If Twos persist in this attitude, they may cross into the unhealthy Levels. If you or someone you know is exhibiting the following warning signs for an extended period of time—more than two or three weeks—counseling, therapy, or other support is highly advisable.

WARNING SIGNS

POTENTIAL PATHOLOGY: Histrionic Personality Disorder, hypochondriasis, somatization, eating disorders, serious, coercive sexual behaviors, "stalking."

▶ Extreme tendencies toward self-deception

▶ Acting with a sense of delusional entitlement

▶ Episodes of manipulating and coercing others

▶ Episodes of obsessive love out of keeping with age or status

▶ Evidence of repressed aggression acted out inappropriately

▶ Physical symptoms of emotional problems (somatization)

PRACTICES THAT HELP TWOS DEVELOP

▲

▶ Do not be so concerned about what others think of you, and be particularly aware of trying to win over everyone. As you probably know, no matter what you do, you will almost always end up displeasing someone. It is therefore not possible for everyone to like you or to be your friend all the time. It is more important for you to think carefully about doing the best that you can do for someone now and let it go at that.

▶ Learn to recognize the affection and good wishes of others, even when they are not in terms that you are familiar with. Although others may not be expressing their feelings in a way that you want, they may be letting you know in other ways how much they care about you. Most people are not as effusive in their feelings as you are, and most are not as naturally inclined to give attention to others. But if you can recognize what others *are* giving you, you will rest more easily in the knowledge that you are loved, and you will not feel as frustrated with others.

▶ It is vitally important for you to develop good boundaries. Boundaries allow you to feel for others without becoming entangled in their problems. To support this, learn how to "sit in your own skin" when others are troubled or need something from you. This does not mean that you should withhold affection or help, but it does mean that you need to stay connected to yourself at the times in which you are most likely to abandon your own best interests in the pursuit of approval. (The meditation practices described in Chapter 17 will be especially helpful in this regard.) If you can respect your own boundaries, saying no when you need to, you are also much less likely to cross others' boundaries. This will make for happier relationships all the way around.

▶ It will be tremendously valuable to you to become more aware of when you are flattering people or in any way trying to ingratiate yourself with them. (There is often a very particular tone of voice that the personality has for such tactics, and it will be extremely helpful for you to learn to recognize it and to silence it when it arises.) Sincere feelings for others are one of your gifts, but they can be undermined by insincerity or excessive flattery.

▶ Your pride is a compensation for something else: an underlying fear of worthlessness, that nobody wants you. Work on your pride by first seeing the many ways in which it subtly manifests itself. You do not have to have "proud thoughts" or an arrogant facial expression to still be in the grip of pride; false humility is as much an expression of pride as trumpeting your own good works. Only real humility and the knowledge that you are loved—in fact, that in your Essential self, you are an expression of love—will dissolve pride.

▶ Twos tend to give too much and then regret it. Be brutally honest with yourself about your motives when you do anything for anyone. Learn to doubt your own rationales. Learn to listen to your body and your heart: when both ache, you know that you are hurting, and giving more to others so that they will appreciate you will not ultimately heal that hurt. On the other hand, closing down and cutting off ties with others will not solve the problem, either. Only brutal honesty about your intentions and your needs will do.

BUILDING ON THE TWO'S STRENGTHS

▲

Insofar as they can, healthy Twos make good things happen for people. They will stay up late to take care of children or older folks, drive across town to bring food, or see to it that others get medical treatment. When there's practical work to be done for people, healthy Twos will be there, throwing themselves into the effort heart and soul.

The gift of their sincere good works speaks more eloquently for them than anything they could say. Thus, Twos are gifted with the extraordinary ability not simply to care about others but to actually do something meaningful for them.

Healthy Twos exhibit a joyful, spontaneous quality that can resemble the *joie de vivre* of healthy Sevens. They laugh easily and deeply and do not take themselves too seriously, simply enjoying life's bounty with people they care about. They possess a childlike enthusiasm for life and enjoy discovering new things about the world, others, and themselves.

Of course, the ability to experience this freedom has much to do with the Two's ability to maintain good boundaries—to say no when necessary and to have a clear sense of their real motivations at any particular time. Healthy Twos are able to distinguish their own needs from the needs of others and to maintain a healthy balance between the two.

Louise comments:

> I am at my best when I am at peace with myself. I can feel what I need and say it directly. I am aware of my inner self. I am calm and do not feel that I have to take care of anyone else. It is a very freeing feeling. I can allow others to be, and I do not attempt to control or manipulate them. Then I can help others and give without resentment.

Healthy boundaries also enable Twos to do good for themselves—to develop their own lives in significant ways. They do not get sidetracked by "helping" or interfering with others; they do not need to become preoccupied with the life of a loved one because they have a life of their own. Being able to be on their own and to stay with their own feelings is a major accomplishment for Twos.

Good boundaries and emotional balance also allow Twos to be less prey to the responses of others. Healthy Twos recognize many different behaviors as positive and loving. If a Two says good morning to someone, and the person says good morning back but fails to hug them or acknowledge them in some other way, high-functioning Twos are not automatically disappointed. Even negative responses will seldom knock them off balance. If a person responds by saying, "I'm having a lousy morning. Leave me alone," a healthy Two will not take it personally; they will be able to back off rather than push for a positive response. In short, healthy Twos have enough self-esteem and self-nurturance not to take the reactions of others as a referendum on their own value.

Healthy Twos also foster independence in others, nurturing self-confidence, strength, and new skills so that people can grow on their own. They really want others to thrive and do not want anyone to be dependent on them, physically or psychologically. They are sincerely encouraging and are extremely appreciative of the talents and strengths they find in others—a quality that is particularly helpful to those who may not see much good in themselves.

"I'm glad to be able to share my gifts with others."

THE PATH OF INTEGRATION: TWO GOES TO FOUR

▲

Twos become actualized and remain healthy by learning to recognize and accept all of their feelings without censoring them, like healthy Fours. Because Twos naturally focus on the feelings of others, their empathy can be developed to a heightened sensitivity, like an antenna attuned to the needs, pain, and states of others. It is as if the Two's own "emotional body" extends to others, picking up subtle changes in their condition. When Twos integrate the qualities of the healthy Four, this sensitivity also extends to their own feelings and inner states.

This does not mean that Twos need to act on their feelings. They might discover, for instance, that they are extremely angry or frustrated with a loved one, and they may experience the anger within them rather than explode at the person or leave them impulsively. Integrating Twos gradually become acquainted and comfortable with the entire panoply of feeling states available to them—including their secret needs and their darkest hatreds. This gives them the ability to know when and how to nurture themselves, as well as the self-knowledge to voice their needs and fears as they arise. Just as Twos respond instantly to distress in others, integrating Twos also respond instinctively to distress in themselves.

Exploring modes of self-expression—music, art, dance—or simply keeping a private journal can be extremely helpful to Twos. Yet each time a Two attempts to pursue more self-knowledge, via art or therapy or simply by asking for help from others, his superego will attack him for being "selfish." ("Why are you spending all of this time on yourself?") Twos can do much to counteract these voices by learning to stop, quiet their minds, and discriminate the strict "voice" of their superegos from real inner guidance.

Twos will not gain much, however, by attempting to imitate the average qualities of the Four. Becoming more emotionally volatile and self-absorbed will do little to enhance the real self-knowledge that Twos need. The Fourish tendency to fantasize romantically and to create heightened expectations of others will only worsen Twos' need to get close to people. Rather, as Twos begin to break down the superego restrictions against "selfishness" and learn to genuinely nurture themselves, the self-knowledge, self-revelation, and creativity of the high-functioning Four naturally unfold.

TRANSFORMING PERSONALITY INTO ESSENCE

▲

Real love is not scarce, but our personality does not know this. We put ourselves through all kinds of contortions, either trying to "get love" from others or to "make love happen." We force ourselves to smile when we are sad, to be generous when we feel empty, and to take care of others when we need to be cared for, as if giving ourselves away one more time might turn the trick. But who could love us in a way that would make all of this effort worthwhile?

It is a major healing for Twos to realize that they are not going to heal their hearts this way—no matter how many self-sacrifices they make. They can, however, turn to the one source that can fulfill them—their own Essential nature. The one and only person who can love us deeply, constantly, and under all circumstances is us. Our own Essence is the source of love we seek because it is an expression of Divine love and therefore cannot be conditioned, withheld, or diminished.

When they learn to nurture themselves and look after their own needs, Twos achieve a balance in which loving and satisfying relationships are not only possible—they will happen as surely as the sun rises. They are free to love others and to give with an open hand. Twos become deeply unselfish and altruistic and are happy to do good, to see people thrive, and to see good being done in the world. Having discovered that it is a privilege to be in the lives of others, they realize a genuine humility and do not need to call attention to themselves or their good works.

More profoundly, Twos grow tremendously when they recognize that love is not a commodity that can be won, demanded, earned, or bestowed by someone else—or that can be given *to* someone else, because it is, in its highest and truest form, not a function of the ego. Love is not a poker chip or a bag of "goodies" that can be given or withheld. If the "love" we seek has these qualities, then it is not real love.

When two people are truly present to each other, love naturally arises. It does not matter whether they have been lifelong friends or have just met. Love is also not primarily a feeling—although various feelings may well arise in its presence. Love is something that cannot be won or lost, because it is always available—but only to the degree that we are present and therefore receptive to it.

We cannot will ourselves to love ourselves or to love others. All we can do, paradoxically, is to *recognize the presence of love in ourselves and others.* As we have seen, our Essential nature is an outpouring of love—the only problem is that it is blocked by the habits and false beliefs of our personality. What *is* in our power is to become aware of those blockages so that our essentially loving nature can once again make itself felt and have a healing effect in our lives. The love that we experience under these conditions is real and deep and quiet. It does not draw attention to itself. It is not demanding, nor does it keep accounts. It lasts because it does not depend on the changing conditions of personality. It is full of joy because nothing can disappoint or frustrate it. Real love in action is unstoppable.

THE EMERGENCE OF ESSENCE

On a very deep level, Twos remember the Essential quality of *unconditional love* and the omnipresence of love. When they remember their Essential nature and the Divine state that it mirrors, healthy Twos are aware of the presence of love all around them, so there is quite literally nothing that they need to get from anyone—and nothing they can give. Twos help all of us to see that love does not belong to anyone, and certainly does not belong to the personality. We could say that our job in life is not to "do good" or to "give" love to anyone, but to be open to the action of love.

This Essential love is experienced as a sweet melting quality—Twos feel flowing, soft, and at one with everything around them. Further, they do not need to have another person with them to experience this love, and when they are experiencing this love in the presence of another person, they do not lose the sense of their own identity. This love is balanced, pure, and nourishing—it allows the soul to relax on a profound level.

The recognition of the true nature of love brings with it a tremendous sense of *freedom*. When love is no longer a commodity and is understood as a part of our true nature, as something we cannot lose, we experience an incredible lightness. Our desperate search for attention ends when we recognize that we not only have love and value, at the level of our souls, *we are love and value.*

Add your scores for the fifteen statements for Type Two. Your result will be between 15 and 75. The following guidelines may help you discover or confirm your personality type.

▶ 15   You are probably not a compliant type (not a One, Two, or Six).

▶ 15–30   You are probably not a Type Two.

▶ 30–45   You most probably have Two-issues, or had a parent who was a Two.

▶ 45–60   You most likely have a Two-component.

▶ 60–75   You are most likely a Two (but could still be another type if you are thinking too narrowly about Type Two).

Twos are most likely to misidentify themselves as Fours, Sevens, and Ones. Nines, Sixes, and Sevens are most likely to misidentify themselves as Twos.

CHAPTER 9

TYPE THREE:

THE
ACHIEVER

▲

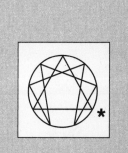

THE MOTIVATOR

THE ROLE MODEL

THE PARAGON

THE COMMUNICATOR

THE STATUS SEEKER

"THE BEST"

"The toughest thing about success is that you've got to keep on being a success."

—IRVING BERLIN

"Most men that do thrive in the world do forget to take pleasure during the time that they're getting their estate, but reserve that till they have got one, and then it is too late for them to enjoy it."

—SAMUEL PEPYS

"All ambitions are lawful except those which climb upward on the miseries or credulities of mankind."

—JOSEPH CONRAD

"A slave has but one master; an ambitious man has as many masters as there are people who may be useful in bettering his position."

—LA BRUYÈRE

"Be content to seem what you really are."

—MARTIAL

THE RISO-HUDSON
T A S

Type Attitude Sorter

Score each of the following statements according to how true or applicable to you it is on the following scale:

1.......*Not at All True*

2.......*Seldom True*

3.......*Somewhat True*

4.......*Generally True*

5.......*Very True*

See page 177 for scoring key.

_____ 1. I see myself as a highly competent person: it really bothers me when I am anything less than effective and efficient.

_____ 2. When things are going well for me, I virtually "glow" with a kind of inner joy in being who I am and having the life that I have.

_____ 3. I try to present myself to others in the best possible light—but doesn't everyone?

_____ 4. My feelings have tended to be foreign to me—I feel things strongly for a little while, and then just get on with things.

_____ 5. It's important to me to feel successful, even if I'm not yet the success I want to be.

_____ 6. For better or worse, I am good at covering up my insecurities—people would never guess what I'm really feeling!

_____ 7. I want to make a good impression on people, so I'm usually polite, well-mannered, and friendly.

_____ 8. I am aware of how well my friends and colleagues are doing, and I tend to compare myself with them.

_____ 9. I often strive to be the best at what I'm doing—if I can't be outstanding at something, I generally don't bother with it.

_____10. Sometimes I've had to cut corners a little to achieve my goals.

_____11. When I am insecure, I can be rather aloof and cool with people.

_____12. It really bothers me when others don't acknowledge the excellence of what I've done.

_____13. I'm more adaptable than most: if things aren't working well, I know how to change my behavior to obtain the results I want.

_____14. I always have a goal in focus and know how to motivate myself to achieve it.

_____15. I have a workaholic streak—I feel adrift if I'm not accomplishing things.

PERSONALITY TYPE THREE: THE ACHIEVER

The Success-Oriented, Pragmatic Type:
Adaptable, Excelling, Driven, and Image-Conscious

We have named personality type Three *the Achiever* because when they are healthy, Threes really can and do achieve success in many areas of life. They are the "stars" of human nature, and people often look up to them because of their graciousness and personal accomplishments. Healthy Threes know how good it feels to develop themselves and contribute their abilities to the world. They also enjoy motivating others to greater personal achievements than others thought they were capable of. They embody the best in a culture, and others are able to see their hopes and dreams mirrored in them.

Threes are often successful and well liked because, of all the types, they most believe in themselves and in developing their talents and capacities. Threes act as living role models and paragons because of their extraordinary embodiment of socially valued qualities. Healthy Threes know that they are worth the effort it takes to be "the best that they can be." Their success at doing so inspires others to invest in their own self-development.

Threes want to make sure their lives are a success, however that is defined by their family, their culture, and their social sphere. In some families success means having a lot of money, a grand house, a new, expensive car, and other status symbols. Others value ideas, and success to them means distinguishing oneself in academic or scientific worlds. Success in other circles might mean becoming famous as an actor, or model, or writer, or as a public figure of some kind, perhaps as a politician. A religious family might encourage a child to become a minister, priest, or rabbi since these professions have status in their community. No matter how success is defined, Threes will try to become somebody noteworthy in their family and their community. They will not be a "nobody."

To this end, Threes learn to be goal-oriented and to perform in ways that will garner them praise and positive attention. As children, they learned to recognize the activities that were valued by their parents or peers, and they put their energies into excelling in those activities. Threes also learned how to cultivate and develop whatever about them is attractive or potentially impressive.

Eve is a successful businesswoman.

My mother trained me to perform. I was about three when I performed my first solo in front of the church congregation. I got a lot

▶ BASIC FEAR: Of being worthless, without value apart from their achievements

▶ BASIC DESIRE: To feel worthwhile, accepted, and desirable

▶ SUPEREGO MESSAGE: "You are good or okay as long as you are successful and others think well of you."

of positive strokes for that and went on to perform in front of audiences throughout high school, either through music or debate. To this day, something mystical happens to me when I get in front of an audience. I "turn it on." I am called on frequently as a public speaker, and some of my professional colleagues say that they hate following me on the program because I am such a hard act to follow!

*"If I work hard I know I
can do it."*

Everyone needs attention, encouragement, and affirmation in order to thrive, and Threes are the type that most exemplifies this universal human need. Threes want success not so much for the things that success will buy (as Sevens do), or for the power and feeling of independence that it will bring (as Eights do). They want success because they are afraid of disappearing into a chasm of emptiness and worthlessness: without the increased attention and feeling of accomplishment that success usually brings, Threes fear that they are nobody and have no value.

The problem is that, in the headlong rush to achieve whatever they believe will make them more valuable, Threes can become so alienated from themselves that they no longer know what they truly want or what their real feelings or interests are. From their earliest years, as Threes learn to pursue the values that others reward, they gradually lose touch with themselves. Step by step, their own inner core, their "heart's desire," is left behind until they no longer recognize it.

Thus, while they are the primary type in the Feeling Triad, Threes, interestingly, are not known as "feeling" people; rather, they are people of action and achievement. It is as if they put their feelings in a box so that they can get ahead with what they want to achieve. Threes have come to believe that emotions get in the way of performance, so they substitute thinking and practical action for feelings.

Jarvis, a well-educated and accomplished business professional, sees that this pattern developed in him at an early age.

> I had no conscious awareness of this at the time, but when I was a child, I wasn't allowed to have my feelings at all. They counted for nothing in the framework of my stepfather's concept of what it took to be successful. I developed the habit of denying my feelings and instead focused on performing and getting good marks in school.

Threes report that when they realize to what extent they have adapted their lives to the expectations of others, the question arises, "Well, then, what do *I* want?" They often simply did not know; it was not a question that had ever come up before. Thus, the fundamental dilemma of Threes is that they have not been allowed to be who they really are and to manifest their own authentic qualities. At a young age, they got the message that they were not allowed to have feelings and be themselves: they must, in effect, be someone else to be accepted. To some degree, all of the personality types have been sent the same message, but because of their particular background and makeup, Threes not only heard it, they began to live by it. The attention they received by performing in a certain way was their oxygen, and they needed it to breathe. Unfortunately, it came at a high price.

Marie, a skilled therapist, describes the contradiction—and the pressure—of this orientation.

> For most of my life, people always noticed when I was involved in any kind of activity, and they have usually looked to me for some sort of direction. This has been a two-edged sword because while I wanted to be noticed and approved, the burden was that I had to be perfect—and that was tough.

THE CHILDHOOD PATTERN

As children, Threes were not valued for themselves—as very few of us were. Instead, they were valued for being and doing certain things extremely well. They learned to get validation of their worth through achievement and performance. But it never really satisfied them because it was a validation not of *them* but of something they had done or something they tried to become.

Marie continues:

> As a child I always felt that I was my mother's favorite. We spent hours together, and she convinced me that there was nothing I couldn't do if I really wanted to do it. That was a blessing and a curse. I remember as a child convincing myself that I really didn't want to do something because underneath I knew it would be too difficult for me. And I knew that if I did anything, I had to do it well and succeed. Once in high school, I stayed home pretending to be sick on the day of a speech competition because I was afraid of not doing so well, and I knew no other way out. I still have guilt feelings about that.

Please note that the childhood pattern we are describing here does not cause the personality type. Rather, it describes tendencies that we observe in early childhood that have a major impact on the type's adult relationships.

Threes have a very deep emotional bond with the person in the family who played the role of the nurturer. Usually the nurturer was the mother, but it may not have been. The child hoped this person would tell them, in effect, "You are wonderful! You are pleasing to me! You are welcomed into the world!" Because they want to continue to be validated by the nurturing figure, Threes as infants learn subconsciously to adapt themselves to do and be those things that will be pleasing to that person.

Often the expectations of the nurturing figure are not directly stated.

Threes may internalize these subconscious expectations and live them out without realizing it. For example, if the mother is a teacher who really wanted to be an actress, the Three child would likely be drawn to the theater, not necessarily liking it but feeling it was something he or she had to do. Even as young adults, Threes may not be at all sure why they are pursuing a certain career, only that they are doing what it takes to make their family (especially their mother) proud of them.

Threes thus learn to play the role of the Family Hero. The child gets the subtle message, "It is not okay to not be okay." The reason for this is that on a deep psychological level, if you are trying to redeem the wounds and the shame of your family, you cannot be hurt or shamed yourself. You have to at least *seem* to have it all together.

Now an outstanding therapist who has a firm grip on his need for attention, Albert reflects back on his early years as a budding show-off.

> Since my dad was in India during World War II, for my first fourteen months, my mom and I lived with my grandparents and an aunt and uncle. I was the first and only child, grandchild, and nephew! I got tremendous attention, doting, and reinforcement, especially for intelligence and achievement. At eighteen months, I was supposed to have had a tremendous vocabulary, and by three years old, I knew all the states and capitals. It's amazing that no one ever pushed me down the stairs for what must have been my really obnoxious vocabulary and geography recitals!

Threes who grow up in highly dysfunctional environments are left to struggle with enormous pent-up rage and hostility because almost nothing they do is enough to please their unhealthy nurturing figure. They can turn themselves inside out like pretzels, trying to come up with something that will win them approval and acceptance, but usually nothing works. Eventually, they split (dissociate) from themselves—burying their genuine desires and inner life—and do more extreme things to get attention. The final result can be a life of deep loneliness and frustration, even if they have achieved some kind of worldly success.

THE WING SUBTYPES

▲

THE THREE WITH A TWO-WING: THE CHARMER

Healthy   People of this subtype are more emotional and spontaneous than the other subtype. Their outgoing, vivacious quality can resemble Sevens'. They can be friendly, helpful, and generous like Twos, while maintaining the poise, self-esteem, and high personal achievement of Threes. They want to be loved and have a drive to be close with people, but they sometimes substitute public life and the recognition they obtain there for a more satisfying private life and domestic stability.

Average   They attempt to suppress any characteristics that interfere with their desirability, feeling that their value comes from the ability to attract and even dazzle others. In short, they want others to like and admire them. They know how to "turn it on" to impress, and this often becomes a preoccupation. Their behavior can have a smooth, artificial quality that undermines their attempt to be popular and credible. People of this subtype are often highly competitive, although usually covertly. They may resort to multiple images to satisfy their social relations and to perform in intimate situations.

THE THREE WITH A FOUR-WING: THE PROFESSIONAL

Healthy   People of this subtype feel that self-esteem comes from their work and career success more than from personal qualities. They want their work to be outstanding and well regarded, often putting great energy into their careers. They take pleasure in whatever profession or "craft" they have chosen and are willing to make great personal sacrifices to maintain their professional integrity. While diplomatic and charming, they are more generally serious and task-oriented and can therefore resemble Ones.

Average   Powerful ambition and self-doubt mix in people of this subtype, inevitably creating tremendous pressures. Their drive for perfection is similar to that of Ones; however, they aspire to embody perfection in some way to avoid being rejected or shamed as inferior. People of this subtype feel they are putting their entire self-worth on the line with every project. They often project competence and poise but can be rather private socially (in contrast to the more outgoing and affable expressions of the other subtype). They may also display pretentiousness and arrogance, mixed with self-consciousness and self-contempt, making this subtype perplexing and sometimes at odds with itself.

THE SELF-PRESERVATION INSTINCT IN THE THREE

Workaholism.   In the average range, Self-Preservation Threes feel that they must constantly work for security and stability (like Sixes) and want to build up a base of material well-being (like Eights). Unlike Sixes, security comes from money, assets, and a stable home, *not* from loyalty to a company, ideology, or person. Self-Preservation Threes strive for efficiency, streamlining their lives as much as possible, seeking to maximize the energy they can put into achieving their goals.

Examples

Bill Clinton
Elvis Presley
John Travolta
Christopher Reeve
Shania Twain
Paul McCartney
Sharon Stone
Dick Clark
Jane Pauley
Kathie Lee Gifford
Tony Robbins

Examples

Barbra Streisand
Oprah Winfrey
Tom Cruise
Ben Kingsley
Madonna
Sting
Richard Gere
Michael Jordan
Whitney Houston
F. Scott Fitzgerald
Werner Erhard

THE INSTINCTUAL VARIANTS

▲

They attempt to impress others not with their sex appeal or their social status but with their stability and material well-being. They are also de-tail-oriented (like Ones), keeping track of all aspects of their particular job or enterprise. While willing to take on responsibility, make sacri-fices, and work long hours, Self-Preservation Threes are motivated by the possibility of advancement. They look for tangible rewards for work well done: raises, promotions, and positive reviews.

Self-Preservation Threes can become excessively focused on their careers. Other aspects of their lives tend to become secondary to work, and they may neglect their health and relationships due to unrealistic schedules. They are unable to relax easily and may even spend vacation time contemplating projects or "doing homework." In the lower-average Levels of Development, Self-Preservation Threes become in-creasingly anxious whenever they are not working and may have difficulty maintaining intimate relationships. Convinced that the material basis of their security could be lost at any time, they believe that they must constantly keep swimming or sink. Stopping their highly stressful work habits feels like courting disaster. Downtime can feel like incapacity or illness. ("What's wrong with me? Why aren't I being more productive?") For this reason, real illness, whether physical or emotional, can be very threatening because it reduces their efficiency and productivity. A few days off could bring down everything.

In the unhealthy range, Self-Preservation Threes make gargantuan ef-forts to remain effective, sacrificing relationships and health for job secu-rity and money. They become highly prone to burnout and nervous breakdowns. When they are no longer able to function well, they desper-ately try to cover over any real physical or emotional health problems. ("I'm fine.")

THE SOCIAL INSTINCT IN THE THREE

The Status Seeker.   In the average range, Social Threes need recognition and reassurance that they are making progress, moving up in the world. Of course, this can look very different in different cul-tures, but all Social Threes need signs that they are valued by their peers. (A Social Three in a Buddhist monastery in Thailand would need to know that he was meditating well—being a model monk!) Degrees, job descriptions, résumés, good grades, and awards are im-portant to them because they are strongly identified with their social roles. ("I am what I do.") They want to have the right pedigree, the right credentials. This instinct can also express itself in the cultivation of professional jargon and dress, as well as the flaunting of brand names, designer fashions, and expensive cars. Again, however, what a particular Three will find important as an indicator of social value will vary from culture to culture and from Three to Three.

As anxiety escalates, Social Threes increasingly feel the need to prove themselves. They can become highly driven in their social ambitions: constantly networking, giving out cards, and making connections. They may also desire fame as a way to compensate for early narcissistic wounds. ("If a million people buy my CD, I must be pretty great!") Narcissism can also lead to compulsive social comparison and competition—keeping up with the Joneses. As they become more insecure, Social Threes are prone to bragging, relentless self-promotion, and exaggeration of their abilities. This is especially true if Social Threes have not succeeded in achieving their idea of success.

In the unhealthy range, Social Threes are desperate for attention and can become dishonest in their pursuit of recognition. They may falsify their accomplishments and background both to get work and to impress. Often they illustrate the Peter Principle—getting into situations that they are not qualified to deal with. Their emotional distress renders them highly ineffective, but as much as possible, they will use charm or exploitation to prevent others from seeing their true condition.

THE SEXUAL INSTINCT IN THE THREE

The Catch.   In the average range, Sexual Threes are characterized by a powerful desire to be desired. This is not just sexual desirability, but an overall drive to be valued and wanted. They work at developing an appealing, alluring image, striving to become the ideal of their gender and cultural milieu, and they often enjoy helping others maximize their attractiveness as well. Sexual Threes want to be the kind of person that their love interest would want to show off to his or her friends. Whether male or female, they tend to cultivate whatever personal qualities they feel will get others interested in them. Sexual Threes desire to impress by dazzling. They can be seductive, but unlike Twos, who seduce by lavishing attention on the other, Threes seduce by drawing attention to their own exceptional qualities. In some cases, this can lead to ambitions to become a movie star, a teen idol, or a fashion model. In contemporary American culture, this type often devotes much time and energy to working out at the gym, to careful grooming, or to finding the right look.

Sexual Threes often know how to attract mates, but they may not know how to sustain relationships. They constantly fear that they will not be able to live up to the image they are projecting. As Sexual types, they possess a strong desire for intimacy, but as Threes, they fear deep emotional connection. They may attempt to achieve emotional intimacy through sexual connection, but in the lower Levels, fears of their own undesirability will cause them to reject even people they deeply care about. In some cases, they may use sexual conquests to dispel fears of being unattractive. Less healthy Sexual Threes also tend to be exhibitionists—wanting to display themselves either to seduce others or to reassure themselves that they are attractive and valued.

In the unhealthy Levels, Sexual Threes can become caught up in promiscuity. Underneath the surface, they are extremely vulnerable but tend to strike out at others who question their value in any way. Slights to their narcissism, real or imagined, can lead to vindictiveness, sexual rage, and jealousy, often out of all proportion to their actual disappointment.

THE THREE'S CHALLENGES TO GROWTH

▲

Most Threes will encounter the following issues at some point in their lives. Noticing these patterns, "catching ourselves in the act," and simply seeing our underlying habitual responses to life will do much to release us from the negative aspects of our type.

THE WAKE-UP CALL FOR TYPE THREE: MY VALUE DEPENDS ON MY SUCCESS

"Discovering real goodness comes from appreciating very simple experiences. We are not talking about how good it feels to make a million dollars or finally graduate from college or buy a new house, but we are speaking here of the basic goodness of being alive."

CHOGYAM TRUNGPA

Most of us think from time to time, "If I could just achieve that— if I just had these credentials, or if I just married this particular person, or if I could go to medical school—then I would know that I am worthwhile, I would have value, and then I would feel okay about myself." For Threes, this has become the driving force of their lives. Threes start to equate their own personal value with their level of success, and this is their Wake-up Call.

Success can mean many different things—in monetary terms, it can mean making millions of dollars a year or saving enough for a new washer-dryer. Average Threes are intensely interested in success and are determined to distinguish themselves through professional achievement and by possessing a variety of status symbols. These can run the gamut from a prestigious address, to a diploma from a major university, to an athletic trophy, to an expensive watch or car, or to having attractive, high-achieving children—anything that makes the statement "I am an outstanding person."

Jarvis, whom we met earlier, describes his intense focus on achievement—and his awareness of what it is costing him.

My viewpoint is focused on being successful and avoiding failure no matter what the situation—working, social situations, hobbies, having fun, relaxing, jogging, reading, listening to music. . . . My preoccupation with success means that I have to work consciously at enjoyment and

H E A L T H Y	Level 1	*Key Terms:* *Inner-Directed* *Authentic*	Threes let go of the belief that their value is dependent on the positive regard of others, thus freeing them to discover their true identity and their own heart's desire. Their Basic Desire is also achieved, and they feel valuable and worthwhile. They become self-accepting, genuine, and benevolent.
	Level 2	*Adaptable* *Admirable*	Threes are attuned to what others value, and adapt themselves to become a person who would be more valuable. Self-image: "I am outstanding, capable, and well-adjusted (unlimited potential)."
	Level 3	*Goal-Oriented* *Self-Improving*	Threes reinforce their self-image by developing themselves and their talents. They are competent, confident, and persistent, becoming exemplary in whatever they do. Effective communicators, they are often popular role models and inspirations for others.
A V E R A G E	Level 4	*Success-Oriented* *Performing*	Threes begin to fear that they will be overshadowed by the accomplishments of others—that their efforts will not bring them the attention they desire. Thus they need to distinguish themselves from others by overachieving. They continually drive themselves to achieve more.
	Level 5	*Image-Conscious* *Expedient*	Threes worry that they will lose the positive regard of others, so they wish to impress people. They strive to cultivate what they believe will be the most attractive image possible. Ambitious but self-doubting, they want to be admired and desired. They typically have intimacy problems.
	Level 6	*Self-Promoting* *Grandiose*	Threes are afraid that others will not notice them unless they are hugely successful or outstanding; thus, they try to convince themselves and others of the reality of their grandiose claims. They are self-promoting, competitive, and arrogant as a defense against secret neediness.
U N H E A L T H Y	Level 7	*Unprincipled* *Deceptive*	Threes fear that they are failing and that their claims may be empty and fraudulent, which may be true. To save their self-image, they begin to deceive themselves and others, saying whatever will impress people or get them off the hook. Inside, they feel empty and depressed.
	Level 8	*Duplicitous* *Opportunistic*	Unhealthy Threes have become so desperate for attention that they will concoct any story or scheme in order to cover over their deterioration. They do not want anyone to know how troubled they are and are willing to go to great lengths to keep their emotional illness and misdeeds hidden.
	Level 9	*Monomaniacal* *Relentless*	Unhealthy Threes feel that there is nothing they can do to win the positive attention of the people whose approval they need, and may lose control of their repressed hostility and rage. They may seek revenge on real or imagined tormentors, attempting to bring down whoever they feel has rejected them.

TYPE 3 LEVELS OF DEVELOPMENT

at appreciating beauty. I find it unnatural to "let go and let flow." There's no guarantee of success emanating from *that* framework!

To borrow a phrase from the recovery movement, Threes are always in danger of becoming "human doings" instead of "human beings." The reason for their compulsive behavior is their need to repress and renounce any hint of shame that they may feel. To lose in any way, on any scale, is potentially to trigger these intolerable feelings of worthlessness. Thus, the more shame Threes feel, the more they will be driven to achieve goals that they believe will make them valuable and successful.

WHOSE GOALS? WHOSE SUCCESS?

What does success mean to you? What did it mean to your parents? What does it mean to your peers? Any connections?

The Social Role: "The Best"

"I can do this better than anyone else."

Feeling that their value depends on shining brightly enough to be noticed, Threes begin to believe that they must *always* shine, that they must always be outstanding. Thus they begin to play the Social Role of the Best (or Golden Boy or Golden Girl) and eventually can only relate to others comfortably in this role. Seeing themselves as the Best compensates for their hidden insecurities about their worth. Not only will average Threes defend their self-image, but like other types, they will try in various ways to reinforce it and to get others to support it. Naturally, needing to be the Best does not allow Threes the luxury of ever being average—and seeing themselves (or allowing anyone else to see them) as a failure of any kind is out of the question.

Tawney is a bright, talented woman, happily married with children. She has learned to embrace many of her true qualities, but she still recalls what it was like to be driven by her Social Role.

I can hardly remember a time in my life that I didn't feel the need to be "the best." To be the most beautiful, have the best clothes, live in the grandest home—the list goes on and on. The problem I faced every day in my pursuit of "the best" was that it shifted with every person I interacted with. It made no difference who I was with. I wanted them to see me in the best possible light, which was my interpretation of who they would most desire—an exhausting process. I always looked outside of myself for validation that I was "okay."

The Social Role of being the Best is related to Threes' role as Family Hero. They are set up to find self-esteem by meeting the expectations and requirements of others, even if those requirements are not explicitly stated. But this is always a losing game in the long run because the requirements can change on a dime: standards of success or beauty can go out of vogue, and an accident of some sort can completely reverse the winner-loser scorecard. Judged from this point of view, a heart attack or a stroke can change a "successful" person into a "failure" overnight.

WHEN DO YOU GIVE YOURSELF A BREAK?

Identify and write down five areas in your life in which you do not feel compelled to be the best. Identify and write down five areas in your life in which you do feel that you must be the best. Read your two lists and see what you can notice about how they make you feel. What differences in your state can you detect? In your tensions or relaxation? In feeling calm or anxious? Think of five more areas where you could learn to relax and just be you.

Deceit, Vanity, and Validation

The Three's Passion is *deceit.* One aspect of the Three's deceit is the tendency to present themselves in a way that does not reflect their authentic self. An even more important aspect is their self-deception: in order to maintain their external performance, Threes must convince themselves that they actually are the idealized image that they project to the world. At the same time, they must also repress their feelings of inadequacy to keep the self-deception going. They fear that if they were to drop their image, other people would see their deficits and reject them—confirming their worthlessness.

"I've got it all together."

Thus, deceit leads Threes to look to others for validation of their excellence and is the reason why they must constantly give themselves internal pep talks. In a sense, Threes must lie to themselves to keep up their self-esteem and to motivate themselves toward greater achievement. ("You're great! A genius! Nobody has ever written a better report!")

Another useful way to think of deceit is to see it as the result of "sloth in real self-development." Average Threes put their energy into perfecting their ego self, their self-image, rather than into discovering their true self, because they believe that the ego *is* the real self. It is much more difficult to develop the authentic qualities of Essence when we are encouraged and rewarded at every turn to adapt and become what others expect us to be.

Performance and Being Out of Touch with Feelings

Since Threes want to stand out from the crowd, they give a great deal of attention to their "performance" in all senses of the word—professional, physical, academic, social. They present themselves to others as someone who has it all together, with a cool, effortless mastery. The problem is that as they become more identified with their image, average Threes must repress any personal feelings since feelings interfere with the smoothness of their performance. Since they are rewarded for functioning, feelings—especially painful ones—need to be resisted.

Tawney recalls one of the most significant moments of her early life, the moment when she realized that she needed to suppress herself and please her mother to survive.

> The most significant experience I can recall as a child was of a fight that I witnessed between my older brother—who was about ten at the time—and my mother. My memory is of her, in a rage, yelling and throwing all of his possessions into a heap in the middle of the floor. I do not know if she physically struck him. It doesn't matter. I was terrified of her and chose then, out of fear, to do or be whatever she told me to do or be. I spent the next thirty years living the results of that moment.

"Feelings are like speed bumps—they just slow me down."

The typical result is that Threes become "achievement machines." But because their activities do not come from the heart, their performance is increasingly joyless and inauthentic. Despite the fact that Threes usually do things well, they do not find much personal satisfaction in the work itself. Nevertheless, their work cannot be abandoned since that is the principal way that Threes have to gain favorable attention and feel valuable. A driven workaholism can begin and devour whatever little emotional freedom and joy they still have left.

The only desire that less healthy Threes can identify in themselves is to become a "star" of some kind. Because they are looking for a big, outstanding public payoff, they may squander whatever genuine talents they do possess, jumping from one opportunity to another. The narcissistic neediness at the root of their activities often strikes others as embarrassing and sad (or questionable and obnoxious, depending on how relentlessly the Threes are promoting themselves). In any case, being so out of touch with themselves and their own feelings begins to backfire in many different ways.

REAWAKENING YOUR HEART

Place your hand on your chest, right over your heart, and take a few deep breaths. Let your attention sense this area of your body. Let it go into this space. What do you experience? Remember that there is no right answer—there is nothing that you are *supposed* to experience. Whatever you find or do not find is *your* experience. Stay with whatever sensations you find in your heart "space," and note how they change over time. Return to this practice at least once a day.

Competition and Driving Oneself

Average Threes may start getting into subtle competitions of all kinds: who is the most successful at work, or who has the best-looking spouse or smartest children, or who is the best in sports or computers or chess, and so forth. The principal way that their self-esteem can be bolstered is by *winning* the comparison (and the overt competition, if there is one). Unfortunately for Threes, their quest for superiority can become exhausting and can undermine the very things they want to achieve.

Threes begin to engage in competitions not because they really want to do them but because they fear being overshadowed by someone else. They fear that they will fall behind and that others will get more attention and be in more demand than they. They then push themselves to do even more—a great waste of time and energy. ("I've been working really hard on my piano recital, but Mary Lou sounds really great on that Chopin piece. I better pick a more difficult piece to perform.")

Not only do average Threes compete with their peers, they may begin to introduce competitiveness into relationships in which it does not belong and can be highly destructive, such as parents competing with their children, or spouses with one another. Ironically, despite their competitiveness, they tend to seek recognition and affirmation from the very people they want to outshine.

Lynn, a successful personal coach and business consultant, understands this well.

If you know the children's story "The Little Engine That Could," you know how it feels to be inside my dynamo personality type. Everything I have ever committed time and energy to doing, I've done from a competitive, striving, goal-oriented stance. Performing everything as close to perfect as possible has fueled my existence since I was potty-trained at eleven months. The fuel motivating my driving force has been the fear of not being outstanding, the fear of failing. To fail means death, swallowed up by a black hole. It's to be avoided at all costs.

DRIVING YOURSELF

In your Inner Work Journal, explore the following questions: In what ways do you see yourself as success-driven and competitive? Why do you hold the goals that you are pursuing? Have you ever gotten into projects that you were not really interested in because of the need to excel or compete? What do you think would happen if you "took your foot off the accelerator" a little bit? How do you deal with the fear or anxiety that comes up when you compare yourself to someone else? How do you feel about your competitors? How have you handled or reframed your own failures?

Image and Self-Presentation

"Without wearing any mask we are conscious of, we have a special face for each friend."

OLIVER WENDELL HOLMES, SR.

Even from their earliest childhood years, Threes have the capacity to adapt themselves to others in order to present an attractive image. In the average range, this can show up either as a forced enthusiasm or as a professional cool that seems to project the message, "I've got it all together." The worlds of advertising, marketing, sales, and fashion frequently promote these images, worlds that seem to be populated by more than their share of Threes. Many politicians, coaches, human potential gurus, and businesspeople have tuned in to this aspect of the Three personality style, particularly their innate talent for reading a situation and being able instinctively to come up with what is expected. Threes can walk into a room and sense the undercurrents between people and know instantly how to act.

As Threes are repeatedly rewarded for this ability, they become so practiced at adjusting themselves that they lose touch with their authentic self. Their private sense of self thus remains undeveloped and largely out of reach, such that average-to-unhealthy Threes often do not know who they are or what they are feeling apart from their image. Rather than express what they actually think or feel, they say and do whatever they sense will be acceptable.

If their image is successful and others applaud it, an entirely new and much more dangerous condition arises. Having a successful image affirms the Three's performance, not his or her own core identity. The more successful their image is, the more tempting it is for Threes to continue to rely on it and to develop *it* rather than themselves. The result is that their own heart is pushed aside and forgotten. Who they really are becomes more and more unknown territory, something they do not want to focus on because when they look inward, they feel an emptiness, a big, black hole.

MEETING EXPECTATIONS

What image are you projecting to others right now? to yourself? at the office? to your social friends? to your parents? to your children? to your pets? Are they the same or different? How do you see yourself as opposed to how you believe others see you? In what specific ways is your self-image different, do you think, from the image you project to others? How do you know? Has the disparity gotten you into conflicts with others or caused problems for you in some way?

Packaging the Self as a Commodity

When Threes feel insecure, they protect themselves by managing their image even more closely. Much of their behavior becomes what amounts to a public relations game. They begin to feel that how they are perceived is everything. Rather than devote their energies to the development of their genuine talents, they allocate their resources to managing others' impressions of them. Trying to find a winning formula, they will do, say, or be whatever will further their goals or save them from potential humiliation, whether they display (false) modesty, apparent agreement accompanied by conciliatory attitudes—or the opposite.

"I can be anything I want to be."

Feeling that they must put their best foot forward all the time is an enormous strain; it is as if they were perpetually on a job interview. Others can only imagine the anxiety and self-doubt that Threes must suppress in order to keep functioning. They are constantly afraid of saying or doing the wrong thing. No moment can be unguarded, so they can never be truly spontaneous or self-revealing lest they be laughed at, questioned, or perceived in a less-than-favorable light.

The problem is that Threes treat themselves as a commodity. ("I have to 'sell' myself to people.") As we have seen, Threes as children were often an extension of someone else's narcissistic needs. They learned that their authentic feelings and needs do not count; they exist only as an object to be admired and desired. The pain of this is so great that Threes must disconnect from their hearts. It is the heart alone, though, that enables us to discern truth, so when we detach from the heart, we detach from our connection with truth. Truth then also becomes a shifting commodity, whatever works at the moment.

This relentless self-adjustment and detachment causes Threes and their intimates much suffering, as Arthur, a hard-working minister, relates.

I've been so competitive in work that I have thought myself better than others and have come across as arrogant and distant. I've gone flat emotionally at home and either get impatient with my wife for not being there for me or simply am so remote that it's as if she weren't really there. I've worried excessively about what "they" think of me without defining who "they" are—I discovered several years ago that I'd dress for work in the morning to impress a nebulous group of downtown professionals I didn't even know or come into contact with!

ADJUSTING YOURSELF

Notice when you are adjusting yourself to your surroundings. How many times do you do this in a day? Observe the differences between your self-presentations with your friends, your coworkers, your family, and so forth. Notice when certain intonations or rhythms creep into your speech patterns. When you notice these self-adjustments, what effect do they have on your own groundedness? On your connection with your heart? When you adjust yourself, do you feel more or less valuable?

Fear of Intimacy

As long as Threes are trying to convince themselves and others that they have it all together, they cannot allow others to get too intimate with them. Closeness will allow others to see that they actually do not have it all together, that they are not the person they seem to be. Privately, average Threes are aware that there is a disparity between who they are and what they show to the world, but they are terrified of letting anyone see this gap. They fear that someone else is going to recognize how lonely, empty, and worthless they actually feel, thus reinforcing their hidden insecurities about themselves. The closer others get, the more they fear that others will see through the facade to the chinks in their armor and reject them. Rather than risk rejection, they will typically try to pull themselves together and achieve more so that others will be satisfied with them (that is, their image) and not question or threaten the relationship.

To keep people at a safe distance—and yet retain their attention and good regard—average Threes cultivate a kind of professional friendliness or an energetic perkiness that substitutes for real intimacy and connection. They may even keep a certain degree of distance from their spouse because of their fear of intimacy. From the outside, their marriage may look perfect, yet to their spouse real intimacy and emotional connection are missing. Threes typically want the image of a successful relationship rather than the substance of a real one, especially if intimacy means risking being vulnerable or needy, or being rejected for not fulfilling the other person's needs.

LETTING OTHERS SEE YOU

Share something vulnerable about yourself with someone you trust. As you do so, focus on the actual feeling of the vulnerability. Is it unpleasant? What is it like? How does it make you feel in relation to the other person? What are you afraid to let them see?

Narcissism and Showing Off

The more unhealthy a Three's childhood environment has been, the more their sense of value will have been wounded, and the more difficult it will be for them to find and hold on to genuine feelings of self-worth. They will be forced to search for these things in the approval and acceptance of others, and yet the approval and acceptance they receive never makes them feel valued and worthwhile. Narcissistic damage usually manifests itself in overcompensation—in other words, in showing off.

Depending on the depth of their narcissistic wounding, average Threes may develop grandiose expectations of themselves. Being merely successful is not enough: they need to be famous or important in some way—"big stars"—who are known and celebrated for something. Of course, this only sets Threes up for frequent disappointments and feelings of being humiliated.

"What do I have to do to impress you?"

Threes may also become seductive and engage in prowling for sexual conquests to bolster their self-esteem. They often groom themselves in attention-getting ways, but then react with hostility or feigned indifference if someone actually does admire them or seek them out. ("I want you to look at me, but I am not going to acknowledge you.") They worry about their reputation as well as about how the people in their lives reflect on them. Not only must they be attractive and desirable, but so must their spouse and children, their friends and even their pets—although, ideally, others must not be more attractive and desirable than they.

Tawney recalls:

At the times in my life when I felt the most isolated, I worked the hardest to be "fabulous." I remember being rail thin, with perfect nails (fake, of course), perfectly applied makeup, fashionable, expensive clothing, dripping with diamonds and fur (real, of course). I remember people looking at me with awe, and I felt nothing. I have realized that when I am that disconnected from myself, I rarely have memories to go back to. I think what helped me to get out of that state was the recognition that I had no recollection of it. I have almost no memory of my wedding day, for instance. The effort to piece together my past was what helped me reconnect with myself.

LETTING PEOPLE DISCOVER YOU

When you are with others in social settings, focus first on *their* lives and accomplishments. Find out what is interesting about them. Notice how this gives them the opportunity to be curious about you without you needing to impress them up front. Consider that others might like you without you needing to impress them. How does that possibility make you feel?

REACTING TO STRESS: THREE GOES TO NINE

▲

Under increased stress, the coping mechanisms of average Threes may break down, leading them to act out some of the qualities of average-to-unhealthy Nines. Threes are highly focused, driven to achieve, and identified with what they do, so going to Nine serves as a shutdown from their relentless pursuit of success.

Because Threes are so eager to make their mark and prove themselves, they inevitably create stresses and conflicts in their relationships with others. At such times, they may slow down, becoming more diplomatic and accommodating like average Nines. Threes at Nine will still want to stand out from the pack, but not too much. They lower their profiles and try to blend in with others.

As we have seen, their quest for success can often lead Threes into situations where they are compelled to do things that hold no real interest for them. While they may be able to handle this for limited periods, a longer stretch or even an entire career or relationship that is not based on a Three's true desires will cause them to become disengaged and dissociated like Nines. Rather than being efficient, they fill their time with busywork and routines, hoping to persevere through difficult situations without being affected by them. Although Threes are usually quick and effective in handling tasks and in responding to others, stress causes them to become strangely unresponsive and complacent.

Experiencing failures or major setbacks in their careers can be particularly devastating to Threes. During such intervals, Threes become disillusioned with life and with themselves. Their underlying emptiness breaks through, and they appear apathetic and burned-out. Rather than using their industriousness to improve their situation, they tend to avoid the realities of their problems and waste their time indulging in wishful thinking and fantasies of their next big success.

THE RED FLAG: THE THREE IN TROUBLE

▲

If Threes have suffered a serious crisis without adequate support or coping skills, or if they have suffered from chronic abuse in childhood, they may cross the shock point into the unhealthy aspects of their type.

A setback that severely damages a Three's self-confidence may lead them to the fearful recognition that their life has been built on a weak or even a false foundation. They may fear that they are actually failing, or that their successes are meaningless, or that their claims about themselves are fraudulent. Some of these fears may be based on fact. If the Three can recognize the truth in these fears, they may begin to turn their life around and move toward health and liberation. On the other hand, they may try even harder to hold on to their illusions of superiority and attempt to deny that they are suffering or even having any problems. ("No problem here! I'm doing fine." "I'll do *whatever* it takes to get ahead.") If Threes persist in this attitude, they may cross into the unhealthy Levels of Development. If you or someone you know is exhibiting the following warning signs for an extended period of time— more than two or three weeks—getting counseling, therapy, or other support is highly advisable.

WARNING SIGNS

POTENTIAL PATHOLOGY: Narcissistic Personality Disorder, hypertension, depression (often anhedonic), narcissistic rage and vindictiveness, psychopathic behavior

▶ Physical exhaustion and burnout from relentless workaholism

▶ Increasingly false self-image, dishonesty, and deceptiveness

▶ Lack of feelings and inner emptiness

▶ Concealing the degree of their emotional distress

▶ Jealousy and unrealistic expectations of success

▶ Exploitation and opportunism

▶ Severe episodes of rage and hostility

PRACTICES THAT HELP THREES DEVELOP

▲

▶ First and foremost, learn to recognize when you are "turning it on" for someone—when you are becoming your image instead of speaking and acting authentically. You may even notice yourself falling into this image when no one else is around! While there may not be anything wrong with the persona you have constructed and you may even want to use it from time to time, awareness alone will give you the ability *to choose* when to employ it. Without awareness, you serve your image.

▶ Like Eights and Ones, you would really benefit from giving yourself a break once in a while and taking time to relax. As a Three, you are not the quickest at noticing that you are getting too stressed, and it sometimes takes a major health or relationship problem to get you to notice that you are overextending yourself. Stop and take deep breaths periodically during the day and take a few moments from your projects to check in with yourself. Are you anxious? Lonely? Angry? Overwhelmed? These breaks may seem like they are slowing you down, but in the long run, they will do much to maintain your emotional and physical well-being and are likely to help you accomplish your tasks with greater ease.

▶ Seek out people you trust with whom you can share your anxieties and vulnerabilities. Threes usually have no trouble finding pals, and they may spend time with friends on a regular basis, but that is not the same as finding some safe people to address what makes you feel vulnerable or hurt or afraid. Look for people who seem able to do this themselves, and realize that you don't have to talk about everything all at once. Just revealing small things about the way you feel can help you to open up in a way that feels safe. (A good psychotherapist can also be extremely helpful in this regard.) Also, contrary to your beliefs, revealing some of your vulnerability to healthy friends will endear you to them—not disappoint them.

▶ Threes really benefit from creativity, especially when the creativity is for themselves and not an audience of some kind. Painting, making pottery, playing music, writing or drawing, and journaling can help you get in touch with your feelings and bring you into greater alignment with yourself. You may even want to create a sacred space in your home that is devoted solely to your creativity and self-discovery. No work-related tasks are allowed here! It is your refuge from the demands in your life, especially the demands you make on yourself.

▶ You are a type that can especially benefit from meditation, although you are one of the types least likely to meditate. Sitting around "doing nothing" doesn't make much sense to your task-driven ego, but it makes a lot of sense to your soul. And meditating is far from doing nothing. In fact, short of child rearing, it is probably the greatest challenge that you will ever face. To be able to simply *be* is a major human accomplishment, but it is especially an accomplishment for Threes. If it seems difficult at first, use your discipline and persist—Threes usually make breakthroughs suddenly and in big ways.

▶ Find areas in your life where you can be of service as part of a team, but *not* as the head of the team! Learning to cooperate and work with others without needing to be the center of attention is not easy for Threes, but it brings enormous and unexpected satisfaction. You might try volunteer work at a local hospital, school, or retirement home. You may well be surprised at what arises in you while working with others—not only in terms of the relatedness that such efforts bring, but also in what it does for your feelings about yourself. You may find a tremendous sense of self-worth that you never dreamed possible.

Healthy Threes are blessed with genuine self-esteem as opposed to inflated narcissism. They have a realistic and deeply felt appreciation of themselves and their lives that gives them confidence as well as a healthy sense of their possibilities. We could say that healthy Threes possess a balanced *love of self*, which also enables them to love others freely and without agenda. This love of self is not easily disturbed or threatened, because it is based on a truthful assessment of their genuine capacities, as well as a respect for their limitations. It almost goes without saying that others immensely enjoy and profit from the company of a person with these admirable qualities.

Because of their genuine self-esteem, Threes understand the value of investing in themselves and their own development: they are ambitious, confident, and persistent, take care of themselves physically, and make it their business to learn about themselves and how to manage their affairs better. They are always trying to find ways to enhance and improve their lives and to teach others how to develop themselves.

"Self-investing" can be literally spending money, time, and energy on themselves, without being self-centered or narcissistic about it. Healthy self-investment is necessary if anyone is to achieve something worthwhile in life—we must get a good education, set our own priorities, and not get deflected from our goals. Threes really apply themselves to developing whatever qualities they have.

"I enjoy being me."

Besides investing in their own talents, healthy Threes help others to be their best; they use their ability to excite and motivate people to achieve more than they thought they could. Threes who are nurses, doctors, teachers, or therapists can have an electrifying effect on their students and clients by the force of their own example. A physical therapist can motivate a physically challenged child on whom others have given up hope to walk again, a music teacher can inspire her students to outdo themselves, a coach can give his team the gift of the pleasure of knowing that they have achieved their best.

Healthy Threes also use their talents and presentation skills to advance worthy causes. As a result, they often become outstanding role models in their fields of endeavor. Many corporations and organizations employ healthy Threes to represent them. They are good communicators and promoters, and they know how to present something in a way that is attractive, appealing, and inspiring. They can be highly effective at building morale and community spirit.

Eve is a lovely and gracious corporate coach:

Most days I love being a Three because I get so much stuff done. I recently approached a new job in the same way. I went about motivating my staff to make them feel like they are really part of a winning team. I also was able to get five of my staff pay raises. Now they are so loyal to me that they'd walk over hot coals. They think I'm the best, which feels great! I love being able to motivate people to do their best.

High-functioning Threes are self-accepting and inner-directed—everything they seem to be. They model an honesty, simplicity, and authenticity that is extremely inspiring to others. High-functioning Threes see themselves realistically, accepting their limitations and appreciating their talents without taking themselves too seriously. They are tender, touchingly genuine, and affectionate—truly admirable people who enjoy the admiration they receive, but do not *need* it.

Having overcome much of the narcissistic wounding she experienced in early life has led Lynn to feel completely differently about herself and others.

I'm imbued with a presence or inner glow that radiates out to others. It is magnetic, drawing people to me without my having to perform or achieve anything. One person recently asked "Do you always glow like this?" I feel transcendent and at the same time very human and grounded.

THE PATH OF INTEGRATION: THREE GOES TO SIX

▲

Threes, like healthy Sixes, become actualized and remain healthy by learning to commit to others and to goals that transcend their personal interest. This shifts their focus from the need to sustain a self-image to the real desire to support the development of something larger than themselves. Integrating Threes begin to find a sense of real self-esteem in ways they could never have anticipated. Further, as they interact cooperatively with others, both in their careers and in their relationships, they begin to discover the courage and sense of inner guidance of the healthy Six, which enables them to reveal more of their authentic qualities. Communication becomes simple, sincere, and direct—there is no need to dazzle people.

No matter how hard they work, Threes' search for validation through the pursuit of goals not dictated by their own hearts never seems to pay off. To their surprise, however, Threes find deep satisfaction and feelings of worth in the selfless acts and shared responsibilities that arise through honoring their heartfelt commitments. They find themselves deeply touched by what they create with others, seeing the beauty and goodness of what they have done, regardless of the acclaim they may or may not have received for their actions. In such moments, without any self-reflection, Threes begin to experience their true identity and value.

Average Threes tend to feel like soloists—capable of motivating others and generating team spirit, but essentially experiencing themselves as alone. The burden of being the Family Hero did not allow them to reach out for support or comfort—the hero is not allowed to need too much help. But as Threes integrate to Six, they start to recognize and take in the support that is available in their lives, and they have the courage to ask for it when they need it. Doing so usually brings intense fears of inadequacy and of disappointing others. ("If they knew how I *really* feel, they'd all abandon me.") But as Threes learn to build solid relationships with select others, based on trust and mutual respect in the manner of healthy Sixes, they begin to make the more powerful journey of finding their own inner guidance and support.

Of course, Threes will not be well served by attempting to imitate the traits of an average Six. Overcommitting themselves and attempting to build up their identity and security through various affiliations will only reinforce their preoccupation with self-image and performance. But as Threes begin to let go of their identification with their performance, the endurance, heartfelt commitment, and courage of the healthy Six naturally unfold in them.

TRANSFORMING PERSONALITY INTO ESSENCE

▲

To liberate themselves, Threes must let go of their belief that their value is dependent on the positive regard of others. Only then can they begin to become inner-directed and authentic. This is a difficult path for Threes, although a very direct one. At first, they encounter only the empty, blank feeling in the heart space, but gradually, with patience and compassion, they are able to open to the hurt and shame underneath it. As this suffering is seen, healed, and released, and without noticing quite when or how the change occurred, they gradually realize that they are quite different people than they had imagined. Free from the burden of dancing to the expectations of others, Threes find the tremendous freedom and lightness of pursuing their own heart's desire.

Threes must understand very clearly that the mask must come off, and the feelings of emptiness inside must be acknowledged if healing is to take place. The saving grace is, of course, that there is no real inner emptiness to the Essential self. When the mask is dropped, the apparent emptiness is filled from the inside. It is as if the mask itself exerted a pressure that kept the true self repressed: once the mask is removed, the real self cannot help but reveal itself. Rather than discover that they are empty and valueless, Threes will find that they are simply less developed in certain areas (while the many areas in which they are already highly evolved remain). It takes courage and ideally the support of a spouse, good friend, therapist, or minister for a Three to embark on this journey of self-revelation.

Tawney tells what a difference it can make.

The difference now is that I am making choices for myself based on what I truly need and not on what will make me more "desirable." I have stopped needing to be "the best" for anyone but myself. I am able to express emotions freely without worrying what others may think of me, and give myself permission to look however I want to without judging myself. I feel softer somehow. For most of my life, I radiated my personality type—I was a typical Three. Today, it's just me.

When Threes are willing to risk losing the approval of others to follow their own heart, they can become the outstanding individuals they have always wished to be. Whatever love and admiration is given to them penetrates deeply into their souls, allowing a beautiful new garden to spring up.

A therapist in her later life, Marie has learned this important secret.

My whole identity was caught up in doing and, of course, succeeding. Until I learned how to just be, there was little hope of honesty or genuineness. . . . I was always quick, competent, and capable. I still am, but now it isn't so important to me that I do well. It is more important that I be true to what has real value for me.

Once their center of gravity has shifted from outside themselves to inside themselves, the feeling of being truly guided by their hearts is like no other they have ever experienced before. Once they have tasted it, they are not likely to trade again for anything.

THE EMERGENCE OF ESSENCE

When they are able to reconnect with their hearts, healthy Threes model the Essential gift of *authenticity* like no other type. Their behavior becomes genuine, not trying to be more or less than they really are. They become simple and available, revealing their true selves with honesty and humility.

Authenticity is not about being brutally honest. Authenticity means manifesting who you are in the moment. When Threes are present, they are simple and able to speak the truth that comes directly from their hearts. At first glance, this may not seem like much of an achievement, but if we think about it, we realize how rarely we present ourselves to others in this way.

As Threes learn to embrace their authenticity, their Essential quality begins to arise. It is difficult to speak about, not because it is so abstract but because it is so fundamental to our existence that we tend to be blind to it. Perhaps the best word for it is *value*—the fact that *we are valuable because we exist.*

This idea flies in the face of popular culture, which insists that we are valuable only if we have a certain income or certain physical qualities or are of a certain age or professional background. But all of these more superficial understandings of value are substitutes created by the personality that is out of touch with the ground of its Being, the source of all real value.

If we stop to consider it, it is we who imbue the things that we value with value. Perhaps being an actor gives us our self-esteem. Yet for another person, this same career might seem pointless or trivial. Their self-esteem might depend on having a certain amount of money in the bank. Not only do values vary from person to person, but they also change in the course of our own lives. Obviously, the one common thread in all of this is *us.* In effect, we project our own Essential value onto a job or a person or a thing or an activity and then try to get the sense of value back by having that thing. But it never quite works.

When we contact our Essential value, however, we know that it is an intrinsic part of our true nature. We cannot be without value, we can only forget that it is there. All of the pains, humiliations, and problems of life do nothing to diminish the Essential value of a person; at most, they only modify the person and give him or her an opportunity for further expansion, acceptance, and understanding. Thus, when Threes are able to perceive their Essential value directly, they become freed from the ego's relentless pursuit of self-esteem through achievement. This affords them the time and space to live with a greatness of spirit, a life of love, richness, and wonder.

Add your scores for the fifteen statements for Type Three. Your result will be between 15 and 75. The following guidelines may help you discover or confirm your personality type.

▶ 15   You are probably not an assertive type (not a Three, Seven, or Eight).

▶ 15–30   You are probably not a Type Three.

▶ 30–45   You most probably have Three-issues or a Three parent.

▶ 45–60   You most likely have a Three-component.

▶ 60–75   You are most likely a Three (but could still be another type if you are thinking too narrowly about Type Three).

Threes are most likely to misidentify themselves as Fives, Ones, and Eights. Eights, Sevens, and Nines are most likely to misidentify themselves as Threes.

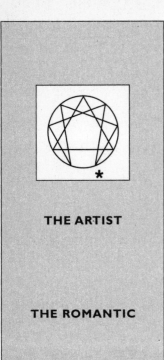

THE ARTIST

THE ROMANTIC

THE MELANCHOLIC

THE AESTHETE

THE TRAGIC VICTIM

THE SPECIAL ONE

CHAPTER 10

▼

TYPE FOUR:
THE
INDIVIDUALIST

▲

"All art is a kind of confession, more or less oblique. All artists, if they are to survive, are forced, at last, to tell the whole story, to vomit the anguish up."

—JAMES BALDWIN

"After all, perhaps the greatness of art lies in the perpetual tension between beauty and pain, the love of men and the madness of creation, unbearable solitude and the exhausting crowd, rejection and consent."

—ALBERT CAMUS

"Happiness is beneficial for the body, but it is grief that develops the powers of the mind."

—MARCEL PROUST

"It is better to drink of deep griefs than to taste shallow pleasures."

—WILLIAM HAZLITT

"It takes a genius to whine appealingly."

—F. SCOTT FITZGERALD

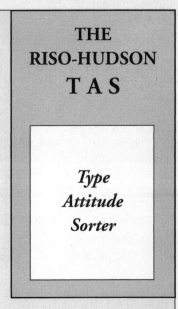

THE RISO-HUDSON
T A S

*Type
Attitude
Sorter*

_____ 1. Many people see me as enigmatic, difficult, and contradictory—and I like that about myself!

_____ 2. I tend to brood over my negative feelings for a long time before getting free of them.

_____ 3. I often feel alone and lonely, even when I'm around people I'm close to.

_____ 4. If I'm criticized or misunderstood, I tend to withdraw and sulk.

_____ 5. I find it difficult to get involved with projects if I don't have creative control.

_____ 6. I tend not to follow rules or to go along with expectations because I want to put my own special touch on whatever I do.

_____ 7. By most standards, I'm fairly dramatic and temperamental.

_____ 8. I tend to spend quite a bit of time imagining scenes and conversations that haven't necessarily happened.

_____ 9. I long for someone to rescue me and sweep me away from all of this dreary mess.

_____ 10. When things get tough, I tend to crumble and give up— perhaps I give up too easily.

_____ 11. I can forgive almost anything except bad taste.

_____ 12. Generally, I don't enjoy working too closely with others.

_____ 13. Finding myself and being true to my emotional needs have been extremely important motivations for me.

_____ 14. I don't like either to take the lead or to be a follower.

_____ 15. I am acutely aware of my intuitions, whether or not I have the courage to act on them.

Score each of the following statements according to how true or applicable to you it is on the following scale:

1.......*Not at All True*

2.......*Seldom True*

3.......*Somewhat True*

4.......*Generally True*

5.......*Very True*

See page 205 for scoring key.

PERSONALITY TYPE FOUR: THE INDIVIDUALIST

▶ BASIC FEAR: Of having no identity, no personal significance

▶ BASIC DESIRE: To find themselves and their significance, to create an identity out of their inner experience

▶ SUPEREGO MESSAGE: "You are good or okay if you are true to yourself."

The Sensitive, Withdrawn Type:
Expressive, Dramatic, Self-Absorbed, and Tempermental

We have named this type *the Individualist* because Fours maintain their identity by seeing themselves as fundamentally different from others. Fours feel that they are unlike other human beings and, consequently, that no one can understand them or love them adequately. They often see themselves as uniquely talented, possessing special, one-of-a-kind gifts, but also as uniquely disadvantaged or flawed. More than any other type, Fours are acutely aware of and focused on their personal differences and deficiencies.

Healthy Fours are honest with themselves: they own all of their feelings and can look at their motives, contradictions, and emotional conflicts without denying or whitewashing them. They may not necessarily like what they discover, but they do not try to rationalize their states; nor do they try to hide them from themselves or others. They are not afraid to see themselves warts and all. Healthy Fours are willing to reveal highly personal and potentially shameful things about themselves because they are determined to understand the truth of their experience—so that they can discover who they are and come to terms with their emotional history. This ability also enables Fours to endure suffering with a quiet strength. Their familiarity with their own darker nature makes it easier for them to process painful experiences that might overwhelm other types.

Nevertheless, Fours often report that they feel they are missing something in themselves, although they may have difficulty identifying exactly what that something is. Is it willpower? Social ease? Self-confidence? Emotional tranquillity?—all of which they see in others, seemingly in abundance. Given time and sufficient perspective, Fours generally recognize that they are unsure about *aspects of their self-image*—their personality or ego structure itself. They feel that they lack a clear and stable identity, particularly a social persona that they feel comfortable with.

While it is true that Fours often feel different from others, they do not really want to be alone. They may feel socially awkward or self-conscious, but they deeply wish to connect with people who understand them and their feelings. The "romantics" of the Enneagram, they long for someone to come into their lives and appreciate the secret self that they have privately nurtured and hidden from the world. If, over time, such validation remains out of reach, Fours begin to build their identity around *how unlike everyone else they are.* The outsider therefore comforts herself by becoming an insistent individualist: everything must be done on her own, in her own way, on her own terms. Fours' mantra becomes "I am myself. Nobody understands me. I am different and special," while they secretly wish they could enjoy the easiness and confidence that others seem to enjoy.

Fours typically have problems with a negative self-image and chronically low self-esteem. They attempt to compensate for this by cultivating a Fantasy Self—an idealized self-image that is built up primarily in their imaginations. A Four we know shared with us that he spent most of his spare time listening to classical music while fantasizing about being a great concert pianist—à la Vladimir Horowitz. Unfortunately, his commitment to practicing fell far short of his fantasized self-image, and he was often embarrassed when people asked him to play for them. His actual abilities, while not poor, became sources of shame.

In the course of their lives, Fours may try several different identities on for size, basing them on styles, preferences, or qualities they find attractive in others. But underneath the surface, they still feel uncertain about who they really are. The problem is that they base their identity largely on their feelings. When Fours look inward, they see a kaleidoscopic, ever-shifting pattern of emotional reactions. Indeed, Fours accurately perceive a truth about human nature—that it is dynamic and ever changing. But because they want to create a stable, reliable identity from their emotions, they attempt to cultivate only certain feelings while rejecting others. Some feelings are seen as "me," while others are "not me." By attempting to hold on to and express specific moods, Fours believe that they are being true to themselves.

One of the biggest challenges Fours face is learning to let go of feelings from the past; they tend to nurse wounds and hold on to negative feelings about those who have hurt them. Indeed, Fours can become so attached to longing and disappointment that they are unable to recognize the many treasures in their lives.

Leigh is a working mother who has struggled with these difficult feelings for many years.

I collapse when I am out in the world. I have had a trail of relationship disasters. I have hated my sister's goodness—and hated goodness in general. I went years without joy in my life, just pretending to smile because real smiles would not come to me. I have had a constant longing for whatever I cannot have. My longings can never become fulfilled because I now realize that I am attached to "the longing" and not to any specific end result.

There is a Sufi story that relates to this, about an old dog that had been badly abused and was near starvation. One day the dog found a bone, carried it to a safe spot, and started gnawing away. The dog was so hungry that it chewed on the bone for a long time and got every last bit of nourishment that it could out of it. After some time, a kind old man noticed the dog and its pathetic scrap and began quietly setting food out for it. But the poor hound was so attached to its bone that it refused to let go of it and soon starved to death.

Fours are in the same predicament. As long as they believe that there is something fundamentally wrong with them, they cannot allow themselves to experience or enjoy their many good qualities. To acknowledge their good qualities would be to lose their sense of identity (as a suffering victim) and to be without a relatively consistent personal identity (their Basic Fear). Fours grow by learning to see that much of their story is not true—or at least it is not true anymore. The old feelings begin to fall away once they stop telling themselves their old tale: it is irrelevant to who they are right now.

THE CHILDHOOD PATTERN

Fours feel that they are not like their parents. Many Fours report fantasizing that they were mistakenly switched at the hospital, or that they are orphans or some kind of changeling. They often express this as feeling that they have not been "seen" by their parents, that they did not connect sufficiently with their parents or their parents with them. In psychological terms, Fours feel that they have not had adequate mirroring, or at least the mirroring of actual qualities and talents that they can make part of their developing identity. (In family systems theory, Fours tend to identify with the Lost Child role.)

The result is that Fours believe that something must be profoundly wrong with them, launching them on a lifelong "search for self." They feel "If I am not like my parents and I cannot see myself in them, then who am I?" This also predisposes Fours to focus on what they lack—on what is missing in themselves, their lives, and their relationships. They feel abandoned and misunderstood by their parents and, later, by other significant people.

Hannah works as an administrator in a university. She is a well-loved wife and mother but still suffers periodically from her type's feelings of alienation.

> I learned very early on not to depend on my mother, to play by myself and seek my own solutions. My father, ambivalent about having children in the first place, began traveling a lot when I was in grade school, so I experienced more abandonment.

Please note that the childhood pattern we are describing here does not cause the personality type. Rather, it describes tendencies that we observe in early childhood that have a major impact on the type's adult relationships.

As a result of this pattern, Fours respond powerfully to people who trigger their desire for mirroring, for being seen and appreciated for who they are. On the most profound level, Fours are always looking for the mother and father they feel they did not have. They may idealize these others as "saviors" who will rescue them from their plight. But just as easily, Fours can become disappointed and enraged with others for letting them down or for not adequately seeing their personal struggles and suffering. The other is seen as the source of love, goodness, and beauty—qualities that Fours usually believe they lack—setting the stage both for expectations of being completed by the other and for terrifying fears of abandonment. People who do not fit into one of these scenarios tend to be of little interest to average Fours; it is as if those who do not produce strong emotional responses in them are somehow less real.

Because they have doubts about their identity, they tend to play "hide and seek" with others—hiding from people, but hoping that their absence will be noticed. Fours attempt to remain mysterious and intriguing enough to attract someone who will notice them and redeem them with their love. But self-concealment and self-revelation alternate and can be expressed with such extremes of intensity and need that Fours inadvertently drive the longed-for rescuer away. Until they can recognize this pattern and see the unrealistic expectations they put on their intimates, Fours run the risk of alienating others with their emotional demands.

THE FOUR WITH A THREE-WING: THE ARISTOCRAT

Healthy   People of this subtype combine creativity and ambition, the desire for self-improvement and an eye toward achieving goals, often involving their personal advancement. They are more sociable than people of the other subtype and want to be both successful and distinctive. They feel the need to communicate themselves and their creative efforts to others, and so they care both about finding the right mode of expression and about avoiding anything off-putting or in bad taste. They create with an audience in mind.

Average   These people are more self-conscious and aware of issues regarding their self-worth and how they are coming across to others than people of the other subtype. They want recognition for themselves and their work, and they typically put more effort into everything having to do with their self-presentation and related matters. They are more practical, but also more extravagant—loving refinement, culture, and sophistication—typically seeing themselves as high class, elegant, and concerned with social acceptance. They can be competitive and

THE WING SUBTYPES

▲

Examples

Jeremy Irons
Jackie Onassis
Tennessee Williams
Judy Garland
Vivien Leigh
Sarah McLachlan
The Artist (Formerly Known as "Prince")
Martha Graham
"Blanche DuBois"

disdainful of others; grandiosity and narcissism are expressed more openly and directly.

Examples

Bob Dylan
Anne Rice
Allen Ginsberg
Alanis Morrisette
Edgar Allan Poe
Johnny Depp
Sylvia Plath
James Dean
Ingmar Bergman

THE FOUR WITH A FIVE-WING: THE BOHEMIAN

Healthy   People of this subtype tend to be extremely creative, combining emotionality and introspection with perceptiveness and originality. Less concerned with acceptance and status than the other subtype, they are highly personal and idiosyncratic in their self-expression, creating more for themselves than for an audience. They enjoy the process of creativity and discovery more than that of presentation and are highly exploratory. For better or worse, they are usually defiant of convention and authority, breaking the rules whenever self-expression is an issue.

Average   More introverted and socially withdrawn than the other subtype, these Fours tend to dwell more exclusively in their imaginations. The real world is less interesting to them than the inner landscapes they create for themselves. They are attracted to the exotic, the mysterious, and the symbolic, and their personal style is often eccentric and unusual. People of this subtype prefer downbeat scenes, choosing a minimalistic lifestyle. They can be intensely private, often seeing themselves as rebellious outsiders. They may have brilliant flashes of insight, but they have trouble sustaining practical efforts in the real world.

THE INSTINCTUAL VARIANTS

▲

THE SELF-PRESERVATION INSTINCT IN THE FOUR

The Sensualist.   In the average range, Self-Preservation Fours tend to be the most practical and materialistic kind of Fours. They love the finer things of life and want to surround themselves with beautiful objects. They relate strongly to the sensuality of the material world and enjoy cultivating a "nest" filled with items that have both aesthetic appeal and emotional resonance. Thus, Self-Preservation Fours are often moved by the presentation and symbolism of gifts and enjoy presenting gifts to others, such as a rose for their beloved. They also tend to be the most introverted Fours; having comfortable, aesthetic surroundings supports them during periods of social isolation. They tend to be very particular, even obsessive, about their physical surroundings, wanting soothing textures, mood lighting, and a comfortable temperature.

Eventually, their desire for emotional intensity begins to interfere with basic life functioning. They often develop a throw-caution-to-the-winds attitude that comes from the excitement of being on a temporary emotional high of some sort. At the other extreme, they tend to be self-indulgent in an attempt to soothe emotional lows. In either case, they typically allow emotional whims to dictate their behavior. Self-Preservation Fours may attempt to maintain a rarefied lifestyle at the expense of their security and physical well-being (buying expensive items when the rent is not quite covered). They (like Sevens) can become frustrated divas, craving rich foods and luxury. They frequently fall into poor eating habits and health routines, staying up late watching movies, listening to music, drinking, and eating to excess, as if to say, "What difference does it make?" Self-indulgent habits become compensations for an unlived life.

In the unhealthy range, Self-Preservation Fours are highly susceptible to alcoholism and drug abuse. They are attracted to situations that undermine the stability of their lives, even to danger—like the proverbial moth to the flame—involving themselves in illicit love affairs or other destructive relationships. Similarly, they can be extremely irresponsible, showing a total disregard of their livelihood, or even of the need to have a livelihood. Feeling emotionally overwhelmed, they may not bother to show up at their job or to pay their bills. Long-term self-destructive behavior through drug abuse and personal neglect is common.

THE SOCIAL INSTINCT IN THE FOUR

The Outsider.   In the average range, of the three Instinctual Variants of Type Four, Social Fours most see themselves as unlike others, as being totally unique. They experience their uniqueness as both the gift they bring to others and the burden they must bear. Not surprisingly, Social Fours also tend to be the most socially active and engaged Fours. They long to be involved with others and to be part of the social world, but they often feel that they do not know how. Like Threes, they constantly compare themselves with others, although always feeling that they come up short. They desire to be among the beautiful, the glamorous, and the elite, yet they doubt that they are really up to it.

Feelings of shame in social settings eventually lead Social Fours to believe that they do not know how to function like normal people. They envy the happiness of others, while rejecting them as crude and insensitive. They frequently adopt a glamorous, exotic image to cover over their social insecurities. Many Social Fours become attracted to alternative lifestyle groups to compensate. ("I'll seek solace with the other outsiders." Beatniks in the 1950s or the Gothic rock subculture in the 1980s and 1990s are examples of this.)

Some Social Fours may aggressively pursue success as a compensation for their nagging feelings of inadequacy. ("They won't make fun of me now!") They react strongly to any statements about themselves, often sifting through past conversations for any hints of a slight. Ironically, they may both defend their defects and feel disadvantaged by them. ("Of course I'm aloof around such coarseness and selfishness—but still I do wish someone loved me!")

In the unhealthy range, fear of rejection can lead Social Fours to withdraw almost completely from involvement with others. Shame and expectations of humiliation become so pervasive that they do not want to risk being seen. At the same time, their insecurities render them unable to work in any consistent way. As a result, Social Fours often become extremely dependent on family, friends, or a significant other. Isolation along with fantasies of achievement may cause unhealthy Social Fours to waste their lives.

THE SEXUAL INSTINCT IN THE FOUR

Infatuation.   In the average range, Sexual Fours most exemplify the romanticism, intensity, and longing for a rescuer that characterize this type. They can be sweetly vulnerable and impressionable, but also aggressive and dynamic, especially in their self-expression. There is an assertive, seemingly extroverted component to Sexual Fours, and unlike the other two variants, they are unlikely to let their romantic fantasies remain fantasies for long. Often turbulent and stormy, their emotional lives revolve around the person they are attracted to. Intense feelings of admiration, longing, and hatred for the object of desire can all coexist. Sensual and seductive, they can also be jealous and possessive like Twos, and they want to be the only person that matters in the other's life. Sexual Fours often have severe doubts about their own desirability, so they strive for accomplishments that will make them acceptable to the other—being a great artist or star—while being resentful of those who achieve those things.

Envy is also most clearly visible in this variant. Relationship problems arise because Sexual Fours often become romantically involved with people who have qualities that Fours admire or want in themselves, but then end up envying and resenting the loved one for having these very qualities. Idealizing the other can quickly shift to rejecting them for their slightest flaws. At the same time, Sexual Fours are often attracted to people who are, for one reason or another, unavailable. They may spend a great deal of time longing to have the desirable other to themselves and detesting anyone who has the other's attention.

In the unhealthy range, intense envy of others can lead to a desire to sabotage them in order to get revenge. Unhealthy Sexual Fours unconsciously live by the adage "misery loves company." ("If I'm going to suffer, so are you.") Sexual Fours may create competitions and rivalries and feel completely justified in undoing their opponents or in hurting those who have disappointed them. (Salieri's envy of Mozart comes to mind, for example.) They are prone to rapid shifts in their feelings toward others, even toward their protectors and loved ones. Their emotional chaos may lead them to rash acts of violence against themselves or the people they believe have frustrated their emotional needs.

Most Fours will encounter the following issues at some point in their lives. Noticing these patterns, "catching ourselves in the act," and simply seeing our underlying habitual responses to life will do much to release us from the negative aspects of our type.

THE WAKE-UP CALL FOR TYPE FOUR: USING THE IMAGINATION TO INTENSIFY FEELINGS

Fours base their identity on their internal feeling states ("I am what I feel"), so they tend to check in on their feelings more than the other types. (Usually Fours are more attuned to their emotional reactions to an experience than to the experience itself.)

But the one sure thing about feelings is that they always change. This presents a problem. *If their identity is based on feelings, and their feelings are always changing, then their identity is always changing.* The way Fours resolve this problem is to cultivate certain feelings that they identify with while rejecting others that are not as familiar or "true."

Rather than allowing the spontaneous arising of their feelings in response to the moment, Fours fantasize about people, events, and scenarios that stir up emotions they feel reflect their identity, even if the feelings that arise are negative or painful. Whatever the feelings might be, Fours try to intensify them to bolster their sense of self. For example, they may select musical pieces that trigger powerful associations for them—such as songs that remind them of a lost lover—playing them over and over to maintain their old feelings, or at least some intense feeling state.

When Fours start trying to create and sustain moods—in a sense, trying to manipulate their feelings—they are going in the wrong direction. All of this leads Fours into the ultimately self-defeating habit of living in their imagination rather than in the real world.

Beverly was a beautiful airline attendant when she was younger; she met many men in her travels but resisted getting involved with anyone.

THE FOUR'S CHALLENGES TO GROWTH

▲

"It's terribly amusing how many different climates of feeling one can go through in a day."

ANNE MORROW LINDBERGH

H E A L T H Y	Level 1	*Key Terms:* *Life-Embracing* *Life-Enhancing*	Fours let go of the belief that they are more flawed than others and are thus freed from their self-absorption. Their Basic Desire, to find themselves and their significance, is also achieved and thus their problems with their identity and its stability are solved. They are self-renewing, redemptive, and revelatory.
	Level 2	*Introspective* *Sensitive*	Fours focus on their own feelings and preferences to establish a clear sense of personal identity. Self-image: "I am sensitive, different, and self-aware."
	Level 3	*Self-Revealing* *Creative*	Fours reinforce their self-image by expressing their individuality through creative action. They are eloquent and subtle, exploring their feelings and impressions and finding ways of sharing them with others. Their creativity is highly personal but often has universal implications.
A V E R A G E	Level 4	*Romanticizing* *Individualistic*	Fours begin to fear that their changing feelings will not sustain them and their creativity, so they use their imaginations to prolong and intensify their moods. They use fantasy and style to bolster their individuality and begin to dream of someone who will rescue them.
	Level 5	*Self-Absorbed* *Temperamental*	Fours worry that others will not recognize or appreciate them and their uniqueness, so they play hard to get—testing others to see if they are really interested in them. Aloof, self-conscious, and melancholy, they believe that their fragility will attract a rescuer and keep others away.
	Level 6	*Self-Indulgent* *Decadent*	Fours fear that life's demands will force them to give up their dreams, and they despair that they will never be rescued. They feel they are missing out on life and envy the stability of others, so they exempt themselves from "the rules," becoming sensual, pretentious, and unproductive.
U N H E A L T H Y	Level 7	*Hateful* *Alienated*	Fours fear that they are wasting their lives, and this may be true. To save their self-image, they reject everyone and everything that does not support their view of themselves or their emotional demands. Their repressed rage results in depression, apathy, and constant fatigue.
	Level 8	*Self-Rejecting* *Clinically* *Depressed*	Fours have become so desperate to be the individual of their fantasies that they hate everything about themselves that does not correspond to it. They loathe themselves and hate others for failing to save them. They may sabotage whatever good is left in their lives.
	Level 9	*Despairing* *Life-Denying*	The realization that they have wasted their lives pursuing futile fantasies is too much for unhealthy Fours. They may attempt to elicit rescue through self-destructive behavior or simply end their lives to escape their negative self-consciousness. In some cases, they may commit crimes of passion.

TYPE 4

LEVELS OF DEVELOPMENT

Since I flew the Atlantic route to Paris, it would have been easy to connect with lots of men. After the meal service was over, there was time to talk with people, and some flirting helped pass the time. But I would rather sit alone in the back of the plane and think about someone on board or someone I had seen in the airport than talk with someone who would probably just disappoint me anyway. I could fall in love, have sex, get married, imagine the house and children we'd have, and so on—all during the flight. Then I wouldn't have to deal with disappointment and having the relationship end.

RECOGNIZING THE "SIREN'S CALL" OF FANTASY

Fours fear that if their emotions are not sufficiently intense, their creativity and even their identity will disappear. Observe yourself during the day to see if you can feel this process of using your imagination to stir up how you feel. Pay attention to your fantasies, daydreams, and self-talk: What are they reinforcing? What purpose do they serve? Do you believe that some feelings are more "you" than others are? What is your personal "baseline mood" most of the time? How do you react if you are spontaneously *not* in that mood? Notice any tendency to run a commentary on your feelings and experiences, as if asking yourself, "What does this experience mean about me?"

Every time you find yourself fantasizing, especially about potential romance, sexual encounters, or becoming your "idealized" self, you are moving deeper into the trance of Type Four.

The Social Role: The Special One

Average Fours insist on being themselves and on putting their personal stamp on everything. Increasingly, their self-image becomes based on *how unlike other people* they are. (Their superego message to "be true to themselves" is more and more intensely heard as they become more entranced.) Similarly, the moods that Fours get into are often in marked contrast to their surroundings. ("If others are happy, I feel sad. If others feel sad, I feel like giggling.") Maintaining feelings unlike those of others reinforces a Four's identity. Thus their characteristic Social Role is the Special One, or the Mysterious Outsider, and they feel ill at ease unless they are interacting with others from this role.

Ironically, the more Fours insist on being different, the more they paint themselves into a corner, depriving themselves of many potential sources of satisfaction. Fours need to understand that if they insist on being unique and different, it is likely that they will overlook or reject many of their positive qualities simply because they resemble the qualities of others, especially in their families. Thus, *they unwittingly create a negative identity:* "I am not like that." "I could never work in an office job." "I would never wear polyester." "I wouldn't be found dead in Kmart." They do not understand that "being oneself" does not require effort since they cannot help but be themselves. When Fours stop trying so hard to "be themselves," they find the freedom to discover the beauty of what they really have to offer.

"No one understands me."

Riva, a gifted visual artist, traces this problem to her childhood.

> As a child, my world was pretty self-enclosed. I didn't share myself easily or reach out. I felt like an outsider and felt rejected—maybe because of how I looked, or talked, or the fact that I'm smart and Jewish. I don't know. While part of me longed to be "normal" and have fun, I started to pride myself on being "special" and more sensitive, more mature and insightful, understanding things on a deeper level. I started to feel like a little adult among my childhood peers. So the inferiority-superiority split began early.

Taken too far, the desire to "be themselves" can lead Fours to feel that the rules and expectations of ordinary life do not apply to them. ("I do what I want to do when and how I want to do it.") Thus they can be privately grandiose, imagining that, because of their great, undiscovered talent, they deserve to be treated better than ordinary people. They feel exempt from the laws of society, dismissive of rules and regulations, and contemptuous of any constraints, particularly regarding their feelings.

Consequently, Fours begin to view many normal aspects of life, such as earning a living or being regular in their work habits, as impediments to their search for self. They want to be free to follow their moods and imagination wherever they take them, although they often end up waiting months (or years) for inspiration to strike. The truth may be that they are unproductively frittering their lives away. Riva continues:

> My sense of entitlement comes from thinking of myself as superior and unusually sensitive, so I shouldn't be expected to do what mere mortals have to do, especially when it's aesthetically distasteful. But my sense of entitlement also has to do with feeling just the opposite about myself—that I am inferior and incapacitated in some way, totally cut off from the everyday abilities that most people take for granted—like holding down a regular job, for instance, or having a steady, satisfying relationship!

BEING DIFFERENT VS. BEING CONNECTED

While it is true that we are all individuals—precious in our own right—it is also true that we share a great deal with other human beings. Notice your tendency to automatically focus on your *differences* with people. What does this cost you in terms of your connectedness with others? Does it prevent you from taking up activities that might be beneficial to you?

Envy and Negative Comparisons

Like all of the Passions (or "Capital Sins"), envy develops as a particular response to the loss of connection with the Essential self. But, unlike many of the types, Fours retain some degree of awareness of this loss of contact with their Essence. They also feel that they alone have experienced this loss. As children, their other family members and their friends seemed to them to be more complete and valued more adequately, while they perceived themselves to have been ignored. The results are chronic loneliness, intense longings to be included, and envy of those who are.

Cass, an actress with a distinguished career, shares some of the feelings that defined her childhood experience.

> I was two years old when my younger sister was born, and she became the center of attention. I felt left out, and my vision of life was as an outsider, the lonely child looking through the window of a house full of light and laughter. At school, I was bullied and isolated, so I became studious, but that just made me feel more different. I always envied other girls who had fair hair and blue eyes and hated my brown hair and brown eyes. My father was cold and aloof and used to say, "You don't know what you want and won't be happy until you get it!"

As adults, envy causes Fours to see everyone as stable and normal while feeling that they are flawed or, at best, unfinished. In effect, their complaint is that they are not as well disguised as others, that everyone can sense their nakedness and vulnerability, and they feel ashamed of themselves. Other people seem to like themselves, have self-esteem, know how to present themselves, and go after what they want in life. Others seem to be spontaneous, happy, unself-conscious, and lively—all the things that Fours feel they are not. They brood about their condition, while enviously longing for the social ease that others seem to enjoy.

Leigh, whom we met earlier, recalls:

"What a wonderful life I've had! I only wish I'd realized it sooner."

COLETTE

I felt so separate. I could see all the other girls having fun and relationships with one another, and I didn't have a clue how to be a part
of it. As a result, I often had a feeling of being isolated and different—
set apart. I didn't feel superior, just painfully different with no way—
absolutely no possibility—of being a part of the group, the fun, the
contact, the friendships—you name it.

Although envy may at times consume Fours, they are usually
ashamed of it and attempt to hide it as much as possible. Often they
cover over their envy with an attitude of aloofness and distance. They
alternate between wanting to express their distress so that others will
know how much they have disappointed them, and periods of withholding their thoughts and feelings. ("I won't give them the satisfaction!") Many Fours resolve this issue by expressing their dark feelings
indirectly, through works of art or through allusions. One Four we know
frequently communicated his feelings to his girlfriend through cassette
tapes with mixes of songs that contained hidden messages to her.

Fours often get caught up in negative comparisons and negative
feelings because of their tendency to imagine the reactions of others
rather than check with them to find out what they are actually thinking. Envy sets them up to be disappointed with themselves and to project this disappointment onto others, anticipating negative reviews
from people even when these people are fond of them. Thus, envious
Fours can spend many hours in melancholic fantasies, wrapping themselves in a shroud of sadness, feeling vulnerable, hurt, and misunderstood by the world—often unnecessarily.

Reinforcing Moods Through Aesthetics and Sensuality

"I do what I want to do when I want to do it."

Fours maintain their moods by cultivating an environment that
supports the feelings they identify with. Thus, they are often drawn to
the aesthetic and exotic, surrounding themselves with beautiful objects,
music, lighting, textures, and scents that both mirror their individuality and intensify their feelings. Atmosphere, style, and being "tasteful"
become of paramount importance. They are extremely particular about
their surroundings and the objects they use. They must have just the
right pen, only the exact shade of paint for the bedroom will do, and
the fabric of the curtains and how they hang must be just so, or else
average Fours feel ill at ease and off-balance.

Left unchecked, the desire to sustain more moods, even negative
ones, may cause Fours to turn to destructive habits that become difficult to break. If they are losing hope that they will ever have a steady
and meaningful relationship, for instance, they may attempt to succor
themselves with substitute pleasures: episodes of anonymous sex, a

devotion to pornography, drinking, drug abuse, or staying up all night to watch old films on television. The many self-indulgences and exemptions Fours give themselves weaken them further. Nicholas is a writer who has been depressed for many years.

> I tend to be both too easy on myself and too hard. I have been too self-indulgent, and as soon as anything painful or difficult appears, I tend to give up and take the easy way out by sleeping too much, or going on a drinking binge. But that behavior quickly leads to self-disgust and big-time guilt. I had a couple of chapters to write in a book several years ago, but rather than just get into it, I couldn't bring myself to face the typewriter, so I drank and watched television and rented movies until I just about made myself sick. Then when I had "bottomed out" in a way, I pulled myself together and started working again. It seems like I almost need to create a crisis for myself.

"INTERIOR DECORATING"

Take some time to examine your home environment, your workplace, and your wardrobe. What are your favorite "props"? What do you use to "create atmosphere"? How attached are you to that atmosphere? Are there specific things you do to "get yourself into a mood" to work? To talk with people? To relax? To exercise or to meditate?

Withdrawal into a Fantasy Self

The types of the Feeling Triad all create a self-image that they believe is preferable to their authentic self. While the self-images of Types Two and Three are more on display, Fours create an internalized self-image we have called the *Fantasy Self*.

As we mentioned before, average Fours spend their time dreaming about their talents and the masterworks they will create instead of actually developing their real skills. Of course, not all of the average Four's self-image exists in their imagination—part of it will be tested with trusted others. But even when Fours reveal some aspects of their inner identity, they keep most of their Fantasy Self to themselves.

While the Fantasy Self gives a Four an occasional persona, it is usually largely unrelated to their actual talents and therefore tends to invite ridicule and rejection. The Fantasy Self tends to be grandiose in proportion to the depth of the Four's emotional damage: they may see themselves as almost magical creatures, and others as highly ordinary or even inferior. Their Fantasy Self is usually based on idealized qualities

"I have a secret self that no one knows."

that would be virtually impossible for them to attain, even with hard work and self-discipline. The Fantasy Self is thus of its very nature unattainable and is inextricably linked with the Four's rejection of his or her own real qualities or capacities.

When Fours become deeply identified with their Fantasy Self, they tend to repel any kind of interference with their lifestyle choices, interpreting suggestions from others as unwelcome intrusiveness or heavy-handed pressure. When called on for practical action, they feel that they are not up to it and tend to postpone or avoid social contacts and professional deadlines for as long as possible. They respond to any questioning of their behavior with disdain, anger, and "hurt feelings." They crave more attention and support but have great difficulty taking in the attention and support that *is* available to them.

Riva comments:

> It's always been hard for me to reach out beyond myself. It's hard for me to ask for what I need. On the one hand, I expect people (as I expected my mother) to read my mind. On the other hand, I don't expect my needs to be met, and don't expect people to care enough to want to help me—since my needs weren't met in my childhood. So I learned to use my fragility, my hypersensitivity, to manipulate my parents into doing things for me so that I wouldn't have to take responsibility for myself, for my own mistakes.

ACTUALIZING YOUR REAL TALENTS

What qualities do you fantasize about having? Of these qualities, notice which ones you might actually be able to develop. For instance, it is true that music requires some talent, but none of that talent will be realized if you do not develop it through practice and discipline. Similarly, being in shape requires exercise and a balanced diet. Which qualities are unattainable, no matter what you do—being taller, or from a different background, for instance? What is it about these qualities that attracts you? Can you feel the self-rejection in wishing to be these things? Can you recognize the value in the qualities you do have?

Hypersensitivity

Continual fantasizing, self-absorption, and negative comparisons lead Fours away from reality-based actions into heightened emotionality and moodiness. As a result, they become hypersensitive or touchy, such that even minor events or offhand statements from others can cause major emotional reactions.

Cass, whom we met earlier, reveals the inner turmoil that her feelings have sometimes created.

> I consider myself volatile and used to think there was nothing between elation and despair, and that I was mentally flawed. I am continually at the mercy of outside influences that affect my moods, and I struggle to maintain a serene center. . . . I feel I am no good at having fun and long to do so, like other people.

As they become more self-absorbed, Fours search for hidden meanings in their every emotional reaction, as well as in the statements of others. They replay conversations in their imaginations from the previous day or the previous year, trying to arrive at what the other person was *really* saying to them. They may experience harmless comments as veiled insults. "You've lost weight!" can mean "She must think I was a fat slob." Or "Your brother is such a talented young man" may be taken as an indictment of how untalented and inadequate the Four is by comparison.

"People are so cruel and insensitive to me."

In this frame of mind, average Fours are extremely uncooperative and resentful—traits that are not likely to win friends or make relationships easy. And yet because these qualities are consistent with their self-image of being "sensitive" and "different," their hypersensitivity is seldom seen by Fours as negative or troublesome.

GETTING REALITY CHECKS

Get reality checks from people when you are feeling that they are judging, criticizing, or rejecting you. Ask them to clarify what they meant, and allow for the possibility that they may be telling you exactly what they feel. Avoid "overinterpreting" or "overreading" every gesture and comment that others are making. Chances are good that they are not scrutinizing you in this kind of detail. Notice, too, your degree of interest in others and the nature of your comments and thoughts about them. Would you find this acceptable in them?

Self-Absorption and Narcissism

Self-consciousness, social awkwardness, and subtle forms of getting attention are related to the narcissism we see in all three types of the Feeling Triad. In Twos and Threes, narcissism manifests directly in a drive to win validation and attention from others; the narcissism of Fours is expressed indirectly, in self-absorption and in the enormous significance Fours attribute to their every feeling. This state of mind can lead to crippling self-consciousness.

Carol, a serious spiritual seeker, has wrestled with these feelings for many years.

> I have suffered greatly in my life from self-consciousness and a shrinking from extending myself to people I don't know or feel comfortable with. I have needed to feel their acceptance before I could really relax and be myself. This is something I strive to push beyond now that I have more self-awareness, but it can still be a struggle. I may find myself suddenly separating myself from a group and then feeling left out.

Fours become so focused on their fragile feelings that they feel completely justified in demanding support for all of their emotional needs. At the same time, they can be surprisingly unaware of the feelings of others. They talk endlessly about every detail of their feelings, dreams, and problems but are often uninterested in learning about the feelings and problems of others; indeed, self-absorbed Fours often have difficulty focusing on anything that does not connect directly with their immediate emotional concerns. They feel that their own sufferings are enough for them to bear.

A sure sign that Fours are becoming self-absorbed is the tendency to continually dwell in unpleasant moods. They tend to parade their hurt feelings (sulking or moping about in various ways) in search of sympathy, acutely feeling shortchanged by life, especially by their parents or by those who are currently dealing with them. No one, it seems to Fours, is giving them their due or recognizing their special state, needs, or suffering. No one understands their depth or sensitivity. They tend, therefore, to wallow in feeling sorry for themselves, which increases their fear of being incapable of getting their lives off the ground.

Once stuck in their moods and reactions, average Fours typically withdraw from others to protect themselves from further self-exposure and from running the risk of humiliation, rejection, and abandonment. But by withholding themselves, they have fewer reality checks, and it becomes increasingly difficult for them to ask others what they think of their emotional reactions. Further, those few people with whom they are willing to communicate are almost never the same people with whom they have grievances or emotional problems.

"Every man supposes himself not to be fully understood or appreciated."

RALPH WALDO EMERSON

> ## WHY WITHHOLD YOURSELF?
>
> Notice when and how you withdraw from people and events, making yourself an outsider when you do not have to be, not participating in social and interpersonal events when you could.
>
> Can you distinguish when this is a legitimate choice arrived at with equanimity and when it is an emotionally charged reaction that is probably the result of an old childhood issue?
>
> Can you stay with your reaction long enough (without acting it out) to see what is at the root of it?

Investment in "Having Problems" and Being Temperamental

As strange as it seems, Fours actually become unconsciously attached to having difficulties. In the average-to-unhealthy range, they can be extremely reluctant to let go of their painful feelings and self-pity, even though they cause them continual suffering.

The roots of this, however, are not difficult to understand. As children, Fours learned to get attention in their family by having emotional problems or by being temperamental and sullen. Many Fours learn that they can be reassured of others' love for them by being difficult and seeing if others will make the effort to respond to them. Rather than throw a tantrum, however, Fours more often pout and refuse to speak for several days, or refuse to go on a family vacation, or dress entirely in black for a week. Sulking lets everyone know that they are unhappy about something, without their having to tell anyone what it is. Indeed, Fours themselves may not know, since they are often overcome by dark and troubling moods seemingly out of the blue. They are often so identified with these moods that they feel they must attend to them before they can do anything else. Unfortunately, they also expect others to attend to them before doing anything else.

William, a talented musician and Internet Web site designer, comments on the emotional storminess that has created difficulty in his career and relationships.

> I rarely have a sense of self that is stable. I spend a great deal of time trying to get emotionally balanced. To be out of balance emotionally is a major source of suffering. Whatever emotional need I am feeling, the desire for contact with others or depression must be dealt with right away and can't be set aside. I like being a Four, but I find it's a high-maintenance situation.

Presenting themselves as needy, however, also enables Fours to get the attention of someone who is willing to be their rescuer, someone to attend to practical affairs so that they will have the time and space to discover themselves. Unfortunately, this only takes them away from a sense of personal responsibility and from the kinds of experiences that might give them a real sense of their value and identity. It is easy to see that this pattern also has its roots in childhood.

William continues:

"Everyone lets me down."

> As a young child, I remember lying on a blanket in my room pretending to be asleep in the hope that my parents would open the door and find me. My fantasy was that they would find me so adorable that they would give me their love. I longed for emotional contact; it is my food. I always knew I was loved by my parents but rarely felt that they could mirror the deepest, most vulnerable parts of me.

Average Fours drive people away with their withdrawals and stormy emotionalism, and yet they demand attention through these very same behaviors. In various ways, they insist on certain rules of engagement, forcing others to walk on eggshells around them. ("You better not bring that up. We don't want to upset Melissa again.") Their dramatic demand to be alone is itself a bid for attention and an invitation to seek them out. Withdrawing Fours secretly hope that someone will follow them into their lair of loneliness.

THE COST OF DRAMA

Many Fours get into a pattern of having stormy conflicts with people and then reconnecting with them by making up. Notice your tendency to create drama in your principal relationships. What are you really frustrated about? What behavior are you trying to elicit from the other person? How close have you come to truly alienating people you love with this pattern?

REACTING TO STRESS: FOUR GOES TO TWO

▲

As we have seen, Fours tend to lose themselves in romantic fantasies and to withdraw from people both for attention and to protect their feelings. The shift to Two represents a Four's effort to compensate for the problems that these behaviors inevitably create. Thus, after a period of withdrawal and self-absorption, Fours may go to Two and unconsciously try to solve their interpersonal problems with a slightly forced friendliness—they try a little too hard. Like Twos, they begin to worry about their relationships and seek ways to get closer to the people they like. They need a great deal of reassurance that the relationship is on solid ground. To this end, they frequently express their affections to the other and remind him or her of how meaningful their relationship is.

In more extreme cases, Fours may precipitate emotional scenes to see if others really care about them. This kind of behavior often wears others down, causing them to lose interest in or even to leave the Four, which inevitably triggers the Four's abandonment issues. Fours may then go to Two and try to hold on to people by clinging. Also, like average Twos, Fours may feel that it is unsafe to express the extent of their neediness and may begin to conceal their problems by focusing on the problems of others. ("I'm here to help *you*.")

Fours will eventually need increasing emotional and financial support to continue their unrealistic lifestyle. They fear that without such support, they might lose the ability to actualize their dreams. To prevent this, Fours under stress begin to exaggerate their importance in others' lives. They remind others of the many benefits that they have derived from their association with the Four, take credit for others' happiness, and find little ways to increase people's dependency on them. They try to create needs to fulfill and become increasingly jealous and possessive of the people they care about. Like Twos, Fours under stress may also compulsively seek credit for whatever they have accomplished while complaining about how unappreciated they are.

THE RED FLAG: THE FOUR IN TROUBLE

▲

If Fours have suffered a serious crisis without adequate support or coping skills, or if they have suffered from chronic abuse in childhood, they may cross the shock point into the unhealthy aspects of their type. This may lead them to a fearful recognition that their fantasies and emotional indulgences are causing them to ruin their lives and to waste their opportunities.

If Fours can recognize the truth in these fears, they may begin to turn their lives around and move toward health and liberation. On the

---

WARNING SIGNS

POTENTIAL PATHOLOGY: Severe depression, Narcissistic Personality Disorder, Avoidant Personality Disorder, crimes of passion—murder and suicide

▸ An oppressive sense of alienation from self and others

▸ Extreme emotional volatility and touchiness (*not* a manic reaction)

▸ Dependency on one or two others, with unstable relationships

▸ Outbursts of rage, hostility, and hatred

▸ Chronic, long-term depression and hopelessness

▸ Episodes of self-sabotage and rejecting positive influences

▸ Obsessions with death, morbidity, and self-hatred

other hand, they may try even harder to hold on to their fantasies and illusions about themselves and attempt to reject anyone or anything that does not support their emotional demands. ("They are all so crude and selfish—none of them understand me." "I know I need to find a job, but I'm just not up to it.") If Fours persist in this attitude, they may cross into the unhealthy range. If you or someone you know is exhibiting the warning signs (page 199) for an extended period of time—more than two or three weeks—getting counseling, therapy, or other support is highly advisable.

PRACTICES THAT HELP FOURS DEVELOP

▲

▶ Remember the adage that "feelings aren't facts." Your feelings may be powerful and may, at times, offer important insights into your own character. However, they do not necessarily provide accurate information about the motivations or feelings of others. Many of our emotional reactions to people are heavily influenced by earlier relationships in our childhood, no matter what type we are. Be especially suspicious of "reading" any apparently negative intentions or comments by others about you.

▶ Emotional volatility and moodiness are not the same as real sensitivity. Further, they are a fairly good indication that our heart is closed down. The deeper qualities of the heart are more subtle and are not reactions to the actions of others or to our environment. Our emotional reactions often prevent us from being affected by our experiences on a deeper level. Ironically, they indicate a fear or unwillingness to explore the deeper, truer feelings that our situation may be triggering in us.

▶ Recognize the aspects of your Fantasy Self that are not in alignment with the reality of your life. Having creative goals is wonderful. Procrastinating because you feel that your "genius" is insufficiently recognized, or because you do not have the particular tools you need, or because it is easier to daydream about your talents, is self-defeating. Similarly, learn to accept and appreciate your genuine talents and not to reject them because some other ability seems more glamorous or desirable. This is envy at its most self-destructive.

▶ Seek out truthful friends who will mirror you honestly and accurately. Find people who can see your genuine good qualities and talents and support you in their development—as well as speak compassionately, but directly, to you about your blind spots. Fours, like most people, benefit from reality checks, especially when it comes to their feelings about themselves and their romantic interests.

▶ Beware of unconsciously expecting friends and intimates to be a dumping ground for your emotional upheavals. People who care about you want to be there in any way they can, but you cannot *demand* that they parent you or that they take on the brunt of your childhood issues. Remember that these people have problems, too, and they may not always be able to handle your intense reactions.

▶ Set up positive, constructive routines for yourself. Fours tend to wait for inspiration to strike, but inspiration has a better chance of getting through to you if your daily schedule and living space are arranged in ways that support your creativity, your physical and emotional health, and above all your active engagement with the world. In your case, a little structure can go a long way in freeing up your creativity.

BUILDING ON THE FOUR'S STRENGTHS

▲

Fours are the deep-sea divers of the psyche: they delve into the inner world of the human soul and return to the surface, reporting on what they have found. They are able to communicate subtle truths about the human condition in ways that are profound, beautiful, and affecting. In a fundamental way, Fours remind us of our deepest humanity—that which is most personal, hidden, and precious about us but which is, paradoxically, also the most universal.

Because of their attunement to their inner states—to their subconscious feelings and impulses—Fours are usually highly intuitive, an attitude that feeds their self-discovery and creativity. Although they may have intellectual gifts, they tend to rely primarily on what their intuitions are telling them about themselves and their environment from moment to moment. Often Fours are not sure how they are able to arrive at their insights; they find the inner workings of their consciousness mysterious and surprising.

Carol, who earlier discussed the limitations of her self-consciousness, here relates the gift of her intuition.

> I feel things without always being aware of what I am feeling. For example, I may get an uneasy feeling inside in certain situations and not know what is causing it. Over the years, I have learned to pay attention to that feeling. . . . At my best, I am highly intuitive. I know things without knowing how. I sit bolt upright in the middle of the night and *know* the answer to a dilemma. At those times there is absolutely no doubt in my mind, even when I would have preferred a different answer.

At the same time, healthy Fours do not take themselves too seriously. They have a subtle sense of humor, often expressed in irony, that sees their own foibles with grace and lightheartedness. Their eloquence of expression and sense of humor can be powerful assets, both in working with others and in healing themselves.

"I've got to be me."

Fours are not the only type to be creative, since any of the Enneagram types can be creative. However, Fours have a particular kind of creativity, a personal creativity, which is fundamentally autobiographical. The creativity of Fours is generally an exploration of their history and feeling world, and particularly of how their family, their loves, and various incidents from the past have affected them. This is why so many playwrights, poets, and novelists are Fours.

Riva shares her excitement about her insights into the human condition and the joy of finding ways to express those insights.

> At my best I have an ability to soar. I can see broad vistas and synthesize different levels and can communicate what I see in poetic and precise language that sweeps other people along and enables them to see it, too. I have an ability to see deep underlying principles, universal truths, and subtle nuances of experiences and communicate them clearly and powerfully. At my best I am anchored in spiritual awareness and can be a source for others of wisdom and healing. At my best, I can express the ineffable.

Healthy Fours receive the mirroring they seek by sharing the depths of their souls. As they do this, they discover with relief that their own nature is, at root, no different from anyone else's. Their connection with their inner life is not a source of alienation but a way of reaching out to and constructively engaging with others.

THE PATH OF INTEGRATION: FOUR GOES TO ONE

▲

Healthy Fours engage with reality through meaningful action. By committing themselves to principles and activities beyond the realm of their subjective reactions, Fours discover not only who they are but that who they are is good. They come more into contact with the immediacy of their instincts and become less entranced by the emotionally charged scenarios that play out in their minds.

Fours at One also realize that self-expression does not mean indulging in their moods. They willingly become self-disciplined, working consistently to contribute something worthwhile to their world. No longer aloof bystanders waiting to be recognized, they participate fully in life and develop a stronger sense of themselves through their work and through their connections with others.

This should not be confused, however, with adopting the critical or perfectionistic traits of the average One. Fours' superegos are already punitive enough, so browbeating themselves with self-improvement projects can easily lead to further self-recrimination. Therefore it is important to develop another healthy One trait—discrimination. Fours learn what healthy Ones know: that the reality of a situation and our emotional responses to it are two different things.

Healthy Ones also exemplify acceptance of reality—working with the real components of a situation rather than resisting or rejecting them. Integrating Fours also understand that acceptance is the key to letting go of their past and creatively engaging with their lives in the present. With self-acceptance comes forgiveness for old mistakes and difficulties. With acceptance of others comes the ability to engage in mutually satisfying relationships. Fours no longer need to idealize others as rescuers or tear them off their pedestals for failing to live up to their unrealistic expectations. They see the other as other and can more accurately perceive their own valuable qualities without resorting to a Fantasy Self.

Finally, integrating Fours are able to build a lasting, genuine sense of identity and self-esteem because it is based on real-life actions and relationships rather than on their imagination or transient emotional states. They recognize qualities in themselves that were previously invisible: strength, willpower, determination, and clarity. Further, once Fours ground themselves in the moment, all aspects of life become occasions for creativity. Rather than being drawn into endless introspection or the turbulent stream of their emotional reactions, integrating Fours stay present to themselves and the world around them and thus begin to awaken to the deeper truths of the human heart. As they allow this process to unfold, their true identity reveals itself in every moment of their existence.

TRANSFORMING PERSONALITY INTO ESSENCE

▲

In the process of transformation, Fours let go of a particular self-image—that they are more inherently flawed than others, and that they are missing something that others have. They also realize that there is nothing wrong with them; they are as good as anyone else. And if there is nothing wrong with them, then no one needs to rescue them. They are entirely able to show up for themselves and create their own lives. Fours discover that their true self is most evident when they are not doing anything to create or sustain it. In other words, "being themselves" does not require any particular effort.

At this stage, Fours no longer *need* to feel different or special, seeing that, indeed, the universe has created only one of them, and that they are part of everything else—not isolated and alone. Life is no longer a burden, something to be endured. They also feel, perhaps for the first time, grateful for all of their past pain and suffering because in their own way these things have allowed them to become the people that they now are. "Who they are" still remains a mystery, perhaps a bigger mystery than ever. But rather than cling to any preconceived notion of their identity, liberated Fours allow themselves to be open to the moment and to experience the renewal of the self that the moment brings.

King is a therapist who, through years of inner work, has come to recognize the richness of his own inner nature.

> At my best, I'm fully alive. I have joy and energy and am connected meaningfully to others and life. I am solid! I express what I am feeling rather than ruminate alone about it. I am fueled by the discipline of accomplishing what I know needs to be done and not finding "reasons" for why I should not have to produce like everyone else. I am creative and imaginative, capable of finding hidden structures, patterns, and meaning in all of life's challenges. I am free!

"It is true of us all, whatever our work, that we are artists so long as we are alive to the concreteness of the moment and do not use it to some other purpose."

M. C. RICHARDS

Once liberated from their Basic Fear, Fours become a work of art and no longer need art as a substitute for the beauty that they find in abundance in themselves. Because they are aware of their Essential self and liberated from enmeshment with their emotional reactions, they can be more profoundly in touch with the ever-changing nature of reality and are inspired and delighted by it.

Diane, an engineer, beautifully describes this feeling of connectedness.

> At my best, I'm unself-conscious and spontaneous. Instead of being continually distracted by the minutiae of my internal states, I'm free to pay attention to the world and to the people around me. It's a wonderfully liberating experience to let go of the usual obsessive process of self-monitoring, self-analysis, and self-inhibition. Then it's as if time slows down, and the world leaps into my awareness in all its richness and subtlety. Things around me look different—more three-dimensional, detailed, and vivid. I'm able to focus intently and effortlessly on other people, to resonate with their emotional states, to listen to their stories, without getting caught up in my own.

THE EMERGENCE OF ESSENCE

Type Four reveals to us the fundamental truth that *our true self is not a thing with fixed attributes, it is an ever-transforming, ever-renewing process.* The manifestations of our true nature are constantly arising and transforming into something else just as marvelous and unexpected, like a magical kaleidoscope. Fours' spiritual work lies in not making the kaleidoscopic self into a snapshot, framed and hung on a wall. Thus, Fours discover that who they really are is a flow of experience that is much more beautiful, rich, and satisfying than anything they could come up with in their imaginations.

The experience of intimate contact with this flow opens us up to deeper contact with others and with more subtle aspects of spiritual reality. This contact always feels personal—precious and of the moment. In a sense, Fours help us recognize the unity of the personal self and other, more universal aspects of our true nature.

Thus, the Four's special Essential quality is the embodiment of the *personal* element of the Divine. That which is eternal in us experiences the world through our personal experience. A fundamental aspect of our souls is *impressionability*—the ability to be touched and to grow from experience. When we are open and present, our hearts are affected and transformed by our experiences. Indeed, every time we allow ourselves to be truly touched by life, we are changed in profound ways. And ultimately, is not this the aim of all creative self-expression—to touch and transform the human heart?

When Fours abide in their true nature, they are one with the ceaseless creativity and transformation that are part of the dynamics of Essence. At their core, Fours represent creation, the constant outflowing of the manifest, changing universe in the eternal now. It is the most profound gift of Fours to be a symbol of this and to remind the other types that they, too, participate in Divine creativity.

Add your scores for the fifteen statements for Type Four. Your result will be between 15 and 75. The following guidelines may help you discover or confirm your personality type.

▶ 15 You are probably not a withdrawn type (not a Four, Five, or Nine).

▶ 15–30 You are probably not a Type Four.

▶ 30–45 You most probably have Four-issues or a Type Four parent.

▶ 45–60 You most likely have a Four-component.

▶ 60–75 You are most likely a Four (but could still be another type if you are thinking too narrowly about Type Four).

Fours are most likely to misidentify themselves as Twos, Ones, or Nines. Ones, Sixes, and Fives are most likely to misidentify themselves as Fours.

CHAPTER II

TYPE FIVE:
THE INVESTIGATOR

▲

THE THINKER

THE INNOVATOR

THE OBSERVER

THE SPECIALIST

THE RADICAL

THE EXPERT

"The first act of insight is to throw away the labels."

—EUDORA WELTY

"Physical concepts are free creations of the human mind, and are not, however it may seem, uniquely determined by the external world."

—ALBERT EINSTEIN

"To be master of any branch of knowledge, you must master those which lie next to it; and thus to know anything you must know all."

—OLIVER WENDELL HOLMES

"Since we cannot be universal and know all that is to be known of everything, we ought to know a little about everything."

—PASCAL

_____ 1. I like to get into things in depth and pore over details until I've figured something out as completely as possible.

_____ 2. I am an extremely private person who doesn't let many people into my world.

_____ 3. I do not feel very big or powerful—more small and invisible: I'd make a good spy!

_____ 4. Other people would think I'm crazy if they knew what I was thinking most of the time.

_____ 5. Only by getting accurate information can you make a rational decision—but then, most people aren't really rational.

_____ 6. My family thinks that I am somewhat strange or eccentric—they've certainly told me that I need to get out more.

_____ 7. I can talk a blue streak when I want to; most of the time, though, I prefer to just watch all the craziness around me.

_____ 8. If you need a problem solved, let me work on it by myself, and I'll come up with the answer.

_____ 9. When you really think about it, you can't get much stranger than so-called normal behavior.

_____ 10. I tend to take a long time fine-tuning projects I'm working on.

_____ 11. Most people are so incredibly ignorant, it's amazing that anything works at all!

_____ 12. I know a lot about a lot of things, and in a few areas, I consider myself an expert.

_____ 13. I am extremely curious and enjoy investigating why things are the way they are—even obvious things are not really so obvious when you really look at them.

_____ 14. My mind is so intense and active that I often feel like it's on fire.

_____ 15. Often I lose all track of time because I'm concentrating so completely on what I'm doing.

Score each of the following statements according to how true or applicable to you it is on the following scale:

1.......*Not at All True*

2.......*Seldom True*

3.......*Somewhat True*

4.......*Generally True*

5.......*Very True*

See page 232 for scoring key.

PERSONALITY TYPE FIVE: THE INVESTIGATOR

▶ **BASIC FEAR:** Of being helpless, useless, incapable (overwhelmed)

▶ **BASIC DESIRE:** To be capable and competent

▶ **SUPEREGO MESSAGE:** "You are good or okay if you have mastered something."

The Intense, Cerebral Type:
Perceptive, Innovative, Secretive, and Isolated

We have named personality type Five *the Investigator* because, more than any other type, Fives want to find out why things are the way they are. They want to understand how the world works, whether it is the cosmos, the microscopic world, the animal, vegetable, or mineral kingdom—or the inner world of their imaginations. They are always searching, asking questions, and delving into things in depth. They do not accept received opinions and doctrines, feeling a strong need to test the truth of most assumptions for themselves.

John, a graphic artist, describes this approach to life.

> Being a Five means always needing to learn, to take in information about the world. A day without learning is like a day without sunshine. As a Five, I want to have an understanding of life. I like having a theoretical explanation about why things happen as they do. This understanding makes me feel in charge and in control. I most often learn from a distance as an observer and not as a participant. Sometimes it seems that understanding life is as good as living it. It is a difficult journey to learn that life must be lived and not just studied.

Behind Fives' relentless pursuit of knowledge are deep insecurities about their ability to function successfully in the world. *Fives feel that they do not have an ability to do things as well as others.* But rather than engage directly with activities that might bolster their confidence, Fives "take a step back" into their minds where they feel more capable. Their belief is that from the safety of their minds, they will eventually figure out how to do things—and one day rejoin the world.

"What's going on here?"

Fives spend a lot of time observing and contemplating—listening to the sounds of the wind or a synthesizer, or taking notes on the activities in an anthill in their backyard. As they immerse themselves in their observations, they begin to internalize their knowledge and gain a feeling of self-confidence. They may also stumble across exciting new information or make new creative combinations (playing a piece of music based on recordings of wind and water). When they get verification of their observations, or see that others understand their work, it is a confirmation of their competency, and this fulfills their Basic Desire. ("You know what you are talking about.")

Knowledge, understanding, and insight are thus highly valued by

Fives, because their identity is built around having ideas and being someone who has something unusual and insightful to say. For this reason, Fives are not interested in exploring what is already familiar and well established; rather, their attention is drawn to the unusual, the overlooked, the secret, the occult, the bizarre, the fantastic, the unthinkable. Investigating unknown territory—knowing something that others do not know, or creating something that no one has ever experienced—allows Fives to have a niche for themselves that no one else occupies. They believe that developing this niche is the best way that they can attain independence and confidence.

Thus, for their own security and self-esteem, Fives need to have at least one area in which they have a degree of expertise that will allow them to feel capable and connected with the world. Fives think, "I am going to find something that I can do really well, and then I will be able to meet the challenges of life. But I can't have other things distracting me or getting in the way." They therefore develop an intense focus on whatever they can master and feel secure about. It may be the world of mathematics, or the world of rock and roll, or classical music, or car mechanics, or horror and science fiction, or a world entirely created in their imagination. Not all Fives are scholars or Ph.D.'s. But, depending on their intelligence and the resources available to them, they focus intensely on mastering something that has captured their interest.

For better or worse, the areas that Fives explore do not depend on social validation; indeed, if others agree with their ideas too readily, Fives tend to fear that their ideas might be too conventional. History is full of famous Fives who overturned accepted ways of understanding or doing things (Darwin, Einstein, Nietzsche). Many more Fives, however, have become lost in the byzantine complexities of their own thought processes, becoming merely eccentric and socially isolated.

The intense focus of Fives can thus lead to remarkable discoveries and innovations, but when the personality is more fixated, it can also create self-defeating problems. This is because their focus of attention unwittingly serves to distract them from their most pressing practical problems. Whatever the sources of their anxieties may be—relationships, lack of physical strength, inability to gain employment, and so forth—average Fives tend not to deal with these issues. Rather, they find something else to do that will make them feel more competent. The irony is that no matter what degree of mastery they develop in their area of expertise, this cannot solve their more basic insecurities about functioning in the world. For example, as a marine biologist, a Five could learn everything there is to know about a type of shellfish, but if her fear is that she is never going to be able to run her own household adequately, she will not have solved her underlying anxiety.

"What if we try it another way?"

Dealing directly with physical matters can feel extremely daunting for Fives. Lloyd is a life scientist working in a major medical research lab.

> Since I was a child, I have shied away from sports and strenuous physical activity whenever possible. I was never able to climb the ropes in gym class, stopped participating in sports as soon as it was feasible, and the smell of a gymnasium still makes me uncomfortable. At the same time, I have always had a very active mental life. I learned to read at the age of three, and in school I was always one of the smartest kids in academic subjects.

Thus, much of their time gets spent collecting and developing ideas and skills they believe will make them feel confident and prepared. It is as if they want to retain everything that they have learned and carry it around in their heads. The problem is that while they are engrossed in this process, they are not interacting with others or even increasing many other practical and social skills. They devote more and more time to collecting and attending to their collections, less to anything related to their real needs.

Thus, the challenge to Fives is to understand that they can pursue whatever questions or problems spark their imaginations *and* maintain relationships, take proper care of themselves, and do all of the things that are the hallmarks of a healthy life.

THE CHILDHOOD PATTERN

Please note that the childhood pattern we are describing here does not cause the personality type. Rather, it describes tendencies that we observe in early childhood that have a major impact on the type's adult relationships.

Fives often report that as children, they did not feel safe in their families; they felt in danger of being overwhelmed by their parents, and so they started looking for a way that they could feel secure and confident. First, they retreated from the family into their own private space—mentally, physically, and emotionally. Second, they turned their attention away from their personal and emotional needs onto something "objective."

Young Fives typically spend long periods on their own; they are quiet children who shy away from playing with others, instead occupying their minds and imaginations with books, practicing a musical instrument or playing with a computer, collecting insects or plants, or playing with board games or chemistry sets. It is common to find young Fives who are exceptionally advanced in some areas (such as spelling or mathematics) but who are unwilling to even try other basic activities (such as riding a bike or going fishing). Others in the family, especially anxious parents who want their Five child to be more "normal," will typically try to pressure them into joining in social activities. These efforts usually meet with intense resistance.

Although brilliant, Michael was isolated as a child and in many ways penalized for his intellectual gifts, even by his own parents.

> As a child I had allergies and many respiratory infections that kept me home from school a lot before age eight. As a result, I had a lot of time to sit around and read and spent less time playing with other kids. My coordination was not good, and I didn't want to do what most of the others wanted to do anyway. So I became known as the nerdy bookworm with a runny nose.

While Fives' imaginations can be a source of creativity and self-esteem, living there almost exclusively fuels their anxieties about themselves and the world. It is not simply that young Fives see the world around them with startling clarity, they also elaborate on it in their minds—a faculty that will have profound repercussions later on, for better or worse.

Mason, an architect and community planner, recalls the difficult events that eventually led to his retreat into the mind.

> I was the youngest child of five children with a blind father and a loving mother who was too busy providing for her kids and husband to spend any time with me. I had a jealous older sister who continually told me that I was a mistake, that nobody wanted or loved me, and that I should just die or go away. I lived my life as though that was true and had ambivalent relationships with my parents and siblings. I just hunkered down and created my own world of reality and fantasized myself as the leader in my own made-up world.

Thus, Fives do not expect anything from others, except to be left alone to pursue their own interests unimpeded by anyone else's demands or needs, especially their emotional needs. It is as if they were saying, "I won't ask much from you if you don't ask much from me." Independence—or perhaps more accurately, *nonintrusion*—is therefore sought by Fives as a way of attaining safety and the feeling that they have control of their lives.

Not being intruded on also allows Fives the time to develop something "to bring to the table" when they eventually do feel ready to connect with others. For example, they may learn the piano principally because they enjoy it and it gives them time alone; it also bolsters their self-esteem and provides a niche for them in the family. Music is a potential bridge to others, but it is also a way of disappearing: rather than talk with anyone, they can play the piano for them.

Fives are psychologically stuck in the separation phase of childhood—the period around two to three-and-a-half years old—when children are learning to operate independently of their mothers. For whatever reasons, young Fives felt that the only way to become independent was *to make themselves not want nurturing and emotional connection with their mothers.* Thus, at an early age, Fives learned to cut off from painful feelings of need and longing by staying in their minds.

Lloyd speculates on what caused his sense of detachment.

> I have felt disconnected from my mother since before I can remember. Her heart was broken at least twice before I was born: she married a man who was unable to consummate their relationship and blamed this on her appearance or lack of appeal; it later turned out that he was gay and trying to "act straight." After she married my father (who was very safe, trustworthy, and unadventurous), they had a son who died three days after birth. Two years and two miscarriages later, I was born. I think my mother was unable to fully give her heart to me after all that.

Learning to cut themselves off from nurturance—even from desiring it—becomes a way of defending themselves against further hurts and frustrations. This becomes significant for adult Fives and explains their reluctance to become more emotionally engaged with others. To leave the safety of their minds, to reoccupy the body and feelings, is to reexperience the primal frustration and anguish of their infant selves. Such feelings completely overwhelm a Five's capacity to focus their mind—their basis of self-confidence—and are therefore powerfully defended against. Even to want something ordinary too much could upset their inner security; thus adult Fives go through life avoiding the things they most want, repressing their longing and finding substitute pleasures in their interests, hobbies, and creativity.

THE WING SUBTYPES

▲

THE FIVE WITH A FOUR-WING: THE ICONOCLAST

Healthy   Curiosity and perceptiveness combine in this subtype with the desire to express a unique, personal vision. These people are more emotional, introspective, and creative than Fives with a Six-wing. They seek a niche that has not been explored by others—something that can truly be their own. Not scientifically oriented, they are often creative loners, mixing passion and detachment. They are whimsical and inventive: their tinkering with familiar forms can lead to startling innovations. Often drawn to the arts, they use the imagination more than the analytic, systematic parts of their minds.

Average Although primarily identified with their minds, people of this subtype struggle with intense feelings that can create difficulties in sustaining efforts and in working with others. They are more independent than the other subtype and resist having structures imposed on them. Their interests tend toward the surreal and fantastic rather than the rational or the romantic: they can easily get lost in their own cerebral landscapes. They often have difficulty staying grounded and can become impractical in the pursuit of their interests. They can be attracted to dark, forbidden subject matter or to the disturbing or grotesque.

THE FIVE WITH A SIX-WING: THE PROBLEM-SOLVER

Healthy Observation combined with organization and detail gives people of this subtype the ability to draw meaningful conclusions from miscellaneous facts and to make predictions based on those conclusions. They seek a niche that will provide security and that fits into a larger context. They are often drawn to technical subjects: engineering, science, and philosophy, as well as inventing and repair work. They can be cooperative, disciplined, and persistent and are more interested in practical matters than the other subtype. They can combine a talent for innovation with business savvy, sometimes with highly lucrative results.

Average Perhaps the most purely intellectual of all of the subtypes, these people are interested in theories, technology, and acquiring facts and details. Analysts and catalogers of the environment, they enjoy dissecting the components of a problem to discover how it works. Extremely restrained and private about their feelings, their attention is more directed at things than at people, although Fives with a Six-wing identify strongly with key people in their lives. Not particularly introspective, they prefer to observe and understand the world around them. They can be more argumentative than the other subtype and more defensive in their views. They tend to be aggressive and to actively antagonize people who disagree with them.

THE SELF-PRESERVATION INSTINCT IN THE FIVE

Isolation and Hoarding. In the average range, Self-Preservation Fives attempt to gain independence and separation by reducing their needs. They are highly conscious of their energy expenditures, considering what activities and pursuits they will take on, and questioning whether they will have sufficient internal resources to meet them. If not, activities will be dropped. Self-Preservation Fives also conserve their energy and resources in order to avoid needing others too much,

THE INSTINCTUAL VARIANTS

▲

trying to take as little from the environment as possible. Thus, they can be very private and protective of their home and work space.

Self-Preservation Fives are the true loners of the Enneagram, loving solitude and generally avoiding social contact. They feel easily over-whelmed by people, especially in group settings. Although they can be friendly and talkative, they are slow to engage with others and often feel drained by social interactions. They then need time in their home space to recharge their batteries. They can be extremely resentful of having expectations placed on them. Often they will find ways to minimize their needs so that they can live on less money, thus avoiding interfer-ence with their independence and privacy. They are also the most emo-tionally detached variant of Type Five. While they can be warm with friends and intimates, they more generally tend to be emotionally dry and have great difficulty expressing their feelings for others.

In the unhealthy range, Self-Preservation Fives can become eccen-tric shut-ins, going to great lengths to avoid social contact. Isolation leads to distorted thinking and delusional ideas. They may exhibit paranoid tendencies, especially with the Six-wing.

THE SOCIAL INSTINCT IN THE FIVE

The Specialist. In the average range, Social Fives engage with others and find a social niche for themselves through their knowledge and skill. They like to see themselves as Masters of Wisdom and want to become indispensable through their particular field of expertise (the only person in the office who knows how to fix the computer, for ex-ample). The most intellectual type of Five, Social Fives are often drawn to academics, science, and other forms of guruhood. They play the so-cial role of the shaman, the wise person who lives at the edge of the tribe and brings back secret knowledge. Social Fives like to talk about weighty topics and complex theories, but they are generally uninter-ested in social banter. They interact with others by debating ideas, cri-tiquing society, and analyzing trends.

Less healthy Social Fives become unable to relate to others except through the role of their expertise. They use the information they have gathered as bargaining chips, as their way of wielding power. They can become socially ambitious in the sense of wanting to be part of the in-tellectual or artistic elite. They would prefer not to "waste their time" on those who cannot understand their work.

In the unhealthy range, Social Fives tend to express extreme and provocative views. They are often anarchistic and antisocial, heap-ing derision on the human race, seeing it as nothing more than a ship of fools. They can develop bizarre theories about society or reality but, unlike Self-Preservation Fives, are determined to propound them to others.

THE SEXUAL INSTINCT IN THE FIVE

"This Is My World."   In the average range, the detachment and avoidance characteristic of Fives clash with the Sexual Variant's desire for intense connection. Sexual Fives like sharing secret information with their intimates. ("I've never told anyone this.") But they are always experiencing some degree of tension between pursuing those they are attracted to and lacking confidence in their social skills. Thus Sexual Fives are driven to engage intensely with people, although often with anxiety and a tendency to withdraw at a moment's notice. They are more affable and talkative than the other two Instinctual Variants of Type Five, but they can cause others surprise and consternation when they unexpectedly drop out and disappear for periods of time. On the one hand, when romantically interested in someone, they can become extremely open and merged, more like Nines. On the other, when they feel unappreciated or misunderstood, they can quickly become emotionally distant. Powerful connections with others alternate with long periods of isolation.

The sexual instinct mixes with intellect to produce intense imagination. Sexual Fives create alternative realities—private "worlds" of various kinds—that they present to potential intimates. They are looking for the ideal mate, the mate for life, who will not be turned off by their strangeness. ("Does this intensity frighten you?") Strong sexuality gives Sexual Fives the impetus to risk emotional contact and also provides relief from their constant mental activity. It becomes a way to ground themselves. But in less healthy Fives, the mix of imagination and sexuality can become dark and fetishistic: they can become lost in disturbing fantasies and dreams.

In the unhealthy range, longing for lost love and feelings of rejection can lead Sexual Fives into isolation and self-destructive behavior. They are often drawn, through voyeurism, into dangerous lifestyles and can be attracted to society's underbelly.

Most Fives will encounter the following issues at some point in their lives. Noticing these patterns, "catching ourselves in the act," and simply seeing our underlying habitual responses to life will do much to release us from the negative aspects of our type.

THE FIVE'S CHALLENGES TO GROWTH

▲

H E A L T H Y	Level 1	*Key Terms:* *Participating* *Visionary*	Fives let go of the belief that they are separate from the environment—an outside observer—and are thus able to confidently engage in life. They also paradoxically achieve their Basic Desire—to be capable and competent and able to live in the world. They then become clear-minded, knowing, profound, and compassionate.	**T Y P E 5**
	Level 2	*Observant* *Perceptive*	Fives focus on the environment so they can feel confident to function in it and develop skills to defend against their Basic Fear. Self-image: "I am smart, curious, and independent."	
	Level 3	*Focused* *Innovative*	Fives reinforce their self-image by mastering a body of knowledge or skills that will make them competent and strong. Not wishing to compete with others, they prefer to explore new ideas and forms. Their "tinkering" can result in profoundly original ideas, inventions, and art.	**L E V E L S**
A V E R A G E	Level 4	*Conceptualizing* *Preparing*	Fives begin to fear that their skills are insufficient and that they need to prepare more before they can take their place in the world. They feel unsure of themselves in many areas, preferring to inhabit the safety of their minds. They study, practice, and collect more knowledge, resources, and skills.	**O F**
	Level 5	*Detached* *Preoccupied*	Fives worry that the needs of others will distract them from their projects, so they shut out "intrusions" by intensifying their mental activity. They minimize their needs, becoming high-strung, cerebral, and secretive. They spend more time alone, speculating and elaborating on alternative realities.	**D E**
	Level 6	*Extreme* *Provocative*	Fives fear that others will threaten the niche they have been creating, so they try to fend people off. They resent the apparent confidence and calm of others and enjoy subverting their beliefs. Their own ideas can be bizarre and disturbing, and they are scornful of those who cannot understand them.	**V E**
U N H E A L T H Y	Level 7	*Nihilistic* *Eccentric*	Unhealthy Fives fear that they are incapable of finding a place in the world, and this may be true. To gain some security, they cut off all connections with the world, retreating into an isolated and increasingly empty world. They reject all but the most basic needs but are still plagued by fears.	**L O P**
	Level 8	*Horrified* *Delirious*	Fives feel so small and helpless that almost everything becomes ominous to them. They are filled with dark fantasies and strange perceptions. They resist all help, shrinking away from people and into feverish nightmares and insomnia. They cannot stop their overheated minds.	**M E**
	Level 9	*Seeking* *Oblivion* *Self-* *Annihilating*	Feeling that they can no longer defend themselves from their pain and terror, unhealthy Fives want to escape from reality. In some cases, they attempt to accomplish this through psychotic breaks or schizoid withdrawal. They may also try to escape through suicide.	**N T**

THE WAKE-UP CALL FOR TYPE FIVE:
RETREATING INTO THEIR MINDS

Whenever Fives feel overwhelmed by people or circumstances, instantly and reflexively they detach from direct engagement with their senses and emotions and retreat into their minds. In effect, they are trying to find a safe vantage point from which they can more objectively assess their situation.

When Fives move into their heads in this way, *they cease connecting directly with their experience and instead become more engaged with their mental commentary on the experience.* They turn experiences into concepts and then see how those concepts fit in with their previous understanding of reality. For instance, a psychologist Five might be having a pleasant conversation with a friend and suddenly find himself considering the friend's thoughts and feelings in the light of a particular psychological structure rather than listening to her. Another Five might spend most of her vacation mentally taking notes on the place for a novel she is working on rather than relaxing and enjoying the trip.

RECONNECTING WITH THE WORLD

Look around the room you are now in, and in your Inner Work Journal list all of the things that you never noticed up to this point. See what you have missed or overlooked. How many new things, colors, irregularities, or features of the room can you now find? When we are present, we notice everything. But when we go into our heads, we do not notice much.

Whenever you are in a new place, you can practice this exercise. First, however, you must become present by sensing yourself and breathing. Then look at your world as if you have never seen it before. If you are a Five, you can use this exercise to reconnect with the world and "activate" your Wake-up Call; if you are not a Five, you will know better what it is like to be one.

Over time, the Five's mental associations, comments, and ideas begin to fit together into what we call the *Inner Tinker Toy.* This Tinker Toy can become the Five's dominant reality—the filter through which they experience the world. Increasingly, adding new ideas, reconstructing old ones, and attempting to see how different parts of this mental structure might fit together become the main pastimes of Fives. Since they are successful at coming up with new ideas all the time, this becomes a powerful way to prop up their self-esteem and to defend the self. But moving their attention more completely into the Inner Tinker Toy causes Fives to abstract and conceptualize the world rather than experience it directly, and this inevitably leads to a loss of contact with Essential guidance. Simply put, playing with ideas gives Fives a temporary sense of confidence but not a solution to their real problems in the real world.

The Social Role: The Expert

As Fives become more insecure, they find it more and more difficult to relate to other people except through the role of being an Expert. Because of their Basic Fear (of being helpless, powerless, and incapable), they want to feel more self-confident and carve out a niche for themselves. They do this by knowing information that no one else in their circle knows (such as the fine points of chess or the more arcane aspects of astrology—or the Enneagram, for that matter). They may also carve out an area of creativity that is uniquely their own.

Knowing a great deal about chess, however, is not sufficient if others in their circle learn as much; average Fives must either surpass everyone else in their understanding of the game or find another game to play: perhaps an obscure game played by the Incas, or a fiendishly complicated computer game.

While Fives are spending more time in their chosen pursuit, they are also aware of the many areas of life that they have not mastered. Being a brilliant physicist or a masterful writer of horror novels cannot entirely compensate for being unable to cook or drive a car or successfully engage in a relationship. Physical activities and athletics are typically a source of shame for Fives, a reminder of something they were not able to master. Social activities and other aspects of relationships may also get short shrift. A Five might have gone out on a few dates, but if she got hurt in some way by the experience, it might be years before she risks dating again. If this pattern continues, the Five's world shrinks down to very few activities that feel safe to them.

WHAT WILL REALLY BUILD CONFIDENCE?

Notice your dependency on certain areas of interest. How does this area of expertise make you feel about yourself? How does it feel to relate to others without discussing your areas of expertise? Are there other areas of your life that you are neglecting that cause you shame or anxiety? Are you focusing on your niche to the exclusion of developing some of these other areas?

Avarice and Feeling Small

The Passion of the Five (their "Capital Sin") is *avarice,* a particular emotional distortion resulting from their feeling that they are small and incapable of defending themselves in the world. Fear makes Fives shrink inward, and avarice makes them try to hoard whatever minimal resources they have at their disposal. Fives feel as though there is not much of them to go around, and that the needs of others can easily·deplete or exhaust them.

Actually, Fives are among the least materialistic of the types and are happy with very few creature comforts. They are avaricious, however, about their time, energy, and resources. They are greedy for knowledge and for the means of improving their skills and expertise. Furthermore, because Fives feel that they must spend most of their time developing their ideas and interests, they do not want anyone to take too much of their time or attention. Because they feel incapable and helpless, they believe that they must gather and hold on to all of those things that will make them capable and secure. They may collect back issues of newspapers or magazines, or compile extensive notes and books on the few areas that interest them, or collect records and CDs until their house is overflowing.

Fives often feel crowded and overwhelmed by the expectations of others. Further, since Fives feel easily intruded upon, they learn to protect themselves by emotionally withdrawing from people.

Mark is a computer specialist with an engaging sense of humor and a touching sincerity. He has been happily married for years, but still struggles with these issues.

> My mother had two sons before I came along, one born with facial skin problems and the other accidentally killed as a pre-teen. When I was born, there was a sense that I had to be overly protected and cared for. Unfortunately, nothing was mine alone. My parents had to know where I was, what I was doing, what I was getting into, everything that was in my room, etc. I learned early on to retreat and withdraw into my mind. There I found the freedom from intrusiveness that was part of my daily life. No one could enter there unless I allowed it—and that never happened. In my early teens, I began to outwardly resist by becoming more aloof, secretive, and emotionally cool. To this day, I remain emotionally distant from my parents, as well as others.

Inability to Bring Closure: Preparation Mode

Average Fives often get locked into what we call *preparation mode.* They gather more and more information, or endlessly practice, never feeling that they are prepared enough to move into action. Fine-tuning and analysis bog them down in details so that they cannot see the forest for the trees. They never feel quite ready to put themselves on the line, like a painter who keeps painting but hesitates to exhibit, or the student who pursues one degree after another but does not want to graduate.

Fives are not necessarily conscious of their underlying anxiety. More often they simply feel that they are not finished with their

"Filling up the hard disk."

"I need more time."

project and require more space and time to fine-tune it. Since so much of their self-esteem rides on their projects, Fives are deeply anxious that their work will be rejected or invalidated by others. But always feeling that they need to prepare more can cause Fives to get stuck for many years. They may awaken one day to realize that they have not lived a life—they have been preparing for one.

Basically, Fives get paralyzed by a recurring superego message that says, "You are good or okay if you have mastered something." But how much knowledge do they need? Who or what lets them know that they have attained mastery and can now move into action? How is mastery sustained?

Morgan recognizes the high cost of this pattern in his life.

> I struggled for many years as a songwriter, and in retrospect, I realize that a lot of people thought my songs were pretty good. But I was never convinced of it. I would toy with them endlessly. This sound wasn't interesting enough or the bridge was too corny or that verse sounded like someone else. Worse, I would not write songs at all and spend my days "doing research," listening to other music for inspiration and understanding. Even when I was involved with other musicians who could have really helped me present my music, I was always very hesitant to play it for them, or to ask them to perform it. I tried to feel better about it by telling myself that I was becoming a better musician in the process and that one day I'd be really good. I wasted many years that way.

BRINGING YOUR IDEAS TO FRUITION

You are most effective when you stop refining concepts and actually get into action. Whenever possible, find people that you can share your ideas with. A group of creative or intellectual peers who are interested in your work can help you to keep things moving. Also, although you are not keen on collaboration, it can be very useful in keeping you from collapsing into preparation mode.

Detachment and Withdrawal

Fives are the most independent and idiosyncratic of the personality types, the ones who could most appropriately be called loners and even misfits. This does not mean that Fives always want to be alone, or that they cannot be excellent company when they are with others. When Fives find someone whose intelligence and interest they respect, they are invariably talkative and sociable because they enjoy sharing their insights and discoveries with anyone who appreciates what they have to say. Their willingness to share their knowledge, however, is not the same as sharing information about themselves.

Unlike Fours, who long to be accepted while feeling like outsiders, Fives are not consciously anguished about not connecting with people. They are resigned about it and focus their attention elsewhere, feeling that their isolation is inevitable—just the way life is. (Tim Burton's movie *Edward Scissorhands* perfectly describes the inner emotional life of a Five.) Their emotional needs and desires are deeply repressed. Beneath their defenses, this causes Fives pain, of course, but they are able to disconnect from their feelings about their loneliness so they can function.

Richard, a successful businessman, traces his emotional reserve back to his childhood.

> I believe that much of my detached personality can be attributed to my lack of relationship with either my father, who was away in the military much of the early part of my life, or my mother, who was more interested in her social life than the needs of her fourth child. The family story was that I was "an accident," and my mother had already done "mom" things with my three older siblings. So I learned to fend for myself very early on and got pretty good at being scarce and not being noticed.

Fives, like Nines, have trouble maintaining their sense of self and their own needs when in relationship with others. Unlike Nines, however, Fives attempt to regain their priorities and sense of self by avoiding people. Being in the company of others obscures their mental clarity and feels like a strain—even if they are enjoying themselves. For these reasons, average Fives come to see most personal interactions as draining. They feel that others want a response from them that they are unable to give.

Mark is quite candid on this topic.

> Sometimes it is just difficult dealing with people, and it always is dealing with people who have expectations. Much to the unnerving of my wife, having to speak, act, dress, behave, and react in an appropriate manner (that is, having to meet social expectations) has never been a strong point of mine. It takes effort to attain social acceptance, to which I wonder, "Why try?"

Fives may actually have a very deep reservoir of feelings, but they are buried underground and are purposely left untapped. In fact, Fives avoid many relationships so that these feelings will not overwhelm them. *Most Fives will also shun those who are trying to help them.* (To be rescued is to have their helplessness and incompetence emphasized, reinforcing their Basic Fear.) This is especially true if the rescuer shows

---

THE ROOTS OF ISOLATION

In your Inner Work Journal, record your observations about isolation. What kinds of situations cause you to detach emotionally? What are your attitudes about people at such times? About social life? About yourself? Can you recall any incidences from your childhood that you feel reinforced this tendency in you? Did you feel engulfed by others' needs or intruded upon? The next time you are with people, see if you can catch yourself emotionally detaching or feeling isolated. What would it take to be in relationship with others and not lose your own sense of purpose?

---

any hint of having an ulterior motive or is in any way manipulative: Fives feel incapable of handling their own needs, let alone the unacknowledged needs of someone else.

Minimizing Needs: Becoming a "Disembodied Mind"

"I don't need much, but I need my space."

The types of the Thinking Triad attempt to make up for the loss of inner guidance by developing *strategies*. The Five's strategy is to get through life by not asking much of it, while hoping that in return others will not ask much of them. (Unconsciously, they often feel that they do not have much to offer others.) They attempt to maintain their independence by *minimizing their needs*. Their personal comforts can be simple to the point of being primitive. They live like "disembodied minds," preoccupied with their theories and visions.

Morgan, the songwriter, speaks candidly about his type's minimalism.

> I lived in my apartment for several months before I got a futon, and before that I slept on an air mattress or just on the floor. I had almost no furniture for years, other than the shelves I had gathered to keep my books and LPs. I think other people felt sorry for me, so they would bring me beat-up old hand-me-down furniture, which I was happy to accept. Nothing matched, but I didn't care. I was living in my head—my apartment was just the place I ate and slept.

Average Fives can become absentminded and increasingly detached, not only from people but from their own bodies. They get high-strung and intense and start to ignore their own physical and emotional needs. They may work at their computer all night eating only candy bars and drinking soda; when they leave, they realize that they have forgotten where they put their keys or what they did with their eyeglasses. Their absentmindedness is not the same as the wool-gathering of Nines, but is the product of an increasing agitation and mental restlessness, a stream of nervous energy pouring into their minds.

STAYING GROUNDED

Fives need to get into their bodies. Yoga, martial arts, working out, running, sports, or just a good brisk walk can all help Fives to reconnect with their physical and emotional presence. Pick one activity that you can commit to on a regular basis. In your Inner Work Journal, write down your chosen activity. Also write a commitment to how many times a week you will engage in your physical activity, sign it, and return to it. Leave some space to write further comments on your experience with your commitment and about what takes place in you as you get more grounded. What feelings arise when you don't keep your commitment? What happens to your sense of yourself when you do your activity? How does it affect your thinking?

Fives at this stage are also highly secretive about their activities. They might seem friendly and conversational with friends or loved ones while harboring whole areas of their lives of which their intimates are completely ignorant. By compartmentalizing their relationships, minimizing their needs, and keeping some of their activities secret, Fives hope to maintain their independence and continue their projects undisturbed.

Getting Lost in Speculation and Alternative Realities

Having created an inner world to which they can retreat from the insecurities of their outer life, average Fives tend to become preoccupied with it. They speculate on various possible ideas, filling out the details of complex fantasy worlds, or developing clever and convincing theories because their thinking is more aimed at keeping their practical and emotional problems at bay than at really attempting to explore or create.

Insofar as Fives have been wounded in their ability to feel strong and capable, they need to spend time engaging in fantasies of power and control. They may gravitate to computer and board games based on themes of conquest, battling monsters, world domination, and techno-erotic elements of sadism and power.

"What if? . . ."

Jeff is a software designer who knows this territory well.

I used to play these very complicated strategy board games. They have them on all kinds of themes, although most of them are about different battles or wars. It would take me days to figure out the rules, and then most of the time, I couldn't find anyone else who was interested in playing them. Sometimes I would play them myself! And when computer versions came out—oh boy! Then I didn't have to depend on anyone. These games take many hours to play, but the appeal of them is in the detail and the feeling of really winning a battle or building a city or whatever. You come away from them fantasizing about your troops marching in and conquering the enemy. I was hooked on playing them until I realized how much time they took, and how much better off I'd be if I applied that energy and strategy to my own real life.

Unhealthy Fives can get trapped in bizarre "realities" entirely of their own making, like dreamers caught in nightmares from which they cannot awaken.

BALANCING THE INNER AND OUTER WORLDS

Fantasizing, theorizing, and speculating can all be enjoyable pastimes, but learn to honestly assess when you are using them to avoid more troubling issues in your real life. How many hours of your day are spent in these pursuits? What might you do with your time if you cut back your investment in these cerebral activities?

Unconscious Anxieties and Terrifying Thoughts

As strange as it might sound, Fives think a lot about the things that they find the most frightening. They may even make a career out of studying or creating works of art out of things that scare them. A Five afraid of diseases might become a pathologist; another Five who suffered from "monsters under the bed" in childhood may grow up to be a science fiction or horror writer or film director.

Now a psychological writer, Rich remembers how he overcame some of his earliest terrors.

Before I was even in kindergarten, some older kids took me with them to see a Saturday afternoon matinee. The movie was about Vikings and was very bloody, at least for a kid my age. I came home really shaken up. I was terrified at the sight of blood and had a lot of nightmares about it. But after that, I wanted to go to every scary movie that came out. Monsters, dinosaurs, aliens, and mass destruction were my favorite topics. I couldn't get enough of it.

Fives try to control fear by focusing their thoughts on the frightening thing itself, not on their feelings about it. But they cannot wholly avoid the emotional impact of these ideas—with the result that they both consciously and unconsciously fill their minds with disturbing images. Over time, their split-off feelings can begin to come back to haunt them in their dreams and fantasies and in other unexpected ways.

This is particularly distressing to them, because average Fives believe that their own thoughts are the only aspect of reality that can be completely trusted. To have their own thoughts seem out of control or frightening causes them to cut off from more activities that might trigger fearful associations. If they once enjoyed astronomy, for example, they might begin to be afraid to go outside at night: the emptiness of the sky completely unsettles them.

Jane, an art director who also sculpts, vividly recounts such an experience.

> When I was about seven years old, I got very interested in studying the human body. I loved to read about the internal organs and look at the transparencies of them in our family encyclopedia. I also started reading books and articles about health and disease. I remember one summer day reading an article about cancer caused by smoking in the *Reader's Digest*. It described people on a cancer ward with tracheotomies, iron lungs, and other forms of radical surgery. I was stunned. Suddenly, at age seven, I understood what death was, and it was not the way my parents had described it. I couldn't stop thinking about it. I grew sullen and stopped eating. Everyone was going to die. I stayed up at night wondering what death was like and if there really was a God. I must say, the more I thought about it, the more skeptical I was. I even went around looking at dead animals. This went on for several years. I guess I just got used to it after a while.

STARING INTO THE ABYSS

Observe your attraction to the "dark side" of life. While this orientation may be useful in understanding this aspect of human existence, beware of a tendency to become obsessed with such matters. Notice how these interests affect your sleep habits. Many Fives also find it helpful to investigate possible traumas in their childhood or infancy. These traumatic events often lead to a compulsive interest in disturbing subjects. Is your interest in these topics harming your ability to function in the world?

Argumentativeness, Nihilism, and Extremism

Every type has aggressions. Because their own ideas are virtually the only source of security Fives have, they propound and defend them with passion—even though they may not actually even believe the position they are taking themselves.

Low-average Fives are antagonistic toward anyone or anything that

"I can't believe what idiots people are."

interferes with their inner world and personal vision. They are offended by others' apparent peace of mind, and they enjoy subverting and undermining people's beliefs. They may affront, provoke, or shock others with intentionally extreme views. Such Fives want to scare people off so that they can be left alone to pursue their interests, and so that they can feel intellectually superior by rejecting the "stupidity" and "blindness" of others. No longer careful thinkers, they jump to conclusions and impose their own extreme interpretations of the facts. If others disagree, Fives can turn nasty and caustic. If this behavior continues, they may well succeed in driving everyone out of their lives.

If Fives are unable to find a niche for themselves, they can quickly fall into a cynical apathy, losing faith in themselves and in the entire human condition. Of all types, Fives are the most prone to feelings of meaninglessness, and many Fives become deeply skeptical about the existence of benevolent forces in the universe.

UNSETTLING OTHERS

When you find yourself getting into debates with people or otherwise worked up, notice what you are feeling in your body. How important is it to make the point you are driving home? What effect are you trying to produce in the other? What motives or beliefs are you ascribing to them? What are you afraid of?

REACTING TO STRESS: FIVE GOES TO SEVEN

▲

Fives attempt to cope with stress by becoming increasingly narrow in their focus and by retreating into the sanctuary of their thoughts. When this method of coping fails to allay their anxiety, they may go to Seven, reacting against their isolation by impulsively throwing themselves into activities. They become restless and agitated—their minds speed up and they feel compelled to distract themselves from their growing fears. Further, anxiety about finding a niche may cause them to become scattered in their pursuits. Like average Sevens, they bounce from activity to activity, from idea to idea, but seem unable to find or connect with anything that satisfies them.

After cutting off from their needs, especially sensory and nurturing needs, Fives going to Seven act out by searching indiscriminately for stimulation and experience. Generally, these diversions have little to do with their professional projects—they may immerse themselves in movies, or in drinking or drug binges, or sexual escapades. They may start to secretly frequent bars, swinger clubs, or stranger, more unusual "scenes" that would come as a surprise to others who believe they know them—if others ever found out.

Under extreme stress, Fives defend against their anxieties by becoming aggressive and insensitive in their pursuit of whatever they feel they want at the time—like less healthy Sevens. They may also take solace in substance abuse of various kinds.

If Fives are overstressed for an extended period of time, if they have suffered a serious crisis without adequate support or coping skills, or if they have suffered from chronic abuse in childhood, they may cross the shock point into the unhealthy aspects of their type. This may lead them to a fearful recognition that the projects they have been pursuing and the lifestyle that they have created are actually ruining their chances of finding a real niche for themselves.

If Fives can recognize the truth in these fears, they may begin to turn their life around and move toward health and liberation. On the other hand, they may attempt to cut off all connection with others, essentially turning their backs on the world in order to further isolate themselves from "intrusions" so that they can follow their train of thought to a "logical conclusion"—usually a dark and self-destructive one. ("To hell with everyone! No one's going to hurt me anymore!") Of course, such a retreat can only undermine whatever shreds of confidence Fives still possess. If Fives persist in this attitude, they may cross into the unhealthy Levels. If you or someone you know is exhibiting the following warning signs for an extended period of time—more than a few weeks—getting counseling, therapy, or other support is highly advisable.

WARNING SIGNS

POTENTIAL PATHOLOGY: Schizoid, Schizotypal, and Avoidant Personality Disorders, psychotic breaks, dissociation, depression, and suicide.

▸ Increasing tendency to isolate themselves

▸ Chronic physical neglect, letting themselves go

▸ Chronic and severe insomnia, nightmares, and sleep disorders

▸ Increasing eccentricity—loss of interest in social skills

▸ Refusing help, or even being hostile to it

▸ Distorted perceptions, hallucinations

▸ Talk of suicide

▸ Remember that your mind is clearest and most powerful when it is quiet. Take the time to cultivate this quiet in yourself, and do not confuse it with an insistence that your external world be silent. Rather, learn to notice your nonstop internal commentary on all of your experiences. What arises when you simply take in an impression of the moment without connecting it with what you think you already know? Being connected with your physical sensations will greatly help you quiet your mind.

▶ Use your body! Of all of the types, you probably feel you could almost do without your body, and it is easy for you to spend many hours at the computer or reading or listening to music. While there is nothing wrong with any of these activities, your balance requires more physical activity. Try running, yoga, dancing, martial arts, working out, even taking a walk. When your body is awake and your blood is flowing, your mind is much sharper and you have more internal resources.

▶ Make the effort to reach out to others, especially when you are feeling vulnerable and afraid. As a Five, you have been conditioned not to expect support from anyone, even to be suspicious of help. But this belief is probably not applicable to your current situation, and you can use your intelligence to figure out who will be stable and there for you when you are having troubles. Speak up. Make your needs known, and you may be surprised. Your tendency to isolate usually only gets you deeper into your own trap.

▶ Think carefully about what areas are most debilitating to your self-confidence. Learning more about world geography will not help you if you feel physically weak, but working out and exercising will. Composing another song will not do much for you if you are really worried about meeting people. You can continue working on whatever projects interest you, but it can be very powerful to explore more directly some of the areas of your life that you have cut off.

▶ Risk feeling your grief. Most Fives split off their awareness from their pains and hurts, especially from feelings of rejection. You know what it is like when those feelings are closer to the surface. Don't swallow them. In a safe and appropriate place, allow yourself to sense your heart and the feelings that are locked there. This can be even more powerful if you can do it with a witness: a friend, your therapist, or anyone that you trust. Ask the person not to give you pep talks but simply to be there as a witness to your pain and struggles.

▶ As you become more balanced and grounded in your body, let your impressions of others and of the world around you affect you— let the world in. You will not lose yourself, you will gain the world. This will give you the sense of confidence and well-being that you have been seeking—and it will give you many new insights in the process. Just remember not to get lost in pondering the insights, and to return to planet earth. Remember, *this is your life:* you are not an abstraction, and your presence here can and does matter.

The Five's main gifts to the world involve their tremendous *insight and understanding,* coupled with some area of expertise. Understanding allows healthy Fives to comprehend many points of view at the same time, to understand both the whole and its component parts. Healthy Fives can entertain many different perspectives without being attached to any of them. They are able to determine which way of looking at a problem will be the most useful in any given set of circumstances.

Fives are extraordinarily observant and perceptive. They are sensitive to their environment and perceive subtle changes or discrepancies that others would likely overlook. Many Fives seem to have one or two of their senses developed to an unusual degree. One Five might have unusual visual acuity with regard to color, while another Five might really be tuned in to sounds, recognizing rhythms and pitches easily.

Fives do not lose their childhood curiosity: they keep asking questions, such as, "Why is the sky blue?" or "Why do things fall down and not up?" Fives do not take anything for granted—if they want to know what is under a rock, they get a spade, dig out the rock, and take a good look. Fives also seem to have an extraordinary ability to concentrate and to focus their attention, and they can do so for long periods of time. Further, they are extremely patient in the course of exploring whatever has captivated them. Focus and patience give them the ability to stay with projects long enough to mine gold from them.

Because of their curiosity and open-mindedness, healthy Fives are highly innovative and inventive. The ability to explore and play with ideas can produce valuable, practical, and original works and discoveries— from paradigms in science or medicine, to startling new achievements in the arts, to finding a new way to store old boxes in the garage. Not satisfied with the sound of a cello, a Five might record the cello and play the tape backward while altering the tone of the recording. Fives who are scientifically oriented make discoveries precisely because they become interested in the *exceptions to the rules.* They focus on the areas where the rules break down or on minor inconsistencies that seem unimportant to others.

Fives enjoy sharing their findings with others, and they often serve up their observations of life's contradictions with a whimsical sense of humor. They are endlessly amused—and horrified—by the unfolding strangeness of life, and they communicate this to others by changing the picture ever so slightly to expose previously invisible absurdities. They enjoy tinkering with things, which can take expression in dark humor, puns, and wordplay. There is a mischievous, sprightly, elfin quality to them. They like to provoke people into thinking more deeply about life and humor often serves as an excellent way of communicating ideas that would otherwise be too threatening.

BUILDING ON THE FIVE'S STRENGTHS

▲

"If you love it enough, anything will talk with you."

GEORGE WASHINGTON CARVER

THE PATH OF INTEGRATION: FIVE GOES TO EIGHT

▲

Fives actualize themselves and remain healthy by learning to reclaim and occupy their physical presence and their instinctual energy in the manner of healthy Eights. This is because the basis of confidence, the feeling of being full, strong, and capable, arises from the instinctual energy of the body, not from mental structures. Thus, integrating Fives grow by coming down out of their heads, and coming into deeper felt contact with their vitality and physicality.

Moving into greater contact with the life of the body usually brings up intense anxiety for Fives. They feel as if they are going to lose their only defense: the sanctuary of their mind. The mind feels safe, reliable, and impregnable; the body feels weak, vulnerable, and unreliable. Further, deeper contact with the body begins to allow powerful feelings of grief and sorrow over Fives' long isolation to come into awareness. Yet only by staying grounded in the body can they feel the inner support to process these long-suppressed feelings.

As they learn to stay with their instinctual energies, Fives begin to participate more fully in their worlds and to apply their knowledge and skill to immediate practical problems. Rather than evading responsibility by retreating from others, integrating Fives feel empowered to take on major challenges and often assume leadership roles. Others intuitively sense that Fives are seeking positive solutions without self-interest and therefore rally to support them in their projects. By joining the real world, Fives do not lose their mental abilities or the expertise they cultivated in isolation; rather, they harness those gifts strategically and constructively like high-functioning Eights.

Fives will not benefit much, however, by attempting to imitate the qualities of average Eights. Focusing on self-protection, cutting off from their vulnerability, and seeing relationships as confrontations will do little to help Fives overcome their detachment and feelings of social isolation. But as Fives begin to directly experience and work through their identifications with their minds, the strength, willpower, and confidence that are the assets of the healthy Eight naturally come into play.

TRANSFORMING PERSONALITY INTO ESSENCE

▲

When we are really present to life, when we are relaxed and engaged in our bodies, we begin to experience an inner knowing or guidance. We are led toward exactly what we need to know and our choices come from this inner wisdom. But when we lose the ground of Presence out of which this Essential guidance emerges, the personality takes over and tries to figure out what to do.

The "wrong turn" that Fives make is to *become identified with their observations of their experiences rather than their experiences themselves.* Fives are the kind of people who try to learn how to dance by watching people dancing from the sidelines. ("Let's see, she made two steps left, then a kick and a kind of twirl. Then he sort of flips her back. . . .") Eventually they might learn the dance, but by the time they figure it out, the dance will be over.

Naturally, Fives face the same dilemma in their entire lives: they try to figure out how to live life without actually living it. When they are present and grounded, however, Fives are able to know exactly what they need to know, when they need to know it. The answer to a question arises not from a chattering brain but from a clear mind that is attuned to reality. Insight arises spontaneously as it is called forth by individual circumstances. Real inner guidance and support can thus be regained if Fives let go of a particular self-image—that they are separate from the environment, mere flies on the wall—and begin to become engaged with reality. Liberated Fives know that they do not have to be afraid of reality because they are part of it.

Further, there is a new immediacy to their perceptions, and they are able to comprehend their experiences without the usual mental commentary. They are awed by the majesty of reality, clear-minded and trusting of the universe. Einstein once said, "The only question worth asking is, 'Is the universe friendly?' " Liberated Fives have an answer to that question. They are enraptured by what they see rather than scared to death, and they become truly visionary, potentially bringing revolutionary change to their field of endeavor.

THE EMERGENCE OF ESSENCE

The Fives drive for knowledge and mastery is the personality's attempt to re-create an Essence quality that we might call *clarity* or *inner knowing*. With clarity comes the Essential quality of nonattachment, which is not emotional repression or detachment but the lack of identification with any particular point of view. Fives understand that any position or idea is useful only in a very limited set of circumstances, perhaps only in the unique set of circumstances in which it arose. Inner guidance allows them to flow from one way of seeing things to another without getting fixated on any of them.

Liberated Fives remember the spaciousness and clarity of the Divine Mind, what the Buddhists call "the shining Void," or Sunyata, the quiet, undisturbed vastness from which everything arises, including all knowledge and creativity. They long to return to an experience of the Void because it was once their home, as it was (from the Buddhist perspective) the origin of everyone and everything in the world. This longing to return to the Void must be understood properly, however, since it is not the emptiness of oblivion, but the "emptiness" of a glass of pure water or of a perfect blue sky: everything else is possible because of their emptiness. In this state, they are liberated

"At the back of our brains, so to speak, there [is] a forgotten blaze or burst of astonishment at our own existence. The object of the artistic and spiritual life [is] to dig for this submerged sunrise of wonder."

G. K. CHESTERTON

from the belief that they are cut off from everyone and everything, and instead, they directly experience their underlying connection with everything around them.

Further, this emptiness and nonattachment does not mean that Fives are removed from their feelings. On the contrary, they can be deeply touched by a sunset or the feeling of a breeze, or by the beauty of a human face. They are free to feel and experience everything while recognizing that everything they behold is temporary—a fleeting gift from a universe of infinite bounty. Seeing more profoundly into the truth of the human condition, they feel great compassion for the suffering of others and are willing to share not only the riches of their minds but also the depths of their own hearts.

Add your scores for the fifteen statements for Type Five. Your result will be between 15 and 75. The following guidelines may help you discover or confirm your personality type.

▶ 15   You are probably not a withdrawn type (Four, Five, or Nine).

▶ 15–30   You are probably not a Type Five.

▶ 30–45   You most probably have Five-issues or a Type Five parent.

▶ 45–60   You most likely have a Five-component.

▶ 60–75   You are most likely a Five (but could still be another type if you are thinking too narrowly about Type Five).

Fives are most likely to misidentify themselves as Fours, Sixes, or Ones. Nines, Threes, and Ones are most likely to misidentify themselves as Fives.

▼

CHAPTER 12

TYPE SIX:
THE LOYALIST

▲

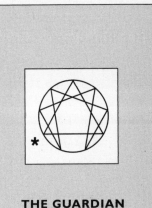

THE GUARDIAN

THE TRUE BELIEVER

THE DOUBTER

THE TROUBLESHOOTER

THE TRADITIONALIST

THE STALWART

"Our imagination and reasoning powers facilitate anxiety; the anxious feeling is precipitated not by an absolute impending threat—such as the worry about an examination, a speech, travel—but rather by the symbolic and often unconscious representations."

—WILLARD GAYLIN

"No man ever quite believes in another man. One may believe in an idea absolutely, but not in a man."

—H. L. MENCKEN

"A man who doesn't trust himself can never really trust anyone else."

—CARDINAL DE RETZ

"Only in growth, reform, and change, paradoxically enough, is true security to be found."

—ANNE MORROW LINDBERGH

Type Attitude Sorter

Score each of the following statements according to how true or applicable to you it is on the following scale:

1.......*Not at All True*

2........*Seldom True*

3.......*Somewhat True*

4.......*Generally True*

5.......*Very True*

See page 259 for scoring key.

_____ 1. I am attracted to authority but distrustful of it at the same time.

_____ 2. I am very emotional, although I don't often show what I feel—except to those I'm close with—and even then, not always.

_____ 3. If I make a mistake, I fear that everyone is going to jump down my throat.

_____ 4. I feel more secure doing what's expected of me than striking out on my own.

_____ 5. I may not always agree with the rules—and I don't always follow them—but I want to know what they are!

_____ 6. I tend to have strong first impressions about people that are difficult to change.

_____ 7. There are a few people I really look up to—they are sort of my heroes.

_____ 8. I don't like making big decisions, but I certainly don't want anyone else to make them for me!

_____ 9. Some people see me as jittery and nervous—but they don't know the half of it!

_____10. I know how much *I* mess up, so being suspicious of what others are up to just makes sense to me.

_____11. I want to trust people, but often find myself questioning their motives.

_____12. I am a real hard worker: I keep plodding along until the job gets done.

_____13. I sound out the opinions of people I trust before I have to make a big decision.

_____14. It's really weird: I can be skeptical, even cynical, about all kinds of things, and then turn around and fall for something hook, line, and sinker.

_____15. *Anxiety* seems to be my middle name.

PERSONALITY TYPE SIX: THE LOYALIST

The Committed, Security-Oriented Type:
Engaging, Responsible, Anxious, and Suspicious

We have named personality type Six *the Loyalist* because, of all the personality types, Sixes are the most loyal to their friends and to their beliefs. They will go down with the ship and hang on to relationships of all kinds far longer than most other types. Sixes are also loyal to ideas, systems, and beliefs—even to the belief that all ideas or authorities should be questioned or defied. Indeed, not all Sixes go along with the status quo: their beliefs may be rebellious and antiauthoritarian, even revolutionary. In any case, they will typically fight for their beliefs more fiercely than they will fight for themselves, and they will defend their community or family more tenaciously than they will defend themselves.

The reason Sixes are so loyal to others is that they do not want to be abandoned and left without support—their Basic Fear. Thus, the central issue for Type Six is a failure of self-confidence. Sixes come to believe that they do not possess the internal resources to handle life's challenges and vagaries alone and so increasingly rely on structures, allies, beliefs, and supports outside themselves for guidance. If suitable structures do not exist, they will help create and maintain them.

Sixes are the primary type in the Thinking Triad, meaning that they have the most trouble contacting their own inner guidance. As a result, *they do not have confidence in their own minds and judgments.* This does not mean that they do not think. On the contrary, they think—and worry—a lot! They also tend to fear making important decisions, although at the same time, they resist having anyone else make decisions for them. They want to avoid being controlled but are also afraid of taking responsibility in a way that might put them in the line of fire. (The old Japanese adage, "The blade of grass that grows too high gets chopped off," relates to this idea.)

Sixes are always aware of their anxieties and are always looking for ways to construct "social security" bulwarks against them. If Sixes feel that they have sufficient backup, they can move forward with some degree of confidence. But if that crumbles, they become anxious and self-doubting, reawakening their Basic Fear. ("I'm on my own! What am I going to do now?") A good question for Sixes might therefore be: "When will I know that I have enough security?" Or to get right to the heart of it, "What is security?" Without Essential inner guidance and the deep sense of support that it brings, Sixes are constantly struggling to find firm ground.

Sixes attempt to build a network of trust over a background of unsteadiness and fear. They are often filled with a nameless anxiety and

▶ BASIC FEAR: Of having no support and guidance, of being unable to survive on their own

▶ BASIC DESIRE: To find security and support

▶ SUPEREGO MESSAGE: "You are good or okay if you do what is expected of you."

then try to find or create reasons why. Wanting to feel that there is something solid and clear-cut in their lives, they can become attached to explanations or positions that seem to explain their situation. Because "belief" (trust, faith, convictions, positions) is difficult for Sixes to achieve, and because it is so important to their sense of stability, once they establish a trustworthy belief, they do not easily question it, nor do they want others to do so. The same is true for individuals in a Six's life: once Sixes feel they can trust someone, they go to great lengths to maintain connections with the person who acts as a sounding board, a mentor, or a regulator for the Six's emotional reactions and behavior. They therefore do everything in their power to keep their affiliation going. ("If I don't trust myself, then I have to find something in this world I *can* trust.")

Although intelligent and accomplished, Connie still has to wrestle with the self-doubt of her type.

> As my anxiety has come under control, so has my need to check out everything with my friends. I used to have to get the nod of approval from several hundred (just joking!) "authorities." About nearly every decision would involve a council of my friends. I usually would do this one-on-one: "What do you think, Mary? If I do this, then that might happen. Please make up my mind for me!" . . . Recently, I've narrowed my authorities to just one or two trusted friends, and on occasion, I've actually made up my own mind!

Until they can get in touch with their own inner guidance, Sixes are like a Ping-Pong ball that is constantly shuttling back and forth between whatever influence is hitting the hardest in any given moment. Because of this reactivity, no matter what we say about Sixes, *the opposite is often also as true.* They are both strong and weak, fearful and courageous, trusting and distrusting, defenders and provokers, sweet and sour, aggressive and passive, bullies and weaklings, on the defensive and on the offensive, thinkers and doers, group people and soloists, believers and doubters, cooperative and obstructionistic, tender and mean, generous and petty—and on and on. It is the contradictory picture that is the characteristic "fingerprint" of Sixes, the fact that they are a bundle of opposites.

The biggest problem for Sixes is that they try to build safety in the environment without resolving their own emotional insecurities. When they learn to face their anxieties, however, Sixes understand that although the world is always changing and is by nature uncertain, they can be serene and courageous in any circumstance. And they can attain the greatest gift of all, a sense of peace with themselves despite the uncertainties of life.

THE CHILDHOOD PATTERN

The Basic Fear of Sixes (of being without support or guidance and of being unable to survive on their own) is a very real and universal fear of every child. A small infant cannot live without Mommy and Daddy; the child is absolutely dependent on them. Clear memories of the terror behind this dependency are repressed in most people. But sometimes they are intense enough to break through, as in the case of Ralph, a consultant in his fifties.

> I remember waking up in my crib and standing up and holding on to the side of it. I heard my parents laughing and talking with the neighbors while they played cards in the living room. I would hear the click of the cards as they were being dealt around the table. I called several times for my mother to come up to my darkened bedroom. Each time my fear increased. In desperation I then called several times for my father. No one came up to see what I wanted, and I finally went to sleep. Until I was eleven years old, I would not let my parents out of my sight if we were more than ten miles from home. I was afraid they would abandon me.

At a certain point in their development, however, toddlers do a remarkable thing. Despite their tremendous dependency, they begin to move away from their mothers, to assert their independence and autonomy; in child psychology, this is called the *separation phase.*

One of the most important ingredients that helps the child find the courage to separate from the mother is the presence of the father-figure. (This is not always the biological father, although it often is. It is the person who provides discipline, structure, and authority in the family.) If the father-figure is present in a strong and consistent way, he provides the guidance and support for the child's bid for independence. He teaches the child about the ways of the world—what is safe and what is not—and mirrors the child's own Essential inner guidance and support. Of course, for most of us, this process has gone somewhat less than perfectly, resulting in our insecurities as adults. But while everyone experiences this to some extent, Sixes are particularly fixated on it.

Further, if the Six child perceives that the father's support for independence is insufficient, he may feel in danger of being overwhelmed by the mother and all she represents to him. This heightens the child's need to keep up his guard and leads to Type Six's deep ambivalence and anxiety about trust, nurturance, and closeness. Thus, Sixes long for approval and closeness but feel the need to defend against it at the same time. They want to be supported but not overwhelmed.

Please note that the childhood pattern we are describing here does not cause the personality type. Rather, it describes tendencies that we observe in early childhood that have a major impact on the type's adult relationships.

Joseph, a journalist in his forties, has explored some of these issues in therapy.

> I had a very powerful, controlling, somewhat dazzling mother. She was capable of withdrawing her love at a moment's notice, angrily, and often inexplicably. It was a highly conditional love, and depended above all on absolute loyalty—to her values, beliefs, and judgments, no matter how erratic and off the wall they might be. I often felt that it was my role to confront my mother—to fight for my own survival. The problem was that my approach was negative: I resisted her and survived but never felt confident that I had prevailed. It was never going to be possible to both win the approval of others (most notably my mother) while also maintaining my independence and developing my own sense of self.

To resolve this dilemma, Sixes try to form an alliance with the father-figure. But this usually leads to ambivalence—the father-figure/authority seems either too strict and controlling, or too unsupportive and uninterested. Many Sixes end up in an uneasy compromise: they offer outward obedience yet retain a feeling of independence through inward rebellion and cynicism, as well as large and small acts of passive-aggression.

THE WING SUBTYPES

▲

Examples

Robert Kennedy
Malcolm X
Tom Clancy
Bruce Springsteen
Michelle Pfeiffer
Diane Keaton
Gloria Steinem
Candice Bergen
Mel Gibson
Janet Reno
Richard Nixon

THE SIX WITH A FIVE-WING: THE DEFENDER

Healthy   People of this subtype often excel at various kinds of technical expertise, making them outstanding practical problem-solvers, analysts, social commentators, teachers, and opinion leaders. They are attracted to systems of knowledge where the rules and parameters are well established, such as mathematics, law, and the sciences. They often have greater powers of concentration than the other subtype, although they can be narrower in their concerns. Political causes and community service are areas of interest, and they often serve as spokespeople or champions for disadvantaged groups or individuals.

Average   They are more independent and serious than the other subtype, and less likely to go to others for reassurance or advice. They are often loners. They get reassurance from systems and beliefs, while remaining skeptical. People of this subtype tend to see the world as dangerous, leading to partisan stances and reactionary positions. Secretiveness can fuel suspicion, and they usually see themselves as rebellious and antiauthoritarian, while ironically constantly being drawn to systems, alliances, and beliefs that contain strong authoritarian elements. Sixes with a Five-wing are reactive and aggressive, typically tending to blame or scapegoat perceived threats to their security.

THE SIX WITH A SEVEN-WING: THE BUDDY

Healthy Engaging and funny, people of this subtype are less serious than the other subtype—they tend to avoid "heavy" topics and restrict their focus to their security needs (taxes, bills, office politics, and the like). They are serious, however, about commitments and make sacrifices to ensure the safety and well-being of their family and friends. They also enjoy good company, kidding around, and emphasizing their connections with others. People of this subtype combine interpersonal qualities with energy, humor, and a zest for experience. They can also be self-deprecating, turning their fears into occasions for joking and bonding with others.

Average These people are eager to be liked and accepted, but they are also more hesitant to speak out about themselves or their problems. While sociable, they are also visibly insecure and depend on loved ones for reassurance and advice before coming to important decisions. They have problems with procrastination and initiating projects on their own. They tend to get into diversions and distractions to quiet that anxiety, including sports, shopping, and "hanging out" with others. Overeating, drinking, and substance abuse are possible. They are not particularly political but can be opinionated and vocal about their likes and dislikes. Anxiety about personal failings or important relationships can lead to depression.

Examples

Princess Diana
Tom Hanks
Meg Ryan
Julia Roberts
Jay Leno
Ellen DeGeneres
Gilda Radner
Katie Couric
Jack Lemmon
Rush Limbaugh
"George Costanza"

THE SELF-PRESERVATION INSTINCT IN THE SIX

Responsibility. In the average range, Self-Preservation Sixes attempt to allay their survival anxieties by working hard to build up security through mutual responsibility. They offer service and commitment with the expectation that it will be reciprocated by others. Although they seek secure partnerships, Self-Preservation Sixes tend to make friends slowly: they observe others over time to see if they are trustworthy and truly "on their side." They are more domestic than the other variants and are frequently concerned with maintaining the stability of their home life. They often take care of the security needs of the household: bills, taxes, insurance, and the like.

Self-Preservation Sixes do not easily disguise their anxiety and neediness. In fact, they may use it to gain allies and supporters—vulnerability can elicit help from others. They tend to fret about small things, which can lead to catastrophic thinking and worst-case scenarios. ("The rent is five days late? We're going to be evicted for sure!") Self-Preservation Sixes are usually frugal, and worry a great deal about financial matters. Conflicts with others over resources are common.

In the unhealthy range, Self-Preservation Sixes are extremely clingy, dependent, and panicky. They stay in punishing situations—bad marriages or overly stressful jobs—because they are terrified of being without support. They may grasp at relationships with such forceful anxiety that they end up alienating the very people they want to bond with. Paranoia may also drive them to become more aggressive: they exaggerate dangers and strike out at "enemies" to ensure that no one will be able to threaten them. Ironically, this often ends up destroying their own security systems.

THE
INSTINCTUAL
VARIANTS

▲

THE SOCIAL INSTINCT IN THE SIX

Generating Support.   In the average range, Social Sixes handle anxiety by looking to friends and allies for reassurance and support. They project friendliness and attempt to create bonds with others, disarming them with warmth and humor. They often make fun of themselves while offering support and affection to others, and they can sometimes be mistaken for Twos. Social Sixes are the most concerned about fitting in. ("There's safety in numbers.") They are fairly idealistic, enjoying the feeling of being part of something larger than themselves—a cause or corporation or movement or group—and are willing to make major sacrifices for the security of that affiliation.

Social Sixes can also sometimes resemble Ones in their adherence to protocols and procedures. They look for reassurance through commitments, obligations, and contracts—insurance that their hard work will not be taken advantage of. When they are more insecure, Social Sixes look for places of safety where like-minded individuals help each other out (twelve-step groups).

Although able to make major efforts for others or for their group, Social Sixes can often have difficulty working for their own success or development. Anxiety can lead them to look for consensus before they act or make decisions; anxiety also leads them to reference the potential responses of others in their imagination. Their own indecisiveness bothers them, however, and leads to ambivalence about depending on allies or authorities. They fear losing the support of the group or authority but chafe at the bit. If frustrated, they can develop passive-aggressive issues with authorities and friends. Under stress, they easily feel pressured, overworked, and underappreciated. At such times, they can be negative and pessimistic.

In the unhealthy range, Social Sixes may become attracted to fanatical beliefs, causes, and groups. They may develop an "us against the world" mentality, feeling besieged by a hostile environment (somewhat like an unhealthy Eight). They can be unquestioning of their beliefs (even if others find their beliefs to be questionable) and slavish to a particular authority while being extremely paranoid about authorities not in alignment with their own belief systems.

THE SEXUAL INSTINCT IN THE SIX

Symbols of Power and Connection.   In the average range, Sexual Sixes develop physical strength, power, and/or physical attractiveness to feel safe. More aggressive Sexual Sixes rely on strength and displays of toughness that can resemble Type Eight ("Don't mess with me"), while more phobic Sexual Sixes use their sexuality and coquettishness to disarm others and attract support in ways that can resemble Type Four. They mask their insecurities through open assertion and defiance of authority, or through flirtation and seduction.

Sexual Sixes are highly aware of their physical attributes—for instance, spending time in gyms—although not for health reasons but to enhance their strength and appeal. Sexual Sixes want to attract a powerful and capable mate, so they frequently test the other, both to see if they will stay with them, as well as to give themselves time to assess the other person's character and fortitude.

Sexual Sixes are more openly defiant of authority than the other Instinctual Variants of the Six, especially when anxious. They are also the most doubting of others and of themselves. They can have explosive emotional reactions when their own insecurities are exposed or their connections with others are threatened. When anxious, they may assert themselves against their own supporters or third parties rather than at the true source of their anxieties. Attempts at sabotaging others, or undermining their reputations in various ways, especially through rumor-mongering, are typical.

In the unhealthy range, Sexual Sixes can be depressive and erratic, especially if they feel that their reactivity has undermined or ruined their intimate connections. Impulsive, self-destructive behavior alternates with irrational lashing out. Paranoia may become part of the picture, although usually with a distinctly focused and obsessive flavor since it is aimed at particular, personal enemies.

Most Sixes will encounter the following issues at some point in their lives. Noticing these patterns, "catching ourselves in the act," and simply seeing our underlying habitual responses to life will do much to release us from the negative aspects of our type.

THE SIX'S CHALLENGES TO GROWTH

▲

H E A L T H Y	Level 1	*Key Terms:* **Self-Reliant Courageous**	Liberated Sixes let go of the belief that they must rely on someone or something outside themselves for support: they discover their own inner guidance. They also paradoxically achieve their Basic Desire—to find security and support, particularly in their own inner guidance. They then become truly secure with themselves, grounded, serene, and valiant.
	Level 2	*Engaging Reliable*	Sixes focus on the environment to find support and to alert themselves to dangers. They are friendly, trustworthy, and engaging, seeking to build connection and stability in their world. Self-image: "I am solid, attentive, and dependable."
	Level 3	*Committed Cooperative*	Sixes reinforce their self-image by responsibly working to create and sustain mutually beneficial systems. They form alliances with others, bringing thrift, hard work, and an attention to details. They are well-disciplined and practical, often foreseeing potential problems before they arise.
A V E R A G E	Level 4	*Dutiful Loyal*	Sixes begin to fear that they will lose their independence but also believe they need more support. They invest themselves in the people and organizations that they believe will help them, but are uneasy about it. They seek reassurance and guidance in procedures, rules, authorities, and philosophies.
	Level 5	*Ambivalent Defensive*	Sixes worry that they cannot meet the conflicting demands of their different commitments, so they try to resist having any more pressure put on them without alienating their supporters. They are anxious, pessimistic, and suspicious, leading to greater caution, impulsiveness, and indecision.
	Level 6	*Authoritarian Blaming*	Sixes fear that they are losing the support of their allies, and they are extremely unsure of themselves, so they look for causes for their anxiety. They are embittered, cynical, and reactive, feeling that their good faith has been betrayed. They blame others and get into power struggles.
U N H E A L T H Y	Level 7	*Panicky Unreliable*	Sixes fear that their actions have harmed their own security, and this may be true. Their reactive behavior may have caused crises in their lives, so they trust themselves even less. They feel panicky, depressed, and helpless and so look for something to save them from their predicament.
	Level 8	*Paranoid Lashing Out*	Sixes become so insecure and desperate that they begin to believe that others will destroy whatever safety they have left. They harbor paranoid fears and delusional ideas about the world. They rant about their obsessive fears and may strike out at real or imagined enemies.
	Level 9	*Self-Abasing Self-Destructive*	The realization that they have committed acts for which they will likely be punished is too much for unhealthy Sixes. Guilt and self-hatred lead them to punish themselves, inviting disgrace and bringing down all that they have achieved. Suicide attempts to elicit rescue are not uncommon.

TYPE 6

LEVELS OF DEVELOPMENT

THE WAKE-UP CALL FOR TYPE SIX:
LOOKING FOR A SURE THING (GUIDANCE AND
SUPPORT OUTSIDE THEMSELVES)

Average Sixes are frequently worried about the future. Because they have serious doubts about themselves and the world, they start to look for a "sure thing" that will guarantee their security—anything from a marriage to a job to a belief system to a network of friends to a self-help book. Most Sixes have more than one sure thing—just in case. They are the type that believes in saving for a rainy day, *and* investing for the future, *and* being loyal to a company in order to ensure their pension.

Simply put, Sixes are *seeking assurance and insurance,* trying to hedge their bets. They feel that life is fraught with dangers and uncertainties so it must be approached with caution and limited expectations. Sixes have personal wishes and dreams, of course, but they are afraid to take actions that might undermine their security. ("I'd love to be an actor, but you need something to fall back on.") They become more concerned with establishing and maintaining their safety nets than with pursuing their true goals and aspirations.

They increasingly turn to safe bets, reliable procedures, and tried-and-true methods for solving problems. Doing things the way they have been done before gives Sixes a feeling of weight and solidity. With other people or with tradition behind them, they feel they have the backup they need to move ahead. For instance, Sixes would generally be hesitant to work for a company that has no track record, or one that looks promising but risky. They prefer an employer that seems to have time-tested staying power. Ironically, however, when Sixes feel uncertain about their situation, they may act impulsively simply to bring closure to their anxieties. Sometimes this works—sometimes it undermines their security.

"What can I believe in?"

DARING TO FOLLOW YOUR HEART

Sixes tend to err on the side of caution, thus missing many possibilities for self-development and fulfillment. In your Inner Work Journal, record any examples of times in your life when you let significant opportunities for growth and challenge pass you by. Why did you decide to let them go? Would belief in your own abilities have changed the outcome?

Recall some times when you did fly against common sense and took a chance. We are not referring to impulsive acting out but rather to those times when you consciously chose to stretch yourself. What was the outcome? How did you feel at the time? Are there areas in your life now where you know that you are resisting your true desires out of fear or doubts about yourself? What can you do differently?

The Social Role: The Stalwart

"You can depend on me."

Average Sixes want to reinforce their support system, to strengthen their alliances and/or their position with authorities. To that end, they invest most of their time and energy in the commitments they have made, hoping that their sacrifices will pay off in increased security and mutual support. Similarly, as a defense against growing anxiety or uncertainty, Sixes become invested in particular beliefs, be they political, philosophical, or spiritual.

Sixes tirelessly volunteer themselves to be "the responsible one." They put in long hours working to ensure that the relationship or job or belief that they have invested in will continue to thrive and support them. This inevitably raises questions in their doubting minds: Are they being taken advantage of? Do others want them around only because of their hard work and dependability? Would they still be wanted if they stopped working so hard? Thus, playing their Social Role ironically begins to create social *insecurities.*

Sixes would like a guarantee that if they do all they are supposed to do, then God (or the company, or their family) will take care of them. They believe that if they and their allies manage their environment well enough, then all unpredictable and potentially dangerous events will be avoided or controlled. But countries rise and fall, and even the largest corporations go out of business or have cycles of growth and recession. There is nothing that Sixes can do in the external world that will make them feel secure if they are insecure within themselves.

WHAT SUPPORTS YOU?

Examine the "social security" systems you have created in your own life. Have they really made you more secure? What have they cost you? What would you do without one of them? Beyond these investments of your time and energy, consider all the different ways that your life is supported every day. (Hint: Did you grow, process, and package the food you had today?)

Fear, Anxiety, and Doubt

While not one of the classic seven "Capital Sins," *fear* has been assigned as the "Passion" (or underlying emotional distortion) of the Six, since the root of so much of Type Six's behavior is based on insecurity and reactions to fear. Sixes' fear can be seen in worry about their security and about potential future problems, but also in chronic self-doubt and anxieties about others. Although Sixes can appear on the surface to be extremely friendly and people-oriented, they often harbor deep fears that others will abandon them, reject them, or harm them. They fear that they will make some mistake that will ruin their relationships and that others will unexpectedly turn against them. Thus, much of their friendliness comes from a desire to "check in" with others to make sure that everything is still okay.

Unlike other types who repress (or at least distract themselves from) their fears and anxieties, Sixes seem to be constantly conscious of them. Sometimes they are energized by their fears, but more often than not, they are confused, enervated, and unnerved by them. However, they may not outwardly seem to be all that nervous since much of their anxiety is internal.

Looking at Laura, a poised and successful lawyer, you would not guess at the terrors going through her mind.

> I worry about all manner of things—like the roof leaking, or my car tires suddenly going flat—most of which would rarely happen and many of which are completely impossible. Fear is something I live with daily, minute by minute, hour by hour. The fear shows itself as nervousness, anxiety, and worry, though seldom as plain fear or terror. I'd say that excitement, anxiety, and anticipation are all rolled up into one. I think generally that I am a positive person—but dread and pessimism rear their ugly heads and can really send me into a tailspin.

Sixes learn to cope with fear either by reacting with it or against it. Some Sixes express themselves more aggressively, while others are more visibly timid. This is not to say that there are two kinds of Sixes; rather, we see that some Sixes express themselves counterphobically more often than others and that much of this probably comes from superego messages learned in childhood. Some Sixes were instructed to be tough and found that they could protect themselves by being relatively aggressive. Other Sixes were taught to avoid trouble and turn the other cheek.

Of course, in most Sixes these two tendencies coexist, alternately taking the upper hand, as Connie knows very well.

> I feel like a frightened rabbit that doesn't know which way to go. I need to find the courage to move. On the other hand, when there is a crisis, I function very well. No fear there. When my loved ones are attacked, watch out! I just put myself on automatic, and off I go to defend and rescue anyone who needs me. But taking the lead or taking responsibility for other people where I have to think and stay in my head just brings up panic.

"I get anxious and then look for reasons why I'm anxious."

EXPLORING ANXIETY

In your Inner Work Journal, can you list ten or more instances or areas where fear, anxiety, or doubt habitually show up?

Can you identify particular times, people, places, or other triggers that get you revved up with anxiety and tension? While there is clearly a negative component to these states, can you also discern a positive payoff that you might also unwittingly be seeking—such as gaining sympathy from others, or their protection? How do you complain or otherwise show your displeasure? What would it be like to not behave this way? What do you think would be gained? What would be lost?

Seeking Support for Independence

"One hand washes the other."

Although Sixes want to feel supported by others, they do not want to feel engulfed by anyone, and it feels uncomfortable when someone starts to overwhelm them with too much attention or closeness. They want distance from others, while still knowing that others are there for them.

Paradoxically, they *run the risk of becoming dependent on someone to become independent.* They may be like a girl who, desperate to leave an oppressive home, marries a controlling and possessive man. Anxiety often makes them jump too fast into an apparent solution, like the entrepreneur who quits his job to start his own business, only to feel even more oppressed by demanding investors or government regulations with which he must contend.

The irony is that the more insecure and lacking confidence they are, the more Sixes rely on external support, and the more they lose their independence. If their self-confidence is severely damaged, their dependency on a person or a belief system can become so deep and extensive that they cannot imagine living without it. In other cases, they can develop a "siege mentality," feeling that others are out to harm or exploit them. These suspicions can lead to social isolation.

UNDOING "AMNESIA OF SUCCESS"

You are much more capable than you realize. Everyone needs assistance and support from time to time, but you sometimes undervalue your contribution to the support of others. Take a moment to list the ways that you have supported significant people in your life. Then make a list of ways that you have supported yourself. In this second list, make sure to include important accomplishments that made you feel good about yourself. Study these lists. Which is longer? How do you feel about each of these lists?

Looking for Answers

Because they do not feel they can trust their own inner guidance, Sixes often look for answers in ideas and insights first propounded by others. Sixes do not just jump on the bandwagon, however; they will subject these ideas to scrutiny and testing and eventually may replace them with yet other ideas. More insecure Sixes will tend to simply accept the ideas of others, but even in this case, they can also resist and question them aggressively. Either way, their natural response is first to look outside of themselves for something to believe, and if that fails, to react against it and look for something else. Doubt, questioning, believing, searching, skepticism, and resistance are always part of the picture.

In general, Sixes tend to be mistrustful of authority until they are reassured that the authority is benevolent and "knows what he's talking about." Once Sixes feel that they have found a "good" authority, however, they strongly identify with it and internalize its values and teachings. (If the boss likes them, it makes them feel great. If they discover a new mentor who seems wise and helpful, they are elated. If they find a political system or leader who seems trustworthy, they can get involved in a very big way.) But Sixes are never entirely convinced: they harbor nagging doubts, while often expressing their adopted views all the more forcefully to suppress their doubts.

Sixes often attempt to solve the problem of finding the "right" answers by aligning themselves with multiple authorities and systems. They may believe in a religious affiliation, have strong political convictions, listen to the opinions of their spouses, take lessons from their fitness trainer, and read self-help books for further advice. If these different messages and teachings conflict, Sixes are right back where they started—uncomfortably trying to make up their own minds.

Thus, Sixes are cautious and skeptical about taking on new beliefs or relationships. This is because Sixes are aware of the intensity of their commitment, once made, and want to avoid making a mistake. Should Sixes have any reason to suspect their authority of being unjust or unwise, their feelings of doubt can blossom quickly into rebellion or rejection. Of course, no belief system or relationship will always provide perfect guidance and support. Until Sixes become aware of this pattern, they will play out their dance of trust and doubt over and over again.

"There is nothing easy about becoming conscious. My own life was much easier before I knew about the deeper meaning of choice, the power of choice that accompanies taking responsibility. Abdicating responsibility to an outside source can seem, at least for the moment, so much easier. Once you know better, however, you can't get away with kidding yourself for long."

CAROLINE MYSS

QUESTIONING THE ROOTS OF YOUR BELIEFS

What are the foundations of your belief-system? Are these based on your own experiences or on the authority of trusted friends, mentors, books, or teachings? How do you evaluate the truth or falseness of a belief?

Seeking Structure and Guidelines

Sixes dislike having too many options. They feel more confident in situations with well-defined procedures, guidelines, and rules, such as the legal profession, or accounting, or academia. When the demands on them are clear, however, they can be highly effective at *creating* structure and organization—often serving as the head of a group or corporation that governs by consensus. Not all Sixes are comfortable in organizations, however, given their suspicion of authority.

Many Sixes find a great deal of flexibility and creativity within the security of known boundaries. For them, it is no more restrictive to play within the rules of an organization than it is to play tennis with the net up or to read a book starting at the beginning. As far as they are concerned, things have a natural order, and they are usually content to work within it—as long as they also retain some choice about whether to ignore it. (They may never exercise this choice, but they still want to know that it is there.) Even artists, writers, therapists, and other creative individuals who are Sixes like working with established forms (the Blues, Country, sonatas, haiku) and find freedom within these structures.

Sixes feel safer when they have some sense of what to expect, so they typically dislike sudden changes. Having a certain amount of dependable predictability is comforting to their anxious minds.

Annabelle, a therapist, notes:

I am a creature of habit and routine. You see, each time I deliberately create a habit, I have one less thing to think about. Otherwise, I would use that much more energy thinking. I hate change. I have a knee-jerk negative reaction to change. Change means that the future will be different. The good news is that I'll adjust as soon as the future gets predictable again or as soon as I get one of my systems or explanations into place. For example, I always go to the same gas station. If I were not already in the habit of going to the same place, I would go around and around in my head about when and where to stop.

TRUSTING YOUR OWN INNER KNOWING

Watch for times in which you or someone else has a question about what to do in a situation. For example, there might be a question about how to approach a problem at work, or a friend might come to you for advice about a marriage. Notice how you approach the problem. Do you rely on precedents? ("The company policy on that is . . ." or "The spiritual teaching that I've learned says . . .") Or do you turn to your own intelligence—especially the intelligence of your heart and instincts?

Overcommitment and "Covering All the Bases"

Sixes try to fulfill their commitments to many different people and situations, but inevitably they find it impossible to satisfy everyone. Then they become like the Little Dutch Boy who has to put his fingers in all the holes to keep the dike from leaking. They become overextended and often feel taken advantage of.

For example, a Six at the office might hear from his spouse that she has made dinner reservations at a fine restaurant—"just for us"—on Friday night. The Six, wanting to reinforce the security he derives from his marriage, agrees and looks forward to a pleasant evening. At about this point, his boss comes in and, knowing the Six to be a reliable and persevering worker, asks if he can stay late on Friday night to meet a Monday morning deadline. Not wanting to disappoint—or get in trouble with the boss—the Six agrees to stay later, while beginning to fearfully figure out what to tell his wife. Later that afternoon, his best friend calls to remind him of their date—made the previous week—for a card game on Friday night. The Six is now in a quandary. Because he has overcommitted himself—trying to cover all the bases—he cannot help but disappoint someone.

The Six will be racked with fear that others will get angry with him, although he may not actually check to see if this is the case. No matter, the Six's anxious mind will fill in the gaps with fearful projections and imagined complaints and tirades. He feels pressured—"damned if you do, and damned if you don't." He becomes irritated that others expect too much from him; he cannot possibly do everything they want!

"Damned if I do, and damned if I don't."

BEING THERE FOR EVERYONE

Look for areas in your life where you have tended to overcommit yourself. What was your motivation for doing so? What prevented you from saying no when you were overbooked? What was the result of your overcommitment for you? For others?

The Inner Committee

While Ones have a powerful inner critic in their heads, Sixes have an *inner committee.* Sixes often check in with them, imagining what their response would be to a given situation. ("Gee, I don't know if I should take this job. What would Julie say? She'd definitely be for it, but Dad would really disapprove. On the other hand, that self-help book said . . .") Thus, when they have to make a decision, Sixes will feel caught between various internal voices arguing for different positions and responsibilities. Sometimes the loudest internal voice will win out; at other times, there is a deadlock and procrastination. Sixes may find themselves unable to come to any closure or final decision because they cannot stop second-guessing themselves.

As a result, Sixes often feel indecisive. Although they may feel strongly about things, they are not certain that they know the best course of action to take. Every choice brings the deliberations of the inner committee, which can lead Sixes around and around in circles. On the other hand, in highly significant matters (such as where to live or which religion to believe in), Sixes usually have strong opinions and can be rather inflexible because they have settled their doubts sometime in the past and have come to a conclusion to which they then doggedly adhere. By contrast, it is in the smaller choices in life where they tend to bounce back and forth, constantly second-guessing themselves. ("Do I get the hamburger or the hot dog?") Their unending inner conversation clutters the quiet of the mind and blocks the inner guidance of Essence. They need to fire their inner committee.

FIRING THE INNER COMMITTEE

Are you aware of your inner committee? Who sits on it? In the past, when you've tried to imagine the responses of your allies and authorities, have their real responses been the way you imagined them?

Vigilance, Suspicion, and Catastrophizing

Because of their feelings of being unsupported, Sixes develop an extraordinary sensitivity to danger signals. This is even truer if they grew up in an environment that was unsafe or unstable, or if they were traumatized in some way. While this kind of awareness can be an asset and can even save a person's life, many Sixes remain hyperalert and hypervigilant even when no danger is present. They can never relax, never feel safe. Their eyes dart about nervously, scanning their surroundings for potential threats or problems. (Many Sixes have reported being aware of where the exits are in any room they are occupying and what stands between them and the exit.) This relationship with the world is extremely stressful and over time can even change their brain chemistry. Further, it begins to shape their imaginations, resulting in *a constant expectation of mishap or danger.*

Joseph knows this state very well.

Being a Six is akin to feeling that the sky is always about to fall in. My view of the world is colored by a constant sense that something is about to go wrong. From the moment that I wake up in the morning, I find myself scanning the environment—internally and externally—for trouble.... Life seems like an accident waiting to happen. Even in the best of moments, the only question is when the other shoe will drop.

"What are they up to?"

Average Sixes can also become very pessimistic and sour. They may have extremely low self-esteem and "amnesia" about their past successes and accomplishments. It is as if nothing in their past can convince them that they will be able to deal effectively with the problems at hand—and they see problems in every direction.

Annabelle vividly describes the tension that this creates.

When I'm a passenger in a car, I look ahead to see what the other cars ahead of us are doing. I see the possibility of something bad happening, and I imagine a scene of disaster. Heart pounds, pulse races, breath becomes shallow, imagination races out of control—no escape! Nothing happens. I move on to the next possibility. Creating a disaster in my mind is automatic. I can do this for hours, then I observe that I'm doing it and make myself stop, but pretty soon I'm lost in it again.

Sixes feel that any small mishap could be their undoing. They make mountains out of molehills and can be relied on to come up with all of the reasons why a project or endeavor will not work. Naturally, this can affect their attitudes at work, but it also affects their personal relationships. Slight misunderstandings or differences of opinion can indicate to the Six that she is facing imminent abandonment, or that her friends and supporters have turned against her. Left unchecked, this tendency can undermine significant relationships, or trigger paranoid responses to what they perceive as injustices directed at themselves.

OVERCOMING PESSIMISM

Learn to discern real dangers from potential ones. How often do you expect bad outcomes? Do you have trouble believing that things will work out? Do you choose to think about problems or is it a reflex? While anticipating future problems may have some usefulness, it more generally leads you away from dealing with the reality of here and now—the one place you can find the steadiness and guidance to move into the next moment.

Blaming and Victimization

To the degree that they feel powerless to do anything constructive themselves, Sixes may act out their anxieties by complaining and blaming others. This is all the more true if they fear that they will be reprimanded or punished in some way by an authority figure for their failures.

Blaming may well begin with the common childhood scenario in which a parent comes home to find a broken knickknack and asks, "Who did this?" To which the guilty Six child responds, "Debbie did it! And you know what else? Debbie made a mess upstairs and said a bad word to me!"

In the adult world, Sixes more commonly discharge their anxieties by complaining to third parties about the people with whom they are frustrated. For many Sixes, the dinner table at home is the favorite place to vent about disappointments at work or to let off steam about someone's incompetence. Similar activities occur around coffee machines at the office or at bars after hours. Simply put, Sixes feel put-upon and victimized and frequently fall into the habit of *complaining without taking any definite action that would change the situation.* Over time, this begins to heighten their self-image of being victims, often leading to paranoia and the destructive modes of "problem-solving" we find in the unhealthy range.

> *"I'm mad as hell and I'm not going to take it anymore!"*

WHY IS EVERYBODY MESSING UP MY LIFE?

How many of your conversations involve complaining? About your job, relationships, children, parents, sports team, politics, town, or even the weather? When you are complaining about a person, have you discussed this matter fully with that person? Who or what are you blaming for the problems in your life?

REACTING TO STRESS: SIX GOES TO THREE

▲

As we have seen, Sixes tirelessly invest their time and energy in their "security systems." When stress increases beyond their normal ability to cope, Sixes may go to Three and become even more driven and potentially workaholic. They also make additional efforts to fit in, adapting themselves to their surroundings and striving to be exemplary enough to maintain their social and financial position. Thus, Sixes at Three become more image-conscious, developing the right look, gestures, jargon, and attitude to be acceptable to their peers. They hope in this way to win people over and avoid rejection. However, others often notice the forced quality of their friendliness or professionalism, leading them to wonder what Sixes are really up to.

Like Threes, Sixes can become competitive, although usually through identification with groups or beliefs (a favorite football team, their company, school, nationality, or religion). They may also become boastful and self-promoting, adopting condescending attitudes, dismissing others, and hyping their own superiority in a desperate attempt to defend against their low self-esteem and feelings of inferiority. Dishonesty about their background or education, exploitation of self or others, and a relentless desire to triumph over rival groups or ideologies can enter the picture.

If Sixes are overstressed for an extended period of time, if they have suffered a serious crisis without adequate support or coping skills, or if they have suffered from chronic abuse in childhood, they may cross the shock point into the unhealthy range of their type. This may lead them to a fearful recognition that their own belligerent actions or defensive reactions are actually harming their security.

If Sixes can recognize the truth in these fears, they may begin to turn their life around and move toward health and liberation. On the other hand, they may become even more panicky and reactive: "I'll do anything for you! Don't leave me!" or, at the other extreme, "They'll be sorry they messed with me!" If Sixes persist in these attitudes, they may cross into the unhealthy range.

If you or someone you know is exhibiting the following warning signs for an extended period of time—more than two or three weeks—getting counseling, therapy, or other support is highly advisable.

THE RED FLAG: THE SIX IN TROUBLE

▲

WARNING SIGNS

POTENTIAL PATHOLOGY: Paranoid, Dependent, and Borderline Personality Disorders, Dissociative Disorders, and passive-aggressive behaviors, intense anxiety attacks.

▶ Intense anxiety and panic attacks

▶ Acute inferiority feelings and chronic depression

▶ Constant fear of losing support from others

▶ Alternating dependency and impulsive displays of defiance

▶ Keeping "bad company" and attachments to abusive relationships

▶ Extreme suspiciousness and paranoia

▶ Hysterical lashing-out at perceived enemies

▶ Notice how much time you spend trying to figure out how to handle possible future problems. In reality, how often do these imagined events come to pass? Also notice how this mental activity actually makes you *less* effective at dealing with the challenges at hand. If you are worrying and obsessing about a meeting you will have tomorrow or next week, you are far more likely to forget an important phone call— or even overlook a real danger signal. Quieting the mind through disciplined meditation practices, especially those that focus on the body,

PRACTICES THAT HELP SIXES DEVELOP

▲

can help Sixes clear out the chorus of voices in their heads. Remember, inner knowing usually does not speak using words.

▶ You tend to have difficulty enjoying those moments when you achieve your objectives without immediately launching into your next round of anxieties—even worrying about how others might resent your accomplishment! When you achieve a goal, large or small, stop long enough to relax, breathe, and savor the moment. Take in the impression of your competence. Remember this impression. This feeling will help you see the ways in which you consistently support yourself and others. This memory will come to your aid when you doubt your ability to cope at other times.

▶ Get in the practice of noticing what you trust and how you come to decisions. Notice especially the procedures or allies you automatically turn to when you are unsure of yourself. Why do you feel that others will know better what to do than you do? Also notice your anger and rejection of them when it is clear that they do not have the answers you seek. You can avoid these situations by turning more to what your heart and instincts are telling you in the moment. Many internal voices may clamor, but understand what they are—fearful aspects of your imagination and your superego, and no more. The more you are able to see the truth of this, the more you will find your quiet mind and come to the right path for yourself.

▶ While you want to be there in a responsible way for everyone else in your life, you tend to shortchange yourself by not believing that your own self-development is worth the trouble. This can be exacerbated by fears of change—of moving into the unknown. Take risks, especially when it comes to moving out of familiar, safe patterns. Having a therapist that you trust or a spiritual group that you work with can be invaluable for creating the kind of support you need to explore difficult issues. But remember, it is your own courage and strength that ultimately are required (and available) for such explorations.

▶ Seek out diversity and variety. Sure, you like cheeseburgers, but maybe you could try the chicken sandwich. You love basketball, but perhaps you could also find another sport or activity interesting. The same is true with your choice of acquaintances. By sometimes interacting with people from very different backgrounds and perspectives, you will learn more about yourself and the world. All of this, far from being threatening or dangerous, will greatly expand your base of support and increase your comfort in the world.

▶ Learn to cultivate quiet time for yourself. By this, we do not mean sitting around in front of a TV for hours, but time in which you get to be with yourself in a simple way. You benefit greatly from contact with nature. Take walks, garden, swim, meditate—and above all, do not use these times to worry, fret, and strategize about your work and relationships. They are times for you to become more comfortable with Being. Getting in greater contact with your surroundings and with the sensations in your body will do much to soothe and quiet that busy mind of yours.

Healthy Sixes are endowed with tremendous endurance and achieve their objectives through steady and persistent efforts. Less flashy than some of the other types, they believe in the adage "Success is 10 percent inspiration and 90 percent perspiration." They give careful attention to details and tend to approach problems carefully and methodically. They organize resources, prioritize tasks, and see projects through, feeling that their personal value rests on their reliability and on the quality of the work they produce. High-functioning Sixes respect dependability and good craftsmanship and, to the best of their ability, provide them.

Because of their underlying vigilance and sensitivity to danger signals, Sixes also foresee problems and can "head them off at the pass." They are natural troubleshooters and often save themselves, their families, or their companies many headaches by spotting irregularities or potential problems. They like to stay on top of things so that their world runs as trouble-free as possible. Keeping insurance and paying bills early are typical Six behaviors.

Sixes like to learn and to think about things, but within known and knowable categories. They are attracted to self-contained systems, such as law, accounting, engineering, languages, and the sciences, where one can arrive at a definite answer. Thus, they tend to be excellent in work that involves careful analysis and an ability to keep track of variables. Their diligence can alert them to discrepancies in systems, to potential problems, or to inaccuracies or contradictions in the statements of others. The world of academia, for example, supports many Six values: observing good structure and form, referring back to authorities through citations and footnotes, careful analysis and systematic thinking.

Sixes are outstanding in their ability to work for a common good without needing to be stars. Sixes ask what needs to be done and then do it, with a sense of being part of something that transcends their personal interests. They teach us all about the benefits and joys of commitment, cooperation, and service. Healthy Sixes are great believers in the age-old observation that people acting with a common purpose can accomplish more than anyone acting alone, particularly in situations where people need to band together to survive—to produce food or

BUILDING ON THE SIX'S STRENGTHS

▲

clothing, to build a house, to improve communities or working conditions, or to defend a city or a country.

While high-functioning Sixes are deeply loyal and committed to others, they are also committed to learning more about themselves. In the process, they often find rich and unsuspected talent for creativity and self-expression. Committing to their own development helps Sixes build strong self-esteem and see themselves as the equal of others—equally competent, equally worthy of respect and rewards, equally able to take responsibility and to hold their own in all areas of life.

Connie's path of growth has involved finding her own center within herself.

"Can we be friends?"

Probably the aspect about my personality that has changed the most is my ability to stand on my own. I now know within myself that I am okay, that things will be all right. At my best, I am strong and can care not only for myself but for those around me. Instead of having fifteen authority figures, I have one or two trusted friends—and I listen to my own counsel. There are actually things that I don't share with anyone. Previously my life was an open book. Now I give myself and others needed respect.

High-functioning Sixes are self-confident and self-affirming because they have learned to recognize and trust their own inner guidance. Their faith in themselves often manifests as outstanding courage and leadership. They lead from a deep understanding of people's insecurities and frailties, and others respond to them, seeing their sincerity and willingness to be honest about their own weaknesses. They nurture an egalitarian spirit, a sense that there really are no leaders and followers, just different people with different talents finding ways to combine them for a common good. This desire to engage, to find common ground, and to work for everyone's mutual safety and benefit is a gift that our species needs for survival.

Sixes become actualized and remain healthy by becoming balanced in their instincts and grounded in their bodies like healthy Nines. For Sixes to find the stability they seek, they need to turn to the steady support of their physical presence: to get grounded in the here-and-now. Many Sixes are active, even athletic, but this is not the same thing as being in contact with the moment-to-moment sensations of the body. Attending to the immediacy of their sensory impressions acts as a counterbalance to the Six's nonstop thinking and gives them something else to identify with.

At first, centering themselves in their physical sensations may produce feelings of panic or dread, particularly if Sixes have suffered trauma in their past. It is not uncommon for Sixes from abusive backgrounds to begin to tremble as they occupy their bodies more completely. At such times, it is important for Sixes to realize that such physical reactions are the body's way of processing old fears and hurts and *are not necessarily indications of present danger.* If Sixes are able to sense themselves *and* their anxious feelings without reacting to them, they begin to come into a more open and trusting experience of life.

Sixes cannot find this steadiness by imitating the traits of average Nines, however. Becoming complacent, attempting to efface themselves, or getting involved in comforting ruts merely reinforces the Six's fearful clinging to people and activities for security. Trying to be easygoing or passive will not negate a Six's anxieties and may even increase the churning of her mind. But as Sixes become more practiced at staying with themselves without reacting to their anxieties, they begin to feel supported, not just by their significant others or by their work but by Being itself. They sense life's benevolence and know that the ground will hold. This is not based on belief or on any trick of the mind but on a quiet and steady inner knowing that requires no explanation or external backup.

From this position of grounded openness, Sixes are able to recognize the common bonds they share with all of humanity. They feel inclusive and accepting of others, regardless of whether their views or lifestyles are familiar to them. They are filled with courage that is not a counterphobic reaction to fear but is an actual force in and of itself. Their courage arises from a feeling of real inner solidity and of profound connection with themselves and with all living things. Thus, integrating Sixes, like healthy Nines, can approach tremendous challenges and even tragedies or threats with inner balance and equanimity.

THE PATH OF INTEGRATION: SIX GOES TO NINE

▲

TRANSFORMING PERSONALITY INTO ESSENCE

▲

All human beings need support and security in order to survive, let alone thrive, *but seldom do we realize how extensively we are supported.* Besides the support of our friends and loved ones, we have been supported by the people who grew the food that we will eat for dinner tonight, by the unknown factory workers who manufactured our clothes, by the people working in the utility company who provide us with heat and electricity, and on and on. No one who reads this book has ever truly been without support, but our personality, based as it is on defenses against fears and feelings of deficiency, cannot recognize this. The ability to recognize and respond intelligently to the support of the world, as well as the inner support and guidance of Being, can be achieved only through Presence—through abiding in our true nature.

The "wrong turn" that Sixes take is to use their fearful and doubting ego minds to figure out where reliable guidance and support can be found. Ironically, the more they question and strategize, the less secure they feel. Rather than give them the security they seek, being identified with their anxious thoughts makes Sixes feel small, helpless, and without direction. Only by seeing through their fearful thinking patterns can Sixes begin to reconnect with their Essential nature. When they do so, they rediscover their own inner authority, and they begin to recognize that the support they have been seeking is everywhere and always available.

Jenny, a therapist in her fifties who had recently undergone a mastectomy, beautifully expresses this transformation.

> I believe I became my own authority with my mastectomy experience. I was able to take in love from my family and friends. It never felt safe before. What a beautiful gift! I had to be my own authority because my survival was at stake and no one really knows what is best for me except me! I feel wonderful when I allow myself to feel healthy! Recently I have been focusing my attention on growing flowers as opposed to pulling weeds all the time. My "inner voices"—my old superego stuff—just keep me in the weeds.

Sixes achieve transformation by confronting their Basic Fear of being without support and guidance. As they do so, they begin to experience a vast, empty inner space, and they may sometimes feel as though they are falling into it. If they can tolerate this sensation, this space may change and feel solid or become intensely shiny and luminous—or it could transform itself in numerous ways. Sixes then come to recognize that the inner space they experience is actually the very support they have been looking for. It is free, open, and infinitely wise and patient. When this spaciousness is present, Sixes feel self-reliant, courageous, and brilliantly intelligent—in short, all of the qualities they have been looking for.

"When eating a fruit, think of the person who planted the tree."

VIETNAMESE SAYING

"You cannot depend on anybody. There *is* no guide, teacher, no authority. There is only you—your relationship with others and with the world—there is nothing else."

KRISHNAMURTI

THE EMERGENCE OF ESSENCE

Deep down, Sixes remember that the universe is benevolent and supports them completely. They know that they are grounded in Being, are part of the Divine Nature, and that grace is always available to them.

When their minds become quiet, Sixes experience an inner spaciousness that is the Ground of Being. They realize that Essence is real and is not simply an idea; in fact, it is the thing that is most real in existence, the very foundation of existence itself. People have associated this inner peace with the presence of God, which is manifesting itself at every moment, and which is available at every moment. When Sixes experience this truth, they feel solid, steady, and supported, as if they were standing on a massive bed of granite. They realize that this ground is the only real security in life, and it is what gives Sixes immense courage.

This is the real meaning of *faith,* their particular Essential quality. Faith is not belief, but a real, immediate knowing that comes from experience. Faith without experience is belief. Faith with experience brings reliable guidance. Much of the personality of Sixes can be seen as an effort to imitate or recreate faith in terms of beliefs, and to find a substitute for the certainty that they are already secure as an expression of the Divine. When Essence emerges, however, Sixes have a certainty that they are grounded in Being in a way that is immutable and absolute. Being supports them because they are part of it: their own existence has Being because it cannot *not* have Being.

Add your scores for the fifteen statements for Type Six. Your result will be between 15 and 75. The following guidelines may help you discover or confirm your personality type.

▶ 15   You are probably not a compliant type (not a One, Two, or Six).

▶ 15–30   You are probably not a Type Six.

▶ 30–45   You most probably have Six-issues or a Six parent.

▶ 45–60   You most likely have a Six-component.

▶ 60–75   You are most likely a Six (but could still be another type if you are thinking too narrowly about Type Six).

Sixes are most likely to misidentify themselves as Fours, Eights, or Ones. Twos, Fives, and Ones are most likely to misidentify themselves as Sixes.

▼

CHAPTER 13

TYPE SEVEN:
THE ENTHUSIAST

▲

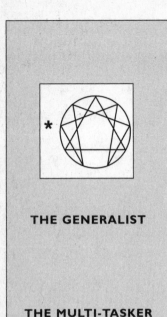

THE GENERALIST

THE MULTI-TASKER

THE WUNDERKIND

THE DILETTANTE

THE CONNOISSEUR

THE ENERGIZER

"Pleasure is the object, the duty, and the goal of all rational creatures."

—VOLTAIRE

"No pleasure is evil in itself; but the means by which certain pleasures are gained bring pains many times greater than the pleasures."

—EPICURUS

"With the catching ends the pleasure of the chase."

—ABRAHAM LINCOLN

"How could there be any question of acquiring or possessing, when the one thing needful for a man is to become—*to be at last, and to die in the fullness of his being."*

—SAINT-EXUPÉRY

*Type
Attitude
Sorter*

Score each of the following statements according to how true or applicable to you it is on the following scale:

1.......*Not at All True*

2.......*Seldom True*

3.......*Somewhat True*

4.......*Generally True*

5.......*Very True*

See page 286 for scoring key.

_____ 1. I love traveling and discovering different kinds of foods, people, and experiences—the whole fabulous whirlwind of life!

_____ 2. My calendar is usually full, and I like to keep it that way: no grass is going to grow under my feet!

_____ 3. What's important to me is excitement and variety rather than comfort and playing it safe—although I'll take my comforts wherever I can find them.

_____ 4. My mind is always chattering—sometimes it seems like I'm thinking about ten things at once!

_____ 5. One thing I absolutely cannot stand is being bored—and I make sure that I am never boring myself.

_____ 6. I'm pretty committed when I'm in a relationship, but when it's over, I move on.

_____ 7. I am curious and adventurous and am usually the first one of my friends to try whatever is new and interesting.

_____ 8. When I no longer enjoy doing something, I stop doing it.

_____ 9. I'm not just a "fun person"—there is a serious, even dark side to me, although I do not like to go there very much.

_____ 10. I'm good at the big picture, not so much the little details: it's more enjoyable for me to brainstorm a lot of new ideas than to get involved with implementing them.

_____ 11. When I really want something, I usually find a way to get it.

_____ 12. Things get me down once in a while, but I quickly pop back up again.

_____ 13. One of my main problems is that I am easily distracted and can get too scattered.

_____ 14. I tend to spend more money than I probably should.

_____ 15. Other people are great to have along—as long as they want to go where I'm going.

PERSONALITY TYPE SEVEN: THE ENTHUSIAST

▶ BASIC FEAR: Of being deprived and trapped in pain

▶ BASIC DESIRE: To be happy, satisfied, to find fulfillment

▶ SUPEREGO MESSAGE: "You are good or okay if you get what you need."

The Busy, Fun-Loving Type:
Spontaneous, Versatile, Acquisitive, and Scattered

We have named this personality type *the Enthusiast* because Sevens are enthusiastic about almost everything that catches their attention. They approach life with curiosity, optimism, and a sense of adventure, like kids in a candy store who look at the world in wide-eyed, rapt anticipation of all the good things they are about to experience. They are bold and vivacious, pursuing what they want in life with a cheerful determination. They have a quality best described by the Yiddish word *chutzpah*—a kind of brash nerviness.

Although Sevens are in the Thinking Triad, this is not immediately apparent because they tend to be extremely practical and engaged in a multitude of projects at any given time. Their thinking is *anticipatory:* they foresee events and generate ideas on the fly, favoring activities that stimulate their minds—which in turn generate more things to do and think about. Sevens are not necessarily intellectual or studious by any standard definition, although they are often intelligent and can be widely read and highly verbal. Their minds move rapidly from one idea to the next, making them gifted at brainstorming and synthesizing information. Sevens are exhilarated by the rush of ideas and by the pleasure of being spontaneous, preferring broad overviews and the excitement of the initial stages of the creative process to probing a single topic in depth.

Devon, a successful businesswoman, shares with us some of the inner workings of her Seven mindset.

> I am definitely a list person. It's not really for memory, since I have a great memory. It's more for downloading information so that my mind won't spin on it. For example, I was at a concert where the tickets were hard to get and very expensive. I couldn't sit through it. My mind was torturing me with the things I needed to do. Finally, I had to get up and leave. This was very upsetting to the person I went with, and I missed a good show.

Sevens are frequently endowed with quick, agile minds and can be exceptionally fast learners. This is true both of their ability to absorb information (language, facts, and procedures) and their ability to learn new manual skills—they tend to have excellent mind-body coordination and manual dexterity (typewriting, piano playing, tennis). All of this can combine to make a Seven into the quintessential Renaissance person.

Ironically, Sevens' wide-ranging curiosity and ability to learn quickly can also create problems for them. Because they are able to pick up many different skills with relative ease, it becomes more difficult for them to decide what to do with themselves. As a result, they also do not always value their abilities as they would if they had to struggle to gain them. When Sevens are more balanced, however, their versatility, curiosity, and ability to learn can lead them to extraordinary achievement.

The root of their problem is common to all of the types of the Thinking Triad: they are out of touch with the inner guidance and support of their Essential nature, and this creates a deep anxiety in Sevens. They do not feel that they know how to make choices that will be beneficial to themselves and others. Sevens cope with this anxiety in two ways. First, they try to keep their minds busy all of the time. As long as they can keep their minds occupied, especially with projects and positive ideas for the future, they can, to some extent, keep anxiety and negative feelings out of their conscious awareness. Likewise, since their thinking is stimulated by activity, Sevens are compelled to stay on the go, moving from one experience to the next, searching for more stimulation. This is not to say that Sevens are spinning their wheels. They generally enjoy being practical and getting things done.

Frances, a successful business consultant, sounds more energetic than is humanly possible—and yet she is a typical Seven.

> I am highly, highly productive. At the office, I am joyful and my mind is running at its best. I might create several marketing campaigns for a client, work on the outline for an upcoming seminar, talk out a difficult problem with a client on the telephone, close two deals, make a project list, dictate a few letters, and look up to see that it's 9:30 A.M. and my assistant is coming in to start our work for the day.

Second, Sevens cope with the loss of Essential guidance by using the trial-and-error method: they try everything to make sure they know what is best. On a very deep level, *Sevens do not feel that they can find what they really want in life.* They therefore tend to try everything—and ultimately may even resort to *anything* as a substitute for what they are really looking for. ("If I can't have what will really satisfy me, I'll enjoy myself anyway. I'll have all kinds of experiences—that way I will not feel bad about not getting what I really want.")

We can see this in action even in the most trivial areas of their daily lives. Unable to decide whether he wants vanilla, chocolate, or strawberry ice cream, a Seven will want all three flavors—just to be sure that he does not miss out on the "right" choice. Having two weeks for a vacation and a desire to visit Europe brings a similar quandary. Which countries and cities to visit? Which sights to see? The Seven's way of

"I still haven't figured out what I want to be when I grow up."

dealing with this will be to cram as many different countries, cities, and attractions into his vacation as possible. While they are scrambling after exciting experiences, the real object of their heart's desire (their personal Rosebud, as it were) may be so deeply buried in their unconscious that they are never really aware of precisely what it is.

Furthermore, as Sevens speed up their pursuit of whatever seems to offer freedom and satisfaction, they tend to make worse choices, and they are less able to be satisfied because everything is experienced indirectly, through the dense filter of their fast-paced mental activity. The result is that Sevens end up anxious, frustrated, and enraged, with fewer resources available to them physically, emotionally, or financially. They may end up ruining their health, their relationships, and their finances in their search for happiness.

Gertrude is busy establishing her career and family now, but she looks back at how this tendency contributed to her getting a rough start in life.

> There wasn't anything to do at home or in the tiny Southern town I grew up in. I was dying to get out of it and go someplace more exciting. When I was sixteen, I started dating, and before long I got pregnant, but the father didn't want to marry me—which was okay since I didn't want to marry him, either. It wasn't too long before I found somebody else, and we got married, and I got to move to a larger city. But it didn't really work out the way I wanted because after I had the baby, we broke up and I had to move back home. I stayed there for a year or two to get my feet on the ground. When things were looking bleak, I married someone else. I'm nineteen now and I guess I've done a lot already.

"If life gives you lemons, make lemonade."

On the positive side, however, Sevens are extremely optimistic people—exuberant and upbeat. They are endowed with abundant vitality and a desire to fully participate in their lives each day. They are naturally cheerful and good-humored, not taking themselves too seriously, or anything else for that matter. When they are balanced within themselves, their joy and enthusiasm for life naturally affect everyone around them. They remind us of the pure pleasure of existence—the greatest gift of all.

THE CHILDHOOD PATTERN

The Seven's childhood is flavored by a largely unconscious feeling of disconnection from the nurturing figure (often, but not always, the biological mother). Generally speaking, Sevens are sensitive to a very deep frustration resulting from feelings of being cut off from maternal nurturance at an early age, as if they had been taken away from the breast too soon (which may have literally been true in some cases). In response, young Sevens unconsciously "decided" to nurture themselves. ("I am not going to sit around feeling sorry for myself, waiting for somebody to take care of me. I'll take care of myself!") This pattern does not mean that Sevens were not close to their mothers in childhood. But on an emotional level, they unconsciously decided that they would have to take care of their own needs.

The reasons for this perception can vary widely. Perhaps another sibling came along, and the young Seven suddenly found he was displaced from his mother's attention. Perhaps an early illness curtailed the Seven's nurturing: either she was ill and needed to be hospitalized or the mother became ill.

Devon, the businesswoman we met earlier, recalls:

> One incident that happened when I was three years old made such an impression on me that I remember it like it was yesterday. My infant brother was having a convulsion. My mother stood screaming and literally pulling handfuls of her long, beautiful black hair out. I remember the hair landing on the rose and cream carpet. It was late at night, and the ambulance took my mother and my brother away, and my father went with them, too. I know that until I was one and a half, I was well nurtured by my mother. Then she became pregnant and was very sick until my brother was born. My brother was sick early, and so I kind of lost my mother along the way.

Sevens are also heavily influenced by the "separation phase" of ego development when they are learning to be more independent of their mothers. One way that children manage the difficult process of separation is by focusing on what psychologists call *transitional objects.* Having toys, games, playmates, and other distractions helps toddlers tolerate their anxiety.

Sevens seem to be still in search of transitional objects. As long as Sevens can find and move toward interesting ideas, experiences, people, and "toys," they are able to repress their underlying feelings of frustration, fear, and hurt. But if, for whatever reasons, Sevens are unable to find any adequate transitional objects, their anxiety and emotional conflicts crowd into conscious awareness. As quickly as possible, they attempt to manage their panicky feelings by finding another distraction. Of course, the more actual deprivation and frustration the Seven child suffered, the more intensely the adult Seven will need to "occupy their mind" with a variety of distractions.

> *Please note that the childhood pattern we are describing here does not cause the personality type. Rather, it describes tendencies that we observe in early childhood that have a major impact on the type's adult relationships.*

THE SEVEN WITH A SIX-WING: THE ENTERTAINER

Healthy   People of this subtype are productive and playful, retaining a belief in life's goodness and the joy of existence. They are often curious and creative, with an excellent sense of humor and a more positive outlook than the other subtype. They have quick minds, a cooperative spirit, and organizational abilities—enabling them to accomplish a great deal, seemingly with little effort. They seek variety and have the ability to interact easily with people—show business, public relations, advertising, media, and the world of entertainment are naturals for them.

Average   Excited by new ideas, fast-talking, witty, and engaging, people of this subtype have high energy and provide moments of high spirits for others. They are generally productive but can lose focus, become scattered, with less follow-through than the other subtype. To the extent that they are insecure, there can be a revved-up, manic, nervous quality to them. Looking for strong experiences, they are often either in a relationship or looking for one. They do not like to be alone but have high requirements of intimates. They often have conflicts between a desire to move on to greener pastures and a fear of losing connection. There is the possibility of substance abuse in this subtype due to anxiety and hidden feelings of inferiority.

Examples

Robin Williams
Steven Spielberg
W. A. Mozart
Jim Carrey
Goldie Hawn
Carol Burnett
Sarah Ferguson
Benjamin Franklin
Timothy Leary
Tom Wolfe

THE SEVEN WITH AN EIGHT-WING: THE REALIST

Healthy   People of this subtype truly enjoy the world and are "materialistic" in the broadest sense of the word. They combine quickness with drive, often leading to material success and positions of power and prominence. They are determined to get what they want from life; they think strategically and can rapidly organize their internal and external resources in pursuit of their desires. They are earthy, practical, and tough-minded. Their sense of humor expresses itself in a biting wit and a taste for the outrageous.

Average   People of this subtype apply their energies in many directions, multitasking or even "multicareering." They can be aggressive and have the willpower and drive to take care of their own needs. They tend to be more workaholic than the other subtype, coming from the strong desire to accumulate possessions and experiences. ("I'm worth it!") Their focus is more on generating activities than on connecting with people. Hence they tend to be pragmatic about relationships—looking for a partner, not a romantic fantasy figure. They are not afraid to be alone and are clear about their own expectations and how much they will tolerate. Directness can verge on bluntness and on pushing

Examples

Jack Nicholson
Lucille Ball
Joan Rivers
Howard Stern
Leonard Bernstein
Lauren Bacall
Bette Midler
Malcolm Forbes
John F. Kennedy
"Scarlett O'Hara"

people out of the way to get what they want. They can be jaded and callous, in contrast to the childish hyperenthusiasm of the Six-wing.

THE SELF-PRESERVATION INSTINCT IN THE SEVEN

Getting Mine. In the average range, Self-Preservation Sevens are determined, energetic people, driven to make sure that their basic needs and comforts will always be met. Their attitudes and concerns tend to emphasize the practical and the material. (In the immortal words of Scarlett O'Hara, "As God is my witness, I will never go hungry again!") They tend to be ambitious and work hard to insure that options will remain open to them.

Self-Preservation Sevens are also classic consumers. They enjoy shopping, traveling, and pampering themselves, making it their business to gather information about potential sources of enjoyment (catalogues, movie listings, travel and restaurant guides). These Sevens are especially on the lookout for sales and bargains, and like discussing these matters with friends. ("I just found the most darling mugs at the Pottery Barn." "That's a great computer monitor. How much did you pay for it?") While they enjoy socializing, Self-Preservation Sevens fear developing dependencies on others and avoid having others depend on them.

Less healthy Self-Preservation Sevens can feel impatient and panicky when their needs are not quickly met. They often experience anxieties about the loss of comforts or of material support and easily feel deprived. (Fears about going hungry are not uncommon.) They can be extremely demanding and cranky when frustrated, expecting others to meet their needs as soon as they are expressed—or even sooner.

In the unhealthy range, Self-Preservation Sevens can be extremely thoughtless and relentless in pursuit of security needs. They aggressively go after whatever they believe will make them feel more secure or stave off their anxiety, and brook no interference. Reckless with their finances and resources, spending out of control or gambling, they can be even more profligate with their own health and inner resources. They push themselves beyond reasonable limits, eating, drinking, and indulging themselves to excess.

THE SOCIAL INSTINCT IN THE SEVEN

Missing Out. In the average range, Social Sevens often cultivate a group of friends and "advisors" who share enthusiasms and interests with them. These people keep the Seven informed of new possibilities and

THE INSTINCTUAL VARIANTS

▲

provide the stimulation and variety that Sevens enjoy. Idealistic people, they like getting involved with social interactions and causes, finding these activities exciting. However, once involved in projects with other people, Social Sevens can become frustrated and feel bogged down by others' slower pace. At such times, social responsibility begins to feel burdensome—they are caught in a conflict between the desire to fulfill their commitments and the desire to go off and do their own thing. Moreover, Social Sevens are always on the lookout for a more stimulating setting ("This New Year's gathering is pretty nice, but I bet Ted's party will really be jumping after midnight!"). Social Sevens also resent authority, seeing it as arbitrary and unnecessary—yet another source of social restriction.

Less healthy Social Sevens tend to scatter their energy and resources, to half commit. They make sure to fill their calendars and date books, but also "pencil in" back-up plans, so that they are not trapped in any particular course of action. They tend to have many pokers in the fire, but are too distracted to get white-hot about any of them. They are friendly and engaging, even charming, but easily feel trapped, and may cancel appointments or dates with little or no notice if anxiety or a more promising social engagement presents itself.

In the unhealthy range, Social Sevens tend to dissipate their force and talent in endless successions of meetings, social gatherings, and "planning sessions" that are never brought to a conclusion. They leave a trail of loose ends and broken hearts, never alighting anywhere for long. They are unsettled and unsettling since flight from anxiety renders them irresponsible and leads them into potentially dangerous and destructive "social scenes."

THE SEXUAL INSTINCT IN THE SEVEN

The Neophile.   In the average range, Sexual Sevens are constantly looking for something new and beyond the ordinary; like Fours, they tend to reject the mundane. In all of their activities and interactions, they want to experience the intense charge of being alive. They see life through heightened imagination, idealizing themselves, their relationships, and reality. They often have wide-ranging curiosity and interests and are fascinated by new ideas and topics they see as being on the cutting edge. Sexual Sevens are magnetized by people whom they find interesting or refreshing. When the radar of their sexual instinct locks on to such a person, they do not hesitate to approach the person with charm and genuine interest. They feel temporarily dazzled and hypnotized by the object of their curiosity and may induce similar feelings in others. Sexual Sevens enjoy the excitement of fantasizing about future adventures and shared interests with the new person. They love wild ideas, wit, and humor—their minds move very quickly, but this can also cause restlessness with themselves and their relationships.

Less healthy Sexual Sevens can become fickle—both with their interests and with their affections. They fear commitment, preferring the intense feelings of infatuation that occur in the earliest stages of a relationship. (They love falling in love.) They revel in romance and in the process of mutual discovery, but as soon as the feelings become familiar, they are ready to explore other possibilities. Similarly, restlessness causes them to lack discernment. They may get involved in faddish or sensational ideas in glitzy packaging that are little more than temporary distractions. Disappointment soon follows.

In the unhealthy range, Sexual Sevens become even more reckless in their pursuit of charged excitement. They may involve themselves in crazy schemes and unrealistic or dangerous love affairs. They become thrill-seekers, looking for more and more extraordinary sources of entertainment while being less and less affected by any of it. They become hardened and dissipated from living on the edge, often burning out or damaging themselves in some permanent way from their excesses.

Most Sevens will encounter the following issues at some point in their lives. Noticing these patterns, "catching ourselves in the act," and simply seeing our underlying habitual responses to life will do much to release us from the negative aspects of our type.

THE SEVEN'S CHALLENGES TO GROWTH

▲

THE WAKE-UP CALL FOR TYPE SEVEN: "THE GRASS IS ALWAYS GREENER"

Sevens' characteristic temptation is the tendency to become dissatisfied with whatever they are doing or are currently experiencing. The grass is always greener somewhere else, and so they begin to look forward to the future, as if another event or activity will be the solution to their problems. ("I'm having dinner with friends now, but I wonder what's going on at that gallery opening tonight? Maybe if I eat quickly, I'll be able to go there, too!") If Sevens ignore their Wake-up Call—getting distracted by the possibilities of the next moment rather than being fully in the present one—they will begin moving in a wrong direction.

Imagine that you are talking with someone in a crowded restaurant and begin to overhear another conversation nearby. Do you shift your attention to the other conversation and eavesdrop while pretending to still be engaged with the first conversation? If so, you have succumbed to the Seven's Wake-up Call—with the result that you would enjoy neither conversation and would subtly insult your dinner partner who would likely sense your relocated attention.

H E A L T H Y	Level 1	*Key Terms:* *Joyful* *Satisfied*	Sevens let go of the belief that they require specific objects and experiences to feel fulfilled, so they are able to fully assimilate their experiences and be nourished by them. They also paradoxically achieve their Basic Desire—to be satisfied and content, to have their needs fulfilled—and they become appreciative, ecstatic, and deeply grateful.
	Level 2	*Anticipating* *Enthusiastic*	Sevens are focused on the world of possibilities and are excited by thinking about all the things they will do. Self-image: "I am happy, spontaneous, and outgoing."
	Level 3	*Realistic* *Productive*	Sevens reinforce their self-image by fully engaging with life and by doing things that will ensure that they will have what they need. Their passionate gusto for life is revealed in great versatility and a prolific output. They are optimistic and bold but also practical and accomplished.
A V E R A G E	Level 4	*Acquisitive* *Consuming*	Sevens begin to fear that they are missing out on other, more worthwhile experiences; thus they become restless and interested in having more and more options available to them. They stay busy, juggling many different tasks and plans and trying to keep up with the latest trends.
	Level 5	*Distracted* *Scattered*	Sevens worry that they will be bored or frustrated and that painful feelings will arise, so they try to keep themselves excited and occupied. They pump up the energy around them by talking, joking around, and pursuing new adventures, but they are often distracted and unfocused.
	Level 6	*Self-Centered* *Excessive*	Sevens are afraid that there will not be enough of whatever they believe they need, so they become impatient, seeking instant gratification. They can be very demanding but are seldom satisfied when their demands are met. Jaded and wasteful, they are cavalier about their habits, denying guilt.
U N H E A L T H Y	Level 7	*Insatiable* *Escaping*	Sevens fear that their actions are bringing them pain and unhappiness, and this may be true. They panic, trying to avoid their pain at any cost. They are highly impulsive and irresponsible and do whatever promises temporary relief from their anxiety, but they are joyless in their pursuits.
	Level 8	*Manic* *(Depressive)* *Reckless*	Sevens become so desperate to escape their anxiety that they fly out of control, recklessly acting out their pain rather than feeling it. Hysterical activity alternates with deep depression as they become increasingly unstable and erratic. Numb and heedless, they go to extreme lengths to suppress their pain.
	Level 9	*Overwhelmed* *Paralyzed*	The realization that they may have ruined their health, their lives, and their capacity for enjoyment is too much for unhealthy Sevens. Feeling that they no longer have options or ways out of their pain, they are panic-stricken and feel trapped. Often their excesses have resulted in severe financial and physical problems, even chronic pain.

TYPE 7

LEVELS OF DEVELOPMENT

This style of wandering attention has far more serious consequences for Sevens since so much of their lives are ruled by it. *Thinking becomes anticipating,* and they do not stay with anything long enough either to experience it deeply or to get any real satisfaction from it. When Sevens miss their Wake-up Call, no matter what they are doing, they are pulled somewhere else. Their wandering attention compels them to jump up and turn on the television set, check the refrigerator for a snack, call a friend on the phone, or doodle on a notepad rather than get down to work—or even stay with the novel they were enjoying.

"I don't want to miss out."

TRAINING THE MONKEY MIND

Choose any ordinary activity and concentrate on it. As you bring your attention to whatever task you have chosen, also notice when your attention has wandered on to something else. Gently bring your attention back to the original task until it wanders again. Then bring it back again to the task and so forth, repeating the attempt to stay focused.

It will generally be difficult to do this, especially in the beginning. If you stay with it, however, and if you are able to identify what is distracting you away from the task, you will have made an enormously valuable insight into the triggers of your Wake-up Call. Are there physical tensions that are also triggers? Does hunger, tiredness, or anxiety cause you to become distracted?

The Social Role: The Energizer

Average Sevens define themselves as the "Energizer," the person who must pump energy and excitement into a situation so that everyone will be charged up—and so that they can stay excited themselves. Since Sevens have a great deal of energy, it is easy for them to play this role. Like all Social Roles, however, once it has begun to be identified with, the person finds it increasingly difficult not to act this way.

Playing the role of the Energizer, the Spark Plug or Catalyst—as well as coconspirator and tempter into mischief—allows Sevens to become the center of attention. Their company is frequently sought after because others' spirits are uplifted by their cheer.

Kansas is an accomplished actress who has also enjoyed a career as a casting agent.

It's nice to know that you can affect the lives of others with your energy. I can often see spirits rise right in front of my eyes. I like to make people feel happy. I enjoy having that power. At times it's a conflict, though, as I attract a few too many people who are basically "downers." Truthfully, I do not think they want to feel better. I'm trying to learn to let them go their own way and save my energy for better uses, where it's appreciated. It's a gift to be able to lift the spirits of others in a natural way.

"Come on everybody! Let's get some juice going."

The problem arises when average Sevens begin to function only as superchargers who are outspoken and outrageous, who must be stimulating and dazzling all the time. This inevitably puts an enormous burden on them—and it becomes wearing on others as well. Most people, even other Sevens, find that relentless energy eventually becomes one-dimensional and tiresome. If others cannot keep up their pace, Sevens often interpret this as a form of rejection or abandonment that angers and frustrates them, leading them to move on to greener pastures and new audiences. Increasingly, however, they may feel trapped in their role, not knowing how to relate to others or get their needs met.

Velma, a multitalented educator and business consultant, experienced this frustration in her early teens.

As a child I felt free, uninhibited, full of life, and aware that I made people laugh. Other children sought me out because I was fun to be with. As a teenager, I wanted to be taken more seriously, but I never felt I was, especially by my family. So I responded to their level of expectation by acting out or by being silly, funny, or dramatic (rather than real) to get attention.

STIRRING THE POT

When you catch yourself entertaining others—getting the juice flowing, so to speak—notice whom you are doing this for. What does this excited state do for your contact with yourself? With others? Is it satisfying? What do you think would happen if you did not pump up the excitement in your environment?

Gluttony and Never Being Satisfied

The Seven's characteristic vice is *gluttony*, literally the desire to stuff oneself with food—and Sevens can be guilty of overeating and overdrinking, just as they can overdo all physical gratifications. Although a literal interpretation of gluttony can sometimes apply to Type Seven, it is more insightful to understand this Passion metaphorically, as the attempt to fill up an inner emptiness with things and experiences.

Gluttony is the emotional response of wanting to stuff the self with external gratifications in response to the experience of feeling frustrated, empty, and needy. Rather than experience emptiness and neediness directly, Sevens attempt to escape from anxiety by distracting themselves both with pleasures of the flesh and with mental stimulation. The deeper their underlying emotional distortions from childhood, the less likely Sevens will feel that they have enough experiences to satisfy them—they must have *more* to completely fill themselves—thus falling into the "Passion" of gluttony.

Because Sevens keep their minds full in order to defend themselves from feeling anxiety, they have trouble taking in sensory information unless it makes a strong impression on them. Their identity is thus based on *staying mentally excited*; the content of their minds—their individual thoughts—are not as important as the degree of stimulation and the anticipation of gratification that is produced. Then again, Sevens seek strong stimuli so that the impressions that do filter in will register on their minds and satisfy them. Since their identity is dependent on staying stimulated, Sevens tend to put few brakes on themselves and dislike boundaries or limitations of any kind. They want to be free to respond to impulses and desires as soon as they arise, without delay. Like all of the Passions, gluttony is self-defeating in the long run because the more Sevens "stuff themselves" indiscriminately in an attempt to find the nurturance they feel they were deprived of in childhood, the more unsatisfied they become.

Seeking Stimulation and Acquiring New Experiences

No matter what type we are, we often pursue what we think will make us happy without considering whether our choices have the *capacity* to make us happy. Under what circumstances does happiness arise? What makes it endure for more than a little while? How can we increase our happiness without running the risk of going overboard in some way? These kinds of questions are the special themes of Type Seven.

Average Sevens are typically sophisticates, connoisseurs, and collectors—those who know the best French restaurant or cognac or jeweler, what new movies are worth seeing, and what the latest news and trends are because they do not want to miss out.

One of the clearest demarcations between the healthy and average Sevens is that healthy Sevens know that they are most gratified by being focused and productive; they are contributing something new and potentially valuable to the world. Average Sevens become less productive because anxiety causes them to focus more on ways of entertaining and distracting themselves. Their creativity becomes supplanted by an increasing desire to acquire and consume.

Tara, a filmmaker, recognizes this pattern in herself.

It's unfortunately true that my tendency is to get very excited about something new, then get bored with it and not follow through. For

> "Life is a progress from want to want, not from enjoyment to enjoyment."
>
> SAMUEL JOHNSON

me, variety is the spice of life. Talking about doing something "inter-esting" makes me feel better, even if we don't do it. I like to learn new things. I love to take classes—whether it's cooking, or ballroom danc-ing, or Rollerblading, whatever. We get at least ten different maga-zines. I also like to bargain-shop because I like to check out all my options and make sure I have the most bang for the buck. It's also been hard for me to commit to a relationship because I'm always looking for something that might be better, making sure I've checked out all my options.

FINDING THE GIFT

Notice how the anticipation and desire for other experiences and things prevents you from savoring what you are experiencing right now. To explore this, you can play a game: take a moment to find something of wonder in your immediate experience. What is the gift you are receiving right now?

Boredom and Keeping Their Options Open

"The essence of boredom is to find yourself in the obsessive search for novelty."

GEORGE LEONARD

Sevens frequently complain about boredom and how much they hate it, although what they call boredom is the anxiety they feel when the environment is not providing adequate stimulation to keep pain and other negative feelings at bay. Similarly, feeling restricted and un-able to move on creates not only boredom but even panic. They do not want to feel stuck in any situation that would "tie them down" or force them to confront painful feelings before they are ready to do so.

To defend against boredom and the feelings that it brings, Sevens want to keep their minds full of fascinating possibilities, and they want to make sure that their supply lines to the new, the exciting, and the fashionable will always be open.

Velma, whom we met earlier, elaborates:

I preferred variety in all things. I had specific friends for my intellec-tual side, different ones for my emotional side, and altogether differ-ent ones for my sexual side. I was driven to seek fulfillment for all of these different sides of myself. It was not possible to resist. The more experiences I had, the more I wanted and then grew to need. My en-ergy was cycled and replenished by the diversity of my experiences. I managed to handle many different things without exhausting my-self—I was compelled to "do" everything, and I had the energy for all of it. I never wanted to do the traditional thing. Everything new and different that I tried fed my desire to continue to seek out the new and different. An unrelenting cycle.

Without inner guidance, Sevens must learn everything by a process of trial and error, and they are not likely to take other people's advice because they want to experience everything for themselves. They believe that by experiencing as many things as possible, they will know which options will make them happiest. But it is not humanly possible to experiment with everything: there are too many places to visit, foods to eat, clothes to wear, experiences to have. Their lives would be over before Sevens could have all the experiences they would need to have to be able to guide themselves from experience alone. Trying everything to see what it is like would take several lifetimes, and the near-infinite possibilities of the world would still not be exhausted. Furthermore, some of those experiences will most likely be damaging and dangerous since there are things in life that one needs to avoid, or at least be extremely cautious about. But for better or worse, Sevens usually have to learn things the hard way.

THE "B" WORD

Study what you are calling boredom. What does it feel like in your body? What is the sensation of boredom? As you are able to sense it, what associations or memories does it bring up?

Being Indiscriminate and Overdoing Their Activities

Average Sevens easily lose a sense of priorities, throwing themselves into constant activity, often overdoing things in many areas of their lives. They tend to be lavish with money to whatever degree their circumstances allow. They typically try to live life in the fast lane, whether they reside in a small town and must content themselves with trips to the local mall and bowling alley, or in a larger city with many more distractions and conveniences available to them. If they cannot get out, indiscriminate Sevens may watch television all day while chain-smoking or talking on the phone, or they may pass the time visiting friends or hanging out at the local bar.

"Why can't everyone keep up with me?"

Overdoing also applies to ideas, and Sevens tend to become stuck on something that catches their fancy, becoming so enthusiastic about it that they wear it into the ground. But the opposite is also true: as they become less healthy, they become less focused and less able to follow through. Many partially completed projects lie in their wake. The fact that many of their good (perhaps even brilliant) ideas are never realized becomes an additional source of frustration to them. If Sevens do not deal with the underlying anxieties that are keeping them in flight from themselves, they ultimately squander many of their best opportunities and inspirations.

Their quick minds and ability to talk can also deteriorate into being glib and facile, although Sevens generally consider this an ability to improvise for the sake of getting things moving or making for a better story. Average Sevens also tend to consider themselves instant experts on all manner of things, often getting in over their heads—and attempting to get through by "winging it."

REALISTIC SCHEDULES

For a few days, keep track of how long it actually takes you to do things: how long it takes to get to work, to a store, to shop, to meet with a friend, and so forth. See how this fits with your intended schedule. Is it possible to drop one or two activities per day to give yourself a little breathing room and to ensure that you will be able to fully enjoy the experiences you have committed to?

Avoiding Anxiety and Painful Feelings

Just as, during wartime, an enemy can jam radio signals by transmitting another, stronger radio signal, Sevens "jam" their own awareness of pain, deprivation, and sadness by constantly keeping their minds occupied with interesting and exciting possibilities. This does not mean, however, that average Sevens do not feel pain or suffer or get depressed—awareness of their suffering eventually penetrates their defenses. But as soon as possible, Sevens are on the go again. In a similar way, Sevens become adept at using their agile minds to reframe their experiences—finding a way to accentuate the positive and deflect their deeper feelings about even major tragedies.

Jessie, a therapist who embodies many of the sparkling qualities of Type Seven, recalls reframing a major loss in her life.

"A man who finds no satisfaction in himself seeks for it in vain elsewhere."

LA ROCHEFOUCAULD

> At age eleven, my dad suddenly died of a massive heart attack. I can remember thinking, "What are my options? What is the best thing I can do now?" Mom is in shock and suicidal, and my little sister is acting out. I can grow up. I decided I can be as happy, cheerful, and helpful as I can be. There is no time to linger in pain. This is the only way I will ever remain free—free from depression and despair.

CONTACTING DEEPER FEELINGS

As an Inner Work task, allow yourself to stop and experience your feelings more deeply. Recall a person or event that you know you have strong feelings about. Contemplate that person or event until your feelings begin to emerge. Notice what happens and how long you are able to stay with your feelings before you become aware that your attention has shifted. Can you identify what prevented you from staying with your feelings? What distracted you?

Frustration, Impatience, and Self-Centeredness

Sevens can be extremely demanding: the more anxious they become, the more impatient they become with others and with themselves. Nothing is happening fast enough. Nothing meets their needs. Without realizing it, Sevens can move through life projecting an underlying feeling of frustration onto all of their experiences.

They can also become deeply frustrated and impatient with themselves. Sevens may avoid dealing with their pain, but they are generally too alert to avoid noticing that they are squandering their talents and resources. Many worthwhile ideas go unrealized because Sevens become too impatient with themselves to allow their projects to fully develop.

This underlying frustration makes them highly intolerant of the foibles of others and unwilling to put up either with expectations placed on them or with other people's inability to meet *their* expectations. Their impatience can also be expressed as exasperation and a cutting, dismissive attitude.

Velma, the business consultant, continues:

> When I was a little girl, I would flop onto my mother's bed for a little chat, she would humor me for a while, then she would try to get rid of me. She told me that I didn't have any problems. She expected me to continue being the same happy girl I always was. I learned to be dismissive from my mother, and I catch myself doing the same thing to those whom I have no patience for.

Among the three frustration-based types (Fours, Ones, and Sevens), Sevens are perhaps the most overt in their expression of displeasure because they are also an assertive type. They are able to openly vent their unhappiness and frustration about whatever does not please them. Their underlying subconscious thought is "If I throw a big enough tantrum, I will get Mommy to come and attend to me." By acting out in such a demanding way, they often get what they want.

"I want it and I want it now!"

Others experience Sevens' impatience as unbridled self-centeredness. While Sevens can be attention-grabbing, they are not doing so because they want to be esteemed and admired by others, which would be a narcissistic motivation typical of types in the Feeling Triad. In fact, in certain situations, Sevens do not mind looking foolish if it will get the energy going and keep them out of contact with underlying anxiety. By contrast, Threes would never willingly let their foibles and imperfections hang out the way Sevens often do.

UNCOVERING FRUSTRATION

Observe the energy of frustration in yourself. When you notice that you are frustrated, stop and take a few deep breaths. What does frustration actually feel like? What happens when you sense it instead of acting it out?

Insensitivity and Impulsiveness

Since keeping up the momentum of their lives is a primary value, Sevens can take a kind of hit-and-run approach that leaves others hurt and confused. Staying in motion means suppressing guilt and regret about their actions. Sevens do not generally wish to hurt others, but their defenses make it difficult for them to acknowledge the pain that they cause—or even to be aware of it.

"It's not my problem."

Avoiding anxiety also causes Sevens to become increasingly impulsive—they leap before they look. Serious physical problems can result from heavy drinking or eating the wrong foods, smoking, or simply pushing themselves too hard in a constant search for stimulation. At their worst, they can be verbally abusive—intensely demanding, pushy, and rather nasty.

Devon speaks frankly about her way of dealing with problems.

There were times when I shut people out of my life on short notice. One day they thought we had a future, the next day I was saying good-bye. At the time, I had no remorse. They had driven me to leave, it was all their doing. Today I feel very bad that I had so little concern for their feelings, but the bottom line was if I began to feel pain, I didn't believe I would survive that pain. So I ran from it and found new pleasure elsewhere. It was a sure bet that when I felt down, I would get up, put my best dress and high heels on, and go out dancing.

CLEANING UP MESSES

People who know you recognize that you do not intend to hurt them, but in more stress-filled periods, you may have done so inadvertently.

When appropriate, have a conversation with a friend or loved one whom you fear you may have hurt. Ask their permission to talk with them first, then after you have apologized, hear what they have to say. Share with them your feelings about any aspects that still remain unresolved. This may not be easy for you, but clearing the air this way can go far in reducing your own underlying hurt and anxiety—and your need to bury them in excess and activity.

Escapism, Excessiveness, and Addiction

Average Sevens see themselves as spontaneous and fun-loving, with a live-for-today philosophy. What they are not always aware of, however, is how much this attitude can cover over an increasingly escapist approach to life. To the degree that Sevens are driven by fears and anxieties, they are not as free and spontaneous as they believe. They may blindly and impulsively pursue whatever promises immediate satisfaction, not considering the costs of their impulses. Their philosophy is "Enjoy now, pay later."

"Whatever gets you through the night."

Even painful, negative experiences can be exciting and can serve as a way of masking over deeper pain. For instance, the pain of alcoholism or drug addiction can be terrible, but for deteriorating Sevens, this pain is preferable to being overwhelmed by deeper grief and panic.

Sevens are caught in a cycle of anticipation, craving, and excess that we call *the chocolate syndrome.* One of the most exciting things about getting a box of expensive chocolate is the anticipation of the first bite. Similarly, it is not so much the experience itself *but their anticipation of the experience* that most excites Sevens. And as everyone (but Sevens) knows, a pleasure overdone can quickly become a source of displeasure. After several chocolates, we begin to experience the opposite of pleasure: pain and disgust.

The Seven's pursuit of gratification can take on the quality of an addiction: they require higher and higher doses of whatever has pleased them in order to stay in a state of stimulation and euphoria. Even dangerous experiences begin to leave them unaffected.

Tara speaks frankly about her past in this regard.

Avoiding things builds up anxiety, and as the anxiety becomes more and more intolerable, the need to distract becomes greater and greater. The distraction has to be "louder" than the anxiety to squelch it. I think this is why I got so out of control at various times in my life. Instead of being with the fear and pain, I'd run from it.

Avoid it at all costs, until it was impossible to run anymore. I could have easily overdosed on drugs, or gotten killed driving 140 mph.

ACCESSING YOUR FOLLOW-THROUGH

In your Inner Work Journal, make two lists. First, make a list of the major projects you have begun as an adult that you did not get around to finishing. Then make a list of the projects you have actually completed. Do you see patterns in both lists? Are you more serious about the excitement of having new plans and possibilities than the excitement of the process and satisfaction of finishing them? To what degree are you "addicted" to staying on the move at the expense of actually accomplishing something important to yourself? What do you think you have been running toward—and what have you been running away from?

REACTING TO STRESS: SEVEN GOES TO ONE

▲

Under increased stress, Sevens become aware that they need to focus their energies if they want to accomplish things. Thus, like average Ones, they begin to feel the need to restrain themselves. They begin to work harder, feeling that they alone can do the job properly, and attempt to impose limits on their behaviors. In effect, they force themselves to stay on track, while quickly becoming frustrated with these structures and limits. They may get either more restless and scattered, or more self-controlled and rigid, in which case their usual vivaciousness can give way to a grim seriousness.

Also like average Ones, Sevens under stress attempt to educate others—whether about an exciting book or workshop, a good place to shop, or a particular political or spiritual viewpoint. Their enthusiasm for their own opinions can rapidly shift into a tendency to debate or critique the views of others. They can become "short," impersonal, and highly impatient with any degree of incompetence in themselves or others. Under high stress, their underlying anger and resentment bubble to the surface, and they vent their frustration by scolding, nitpicking, and delivering withering sarcastic comments.

THE RED FLAG: THE SEVEN IN TROUBLE

▲

If Sevens are overstressed for an extended period of time, if they have suffered a serious crisis without adequate support or coping skills, or if they have suffered from chronic abuse in childhood, they may cross the shock point into the unhealthy aspects of their type. This may lead them to a fearful recognition that their lives are becoming out of control and that their choices and actions are actually increasing their pain.

If Sevens can recognize the truth in these fears, they may begin to turn their lives around and move toward health and liberation. On the other hand, they may become even more scattered, impulsive, and manic, desperately throwing themselves into reckless activities to avoid their pain at any cost. ("Whatever gets you through the night is okay.") If Sevens persist in this attitude, they may cross into the unhealthy range. If you or someone you know is exhibiting the following warning signs for an extended period of time—more than two or three weeks—getting counseling, therapy, or other support is highly advisable.

WARNING SIGNS

POTENTIAL PATHOLOGY: Manic-Depressive Disorders, Borderline Conditions, some elements of Histrionic Personality Disorder, Obsessive-Compulsive Disorders, substance abuse.

▶ Extreme dissipation and attempts to escape anxiety

▶ Serious longstanding and debilitating addictions

▶ Impulsiveness, offensiveness, and infantile reactions

▶ Compulsive activities and highly elated mood

▶ Periods of being out of control

▶ Mania, depression, and wild mood swings

▶ Periods of panic and paralyzing terror

PRACTICES THAT HELP SEVENS DEVELOP

▲

▶ When you are mentally revved up, take a moment to breathe and see what is really going on with you. Notice especially if you are afraid or upset about something, and see if you can observe how the velocity of your thoughts leads you away from experiencing these feelings. When you see your mind racing and free-associating, it is a good time to ask yourself, "What's up?" Almost always you will see that you are masking some source of anxiety. The word *boring* can be a big clue. Any time you feel in danger of being "bored," stop and see what you are avoiding.

▶ It is not so much that you ignore your negative feelings as that you process them *incompletely*. You more or less notice them and then want to move on to the next thing. Really allowing things to affect you, to impact you on a deeper level, is not the same as wallowing in negativity. On the contrary, letting the events of your life, even the painful ones, touch you deeply will only enrich your experience and make your joy more meaningful and real. See how your feelings are experienced in your body. What does sadness feel like? Where do you notice it? In your stomach or your chest or your face? How about eagerness? Simply identifying a feeling, saying to yourself, "I feel sad," is a beginning, but it is not the same as fully experiencing and being affected by your sadness—or your happiness, for that matter.

▶ Learn to notice your impatience and its roots. As a Seven, you can be extremely impatient with the pace and energy levels of others but also extremely impatient with yourself. Because you are talented in many areas, you tend not to develop any one fully. You shortchange yourself both because of your impatience with yourself and with the process of learning and acquiring skills. Also be on guard for the "instant expert" syndrome. A basic grasp of a subject or a certain facility with a skill, combined with your charm and bravado, can certainly open doors for you. But if you do not really know what you are talking about, if you have not really done your homework, if your ideas are half-baked, others will soon catch on, and your reputation—despite your talents—will suffer. Sevens hate being referred to as superficial, but it is your impatience that causes others to perceive you that way. Take the time to bring your abilities to fruition.

▶ Find the joy of the ordinary. Like Fours, Sevens tend to seek out heightened reality—you like things to be extraordinary, fabulous, exciting, and stimulating. The amazing thing, however, is that when we are present, *all of our experiences are extraordinary.* Cleaning your room or eating an orange can be a totally fulfilling experience if you are in it one hundred percent. Each moment is a unique source of delight and amazement. Your fear of deprivation and your desire to entertain yourself prevent you from finding the fulfillment you seek. Think about which moments from your past were the most alive and fulfilling—a child's birth, a wedding, a picnic with friends during college, a perfect sunset. What about them made them so satisfying and real? Also notice that these moments do not necessarily make exciting stories, although they have another quality that makes them fulfilling. Your life will change to the degree that you find out what that quality is.

▶ Meditation can be extremely helpful for Sevens, as for Type Six, especially for quieting down the mind. If you begin to meditate, you will soon recognize the intensity of your mental chatter, and the effort to relax and identify more with your presence in the moment will be challenging. It is also extremely important to notice how you *end* your meditation. Sevens tend to lurch out of the meditation, as if the personality cannot wait two seconds to start revving up again. Be mindful as you end the sitting, and see if you can carry your inner quiet into your actions. The quality of the meditative mind will do little to transform us if it is confined to those few minutes a day we allot for our inner life.

▶ You do tend to be happier and more exuberant than most people. See what happens when you can share that feeling with others without pushing—and without "demonstrating" it to them. You are most profound and effective when you are grounded and steady—at such times your joy is evident and affecting to everyone. Besides, if your joy is genuine, it does not depend on "stirring the pot" and cannot be reduced or lost if people are not reacting to it.

Even average Sevens tend to be creative, but when they are more balanced and grounded, they can be brilliant, multifaceted people, synthesizing and cross-fertilizing their many diverse areas of experience. Their varied abilities and interests, enjoyment of work, and extroverted qualities often lead them to success in the world.

Sevens, as they say, have their feet on the ground. They are not wool-gatherers or idlers—they are engaged with the reality and with the practical business of living life. They understand that they must be realistic, productive, and hardworking to have the financial means to support their many dreams.

Thus, healthy Sevens are not satisfied with merely consuming the work of others—whether that work is a hamburger or a piece of designer clothing. They know that their primary enjoyment of life comes from *contributing* something to the world. Healthy Sevens would rather design a dress than buy one. They would rather make a movie than watch someone else's. After all, then they can have it be exactly the way they want it to be.

One way that Sevens constructively work with their versatility and desire for different experiences is through multitasking. By maintaining several different tasks at any given time, they are able to shift from one to the other, to use a variety of skills, and to see ways that their different skills or interests relate with each other. All of this can be satisfying for Sevens, and as long as they can prioritize and set limits, they excel at this style of working.

Similarly, Sevens have a talent for generating ideas quickly and spontaneously. They are big-picture people who like getting projects started and are good at brainstorming fresh approaches to problems. Their minds almost overflow with creative concepts and possibilities, and they excel at considering options that others might not perceive. Healthy Sevens also maintain the discipline required to develop their ideas to fruition.

Perhaps Type Seven's greatest gift is the ability to maintain a positive outlook and sense of abundance. When this outlook is tempered by realism and a willingness to deal with difficult feelings, Sevens are able to generate an infectious enthusiasm for whatever situation is at hand. Far from timid, they live fully and encourage others to do the same. ("You only go around once.") Further, their willingness to explore and to be open to new experiences can lead them to be well rounded and knowledgeable. They truly make the world their home and enjoy sharing with others the riches they find on their journeys.

Tara continues:

BUILDING ON THE SEVEN'S STRENGTHS

▲

"The world is my oyster."

Life is a big playground. Everything is interesting. There's a kind of spontaneous joy and curiosity I have about life. I feel supported by the universe, like everything will turn out okay. Even when things are dark and bad, something in me really believes that it will turn out all right in the end. The world can be cruel and awful, but my sense is that it isn't personally hostile toward me. Because of this basic feeling of security, I'm more willing to be open and curious about things.

THE PATH OF INTEGRATION: SEVEN GOES TO FIVE

▲

Sevens actualize themselves and remain healthy by learning to slow down and quiet the rapid activity of their minds so that impressions can affect them more deeply, in the manner of healthy Fives. No longer addicted to seeking extraordinary experiences and distractions, integrating Sevens are able to stay with their observations and experiences long enough to discover all sorts of amazing things about themselves and the world around them. This both gives them more of the guidance they seek and enhances their productivity and creativity. Further, what they produce has far more resonance and meaning for others.

Cultivating a quieter, more focused mind brings Sevens into closer contact with their own Essential guidance; thus they are able to recognize which experiences will be of real value to them. No longer distracted by anxiety about making wrong choices and missing out on the best course of action, integrating Sevens simply *know* what to do. Exploring reality in greater depth does not cause integrating Sevens to lose their spontaneity or enthusiasm; on the contrary, they become more free to savor each moment.

Imitating the average qualities of Fives, however, will do little to help integrating Sevens. Getting lost in thoughts, emotional detachment, and anxieties about coping with the needs of others will only exacerbate the Seven's cerebral circus. Trying to force themselves to concentrate will not work either, because such efforts are based on repression. But as Sevens learn to quiet their minds and tolerate the anxiety that arises, they gradually and naturally begin to open to the clarity, innovation, insight, and knowing qualities of the healthy Five.

TRANSFORMING PERSONALITY INTO ESSENCE

▲

The key thing for Sevens to understand about themselves is that as long as they are directly pursuing happiness and satisfaction, they will never attain them. Fulfillment is not the result of "getting" anything: it is a state of being that arises when we allow the richness of the present moment to touch us. When Sevens understand this and are able to let go of the conditions they place on their happiness, an inner spaciousness opens up, and the simple pleasure of existing arises in them. They understand that Being itself, pure existence, is pleasurable. Thus, they become deeply and profoundly appreciative of life itself.

After years of inner work, Tara has also discovered this for herself.

I began to understand that life isn't always fun. I have redefined what is fun and not fun and realized that those ideas are generally false. A lot of what I thought was not fun, like washing the dishes, is actually just fine and is really no different or any worse from other activities I thought of as fun.

Certainly there is nothing wrong with thinking about the future, but with Sevens, it is the primary way that they lose their connection with Presence. The most challenging part of the transformative process for Sevens involves their ability to stay in contact with present reality. This is difficult because staying more awake and present eventually brings into consciousness the very pain and deprivation that Sevens have been fleeing. At such times, Sevens might well remember that the suffering they truly fear has already occurred—and they survived. With the support of Presence, then, Sevens are able to be with their pain long enough to really metabolize it. Grieving, like any organic process, has a cycle and requires a definite period of time—it cannot be rushed. Further, if we cannot be with our pain, we cannot be with our joy.

When this work has been done, high-functioning Sevens have the ability to be satisfied with very little because they realize there will always be enough for them and for everyone else. Perhaps their greatest gift is their *ability to see the spiritual in the material world*—to perceive the Divine in the ordinary.

Jessie, the therapist we met earlier, shares a moment in which this ability served her well.

> "Gratitude unlocks the fullness of life."
>
> MELODY BEATTIE

When my stepson was dying of AIDS, I held him in my arms and asked myself, What is the best option right now? What is the most wonderful thing he can experience in this moment? So I guided him toward the peace and comfort of the other side. Gregory was able to gently release the physical aspect of his life, to feel that his life was done, and to actually choose the moment of his last breath. Everything was complete and perfect, and we were with him.

THE EMERGENCE OF ESSENCE

The Hindus say that God created the universe as a dance so that He could enjoy the pleasure of His own creation reflecting back to Himself. It is this feeling of wonder and awe at the beauty of life that fully infuses Sevens.

From this Essential point of view, the Seven personifies the quality of

"The fullness of joy is to behold God in everything."

JULIAN OF NORWICH

joy, the final state that human beings were meant to be in. Joy is a natural experience that arises spontaneously when we experience ourselves as Being—when we are free of the endless chatter, planning, and projects of our ego minds. In the Christian view, human beings were created to go to Heaven and to enjoy the Beatific Vision—to spend all eternity contemplating God in utter and complete bliss. Thus, *ecstasy* is our final and rightful state. When Sevens remember this truth, they are drawn back to joy as their essential state, and they embody it and spread it to others.

Jessie continues:

> I have learned to recenter myself through quiet times of contempla-
> tion and reflection. I have discovered another whole world inside of
> myself. The spirit that is me is free, and I have found so much to feast
> on. My inner world transcends my outer doings, but it also spills out
> and colors all of it. The joy sometimes just bubbles up and life is a de-
> light. I find that I do not need a lot, yet my life is filled. At my best, I
> am overcome with awe and gratitude. I live in the moment and trust
> that all of my needs will be met

Above all, Sevens realize on the most profound level of their consciousness that life really is a gift. One of the big lessons that the Seven offers is that there is nothing wrong with life, nothing wrong with the material world. It is the gift of the Creator. If we were not to take anything for granted, we would be flooded with joy and gratitude all the time. When we have no claims on life, everything becomes a Divine gift capable of sweeping us into ecstasy. Of all the types, this is the struggle of the Seven—to remember the real source of joy and to live out of that truth.

Add your scores for the fifteen statements for Type Seven. Your result will be between 15 and 75. The following guidelines may help you discover or confirm your personality type.

▶ 15   You are probably not an assertive type (not a Three, Seven, or Eight).

▶ 15–30   You are probably not a Type Seven.

▶ 30–45   You most probably have Seven-issues or a Seven parent.

▶ 45–60   You most likely have a Seven-component.

▶ 60–75   You are most likely a Seven (but could still be another type if you are thinking too narrowly about Type Seven).

Sevens are most likely to misidentify themselves as Twos, Fours, and Threes. Nines, Threes, and Twos are most likely to misidentify themselves as Sevens.

CHAPTER 14

▼

TYPE EIGHT:
THE CHALLENGER

▲

THE LEADER

THE PROTECTOR

THE PROVIDER

THE ENTREPRENEUR

THE MAVERICK

THE ROCK

"From this arises the question whether it is better to be loved rather than feared, or feared rather than loved. It might perhaps be answered that we should wish to be both: but since love and fear can hardly exist together, if we must choose between them, it is far safer to be feared than loved."

—NICCOLÒ MACHIAVELLI, *THE PRINCE*

"It is fatal to enter any war without the will to win it."

—DOUGLAS MACARTHUR

"Power doesn't have to show off. Power is confident, self-assuring, self-starting and self-stopping, self-warming and self-justifying. When you have it, you know it."

—RALPH ELLISON

"Man must evolve for all human conflict a method which rejects revenge, aggression, and retaliation. The foundation of such a method is love."

—MARTIN LUTHER KING, JR.

THE RISO-HUDSON TAS

Type Attitude Sorter

Score each of the following statements according to how true or applicable to you it is on the following scale:

1.......*Not at All True*

2.......*Seldom True*

3.......*Somewhat True*

4.......*Generally True*

5.......*Very True*

See page 313 for scoring key.

_____ 1. I am extremely independent and don't like having to rely on others for what I really need.

_____ 2. I feel that "you have to break some eggs to make an omelet."

_____ 3. When I care about people, I often begin to think of them as "my people" and feel like I need to watch out for their interests.

_____ 4. I know how to get results: I know how to reward people and how to put pressure on them to get things done.

_____ 5. I do not have much sympathy for those who are weak and vacillating—weakness just invites trouble.

_____ 6. I am strong-willed and do not give up or back down easily.

_____ 7. I am never prouder than when I see someone I've taken under my wing make it on their own.

_____ 8. I have a tender, even somewhat sentimental side that I show to very few people.

_____ 9. People who know me appreciate the fact that I talk straight to them and tell them exactly what's on my mind.

_____ 10. I've had to work hard for everything I have—I think struggle is good because it toughens you up and makes you clear about what you want.

_____ 11. I see myself as a challenger, as someone who pushes people beyond their comfort zone to achieve their best.

_____ 12. My sense of humor is earthy, sometimes even crude, although I think most people are too prissy and thin-skinned.

_____ 13. I can get into a towering rage, but it blows over.

_____ 14. I feel most alive when I do what others think is impossible: I like to go to the edge and see if I can beat the odds.

_____ 15. Somebody usually has to come up on the short end of the stick, and I don't want it to be me.

PERSONALITY TYPE EIGHT: THE CHALLENGER

The Powerful, Dominating Type:
Self-Confident, Decisive, Willful, and Confrontational

We have named personality type Eight *the Challenger* because, of all the types, Eights enjoy taking on challenges themselves as well as giving others opportunities that challenge them to exceed themselves in some way. They are charismatic and have the physical and psychological capacities to persuade others to follow them into all kinds of endeavors—from starting a company, to rebuilding a city, to running a household, to waging war, to making peace.

Eights have enormous willpower and vitality, and they feel most alive when they are exercising these capacities in the world. They use their abundant energy to effect changes in their environment—to leave their mark on it—but also to keep the environment, and especially other people, from hurting them and those they care about. At an early age, Eights understand that this requires strength, will, persistence, and endurance—qualities that they develop in themselves and that they look for in others.

Thayer is a stockbroker who has worked intensively on understanding her Type Eight personality. She recounts a childhood incident in which she could clearly see the development of this pattern.

> Much of my tenacity and toughness comes from my dad. He always told me not to let anybody push me around. It was not okay to cry. I learned to master my weaker side early on. At the tender age of eight, a huge horse ran away with me. When an adult caught the horse, I resolutely dismounted without a tear. I could tell my father was proud.

Eights do not want to be controlled or to allow others to have power over them (their Basic Fear), whether the power is psychological, sexual, social, or financial. Much of their behavior is involved with making sure that they retain and increase whatever power they have for as long as possible. An Eight may be a general or a gardener, a small businessman or a mogul, the mother of a family or the superior of a religious community. No matter: being in charge and leaving their imprint on their sphere is uniquely characteristic of them.

Eights are the true "rugged individualists" of the Enneagram. More than any other type, they stand alone. They want to be independent and resist being indebted to anyone. They often refuse to give in to

▶ BASIC FEAR: Of being harmed or controlled by others, of violation

▶ BASIC DESIRE: To protect themselves, to determine their own course in life

▶ SUPEREGO MESSAGE: "You are good or okay if you are strong and in control of your situation."

"We either make ourselves miserable, or we make ourselves strong. The amount of work is the same."

CARLOS CASTENEDA

social convention, and they can defy fear, shame, and concern about the consequences of their actions. Although they are usually aware of what people think of them, they do not let the opinions of others sway them. They go about their business with a steely determination that can be awe-inspiring, even intimidating to others.

"I am the master of my fate."

Although, to some extent, Eights fear physical harm, far more important is their fear of being disempowered or controlled in some way. Eights are extraordinarily tough and can absorb a great deal of physical punishment without complaint—a double-edged blessing since they often take their health and stamina for granted and overlook the health and well-being of others as well. Yet they are desperately afraid of being hurt emotionally and will use their physical strength to protect their feelings and keep others at a safe emotional distance. Beneath the tough facade is vulnerability, although it has been covered over by a layer of emotional armor.

Thus, Eights are often extremely industrious, but at the price of losing emotional contact with many of the people in their lives. Those close to them may become increasingly dissatisfied with this state of affairs, which confounds Eights. ("I don't understand what my family is complaining about. I bust my hump to provide for them. Why are they disappointed in me?")

When this happens, Eights feel misunderstood and may distance themselves further. In fact, beneath their imposing exterior, Eights often feel hurt and rejected, although this is something they seldom talk about because they have trouble admitting their vulnerability to themselves, let alone to anyone else. Because they fear that they will be rejected (divorced, humiliated, criticized, fired, or harmed in some way), Eights attempt to defend themselves by rejecting others first. The result is that average Eights become *blocked in their ability to connect with people or to love* since love gives the other power over them, reawakening their Basic Fear.

The more Eights build up their egos in order to protect themselves, the more sensitive they become to any real or imaginary slight to their self-respect, authority, or preeminence. The more they attempt to make themselves impervious to hurt or pain (whether physical or emotional), the more they shut down emotionally to become hardened and rock-like.

When Eights are emotionally healthy, however, they have a resourceful, can-do attitude as well as a steady inner drive. They take the initiative and make things happen with a great passion for life. They are honorable and authoritative—natural leaders who have a solid, commanding presence. Their groundedness gives them abundant common sense as well as the ability to be decisive. Eights are willing to take the heat, knowing that any decision cannot please everyone. But as much as possible, they want to look after the interests of the people in their charge without playing favorites. They use their talents and fortitude to construct a better world for everyone in their lives.

THE CHILDHOOD PATTERN

Most Eights have told us that they felt that they had to become "adults" at an early age, perhaps to help bring in money to raise the other children in the family because of an absent father or some other calamity. They may have had to deal with a dangerous environment (such as drug dealers, or street gangs, or some kind of war zone), or with an erratic or violent adult in their home. Other Eights grow up in fairly normal families but may have felt the need to protect their feelings for other reasons. In short, Eights tend to grow up quickly, and *survival issues* are foremost to them, as if they were asking, "How can I—and the few people I care about—survive in a cruel, uncaring world?"

Roseann is an Eight who recalls the enormous pressure created by her childhood situation.

> Being tough with my tough father set up a relationship with my mother as I got older. She would often ask me to go to my father with a request regarding a family outing, a movie—stuff like that. "You ask him," she'd say. "If I suggest it, he'll say no." On the one hand, this made me feel proud that she thought I was strong and tough enough to deal with him. But on the other hand, I resented it because even though my father and I seemed to be respectful of each other's temper, I was always afraid of him. I was just a little girl, after all. I just knew that I couldn't show it or ever admit it.

Young Eights soon get the idea that it is not safe to be gentle or giving. These attitudes feel "soft" and "weak" and in their minds only invite rejection, betrayal, and pain. They feel that it is best not to let down their guard, so if there is going to be any nurturing or warmth in their lives, someone else will have to provide it.

Eights often report that as children, they struggled with powerful feelings of having been rejected or betrayed. They were typically assertive and adventuresome and got into "situations" that led to being punished frequently. Rather than detach or withdraw from their punishers, young Eights defended themselves against the feeling of rejection with the attitude, "To hell with them. Who needs them? No one tells me what to do!" Of course, like anyone else, Eights want to be loved, but the more they felt rejected and treated like misfits, the more they hardened their hearts.

Please note that the childhood pattern we are describing here does not cause the personality type. Rather, it describes tendencies that we observe in early childhood that have a major impact on the type's adult relationships.

Arlene is a member of a religious order, and has been a constant source of strength and support for those in her community. She recalls an unhappy early event that brought out her Eight defense.

> When I was two and a half years old, my younger sister was born. My mother was in bed nursing her, and I kept crawling into bed to be with my mother. She told me several times to stay with my aunt who would put me on her lap. My mother was concerned that I would hurt the baby. But I was persistent and kept crawling off my aunt's lap and getting back into the bed with my mother. My mother finally just pushed me off the bed, and when that happened, I think my feelings said, "I'll get even!" Later, when I was somewhat older, I determined that I would leave home for the convent after eighth grade, even though this deeply hurt my folks. But I didn't consider my parents' wishes and just did it anyway.

Young Eights may learn to play the role of the Scapegoat (the Black Sheep or Problem Child). In family systems theory, "scapegoats" typically make explicit the hidden problems in a family, through either word or deed. As adults, Eights become mavericks, rebelling against restraints and bucking the system wherever possible.

Sometimes the "decision" to steel themselves came when the child *felt betrayed by a parent* or another significant adult. The child may have been abandoned by the parents in a boarding school, or left with relatives, or had their savings or some other valuable taken from them unfairly. They may also have been the victims of physical or sexual abuse. But because of the gross imbalance of power between young Eights and those who treated them unfairly, they could do little or nothing about it except to make the decision never to allow this to happen to them again.

Kit is an accomplished entrepreneur in the fashion industry. Here she recounts a momentous decision she made as a young girl.

> The sudden death of my black nanny when I was seven was an important turning point for me. She was secretly supportive of me and would comfort me in different ways when I was punished by my parents. But when she died unexpectedly, I felt truly alone. I was furious at my parents for not allowing me to attend her funeral, angry at my brothers for their apparent indifference, and irate at my nanny for leaving me. Yet I never shed a tear. I decided that I was truly on my own, and that I didn't need anyone.

Eights consider betrayal to be a pivotal point in their lives because it marked the death of their innocence and goodness. When their inner core was betrayed by someone important, Eights decided that they would never allow themselves to be vulnerable or innocent again. They would never allow themselves to drop their guard. For a time, Eights may secretly grieve their lost innocence, but eventually they accept this as the way they must be to meet life's challenges. If they have come from backgrounds that were remorselessly threatening, Eights tend to become as remorseless to themselves as they are to others. Once the heart has been buried, even grief over lost innocence can be forgotten.

THE EIGHT WITH A SEVEN-WING: THE INDEPENDENT

Healthy Having a quick mind combined with a vision for practical possibilities, people of this subtype are often charismatic and able to attract the support of others to join them in their vision. They are action-oriented, and want to have an impact on their world. They are also good at challenging others to stretch their abilities and to surpass their own expectations so that their lives can be better in some practical way. This is the most independent subtype, often entrepreneurial, and interested in creating projects that will ensure their independence.

Average People of this subtype are adventurous risk-takers; they tend to have "big plans" and, in order to enlist the cooperation of others, to make big promises and exaggerate the potential of their ventures. They are also one of the most sociable types, talkative and outgoing, with great self-confidence. They are pragmatic, practical, and competitive and are not overly concerned with pleasing others or with putting up with what they perceive as weakness or inefficiency. They can become impatient, impulsive, and more likely to be led by their feelings than the other subtype. They are more openly aggressive and confrontational and less likely to back down from a fight.

THE EIGHT WITH A NINE-WING: THE BEAR

Healthy People of this subtype combine strength, self-confidence, and determination with quiet groundedness and a certain laid-back quality. They are noticeably steadier in the pursuit of their aims and are not as openly aggressive or as easily perturbed as other Eights. They are also warmer and more family-oriented, asserting power and leadership through protectiveness. There is less of a "wheeler-dealer" quality in their makeup: while they also want to be independent, they want to do so at their own pace. The ability to reassure and calm others enhances their capacity for leadership.

THE WING SUBTYPES

▲

Examples

Franklin D. Roosevelt
Mikhail Gorbachev
Donald Trump
Barbara Walters
Don Imus
Frank Sinatra
Courtney Love
Susan Sarandon
Bette Davis
Joan Crawford

Examples

Martin Luther King, Jr.
Golda Meir
Toni Morrison
John Wayne
Sean Connery
Sigourney Weaver
Paul Newman
Indira Gandhi
Glenn Close
Norman Mailer

Average   These people seem to have a dual nature, manifesting themselves differently in different areas of their lives. For instance, they can be warm and affectionate at home but highly determined and aggressive at work. People of this subtype generally like to live quietly and unobtrusively, preferring to control their affairs from behind the scenes. They also tend to speak slowly and to be highly attuned to the nonverbal cues and body language of others—friendly while secretly sizing people up. Strategic and watchful, they almost dare others to underestimate them. Eights of this subtype can be stubborn, impassive, and quietly menacing. When they lose their tempers, the explosion comes suddenly and violently, and then is gone.

THE INSTINCTUAL VARIANTS

▲

THE SELF-PRESERVATION INSTINCT IN THE EIGHT

The Survivor.   In the average range, Self-Preservation Eights are the most no-nonsense kind of Eights. They focus intently on practical matters and on "bringing home the bacon" so that they will have enough money and power to ensure their well-being as well as that of their loved ones. They are the most domestic Eights, enjoying the privacy of their homes; but whether male or female, they definitely insist on ruling the roost. Self-Preservation Eights tend to be more materialistic than the other two Instinctual Variants, wanting money for the power it gives but also looking to acquire prized possessions (such as cars or homes) as symbols of their impact and importance. They are the most prone to workaholism and may work several jobs or unusually long hours to earn enough income to feel satisfied and protected.

Self-Preservation Eights tend to worry about protecting their possessions and investments. Indeed, even within their homes, they can be extremely territorial about their personal belongings. ("No one goes into the garage without *my* permission!") It makes them feel secure if they have a clear idea of where their possessions are and that they are safe. Thus, they are constantly checking to ensure that their finances, personal and professional position, and belongings are not threatened in any way.

In the unhealthy range, Self-Preservation Eights can become bullies and thieves, justifying their destructive behavior by the belief that they are "toughening up" others. After all, it is a jungle out there. At the very least, they often feel justified acting selfishly, going after their needs—often financial and sexual—without regard for consequences or for others' feelings. They do not hesitate to undermine or attack others to protect their interests and to make sure that no one has the ability to threaten their material security.

THE SOCIAL INSTINCT IN THE EIGHT

Gusto and Camaraderie. In the average range, Social Eights express their intensity through the powerful bonds that they make with others. Honor and trust are big issues for them, and they enjoy making pacts with those who have proven themselves trustworthy. They will test the people they care about so that friendships feel solid and safe. Feelings of social awkwardness or rejection are eased by surrounding themselves with friends who are predictable and who accept them as they are. (Not everyone will be let into their inner circle, but for those who pass the test by demonstrating loyalty and solidity, the sky is the limit.) Having a night out, going on a big weekend jaunt, or holding court with the inner circle are Social Eight ways of relaxing, and Social Eights will do anything for the few that they care about. They enjoy hosting social events, wining and dining their friends, and sharing adventures with "real people." They also enjoy debates about politics, sports, or religion—the more heated, the better.

Lower in the Levels, Social Eights may take friends for granted or reject them over a disagreement. They can easily feel betrayed and tend to hold grudges longer than most. Once someone has been exiled from the inner circle, Eights are extremely reluctant to let the person near them again. Also, their penchant for storytelling can degenerate into gross exaggeration and "snowing" people. They become charming rogues and con artists, full of promises but offering little real support for others.

In the unhealthy range, due to feelings of rejection and betrayal, Social Eights can become extremely antisocial loners. They are often reckless and self-destructive and are particularly prone to substance abuse. The combination of intoxication and rage can rapidly destroy much of the good in their lives. In this state, Social Eights are generally unable to comprehend the damage they are doing to themselves or others.

THE SEXUAL INSTINCT IN THE EIGHT

Taking Charge. In the average range, Sexual Eights are the most quietly intense and charismatic kind of Eights. They are passionate about whomever they care about and want to feel that they have had a major impact on the lives of those in their sphere of influence. (This can be a positive or negative impact, of course, depending on the Level of Development.) Like Social Eights, they enjoy rabble-rousing good times, although there is more of a rebellious streak in Sexual Eights. They have a sly sense of humor and enjoy being "bad." Sexual Eights can be deeply loving and devoted, but they can also see

H E A L T H Y	Level 1	*Key Terms:* *Self-Surrendering Heroic*	Eights let go of the belief that they must always be in control of their environment, which allows them to let down their guard and heal their hearts. They also paradoxically achieve their Basic Desire—the desire to protect themselves, and become magnanimous, self-surrendering, courageous, forgiving, and sometimes heroic.
	Level 2	*Self-Reliant Strong*	Eights use their energy and willpower to become independent and in control of their lives. They are vigorous and action-oriented. Self-image: "I am assertive, direct, and resourceful."
	Level 3	*Self-Confident Leading*	Eights reinforce their self-image by taking on challenges. They prove their strength through action and achievement, through protecting others and providing for them, and through bringing out others' strengths. They are strategic and decisive and enjoy realizing constructive projects.
A V E R A G E	Level 4	*Pragmatic Enterprising*	Eights begin to fear that they do not have enough resources to succeed with their projects or to carry out their role as provider. Thus, they become more shrewd and expedient about getting the resources they want. Businesslike and competitive, they are more guarded about their feelings.
	Level 5	*Self-Glorifying Dominating*	Eights worry that others will not respect them or give them their due, so they try to convince others of their importance. They boast, bluff, and make big promises to get people aligned with their plans. Willful and proud, they want others to know that they are in charge.
	Level 6	*Confrontational Intimidating*	Eights are afraid that others are not backing them up, and they may lose control of their situation as a result. They try to pressure others to do what they want through threats and oppression. They are also bad-tempered and defiant of any demands placed on them, pushing others to the limit.
U N H E A L T H Y	Level 7	*Ruthless Dictatorial*	Eights fear that others are turning against them, and this may be true. They feel betrayed and unable to trust anyone, so they become determined to protect themselves at any cost. Seeing themselves as outlaws, they feel they are beyond the pale of society and can be predatory, vengeful, and violent.
	Level 8	*Megalo-maniacal Terrorizing*	Eights become so desperate to protect themselves and so fearful of retaliation for their actions that they begin to attack potential rivals before they can threaten them. They respect no boundaries, and rapidly overreach themselves. Delusions of invulnerability lead them to endanger themselves and others.
	Level 9	*Sociopathic Destructive*	The realization that they have created powerful enemies who are capable of defeating them is too much for unhealthy Eights. They try to destroy everything rather than let anyone triumph over them or control them. They can go on rampages, remorselessly ruining everything in their path, possibly murdering others in the process.

intimacy as a struggle for control or an opportunity to build their self-esteem. They can play rough with intimates, are stimulated by a good argument, and can be impatient with niceness. Like the Self-Preservation Eights, they can be competitive, but more for the thrill of competition and less for security reasons. In fact, Sexual Eights lose interest if they win too easily, and this extends into their intimate relationships as well.

Lower in the Levels, they demand loyalty, consistency, and attention and have little tolerance for wandering interests in the other. In fact, they see themselves in a parental, mentoring role and want to remold people into shapes that better fit their needs and plans. They have an opinion about every aspect of the other's life. Needless to say, this makes it difficult for them to maintain a relationship of equality.

In the unhealthy range, Sexual Eights can attempt to completely control and dominate their partner. They are extremely jealous, seeing the other as a possession, and may seek to isolate their significant other from friends or other contacts. In worst-case scenarios, spouse abuse, impulsive acts of revenge, and crimes of passion are possible.

Most Eights will encounter the following issues at some point in their lives. Noticing these patterns, "catching ourselves in the act," and simply seeing our underlying habitual responses to life will do much to release us from the negative aspects of our type.

THE WAKE-UP CALL FOR TYPE EIGHT: STRUGGLING FOR SELF-SUFFICIENCY

Eights feel they need to protect themselves—which can become a fear of dependency of any kind. ("I do not feel safe, so I need to toughen myself and get more resources to protect myself.") Because Eights do not feel that they can look to others for support or help without losing their autonomy, they tend to feel at war with the world. Everything in life is difficult, a struggle, and Eights are constantly straining to assert themselves against what they see as an uncooperative or even hostile environment. ("I have had to fight for everything I have." "You've got to be tough or they'll eat you alive.")

Eights generally do not like working under others, preferring instead the risk and adventure of running their own activities. Many Eights are enterprising "wheeler-dealers" who are always thinking of getting a new project under way. They can also be openly competitive—not to feel superior but to ensure that they have the resources they need to maintain their well-being and security. As long as Eights feel that they are in control of their situation, they are able to relax.

THE EIGHT'S CHALLENGES TO GROWTH

▲

Of course, no one in life is truly self-sufficient. Everyone, including Eights, needs others to help them and support them and accomplish common goals. If Eights were to examine their lives objectively, they would see that, in fact, they are actually dependent on many people to fulfill their vision and accomplish their goals. Yet because of their fear of dependency and betrayal, Eights do not want to acknowledge this or share the glory with others. They persuade themselves that they alone are working hard and that they must pressure others to follow their lead.

If this viewpoint becomes habitual, and if they ignore their Wake-up Call, Eights are in danger of becoming trapped more narrowly in their fixation. When Eights find themselves feeling that others have to be controlled and life conquered, they are going in the wrong direction. This can manifest in attitudes at work, in conflicts with loved ones—or simply in swearing at a jar of peanut butter that will not open.

PUSHING AGAINST THE WORLD

Begin to notice when you are using more energy than is necessary for any task or activity. When you are opening a door or holding something, notice how tightly you grip it. When you work, sweeping or scrubbing or using tools, could you use less force and still be effective? When you are speaking to someone, listen to your voice. What is the exact economical amount of energy you need to express what you want to say?

The Social Role: The Rock

Average Eights start to see themselves as the Rock, the strong and impregnable one, the foundation for others in their family or professional circle. ("I'm tough. I'm the one everyone else has to depend on.") Consciously or unconsciously identifying themselves with the strength and immovability of a rock has benefits, reinforcing their self-confidence and can-do spirit, but it also means that Eights must suppress their weaknesses, self-doubts, and fears. Also, like other types, average Eights begin to be uncomfortable around others unless they interact from their Social Role.

If they are like a rock, Eights believe that they will be able to defend themselves and avoid being hurt. Unfortunately, being like a rock makes them defend against many of the good things that come into their lives—caring, intimacy, gentleness, and self-sacrifice. They must be stony and unmoved by difficulties and suffering, either in others or in themselves.

Arlene, whom we met earlier, sees this simply as a matter of fact.

I'm a gut person. It takes a while for my head to catch up. I live a lot
in the future. I can also deny or obliterate feelings very easily and just
go on with life when loss happens.

The more threatened or stressed Eights are, the more tough and aggressive they become. Lower-average Eights feel entirely justified in
taking a hard line with others, as if declaring, "Deal with me!" They see
themselves as someone who is just trying to survive in a tough, cold
world.

Kit recalls the difficulty that this created for her in her childhood.

It wasn't that I wanted to disobey. I would have liked to have been a
"good girl," or at least an acceptable one. But I was impulsive, driven
to prevail at all costs, and compelled to follow my heart and stand up
for myself and my beliefs. I regularly told off my parents and was considered rather sassy and impudent. As a child, I was bewildered to
see that my intentions were misunderstood and viewed negatively. So
very early I began to cut off my feelings and pretend as though I didn't
care.

RECOVERING INTIMACY

Identify at least one area in your life—a relationship, a place, a time—in which you do not feel the need
to be tough. Observe yourself in this setting or with this particular person. How does it feel? How is it different from other areas of your life?

Lust and "Intensity"

Eights want to feel strong and autonomous; simply put, *they want
to feel solid and alive.* Thus, the traditional Passion of *lust* (their "Capital
Sin") compels them to act in ways that stimulate feelings of aliveness,
leading them to live *intensely.* Interactions with others must be intense,
work must be intense, and play must be intense, as if Eights had to
constantly push against life.

But to the extent that they succumb to the Passion of lust, Eights
become trapped in a pattern of asserting their will against the environment (including other people) to gain the intensity they crave.
Ironically, the more they push themselves, the less energy they have to
connect either with themselves or with anyone else. Ultimately, the
more they push, *the less real sense of being they have.* They—and others—become ciphers, objects in the environment to be manipulated.
The result is actually an inner deadening that then tempts them to

make even greater exertions to overcome it. Intensity only begets the need for more intensity.

There is also something of the daredevil in average Eights. They may not be race-car drivers or big-game hunters, but all Eights get hooked on the intensity and adrenaline rush of taking on a challenge and beating the odds. This can be exciting, but over time, it can also be exhausting and eventually wears down their health. For some Eights, the risk might simply be ignoring warnings about bad eating habits, cigarettes, or alcohol. ("It won't happen to me. I'm too strong to be affected by this stuff.") Prevailing becomes an addiction for Eights—the more often they win, the more this builds up a false sense of invulnerability that can lead them to make tragic miscalculations.

A further irony arises with lust in relation to control. As we have seen, Eights want to feel that they are in control of their situation. But being in the grip of lust is the antithesis of control: lust is a reaction to something outside the self that inspires it. To lust after a person or an object is to be under its power, whether it is lust for money, a sexual partner, or power. As with all the types, the Passion is a distortion that ultimately brings the opposite of what the type truly wants.

GETTING WORKED UP

Part of the reason you like to get into competitions and take risks is because of the sense of aliveness you get from these activities. How is this different from the sense of aliveness you get from relaxing? Can you consciously relax more right now? What does this do to your sense of yourself?

The Price of Running Things

Being practical-minded people, average Eights usually have some kind of dream for themselves, usually involving a money-making scheme, a business venture, or the stock market. This can be as complex as starting and running their own business, or as simple as playing the state lottery on a regular basis. Not all Eights have a lot of money, but most are looking for some kind of "big break" that would give them the independence, respect, and bargaining power that they typically want.

Ed, a therapist, recalls how his entrepreneurial spirit developed at a tender age.

When I was five years old, I remember going to a nearby vacant lot and gathering some seeds from the weeds. I then went to our landlady who lived across the street and told her that they were great birdseed. I sold her the seeds for five cents. I took the money and went to the local deli and bought two cupcakes. I then went to a local tennis court and sold the cupcakes for a nickel apiece. I returned to the deli with my dime and bought four cupcakes. There the tale ends, for when I went back to the tennis court, the man behind the snack counter yelled at me and threw me out.

To the extent that Eights fear depending on others, they want to make sure that they are in charge. While they have the satisfaction of being in control, they put a heavy burden on themselves to run everything. If they are parents, they focus on practical survival issues such as making sure that their children have food, shelter, and decent clothes and are getting a good education. If they have more money, they may feel that it is their place to provide cars and houses for their children and to set them up in a well-paying job or career. ("The old man will take care of everything.") They expend a lot of energy, having the vision, taking initiatives, constantly making all the decisions, and prodding others to implement them. Eights constantly radiate a kind of force field around themselves that can be energizing and protective for some, intimidating to others, and a subtle but real drain on the Eights themselves.

Intimacy therefore becomes a problem even for average Eights. They would often like to be close to people and to express the strong feelings they have, but do not know how to relax their defenses, especially their need for control. Given their inability to sustain more direct emotional contact, Eights begin to connect with others through competition, challenge, and physicality. They are stimulated by conflict, and this often becomes a source of misunderstanding with others. Eights like to get into intense discussions—even arguments—and passionately push home their point, only to be surprised that others have been hurt by their forcefulness. Many Eights express their connection with others through sexuality and physical contact. Or they may show affection by roughhousing or getting into verbal sparring.

Average Eights do not want people to know how much stress they are under, however. They try to handle all of their problems without telling anyone about them or at least not the extent of them. They tend to overwork, living on adrenaline and stress, and are unwilling to take steps to manage their stress until they are forced to by their deteriorating health. Constantly expending energy to the point of exhaustion, Eights frequently suffer from heart attacks, high blood pressure, strokes, and cancer.

"I've got to bring home the bacon."

DENYING YOUR TENDERNESS

Eights put themselves under tremendous pressure to provide for others, to be strong for them, to never cry, show weakness, doubt, or indecision.

Explore the various circumstances in which you have put yourself under this kind of pressure. Who were you doing it for? Was the outcome worth the effort? What do you think would have happened if you had been a little easier on yourself?

Self-Importance and Being "Larger than Life"

"You've got to deal with me."

When average Eights fear that others do not recognize how much energy they are expending to "run things," they put people on notice about who is in charge. They let everyone know who is most important by making a lot of noise—much of it bluster and bravado—like the dominance displays of alpha males in the animal world. Average Eights want others to know that they are "big shots" and can get things done. ("I know somebody who can really help you out. I'll talk to her for you.") They may use expressions of apparent generosity to get people to cooperate with them, the well-known carrot-and-stick approach. They also make deals with people—"You do this for me, and I'll take care of you." Average Eights would prefer to use persuasion and incentives to get people to fall in line with their plans, although if they encounter resistance, they usually try to dominate people more aggressively.

Having the means to do favors for others becomes essential. Without bargaining chips of some kind, average Eights feel that they would have to deal with others from a disadvantaged position. Worse, they may end up indebted to someone without the means to pay back the debt—a situation that could trigger their Basic Fear.

They also try to keep extending their influence—in a sense, expanding their ego boundaries. They identify with their projects and possessions as extensions of themselves. ("This is mine—my castle, my property, my business, my spouse, my children. It all reflects me.") Conceiving projects and seeing them to completion is a way of gaining some degree of immortality; it announces to the world, "I have been here." The size of their empire is not as important as the fact that it is *theirs*—and that they are running things. If they are successful financially, they may have an entourage and travel like royalty, expecting deference, respect, and obedience. When they give an order, they want it to be carried out right away and without question.

RETIRING THE BIG SHOT

You pride yourself on being direct and truthful. How truthful are you being when you are trying to impress or overwhelm people? Does getting people "in line" this way make you feel more or less comfortable with yourself? Can you think of more effective ways of gaining the support and cooperation of others?

Self-Assertion Versus Aggression

Eights like straight talk and become suspicious when others seem to be beating around the bush, which is why the communication style of some of the other types can be a problem for Eights. They have difficulty understanding why others are not as forthright as they are. At the same time, some other types are confounded by how audacious and forceful Eights can be.

The reason is that Eights need clear boundaries: they want to know where they stand with others and, on an instinctive level, where they end and where others begin. They want to know what others will tolerate and what they will not. *Eights discover boundaries by testing them.* If a person in relationship with an Eight does not react to him or her, the Eight will continue pushing the boundaries until they get a reaction. Sometimes this can take the form of needling or teasing the other. Sometimes the pressure can be sexual, or it may simply be an insistence that the other answer the Eight immediately in a conversation.

Because of their self-assertion and directness, Eights tend to intimidate people. Others often interpret their in-your-face communication style as anger or criticism, although Eights say that they are just trying to get others' attention and let others know where they stand. Part of the problem is that Eights do not know their own strength. As we have seen, they tend to use more energy than is necessary for many of their activities. The more insecure Eights are, the more likely they will be to aggressively assert themselves, ironically creating more resistance and less cooperation in others.

Arlene comments on her large-scale Eight style:

> I come across as invulnerable, or so I've been told. In general, I am sure of myself and am willing to take risks quite easily. I've "winged" it many times without knowing all the details of a situation. Almost always, I come out on top and as successful. Inside, however, I do not always feel as secure as I come across to other people. This has been quite difficult for me since it creates the problem of being a "threat" to people.

"What are you made of?"

When Eights feel threatened and insecure, they can become explosive and unpredictable. It is difficult for others around them to know what will set them off. It could be something as minor as a meal that is not ready on time, or a room that is not organized the way they want it, or simply a tone of voice. Fearing that others will defy them or get an advantage over them, more troubled Eights begin to impose their will indiscriminately. ("It's my way or the highway!" "Do it because *I* said so!")

Other typical ways of getting their way without resorting to outright aggression include undermining the confidence of others, and the strategy of divide and conquer. Eights may also resort to verbal abuse, screaming in someone's face if they are angry or frustrated. Of course, if they carry on this way for long, they often cause others to band together against them—one of the very things Eights most fear. Once caught up in their fears of violation and rejection, Eights seem unable to discriminate between the people who have actually harmed them in the past and the people they are currently dealing with. They feel as though others will almost certainly treat them unfairly, and they are determined to use whatever power they have to prevent this.

FEELING YOUR INSTINCTIVE ENERGY

The next time you feel reactive in a situation, try a little experiment. Instead of acting on your impulse, stop, breathe deeply, and see how the energy of the impulse moves inside you. See if you can follow it. How long does it last? Does it change over time? Does paying attention to it bring up other feelings? Take one of your hands and gently touch the area where you most feel this energy. What happens?

Control and Relationships

Eights' fears of being controlled are easily triggered; as a result, they may feel controlled even when nothing out of the ordinary is being asked of them. Not surprisingly, this can create major problems for Eights in their careers and in their relationships. For example, they have great difficulty taking direction from others, let alone orders. ("No one tells me what to do!") Eights' primary resource, their abundant energy and willpower, often ends up squandered on unnecessary conflicts.

The more dysfunctional their childhood background, the more control Eights will require in order to feel protected. For dysfunctional Eights to feel strong and in control of their situation requires more and more "proof" that this is so.

A former airline pilot, Ian, talks candidly about his need for control of his family, particularly of his wife.

I don't feel good about this now, but when I was younger, I needed to prove to myself that I was the king of the roost in every way. I made my sons get up early in the morning like a drill sergeant, and I completely controlled the finances in the house. My wife had to come to me for every nickel, and I made sure that she didn't have any spending money of her own so she couldn't have much freedom to stray. If she didn't have money, she couldn't leave me.

"My way or the highway."

Eights' tendency to struggle for control can escalate into open conflict if they feel that others may get an unfair advantage over them. They marshal their powerful instinctual energies and steely determination, effectively drawing lines in the sand and daring others to cross them. ("There will be no raise, and if you don't like it, you can quit right now!") Unfortunately, once Eights have delivered their ultimatums, even if they were uttered impulsively, they feel that they must follow through with them. To back down or soften their stance feels like weakness—and potential loss of independence and control.

Left unchecked, the desire for control can cause Eights to see significant others as possessions. They begin to view those who depend on them as impractical and weak and therefore unworthy of respect or equal treatment. Having ignored their own emotional reactions and sensitivities, they can ridicule or dismiss others' pain or emotional needs. More troubled Eights are also threatened by subordinates who show strength and may attempt to weaken them by undermining their confidence, keeping them off balance with arbitrary commands, and when all else fails, launching withering verbal attacks.

WHAT IF SOMEONE DID THIS TO ME?

Remember an incident in which you pressured someone to do something against his or her will. Can you now think of a way in which you could have gotten what you needed or wanted differently? Was what you were after legitimate? What would it have been like if the other person had simply given you what you were after without your having to pressure them? Similarly, recall times when someone attempted to pressure you. How did their methods influence your desire to cooperate with them?

Defiance and Rebellion

As a way of asserting themselves and defying authority, Eights may get married young or to a person their family disapproves of, or refuse to go to school—or perform any number of other acts of defiance. Even as small children, Eights can show remarkable resistance to authority.

Ed recalls:

> One of my problems as a child was a furious temper. What would make me see red was anyone trying to boss me around. I remember coming home from school when I was about eight years old and seeing some construction in the road. Curious, I walked up to the site. A policeman told me to stay away. I said "No way!" He took me home to my parents and described me as "the freshest kid I ever met."

"No one tells me what to do!"

More troubled Eights have a chip on their shoulder and tend to confront and intimidate others to get their way. Eights may attempt to bulldoze people with escalating degrees of intimidation. Expecting rejection and noncooperation, they create adversarial relationships even with former allies and friends and can inadvertently turn family members against them. Eights may then wonder why they are resisted and resented. From their point of view, they feel that their actions have been largely for the good of others. Others will benefit—eventually. Their own feeling of hurt and resentment makes them feel justified in further hurting others or bullying them to get cooperation.

They usually do not want a fight but are willing to take confrontations to the edge to get the other person to back down. Eights threaten that there is "worse to come" if the other does not yield. ("You are really pushing your luck! You do *not* want to make me mad.")

Kit well illustrates the Eight's strong willpower and spirit of defiance.

> I was usually being punished when the rest of the family had privileges. Determined to win the battle of wills, I endured all punishments, feeling that "No one can make me do anything I do not want to do!" I would laugh when I was whipped so as not to show weakness, and I would sit in my room for hours rather than give in.

COSTLY TRIUMPHS

Many of the Eight's health and relationship problems have their root in not wanting to back down, give in, or appear afraid. In your Inner Work Journal, answer the following questions:

In what early incidents did you see yourself as refusing to yield or concede to others? Can you remember any incidents from your school years, and from more recent times? How did these incidents make you feel physically? Emotionally? Psychologically? (Be as specific as possible.) What did it take to let you know that you had "won" the contest? What did the other person have to do first? How did this make you feel? For how long?

REACTING TO STRESS: EIGHT GOES TO FIVE

▲

As pressures build, Eights can only push their particular methods of dealing with problems so far. Eventually, their self-assertive, confrontational stance leads them into challenges that feel overwhelming. When Eights have bitten off more than they can chew, they may go to Five, effectively retreating from conflicts to strategize, buy time, and gather their strength.

At such times, Eights may become solitary figures, spending many hours brooding, reading, and gathering information so that they can better size up the situation. They insist on having the time and space and privacy to sort things out before they are able to jump back into action. Like Fives, they can become deeply preoccupied with their plans and projects—staying up late working, while avoiding others and being secretive about their activities. They can also seem strangely quiet and detached, which often comes as a surprise to those who are more used to their more assertive, passionate qualities.

Periods of stress may also cause Eights to become high-strung, like average Fives. They tend to minimize their comforts and needs and generally take poor care of themselves. Insomnia and unhealthy diets are not uncommon.

Feelings of rejection may also lead Eights into some of the darker aspects of Type Five. They can become extremely cynical and contemptuous of the beliefs and values of others. Deteriorating Eights may become nihilistic outsiders, with little hope of reconnecting with others or of finding anything positive in themselves or in the world.

THE RED FLAG: THE EIGHT IN TROUBLE

▲

If Eights have suffered a serious crisis without adequate support or coping skills, or if they have suffered from chronic abuse in childhood, they may cross the shock point into the unhealthy aspects of their type. This may lead them to a fearful recognition that their defiant reactions and attempts to control others are actually creating more dangers for them—they are less safe, not more. Eights may experience this as a fear that others, including trusted loved ones, are actually leaving or even turning against them. Indeed, some of these fears may be based on fact.

Coming to these realizations, while terrifying, can be a turning point in an Eight's life. On the one hand, if Eights can recognize the truth in these fears, they may begin to turn their life around and move toward health and liberation. On the other hand, they may become even more belligerent, defiant, and threatening and desperately attempt to stay in control at any cost. ("It's me against the world." "Nobody better even think about messing with me—I'll smash them!") If Eights persist in this attitude, they may cross into the unhealthy Levels. If you or someone you know is exhibiting the following warning signs for an extended period of time—more than two or three weeks—getting counseling, therapy, or other support is highly advisable.

WARNING SIGNS

POTENTIAL PATHOLOGY: Antisocial Personality Disorder, sadistic behavior, physical violence, paranoia, social isolation

▸ Paranoid feelings of being betrayed by "their people"

▸ Increasing social isolation and bitterness

▸ Lack of conscience and empathy; callous hard-heartedness

▸ Episodes of rage, violence, and physical destructiveness

▸ Plotting vengeance and retaliation against "enemies"

▸ Seeing self as an "outlaw"; involvement with criminal behavior

▸ Episodes of striking back at society (sociopathy)

PRACTICES THAT HELP EIGHTS DEVELOP

▲

▸ The suggestion to get in touch with your feelings may be something of a psychological cliché, but in your case, it is a helpful one. No one would question an Eight's passion, and no one knows as much as you do how much you secretly want to feel closer to people, but only you can learn to allow those feelings to surface. Vulnerability lets others know that they matter, that you care about them. No one is suggesting that you walk around with your heart on your sleeve, but denying your hurt or acting it out is not the solution.

▸ Grief work is very helpful for Eights. You are not the kind of person to sit around feeling sorry for yourself for long, but if you are suffering, it is important to find constructive ways of grieving your losses and hurts. That tough shell of yours got there for a reason. Maybe it's time to explore what some of the reasons were.

▸ Eights generally have a hearty sense of camaraderie and enjoy good times with others, but that is not the same thing as intimacy. Find people you can really trust, and talk with them about matters that are eating at you. If you already have someone like that in your life, dare to open up to them more and give them the same opportunity. Don't presume that others do not want to hear about your feelings or your troubles. Also, when you are unburdening yourself, listen to what others are saying to you. Notice that you are being heard when you are—and do the same for others.

▶ Take some quiet time to restore your soul. This doesn't mean watching television, eating, or drinking—really take time to be with yourself and enjoy simple things. Take a tip from your next-door neighbors, the Nines, and let your senses be revitalized by nature. Although your type would not be among the first in line for a class in meditation, quiet, centering practices are tremendously helpful to reduce your stress levels.

▶ Work is important, and your family and friends really do need you and appreciate your efforts to support them. At the same time, you will not be nearly as helpful to them if you work yourself to death. The same is true for immoderation in your "vices." Eights work hard and play hard. A little restraint on the intensity levels in both departments can help ensure that you will be around longer to enjoy your life in deeper and subtler ways. Question your need for intensity. What does it come from? What would happen to you if you or your life were a little less driven?

▶ Examine your expectations of rejection. Do you notice how often you expect people not to like you, or feel that you have to behave in ways that will head rejection off at the pass? These feelings underlie most of your sense of isolation, and in the long run they are what get you so angry. All of us feel deeply angry and even hateful if we sense that we have been continually rejected. Perhaps you are sending out signals that others are reading as a rejection of them, both because of their own issues and because of your self-protection. This leads us back to the vulnerability issue: the good feelings that you want are only going to touch you to the degree that you allow yourself to be affected.

BUILDING ON THE EIGHT'S STRENGTHS

▲

Eights are people of action and practical intuition. They have vision and derive great satisfaction from being constructive—both literally and figuratively. A key element to their leadership is their practical creativity. They enjoy building things from the ground floor, transforming unpromising materials into something great. Eights are able to see possibilities in people and in situations; they look at a garage full of junk and see a potential business. They look at a troubled youth and see leadership potential. They like to offer incentives and challenges to bring out people's strengths. ("If you get straight A's, I'll get you that car.") In this way, they help others to recognize resources and strengths that others did not know they possessed. A key word for Eights, therefore, is empowerment. Healthy Eights agree with the saying, "Give a person a fish and they eat for a day. But teach them how to fish, and they can feed themselves for life." Eights know this is true because they have often taught themselves "how to fish."

Honor is also important to healthy Eights: their word is their bond. When they say, "You have my word on this," they mean it. They speak directly and without subterfuge. Healthy Eights look for similar qualities in others and feel gratified when people recognize this quality in them—although they will not change when others do not appreciate their honesty.

Furthermore, Eights want to be *respected,* and healthy Eights respect others and the dignity of all creatures. They feel personally hurt by any violation of the needs and rights of others, and injustice causes healthy Eights to respond viscerally and to take action. They will step in and stop a fight to protect the weak or disadvantaged, or to even the score for those who they feel have been wronged. Courageous and strong but also gentle and humble, they are willing to put themselves in jeopardy for the sake of justice and fairness. Very high-functioning Eights have the vision, compassion, and strength to be a tremendous influence for good in the world.

Says Roseann, whom we met earlier:

> It feels good to be an Eight, to be strong and in charge of the situation and have others respect me and want me around them. I remember feeling pretty good about the time I rushed to a friend's house in response to her call for help in handling an ex-lover who was stalking her. "Thank God you're here," she said. "You make me feel like the Marines have landed!"

Control, in a healthy Eight, takes the form of self-mastery. They understand that it is actually counterproductive to try to "beat the world" every day. On a deeper level, control is not really a healthy Eight's ultimate goal; rather, it is the desire to have a beneficial influence on people and on their world. Balanced Eights understand that this kind of influence comes from true inner strength, not from outward muscle-flexing, forcefulness, or trying to bend things to their will. They recognize that controlling situations or people is actually a form of imprisonment. Real freedom and independence arise through a much more simple and relaxed relationship with their world.

Finally, healthy Eights are magnanimous or big-hearted, possessing a generosity that allows them to transcend their self-interest. They feel

"I can look out for you."

confident enough to allow themselves some degree of vulnerability, and this enables them to experience their concern and caring for people. They express this in their protection of others, defending friends from schoolyard bullies or taking a stand for coworkers against an unfair policy. Healthy Eights are willing to take the heat and to do whatever is necessary to protect the people they see as under their charge.

When this happens, Eights achieve a degree of greatness on whatever scale they have been operating—the family, the nation, the world—and are honored and respected as a result. They achieve a kind of immortality that lifts them to the rank of hero. They are like forces of nature whom others intuitively honor and respect. History records many healthy Eights who were willing to take a stand for something beyond themselves—sometimes even beyond their immediate understanding—and much of the enduring good in our world has been achieved through their determination and struggles.

THE PATH OF INTEGRATION: EIGHT GOES TO TWO

▲

Eights become actualized and remain healthy by learning to open their hearts to others in the manner of a healthy Two. Eights do not need to add any new qualities for this to occur; rather, they need to reconnect with their hearts to see how much they care about people. Many Eights discover this side of themselves through their love of children or a pet. Children can bring out the best in many Eights because they cherish and respect the innocence of children and want to protect it. With children and animals, Eights can let down their guard and allow some of their tenderness to come to the surface.

For Eights to be able to embrace their bigness of heart, they must first gather the courage to reveal it. This requires that they trust in something beyond their own wits and power—and that, of course, requires letting go of many of their fundamental defenses. No matter how full of rage and shut down an Eight may be, the sensitive child that made the decision to protect itself still lives inside, waiting for the opportunity to contact the world again.

It is important to understand, however, that the movement to Two is not accomplished by imitating the average qualities of the Two. Flattering others and attempting to please them in a forced way will not lead to much heart-opening and will often strike others as false. Rather, the path for Eights lies in letting down their defenses and getting in greater contact with their hearts. Of course, an instant fear of vulnerability will arise, but as Eights learn to acknowledge this fear and let it pass, they become more comfortable with their gentler feelings.

Integrating Eights make outstanding leaders because they clearly communicate their profound respect and appreciation of other human beings. They are also effective because, like healthy Twos, they recognize boundaries and limits—especially the latter. As they learn to nurture themselves and to accept vulnerability in their lives, their health and sense of well-being improve. They work hard but also know when it is time to rest, to eat, and to restore their strength. They choose leisure activities that really nurture themselves, not overindulging their appetites or seeking more intensity.

TRANSFORMING PERSONALITY INTO ESSENCE

▲

As Eights are able to allow their vulnerability to surface, they learn to come to Presence again and again and gradually let go of their self-image of always needing to be strong and in control. If they persist, they eventually come into direct contact with their Basic Fear of being harmed or controlled by others and understand the roots of this fear in their personal history. As they work through old fears and hurts, they become less attached to their Basic Desire to always protect themselves.

When a person becomes liberated from their Basic Fear and Basic Desire, there is a reversal of everything that has happened in the lower Levels of Development. The self-reliance and self-assertion of the Eight personality structure dissolves, creating the space for real Essential strength to emerge. This enables Eights to surrender to some larger plan than the one they have for themselves. Eights who do so can become extraordinarily heroic, like Martin Luther King, Jr., Nelson Mandela, or Franklin Roosevelt. These people surrendered concern about their individual survival to become vessels for a higher purpose. ("If they kill me, they kill me. I yield my life. The vision will live on.") Something inspiring and ennobling arises out of the freedom that has been created when their Basic Fear has been overcome.

THE EMERGENCE OF ESSENCE

In their deepest self, Eights remember the simple joy of existence: the exquisite satisfaction of being alive, especially at the primal, instinctive level. They still have some degree of contact with the purity and power of the instinctual responses and remind us that these, too, are part of the Divine order. Without a real connection to the wellspring of our native instincts, we are cut off from the basic fuel we need for our transformation.

The Essential core of the Eight cuts through the falsehoods and niceties of the personality, bringing forth a simple, unself-conscious embodiment of truth. Oscar Ichazo called this quality "Innocence," and in a way, Eights also long for the innocence they knew as children—an innocence they felt they had to leave behind in order to be strong.

Eights also express the innocence of the natural order, the innocence in which all creatures in the world manifest their nature. Cats innocently function as cats, even as they stalk their prey. Birds innocently function as birds, and fish as fish. It is humankind alone that seems to have lost touch with this innate capacity. We could say that the Essential nature of Eights reminds us of what it is like to be completely human, living beings, functioning as part of a vast, perfectly balanced natural order.

When Eights give up their own willfulness, they discover the Divine Will. Instead of trying to have power through the assertion of their egos, they align themselves with Divine Power. Instead of a me-against-the-world attitude, they see that they have a role to play in the world, which, if followed wholeheartedly, could earn them a place of immortality among the great heroes and saints of history. The liberated Eight has the power to inspire others to be heroic as well, influencing people possibly for centuries.

Eights also remember the omnipotence and strength that comes from being a part of the Divine reality. The Divine will is not the same as willfulness. As Eights understand this, they end their war with the world and discover that the solidity, power, and independence that they have been seeking are already here. They are a part of their true nature as they are part of the true nature of every human being. When they experience this deeply enough, they are able to relax fully into Being, feeling effortlessly at one with the world and with the unfolding mystery of life.

"Unless you change your life and become like a child, you cannot enter the kingdom of Heaven."

JESUS OF NAZARETH

Add your scores for the fifteen statements for Type Eight. Your result will be between 15 and 75. The following guidelines may help you discover or confirm your personality type.

▶ 15   You are probably not an assertive type (not a Three, Seven, or Eight).

▶ 15–30   You are probably not a Type Eight.

▶ 30–45   You most probably have Eight-issues, or an Eight parent.

▶ 45–60   You most likely have an Eight-component.

▶ 60–75   You are most likely an Eight (but could still be another type if you are thinking too narrowly about Type Eight).

Eights are most likely to misidentify themselves as Sevens, Sixes, or Fours. Sixes, Threes, and Sevens are most likely to misidentify themselves as Eights.

CHAPTER 15

TYPE NINE:
THE PEACEMAKER

▲

THE HEALER

THE OPTIMIST

THE RECONCILER

THE COMFORTER

THE UTOPIAN

NOBODY SPECIAL

"Most people think of peace as a state of Nothing Bad Happening, or Nothing Much Happening. Yet if peace is to overtake us and make us the gift of serenity and well-being, it will have to be the state of Something Good Happening."

—E. B. WHITE

"There is a price which is too great to pay for peace, and that price can be put in one word. One cannot pay the price of self-respect."

—WOODROW WILSON

"Men need some kind of external activity, because they are inactive within."

—SCHOPENHAUER

"Indolence is a delightful but distressing state: we must be doing something to be happy."

—WILLIAM HAZLITT

_____ 1. What people seem to like about me is that they feel safe around me.

_____ 2. I don't mind being around people, and I don't mind being alone—either way is fine, as long as I'm at peace with myself.

_____ 3. I've found a certain balance in my life, and I see no reason to mess with it.

_____ 4. Being "comfortable" in every sense of the word appeals to me a lot.

_____ 5. I would rather give someone else their way than create a scene.

_____ 6. I don't know exactly how I do it, but I don't let things get to me.

_____ 7. I'm pretty easy to please and usually feel that what I have is good enough for me.

_____ 8. I've been told that I seem distracted and absentminded—the fact is I understand things, but I just don't want to react to them.

_____ 9. I don't think I'm particularly stubborn, but people say that I can be hard-headed once I make up my mind.

_____ 10. Most people get themselves worked up too easily: I'm much more even-keeled.

_____ 11. You've got to take what life brings, since there's not much you can do about it anyway!

_____ 12. I can easily see different points of view, and I tend to agree with people more than I disagree with them.

_____ 13. I believe in emphasizing the positive rather than dwelling on the negative.

_____ 14. I have what might be called a philosophy of life that guides me and gives me a great deal of comfort in difficult times.

_____ 15. During the day, I do everything that needs to be done, but when the day is over, I really know how to relax and take it easy.

THE RISO-HUDSON TAS

Type Attitude Sorter

Score each of the following statements according to how true or applicable to you it is on the following scale:

1.......*Not at All True*

2.......*Seldom True*

3.......*Somewhat True*

4.......*Generally True*

5.......*Very True*

See page 340 for scoring key.

PERSONALITY TYPE NINE: THE PEACEMAKER

▶ BASIC FEAR: Of loss and separation; of annihilation

▶ BASIC DESIRE: To maintain their inner stability and peace of mind

▶ SUPEREGO MESSAGE: "You are good or okay as long as those around you are good or okay."

"I go with the flow."

The Easygoing, Self-Effacing Type:
Receptive, Reassuring, Agreeable, and Complacent

We have called personality type Nine *the Peacemaker* because no type is more devoted to the quest for internal and external peace for themselves and others. They are often spiritual seekers who have a great yearning for connection with the cosmos, as well as with other people. They work to maintain their peace of mind just as they work to establish peace and harmony in their world. The issues encountered in the Nine are fundamental to all inner work—being awake versus falling asleep to our true nature; presence versus entrancement, tension versus relaxation, peace versus pain, union versus separation.

Ironically, for a type so oriented to the spiritual world, Nine is the center of the Instinctive Triad and is the type that is potentially most grounded in the physical world and in their own bodies. The contradiction is resolved when we realize that Nines are either in touch with their instinctive qualities and have tremendous elemental power and personal magnetism, or they are cut off from their instinctual strengths and can be disengaged and remote, even lightweight.

To compensate for being out of touch with their instinctual energies, Nines also retreat into their minds and their emotional fantasies. (This is why Nines can sometimes misidentify themselves as Fives and Sevens, "head types," or as Twos and Fours, "feeling types.") Furthermore, when their instinctive energies are out of balance, Nines use these very energies against themselves, damming up their own power so that everything in their psyches becomes static and inert. When their energy is not used, it stagnates like a spring-fed lake that becomes so full that its own weight dams up the springs that feed it. When Nines are in balance with their Instinctive Center and its energy, however, they are like a great river, carrying everything along with it effortlessly.

We have sometimes called the Nine *the crown of the Enneagram* because it is at the top of the symbol and because it seems to include the whole of it. Nines can have the strength of Eights, the sense of fun and adventure of Sevens, the dutifulness of Sixes, the intellectualism of Fives, the creativity of Fours, the attractiveness of Threes, the generosity of Twos, and the idealism of Ones. However, what they generally do not have is a sense of really inhabiting themselves—*a strong sense of their own identity.*

Ironically, therefore, the only type the Nine is not like is the Nine itself. Being a separate self, an individual who must assert herself against others, is terrifying to Nines. They would rather melt into someone else or quietly follow their idyllic daydreams.

Red, a nationally known business consultant, comments on this tendency.

> I am aware of focusing on other people, wondering what they are like, how and where they live, etc. In a relationship with others, I often give up my own agenda in favor of the other person's, I have to be on guard about giving in to other's demands and discounting my own legitimate needs.

Nines demonstrate the universal temptation to ignore the disturbing aspects of life and to seek some degree of peace and comfort by numbing out. They respond to pain and suffering by attempting to live in a state of premature peacefulness, whether it is in a state of false spiritual attainment or in more gross denial. More than any other type, Nines demonstrate the tendency to run away from the paradoxes and tensions of life by attempting to transcend them or by seeking simple and painless solutions to their problems.

To emphasize the pleasant in life is not a bad thing, of course—it is simply a limited and limiting approach to life. If Nines see the silver lining in every cloud as a way of protecting themselves from the cold and rain, other types have their distorting viewpoints, too. For example, Fours focus on their own woundedness and victimization, Ones on what is wrong with how things are, and so forth. By contrast, Nines tend to focus on the bright side of life so that their peace of mind will not be shaken. But rather than deny the dark side of life, what Nines must understand is that *all of the perspectives presented by the other types are true, too.* Nines must resist the urge to escape into "premature Buddhahood" or the "white light" of the Divine and away from the real world. They must remember that the only way out is through.

THE CHILDHOOD PATTERN

Many Nines report that they had a happy childhood, but this is not always the case. When their childhoods were more troubled, young Nines learned to cope *by dissociating from the threatening and traumatic events around them* and by adopting the role of Peacemaker or Mediator during family conflicts. They learned that the best way to keep harmony in the family was to "disappear" and not cause anyone any trouble. They learned that if they were undemanding and had few expectations—in short, if they were a low-maintenance child—they could effectively protect themselves while calming down Mommy and

Please note that the childhood pattern we are describing here does not cause the personality type. Rather, it describes tendencies that we observe in the early childhood that have a major impact on the type's adult relationships.

Daddy. (In a dysfunctional family system, the term that most applies here is Lost Child.) The feeling is, "If I show up and assert myself, I am going to create even more problems, so if I stay out of the way, the family will stay together."

Georgia, a well-known therapist, has been doing Inner Work for many years.

> My mother was alcoholic and had a volatile temper, so a lot of my energy as a child was directed to keeping out of the way and not rocking the boat. In this way I learned to stand on the sidelines of life and be accommodating to the needs of other people. I was afraid I wouldn't be loved if I asserted myself. I chose to live my life in a more inward way, which was actually very rich to me, without confronting other people.

Nines grew up feeling that having needs, asserting themselves, getting angry, or creating difficulties for their parents was not allowed. As a result, Nine children never learned to assert themselves adequately or, by extension, *to actualize themselves independently* of their parents and significant others. Young Nines learned to stay in the background where things could not get to them. In adulthood, their psychic space is so crowded with the issues and agendas of the people whom they are trying to accommodate that they are often unable to hear the voice of their own needs or desires.

They also learned to repress anger and their own will so completely that they became unconscious of even having anger or a will of their own. They learned to adjust and go along with whatever life or others presented to them. Seldom did it occur to them to ask themselves what they wanted or thought or felt. As a result, it usually takes some digging for Nines to get in touch with what they want for themselves.

Red has spent years working on the issues of self-effacement and repressed anger.

> I have a clear sense of being left alone because I was such a "good little boy." My mother always tells people what an "angel" I was because I could be left alone for hours and would amuse myself. I think my mother is a Nine and I picked up a lot of her philosophy of life. . . . When conflicts between her and my father would break out, she would use expressions such as "Don't rock the boat" and "If you don't have anything nice to say, don't say anything at all." Another favorite was "It takes two to tango," which was her way of telling me that she could end an argument by refusing to argue.

In highly dysfunctional families, the young Nine may have been traumatized emotionally, physically, or sexually. Such Nines learn to protect themselves from intolerable feelings by dissociating or shutting down. From one point of view, it is a kind of blessing that they are not aware of their traumatic memories or of their rage, but on the other hand the result is a widespread deadening of their ability to allow reality to touch them with any depth or vividness. Such individuals may become lost in fantasies or focus exclusively on whatever is positive and peaceful in their environment—no matter how much of an illusion this may later turn out to be.

André is a successful real estate salesman in a major metropolitan area; much of his success comes from being natural and unassuming, common Nine traits, although these were learned at a high price.

My mother was very depressed for much of my childhood. I knew that the less trouble I was for her, the safer I'd be, so I just tried to blend in as much as possible. I would escape to my grandmother's backyard, where I loved the tall trees and her collection of animals.

THE NINE WITH AN EIGHT-WING: THE REFEREE

Healthy   People of this subtype mix the ability to be agreeable and to comfort others with endurance and strength. They are both powerful and gentle, able to easily engage with people and with things in the world, mediating between people and lessening conflicts. They often seek new projects to have an occasional change of pace from their normal routines. They are also practical and are typically concerned with their immediate needs and physical and financial circumstances. More sociable than the other subtype, they generally prefer to work with other people. They excel in the helping professions and consulting and can be effective in business, especially in negotiations or in human resource capacities.

Average   These people enjoy socializing and good times and are more attracted to losing themselves in sensuality and comforting routines that interfere with their ability to stay focused on significant goals. They can be stubborn and defensive, tending to dig in their heels and refusing to listen to anyone. People of this subtype often have bad tempers, although it is difficult to predict what will set them off—threats to their sense of personal well-being or to their family, job, or beliefs are typical. They can be blunt and explosive but suddenly return to a state of calm and placidity.

THE WING SUBTYPES

▲

Examples

Ronald Reagan
Gerald Ford
Lady Bird Johnson
Kevin Costner
Sophia Loren
Walter Cronkite
Whoopi Goldberg
Janet Jackson
Ringo Starr
Ingrid Bergman

THE NINE WITH A ONE-WING: THE DREAMER

Healthy   People of this subtype are imaginative and creative, often able to synthesize different schools of thought or points of view into a vision of an ideal world. They are particularly good at nonverbal forms of communication (art, instrumental music, dance, sports, or work with animals and nature) and can thrive in large institutions. They are typically friendly and reassuring but have a distinct sense of purpose, especially about their ideals. They often make good therapists, counselors, or ministers, balancing nonjudgmental listening with the desire to be of help to others.

Average   They want external order as a way of giving order to their internal world. People of this subtype tend to get caught up in nonessential activities and busy-ness. They can be energetic but in a detached and uninvolved way that interferes with their ability to stay with long-range goals or to enlist others in joining them. They are less adventurous and more reserved than people of the other subtype, expressing anger with restraint and smoldering indignation. They are also concerned with respectability and often feel morally superior to different classes, cultures, and lifestyles. There may be a puritanical streak to them, as well as a prim and proper, perfectionistic quality to their personal style.

Examples

Abraham Lincoln
Queen Elizabeth II
Carl Jung
George Lucas
Audrey Hepburn
Dame Margot Fonteyn
Rose Kennedy
Walt Disney
Garrison Keillor
Norman Rockwell

THE INSTINCTUAL VARIANTS

▲

THE SELF-PRESERVATION INSTINCT IN THE NINE

The Comfort Seeker.   In the average range, this variant is the pleasant, easygoing Nine who does not ask much from life. Self-Preservation Nines prefer simple pleasures that are readily available—eating at the nearest fast-food restaurant, watching a favorite rerun on television, or "zoning out" in a comfy chair. They are usually not ambitious, although they may be quite talented. They generally deal with anxiety by getting involved in busywork—puttering and routines—and may use small tasks to avoid dealing with bigger projects. They become increasingly attracted to minor rewards as compensation for not being able to pursue real desires—but always with some repressed underlying anxiety about not attending to their real needs.

Nines' inertia shows up most clearly in this variant. Apathy and self-neglect can cause Self-Preservation Nines to have difficulty mobilizing themselves to obtain what they really want or to take care of their genuine self-preservation needs. Increasingly, they use food and drink to suppress feelings of anxiety or anger and often possess large appetites and a tendency toward addiction. They do not want their pleasant moods to be disturbed by others and often resist others simply by not responding to them, remaining stubbornly silent.

In the unhealthy range, Self-Preservation Nines fall into deep apathy about their lives and can become fatigued and ineffectual. They become the chronic couch potato, emotionally shut down and slowly wasting their health, relationships, and possibilities. Addictions are common.

THE SOCIAL INSTINCT IN THE NINE

One Happy Family. In the average range, these are the Nines most interested in bringing people together and in making peace. They like to be involved with others, to be part of whatever is going on, but they also resist having too many expectations placed on them. They can be emotionally and mentally disengaged while physically involved. Social Nines generally have a good deal of energy and like to stay active but within defined, familiar structures. They do not mind working or helping others, but they like to have a clear sense of what will be expected of them. They can be surprisingly conventional and conformist, in the sense that they will meet the expectations of their social circle, but they are also anxious about losing their identity, of becoming a "clone" or an appendage of someone else.

Insecurities about their worth plus their desire to please and fit in also cause Social Nines to have difficulty saying no to people. They often end up resisting others anyway, usually passive-aggressively. Trying to please various people or groups in their lives can lead them to being scattered and disenchanted, like average Sevens. They often have trouble setting independent goals and following through with their intentions.

In the unhealthy range, Social Nines can become resigned and depressed about their lack of development. Their neediness and intense insecurity are usually masked by emotional flatness. Displays of indignant anger may alienate people, thus heightening their feelings of social isolation.

THE SEXUAL INSTINCT IN THE NINE

Merging. In the average range, Sexual Nines want to take on the energetic qualities of the other, often gravitating to aggressive types. They can display minor aggressive traits themselves. They tend to be sassier than the other two variants, and their anger can be easily aroused if they feel that their connection with others is threatened. They seek a complete partnership, thinking of it as "our life" rather than "my life." It is as if they want the other to fuse with them. Sexual Nines often idealize the other, not wanting to see his or her flaws, but they can also become critical and demanding, especially if they have a One-wing. Compliments to the other are compliments to the self; the same is true for insults or disappointments.

The other becomes the center of gravity, the axis of the Sexual Nine's identity. As a result, people of this variant may fail to develop their own identity or any real sense of independence. Sexual Nines can be highly romantic and resemble Fours. Unrealistic rescue fantasies, the "Cinderella complex," wishful thinking, and clinging to loved ones can all be part of the picture.

In the unhealthy range, Sexual Nines become highly dissociated and depressed and seem to lack a core self. Unable to merge with the other adequately, they feel lost. Fantasies of the other mix with fantasies of anger and vengeance, but the latter are rarely acted on. These types end up either in highly dependent relationships or floundering on their own, waiting for one. Or the self may become a function of past relationships. ("Meg and I were the most loving couple. I miss her so much since she died.")

THE NINE'S CHALLENGES TO GROWTH

▲

Most Nines will encounter the following issues at some point in their lives. Noticing these patterns, "catching ourselves in the act," and simply seeing our underlying habitual responses to life will do much to release us from the negative aspects of our type.

THE WAKE-UP CALL FOR TYPE NINE: GOING ALONG WITH OTHERS

"I don't care. It doesn't matter to me."

Beginning in the average Levels, Nines experience the temptation to be overly accommodating to others because they fear that if they get into conflicts with people, they will lose their connection with them. For instance, when asked by a spouse where they would like to go for dinner, the Nine may well answer, "I don't care, honey—wherever *you* want to go is fine with me."

Simply put, Nines get into the habit of saying yes to things that they do not really want to do. This strategy may avoid disagreements in the short run but almost inevitably leads to resentment on both sides. Further, the Nine's resentment usually causes passive-aggressive behavior—agreeing to do something and then not doing it—which ultimately creates much greater conflicts and misunderstandings with others. Their accommodation also puts them in danger of being taken advantage of since they are willing to pay a high price to keep the peace.

Hope, a talented therapist, recognized this pattern in herself.

H E A L T H Y	Level 1	*Key Terms:* *Self-Possessed* *Indomitable*	Nines let go of the belief that their participation in the world is unimportant or unwanted; thus they can truly connect with themselves and with others. They also paradoxically achieve their Basic Desire—to have inner stability and peace of mind. As a result of their self-actualization, they become self-possessed, dynamic, serene, and present.
	Level 2	*Unself-conscious* *Peaceful*	Nines focus on the environment or on relationships as a whole, desiring to maintain a harmonious stability within them and in their environment. Self-image: "I am steady, easygoing, and kind."
	Level 3	*Unselfish* *Comforting*	Nines reinforce their self-image by creating and maintaining peace and harmony in their world. They use their patient, levelheaded approach to mediate conflicts and to soothe others. They are often highly imaginative, inspiring others with a healing, positive vision of life.
A V E R A G E	Level 4	*Self-Effacing* *Agreeable*	Nines begin to fear that conflicts in their lives will ruin their peace of mind, so they begin to avoid potential conflicts by going along with others. They consider many matters not worth arguing about, but will also begin to say yes to things they really do not want to do.
	Level 5	*Disengaged* *Complacent*	Nines worry that any significant changes in their world or any strong feelings will disrupt their fragile peace, so they set up their lives in ways that will prevent things from getting to them. They lose themselves in comforting routines and habits, putter around, and tune out problems.
	Level 6	*Resigned* *Appeasing*	Nines are afraid that others will demand responses from them that may arouse anxiety and ruin their inner peace, so they downplay the importance of problems and try to deflect others. They stoically trudge through their lives, hanging on to wishful thinking and suppressing their anger.
U N H E A L T H Y	Level 7	*Repressed* *Neglectful*	Nines fear that reality will force them to deal with their problems, and this may be true. They may react by defending the illusion that everything is okay and stubbornly resisting all efforts to get them to confront their problems. They are depressed, ineffectual, and listless.
	Level 8	*Dissociating* *Disoriented*	Nines are so desperate to hold on to whatever shred of inner peace they have left that they fear acknowledging reality at all. They try to block out of awareness anything that could affect them through dissociation and denial. They appear desolate, numb, and helpless, often experiencing amnesia.
	Level 9	*Self-* *Abandoning* *"Disappearing"*	Very unhealthy Nines feel unable to face reality at all. They withdraw into themselves and become completely unresponsive. They may attempt to eliminate their awareness to save their illusions of peace through fragmenting themselves into subpersonalities.

TYPE 9

LEVELS OF DEVELOPMENT

I have been too placating, "mealy-mouthed," and a pushover. I can remember times when I needed to act, to stand up on my behalf or for others, and I couldn't. Often it was out of some combination of the fear of conflict, fear that the situation would get worse, and the desire that everyone "should get along with one another." For a large portion of my life I would downplay my ability, whether it was in sports or in my profession, in order to take a backseat and not stand out. It was important that I help others be in the front, not me.

Accommodation and self-effacement mark the beginning of Nines' "disappearing act." Rather than assert themselves and run the risk of alienating others, Nines begin to disappear into conventional roles, as well as hide behind platitudes and slogans. If anxiety and conflicts increase, Nines become almost invisible. This occurs because Nines are trying to adapt to their circumstances, to "not be a problem," but they lose themselves in the process.

Hope pinpoints such a pivotal moment.

In first grade I was still exhibiting my independence and told my teacher I wouldn't copy what she wrote on the board. She walked back to me and shook my chin as hard as she could. I never was a difficult student again in school or church. I became a "good girl," doing what I was told.

SAYING "YES" WHEN YOU MEAN "NO"

Think of times in which you went along with the plans, preferences, or choices of others and submerged your own choices. What did this do to your sense of involvement? To your contact with yourself and your experience? Did you resent having to go along? How did you dispense with your own choice? What did you hope to gain by doing so?

The Social Role: Nobody Special

Average Nines begin to create a particular Social Role by seeing themselves as Nobody Special, the modest person who is content to stay in the background and not cause any inconvenience to others. ("Don't buy me a birthday present. I know you love me.") They feel that their presence, opinions, and involvement do not really matter and are of no particular consequence. As confining as this is from one point of view, Nines find comfort in this self-definition—it allows them to minimize their own hopes and expectations so that they will not be frustrated or feel rejected, angry, or disappointed.

The Social Role of Nines is subtle to grasp, although it is palpable once you have experienced it. The identity of Nines is like a ring that holds a stone or like the frame of a painting. Their attention is on the stone or the picture, not on themselves, and their identity and self-esteem arise by having a relationship (if only imaginary) with those who seem to them to have more value.

Identifying themselves as Nobody Special also offers Nines a certain camouflage, an ability to blend into the background where they will not be intruded on. Their Social Role also gives them the hope that if they do not take care of themselves, others will see their self-effacing humility and rush to their side. They may also believe that because they are humble and self-effacing, life will never present them with sorrow or tragedy. Unfortunately, things do not always work out this way, and by putting themselves last in line, Nines tend to court a certain amount of loneliness and depression. Opportunities pass them by, and others begin to not take them seriously.

Philip is a distinguished college professor whose active academic life does not betray his inner sense of himself.

> I've lived with a sense of not being important. I've always assumed that other people count more than I do, that they should be considered first, that their needs are more consequential than mine. A good example of this is the way in which I have responded to health problems. If I'm experiencing symptoms, say, I'll usually live with them for quite a while. On the other hand, when my children were small, if one of them took ill, I immediately made an appointment and took them to a doctor.

Left unchecked, the Nobody Special role can leave Nines with limited energy and little confidence in their ability to cope with life. They become depressed, easily fatigued, and need frequent naps and many hours of sleep. Taking any positive action for themselves becomes more and more difficult.

I'M WORTH IT

Make a list of the things in your life that excite you. Don't edit yourself. What kind of person would you be if you could? What steps could you take today to become more like that person? This week? This year?

Sloth and Self-Forgetting

Sloth in Nines has to do with not wanting to be internally engaged with what they are doing. They are not necessarily lazy about doing ordinary daily things—on the contrary, they might be extremely busy at work or running a business or a household. Their sloth is internal, a spiritual sloth that makes them not want to be deeply touched or affected by reality. They do not want to show up in their lives in an active, self-initiating way. The result is that even average Nines go on automatic pilot, so that life becomes less immediate and less threatening to them. Life is lived at a safe distance, so to speak.

The sloth is thus a sloth in self-remembering and self-awareness. Nines do not put energy into making contact with themselves, with others, or with the world. To identify with the body and its instincts is to become directly aware of our mortality. Nines hold on to certain comfortable inner states or identify with something beyond themselves, in effect, *diffusing their awareness* so that the full impact of mortality does not touch them. The world goes into soft focus, and Nines feel safer, but at the expense of their full vitality and aliveness.

Despite the fact that they may be spiritual seekers, Nines often attempt to get the emotional and psychological benefits of inner work by doing the opposite of being present. They go to sleep, numbing themselves to what they really feel and tuning out reality while still expecting to function effortlessly in it. Ironically, Nines want unity between themselves and the world but end up achieving only an ersatz peacefulness, the false peace of numbness and dissociation—such a tenuous "peacefulness" that it is disturbed by everything. Like all ego projects, it is doomed to failure.

Unself-Consciousness and Numbing Out

As paradoxical as it sounds, Nines create and maintain their sense of identity by being unself-conscious, by not being too aware of themselves as individual persons. All of the other types *do something* to create and maintain their sense of self—for instance, Fours constantly dwell on their feelings and inner states, and Eights constantly assert themselves in various ways. By contrast, Nines create their identity by not being directly aware of themselves. Instead, they *focus on their relationships with others*. It is as if they are the room in which others gather, or the page in a photo album in which pictures of others are pasted. Their sense of self is thus a "negative capability," a capacity for holding the other—not themselves.

This allows healthy Nines to be extraordinarily supportive of oth-

"It is nothing to die; it is frightful not to live."

VICTOR HUGO

ers. But the fundamental mistake Nines make is to believe that to stay connected with others, they must not be connected with themselves. It also causes problems for Nines, because to maintain their negative capability, they must increasingly *resist* whatever would disturb their sense of harmony and connection. Their sense of self depends on keeping many impressions out. They particularly must resist anything that would make them aware of their rage, pain, frustration, or any other negative feeling.

Outwardly, Nines may do many things, but much of their activity has the quality of busywork. They putter around and run errands but postpone dealing with more critical problems. In this state, Nines do not understand why people get frustrated with them. They are not bothering anyone, so why should anyone be upset with them? What they do not see is how frustrating their lack of appropriate response can be for others. They also do not see that they are laying the groundwork for a self-fulfilling prophecy: the disengagement of average-to-unhealthy Nines will eventually bring about the very thing they fear most—loss and separation from others.

It is important for Nines to understand that *numbness is not relaxation*. In fact, numbness depends on maintaining physical tension. When we are relaxed, we are deeply aware of our breathing, our body sensations, and our surroundings. Real peace has the quality of aliveness and energy and is not the flat detachment that we see here.

André continues:

At my worst, I feel numb. Not even really depressed, just numb. The smallest things can feel like an enormous effort. Long stretches of time can pass by while I simply stare out the window and think, or crash in front of the TV and channel surf. Time simply stops. It's like becoming a zombie. I can still function in terms of going to work and appearing friendly, but inside I'm feeling completely shut down. There is a sense of hopelessness about finding a direction in life.

CHECKING OUT

Whenever you become aware that you have "checked out" and have been unself-conscious for any noteworthy period of time, think back to what circumstances preceded your checking out. What seemed to be threatening you in some way that made you want to remove yourself from the scene? Did the threat seem to be only in the environment, or to be a state or reaction in yourself? As you become aware of what you uncover, use this information as an early warning system to help prevent you from becoming shut down in the future.

Moving into the Inner Sanctum

"I don't let things get to me."

Appearances to the contrary, Nines are actually the most withdrawn of all the types, although because their withdrawal is not physical, this is not as obvious as it is in other types. Nines continue to participate while withdrawing their attention from an active engagement with the world. They seek to create and maintain an Inner Sanctum, a private place in their minds that no one can tamper with. ("In here, I'm safe, and nobody can tell me what to do.")

Nines withdraw to this Inner Sanctum in times of anxiety and upset, or even when conflicts merely threaten. They populate their Inner Sanctum with idealized memories and fantasies; real people and the real world with their real problems are not allowed to intrude. Their Inner Sanctum is the one place Nines feel they can go and be free of the demands of others. Positively, this can allow them to remain calm in a crisis, but it can also lead to interpersonal problems and to a lack of self-development.

On the higher levels, this can manifest as an inner reserve of calm, as André recounts.

> Most of the time I feel calm and tranquil—a contained, safe feeling. I like that about being a Nine. For example, during a recent earthquake when my house sounded as if it were being ripped apart, I wasn't particularly frightened. I had guests in from New York, and I heard them yelling in the living room, but I felt as if I were observing the quake from some other plane. I actually found it rather interesting. It seemed pointless to get upset; I couldn't control what the earth was doing, so why worry?

The more they inhabit their Inner Sanctum, the more Nines lose themselves in hazy daydreaming. Obliviousness to what is going on around them gives them the illusion of peace and harmony, but they are increasingly absentminded, which only frustrates others and makes Nines less productive and capable. If they fall deeply into this trance, Nines may well have feelings for their loved ones, or even for strangers and animals in distress, but their feelings do not connect with meaningful action. Increasingly, their relationships occur primarily in their imaginations.

EXPLORING THE INNER SANCTUM

Your Inner Sanctum is calm, peaceful, and safe, but living there comes at a high price, as perhaps you are beginning to understand. Can you identify moments when you shift your attention into your Inner Sanctum? What are the elements or qualities of your Inner Sanctum that make it a safe haven for you? What are its unrealistic elements? Become more clear in your own mind about how much you would gain if you could stay engaged in the real world more often rather than seek sanctuary in your Inner Sanctum.

Idealizing Others in Relationships

Nines idealize others and live through a handful of primary identifications, usually with family and close friends. As one Nine put it, "I do not have to be in constant contact with somebody as long as I know they are there." As this continues, Nines begin to relate to the idea of the other rather than to the other as he or she actually is. For example, a Nine may idealize his family, but if one of his children actually has a drug problem or some other serious crisis, he will generally have a very difficult time dealing with that reality.

Idealization allows Nines to focus on someone else rather than on themselves. It also allows Nines to have a positive emotional reaction toward others, satisfying their superego message. ("You are good or okay as long as those around you are good or okay.") Idealizing Nines are often attracted to stronger, more aggressive people, looking to them to supply the "juice" in relationships. Their more energetic, dynamic friends and intimates provide them with the vitality that they tend to suppress in themselves. Often this unstated bargain works relatively well, since more assertive types generally look for someone to go along with their plans and adventures. Idealizing others also indirectly maintains (or even increases) their self-esteem: if an outstanding person is in some kind of relationship with them, their sense of self-worth is increased.

But there are three major dangers with this arrangement. First, Nines can be taken advantage of by these more assertive, independent, and aggressive types. Second, the more freewheeling, independent types will often lose interest in the more complacent and unadventurous Nines. Last, and most important, as long as Nines are trying to fill themselves by merging with the vitality of another, it is unlikely that they will do the work necessary to recover their own vitality.

FINDING YOUR HIDDEN STRENGTHS

Whenever you idealize someone in a relationship, notice what qualities about the other person you tend to focus on. Are these qualities that you feel you are missing in yourself? Remember that in your Essential nature, you already have these qualities—and that, from this point of view, the other person is simply acting as a reminder to you of what is blocked in yourself. Your idealizations can therefore act as a trustworthy guide for your own Inner Work to uncover and claim more of your own positive qualities.

Living by Formulas or a "Philosophy of Life"

"One day my ship will come in."

Average Nines increasingly rely on a "philosophy of life," which is usually a mixture of homey aphorisms, common sense, scriptural texts, and proverbs, as well as folk sayings and quotations of all kinds. These formulas give average Nines a way to deal with people and potentially upsetting or troublesome situations. They have ready-made answers for life's problems, but although their "answers" may be true in some circumstances, they tend to be simplistic and not allow for nuance or individual cases. The problem is that Nines use these airtight philosophies to shield themselves from upset rather than to guide them toward deeper truths or real understanding. Furthermore, many of the philosophies embraced by average Nines offer solace. ("I am God." "All is One." "Everything is love.") Without requiring any effort, they can then become excuses for further disengagement and passivity.

Less healthy Nines may use spirituality to defend a kind of fatalism, accepting negative or even damaging situations as if there were nothing that they could do about them. ("It's God's will.") Deeply defended Nines also dismiss their own intuitions, commonsense judgments, sense perceptions, and even personal experience and professional expertise in order to cling to what they wish to be true. It is as if they could ignore their own inner warning bells without consequences to themselves or others. They become prematurely resigned, trying to convince themselves and others not to worry about anything or to get upset. After all, the angels will take care of it.

AIRTIGHT PHILOSOPHIES

Whenever you "catch yourself in the act" of thinking or saying some kind of aphorism or proverb, notice two things. First, note what unpleasant or negative feeling you are using the saying to counteract. Can you move your attention into your body and become aware of whatever sensations you are feeling? Second, begin an exercise in which you see how the proverb is not true—that perhaps the exact opposite of it could be called for. Perhaps the real truth lies somewhere in the middle.

Stubbornness and Inner Resistance

Nines may well know that their attention and energy are required for their own self-development, for addressing problems, or for meaningfully engaging with others. But they feel an indefinable hesitancy, as if some extraordinary effort were required to participate more fully in their own lives. It all seems like too much trouble. Most of us can recall mornings in which we have been enjoying a pleasant dream but have to get out of bed and face some challenging task in the day ahead. We are often tempted to hit the snooze button to allow ourselves a few more minutes of pleasant dreaming. We may even hit the snooze button several times—enough to make us late. Average Nines have a similar mechanism in their psyches that causes them to postpone awakening.

The more others pressure average Nines to wake up and respond, the more they withdraw. They want to get people "off their backs," so they appease others, seeking peace at any price.

André talks about the futility of trying to stand up for himself against his mother's demands.

> The only thing that seemed to give my mother any satisfaction was decorating our home. A Four, she worked hard at making our ordinary suburban home distinctive. When it was time for my room to be decorated, she removed all my posters and replaced them with foil wallpaper in a variety of pastel shades. I felt erased. I hated it, but knew she wouldn't change it, so I just didn't get upset. It was a waste of energy to even become involved in a discussion with her about it.

Even though Nines tend to be accommodating, they have an inner core of stubbornness and resistance, a desire to not be affected by anyone or anything they see as threatening to their peace. Others may see such Nines as passive, although they internally harbor enormous strength and determination—in service of being left undisturbed. Beneath the surface calm, average Nines are brick walls; beyond a certain point, they are not going to budge.

While many Nines do not want to be changed or influenced by others, less healthy Nines also do not want to be affected by their own reactions to events. They feel that anything that could rock the boat is threatening. This includes not only negative emotions but, ironically, positive ones as well. Allowing themselves to get too excited about something can be as threatening to their emotional stability as a legitimate disaster.

Strangely, no matter how unpleasant the circumstances of their lives, less healthy Nines powerfully resist any effort to help them get out of them. Their patience has turned into grim endurance: life is to

"I'll deal with this a little later."

be gotten through, not to be lived, and certainly not to be actually enjoyed. What pleasures they allow themselves are used to distract them from their growing internal deadness. But eating snacks while watching reruns on TV, or hanging out with friends, or living vicariously through others cannot entirely cover the pain of realizing that their lives are stalled.

STOP POSTPONING YOUR LIFE

Take a few moments in your Inner Work Journal to inquire about the many different ways in which you postpone showing up more fully in your life. Where and how do you typically hit your snooze button? Are there particular conditions that trigger this behavior? At home? At the office? With particular people or circumstances? What conditions do you require to wake up?

Suppressed Anger and Rage

Lower-average Nines seem not to have an aggressive (or even an assertive) bone in their bodies. Underneath their outward appearance of contentment and neutrality, however, we often find a great deal of hidden anger and resentment that Nines do not want to acknowledge, much less deal with.

"The more you bring it up, the less I'm going to do it."

Anger is an instinctual response, and if it is not processed, it is eventually transformed into rage. If their rage remains bottled up, many other powerful human feelings and capacities—even the capacity to experience love—do, too. Average Nines fear that if they were to allow their rage to surface, they would lose the two most important things in their lives: their peace of mind and their connections with other people. Actually, the opposite is true. Once Nines become aware of it, repressed rage can serve as the very fuel they need to escape their inner inertia.

Nines are angry (rageful, negative) for a number of reasons, not all of them obvious. Subconsciously, they are angry because they feel that they do not have "space" to have a life of their own. They are so busy trying to accommodate everyone else and maintain harmonious relationships that a good deal of resentment builds up. They are also angry because they feel that others are continually upsetting them, trying to prod them into action when they want to be left alone, or reminding them of problems and difficulties when they would rather not think about them. Last, Nines are angry because others may have been abusive or have taken advantage of them in some way, and they have felt powerless to do anything about it.

Less healthy Nines have the tendency to become "doormats" and to passively suffer whatever others dish out. Average Nines freeze up whenever their instinctive self-protective responses are needed. They feel unable to defend themselves appropriately, to speak up for themselves, or to take timely action to further their own interests. Feeling powerless is one of the most powerful causes of suppressed rage.

We often think of anger as something negative. But the less understood positive side of it is its ability to sweep away the blockages that keep us locked in our old patterns. There is a salutary side to anger which might be called *holy anger*—the ability to put one's foot down, to draw a boundary, and to defend oneself. Much recovery work for Nines involves getting in touch with how clamped down their energy is and with allowing themselves to feel their anger.

INTEGRATING YOUR ANGER

You need to practice being okay with being angry and with seeing anger as a force that you have a legitimate right to experience and exercise. From a spiritual point of view, anger gives us the ability to say no—to protect ourselves from something we do not want to have in our lives. It will therefore be helpful if you could start by allowing yourself to say no to the things that you really do not want. If you feel guilty or fearful as a result, just note those reactions and stay calm and centered. Be mindful, however, of learning to say no in meaningful, legitimate situations: but if you err, err on the side of overdoing no-saying, at least for a while, until you become more practiced at it.

REACTING TO STRESS: NINE GOES TO SIX

▲

As we have seen, Nines attempt to manage stress by downplaying their own choices and desires and by retreating to their Inner Sanctum. When these coping skills are insufficient to contain their anxieties, Nines go to Six, investing themselves in ideas or relationships that they believe will give them more security and stability.

When worries and anxieties surface, Nines focus intensively on work and projects. It is as if, after letting things go for a while, they snap to and try to cover all of the bases at once in a high-pressured phase of frantic activity. At the same time, they are often highly reactive to the demands of others, becoming more passive-aggressive and defensive. Their positive "philosophies of life" crack to reveal the doubts and pessimism that they have been defending against. Also like Sixes, Nines under stress may bring up long-hidden complaints about others and their lot in life. While venting does temporarily lower their stress, its benefit is usually short-lived because Nines are still reluctant to come to terms with the roots of their unhappiness. Under extreme stress, they may develop a siege mentality. Paranoid suspicions can rapidly escalate into blaming others for their problems and reacting defiantly. Angry outbursts and displays of temper can be as surprising to Nines as they are to those who witness them.

THE RED FLAG: THE NINE IN TROUBLE

▲

If Nines have suffered a serious crisis without adequate support or coping skills, or if they have suffered from chronic abuse in childhood, they may cross the shock point into the unhealthy aspects of their type. This may lead them to a fearful recognition that the problems and conflicts in their lives are not going away and may even be getting worse—especially because of their own inaction. They may also be forced by reality to deal with their problems. (Despite the Nine's denial, the police bring a child home, or the spouse with a "slight alcohol problem" gets fired for drunkenness, or the lump in the breast has not gone away as hoped.)

Coming to these realizations, while terrifying, can be a turning point in a Nine's life. They may begin to turn their lives around and move toward health and liberation. On the other hand, they may become even more stubborn and determined to maintain the comforting illusion that everything is okay. ("Why is everyone trying to upset me?" "The more you bring it up, the less I'm inclined to do anything about it!") If Nines persist in this attitude, they may cross into the unhealthy Levels. If you or someone you know is exhibiting the following warning signs for an extended period of time—more than two or three weeks—getting counseling, therapy, or other support is highly advisable.

WARNING SIGNS

POTENTIAL PATHOLOGY: Dissociative Disorders, Dependent and Schizoid Disorders, anhedonic depression, extreme denial, severe long-term depersonalization

▶ Denial of serious health, financial, or personal problems

▶ Obstinacy and long-standing resistance to getting help

▶ General awareness and vitality dampened and repressed

▶ A sense of inadequacy and general neglectfulness

▶ Dependency on others and allowing themselves to be exploited

▶ Chronic depression and emotional flatness (anhedonia)

▶ Extreme dissociation (feeling lost, confused, deeply disconnected)

▶ While real humility is an admirable trait in human beings, it is not one that you have to work at. Learn to discriminate between genuine humility and the tendency to discount yourself and your abilities. In other words, remember the Nine's Social Role, Nobody Special, and notice when you are falling into it. You may feel overwhelmed by life's problems and that you have little to offer others, but a quick look at the discord, violence, and pain in the world may guide you to a quiet wisdom about what you *can* do. If there is an energy that is needed to restore a balance on this troubled globe, it is certainly the calm, healing, reconciling energy of healthy Nines. Know that when you are truly connected to yourself, you have all the power and capacity you need for whatever situation you face.

▶ Learn the value of the word *no.* It is quite natural to not want to disappoint others, but when you are presented with a proposition that you are uncomfortable with, it is better to make your misgivings known at the outset rather than silently acquiescing and regretting it later. Further, others are much more likely to be upset with you if you resist their plans passive-aggressively after you have initially agreed to them. Most people want to know what your real opinion or preference is—even if it seems unimportant to you at the time.

▶ Learn to recognize what *you* want from a given situation. Often you will be so busy taking into account the positions and views of others that you will tend to neglect your own. Because of this habit of mind, you may not know what you want immediately. If necessary, do not be afraid to ask others to give you a moment to consider the options. And don't be afraid to pursue the option you prefer when it arises. Remember that you are allowed to have wants.

▶ Take a tip from healthy Threes and invest time and energy in developing yourself and your talents. There are many pleasant, perfectly valid ways to spend your time, entertaining yourself or hanging out with friends or loved ones—but make sure you do not shortchange yourself by neglecting your own development. The initial struggles may bring up many of your anxieties about yourself, but the rewards of persisting in your development will be much greater and more deeply satisfying. Further, investing in yourself will not lead you away from your connection with others: everyone will benefit from a stronger, more fully actualized you.

▶ Notice when you are imagining a relationship with someone instead of actually relating with him or her. For most people, sitting on a couch with you while you daydream about a camping trip or a recent episode of your favorite TV show is not very satisfying. If you find that you are "checking out" with a particular person, you might well ask yourself if you are uncomfortable or angry with them about something.

PRACTICES THAT HELP NINES DEVELOP

▲

In any event, talking about it may help you reconnect with yourself and with them.

▶ Learn to recognize and process your anger. For most Nines, anger is very threatening. Of all the emotions, it feels like the one that can most easily destroy your inner peace. Yet it is only through anger that you will connect with your own inner power—it is the fuel that will burn away your inertia. This does not mean, of course, that you need to go around yelling at people and being aggressive with strangers. But it does mean that if you feel angry, it is all right to tell others that you are upset with them. Learn to *sense* your anger in your body. What does it feel like? Where does it register most strongly in your body? Becoming familiar with it as a sensation can help you to be less afraid of it.

BUILDING ON THE NINE'S STRENGTHS

▲

One of the greatest sources of strength for Nines is their profound patience: a deep "letting be" of other people that allows others to develop in their own way. This is the quality shown by a good parent who patiently teaches his or her children new skills while remaining at a respectful but watchful distance.

Nines' patience is supported by a quiet strength and tremendous endurance. They are able to "hang tough" through hardships and difficult experiences. Nines often report their ability to outlast flashier competition in work settings or in relationships—much like the parable of the tortoise and the hare. When they are healthy, Nines are able to work steadily and persistently toward their goals and often achieve them. Their willpower is liberated, and they discover incredible grit and stamina—as befits the type at the center of the Instinctive Triad.

Healthy Nines are also highly effective in handling crises because they have an extraordinary inner stability. The little ups and downs of life do not knock them off balance; nor do major problems, setbacks, and disasters. When everyone else is overreacting with anxiety, Nines become the still, calm center that moves ahead and gets things done.

André knows how simple—and how challenging—this can be.

Getting out of a period of malaise and numbness is simple: admitting to myself there is something wrong, then telling someone I trust how I feel. It is painful connecting with "messy" emotions, but doing so seems to diffuse them. Another strategy that helps is reconnecting with my body by going to the gym, getting a massage, etc. Having a dog has also been great for me. He is so "in the moment" and demanding of my full attention that it's hard to go into zombie mode.

Healthy Nines are extraordinarily inclusive of others, an especially important talent in today's diverse global society. (This indicates why Sixes who tend to be exclusive and to segregate people into "in" and "out" groups need to integrate to Nine.) While Nines see the good in others (and desire to merge with them), really healthy Nines can also see the good in themselves (and desire to become more independent and personally engaged with their world).

Although Nines are clearly interested in supporting others, they are not identified with the role of the Rescuer or the Helper. They are valued because they listen without judgment, offering others the freedom and dignity of a live-and-let-live philosophy. They are forgiving and give others the benefit of the doubt, always looking for the positive interpretation of a situation. Their ability to create space for others and to give everyone a fair hearing causes people to seek them out. They can entertain different points of view, but they are also able to take a firm stand when necessary. Their simplicity, innocence, directness, and guilelessness put people at ease and make others trust them.

In healthy Nines, differences of opinion, conflicts, and tensions are permitted and even valued. They often have the ability to arrive at a new synthesis that resolves the contradiction or conflict at another level. Thus, Nines can be highly creative, although they tend to be humble about their talents. Further, Nines typically like to express themselves nonverbally—through music, art, painting, or dance. They can be extremely imaginative and enjoy exploring the world of dreams and symbols. Nines think holistically and desire to maintain a sense of being at one with the universe. Myths are a way of talking about the larger themes of human nature and about the moral order of existence: in the end, everything is good and working out as it should.

"We can all get along."

Nines become actualized and remain healthy by learning to recognize their own Essential value, like healthy Threes. In effect, they overcome their Social Role, Nobody Special, and recognize that they are worth their own time and energy. They work at developing themselves and their potential and put themselves out in the world, letting others know what they have to offer.

The biggest obstacle to their self-actualization is their tendency toward inertia. Integrating Nines will frequently encounter feelings of heaviness or sleepiness whenever they try to do something good for themselves. But as they integrate, they will find their energy increasing, and with it their charisma. After thinking of themselves as invisible for most of their lives, integrating Nines are amazed that others not only listen to them but in fact seek them out. As they recognize their own value, others appreciate them more as well. As they reclaim the vitality

THE PATH OF INTEGRATION: NINE GOES TO THREE

▲

of their instinctual nature, they become energizing to others. Thus, as integrating Nines discover their innate value, they find it mirrored by other people, which surprises and delights them.

Integrating Nines also come in contact with their heart, the seat of their identity, and express themselves with a simple authenticity that can be very moving. They are able to assert themselves as they need to, understanding that self-assertion is not the same as aggression. Further, their resistance to reality falls away, making them more flexible and adaptable to circumstances.

Of course, integration for Nines does not mean imitating the average qualities of Type Three. Becoming driven, competitive, or image-conscious will do little to build genuine self-esteem—on the contrary, it will sustain their anxieties about their own worth and keep them dissociated from their true identity. But as Nines find the energy to invest in their own self-development, the love and strength of their own heart becomes an indomitable, healing force in their world.

TRANSFORMING PERSONALITY INTO ESSENCE

▲

"Unity is not something we are called to create; it's something we are called to recognize."

WILLIAM SLOAN COFFIN

Ultimately Nines reclaim their Essential nature by confronting their Basic Fear of losing connection and by letting go of the belief that their participation in the world is unimportant—that they do not have to "show up." They realize that the only way to truly achieve the unity and wholeness they seek is not by "checking out" into the realms of the imagination but by fully engaging themselves in the present moment. Doing so requires that they reconnect with their instinctual nature and with their physicality in an immediate way. Often this requires confronting repressed feelings of anger and rage that can be extremely threatening to their ordinary sense of self. But when Nines stay with themselves and are able to integrate their anger, they begin to feel the stability and steadiness that they have been seeking. From this platform of inner strength, actualizing Nines become indomitable forces, graceful and powerful and aligned with the Divine will. We can see such qualities in extraordinary Nines such as Abraham Lincoln, or His Holiness the Dalai Lama.

In order to achieve true connection and wholeness, this realm of mortal experience is what Nines must learn to accept and embrace. While it is true that there are many aspects of reality beyond the manifest world, we do not become realized by *negating* or denying that world. In other words, we cannot really transcend the human condition: only by embracing it fully do we arrive at the fullness of our true nature.

When Nines realize and accept this truth, they become extraordinarily self-possessed and independent. They learn to assert themselves more freely and to experience greater peace, equanimity, and contentment. Their self-possession enables them to create profoundly satisfying relationships with others because they are truly present to themselves—alive, awake, exuberant, and alert. They become dynamic, joyful people, working for peace and healing their world.

Far from being detached or repressed, they discover that they enjoy being engaged with life and make amazing discoveries for themselves, as Red notes.

> I know exactly what I need to say and do, and I have the strength and conviction to do it. I stop trying to please others and focus on pleasing myself. Strangely enough, this effort to meet my own needs very often meets the needs of the group, as if by concentrating on my own needs I have intuitively anticipated the needs of the group.

THE EMERGENCE OF ESSENCE

Nines remember the Essential quality of wholeness and completion. They remember the interconnectedness of all things—that nothing in the universe exists separate from anything else. This knowledge brings great inner peace, and the Nine's purpose in life, from an Essential point of view, is to be a living reminder of the spiritual nature of reality and, consequently, of the underlying unity of our true nature.

Liberated Nines are fully present to and conscious of the wholeness and unity of existence while simultaneously retaining a sense of self. Less healthy Nines have a capacity to perceive some of the boundless qualities of reality but tend to get lost in or merge with their surroundings. Liberated Nines do not forget themselves in these states or lose themselves in idealistic fantasies. They see how good and evil are mixed together. ("God sends rain on the just and the unjust alike.") They accept the paradoxical union of opposites—that pleasure and pain, sadness and joy, union and loss, good and evil, life and death, clarity and mystery, health and illness, virtue and weakness, wisdom and foolishness, peace and anxiety—are all inextricably linked.

This is a lesson that Martin, a business consultant, has come to for himself.

> When my wife died last year, I was devastated until I realized that her life and her death were all part of some larger event. Maybe one that I couldn't quite wrap my brain around, but one that seemed to be of a piece. Once I accepted the wholeness of her life, then her death was just part of that bigger whole, and I could and did accept it.

"Happiness—to be dissolved into something complete and great."

WILLA CATHER

Another Essential quality of the Nine is what Oscar Ichazo called "Holy Love," although this must be understood rightly. The Essential love to which we are referring is a dynamic quality of Being that flows, transforms, and breaks down all barriers before it. It overcomes feelings of separateness and isolation within ego boundaries, issues that plague the Instinctive Triad. This is why real love is frightening—it entails the dissolution of boundaries and the death of the ego. Yet as we learn to surrender to the action of Holy Love, we reconnect with the ocean of Being and realize that at our core, we are this Love. We are this endless, dynamic, transforming Presence of loving awareness, and it has always been so.

Add your scores for the fifteen statements for Type Nine. Your result will be between 15 and 75. The following guidelines may help you discover or confirm your personality type.

▶ 15   You are probably not a withdrawn type (not a Four, Five, or Nine).

▶ 15–30   You are probably not a Type Nine.

▶ 30–45   You most probably have Nine-issues or a Nine parent.

▶ 45–60   You most likely have a Nine-component.

▶ 60–75   You are most likely a Nine (but could still be another type if you are thinking too narrowly about Type Nine).

Nines are most likely to misidentify themselves as Twos, Fives, or Fours. Sixes, Twos, and Sevens are most likely to misidentify themselves as Nines.

PART III

▼

*Tools for
Transformation*

▲

CHAPTER 16

▼

THE
ENNEAGRAM AND
SPIRITUAL PRACTICE

▲

IN ITSELF, the Enneagram is not a spiritual path. It is an exceptional tool and a tremendous help to us for *any path* that we might be on. Nevertheless, the insights gained from it must be combined with some kind of daily practice. Practice grounds the information that the Enneagram provides in our daily experience, and it helps us return to the fundamental truths that the Enneagram is revealing to us.

Combining knowledge of the Enneagram with spiritual practice consists of:

1. Becoming present and aware as much as possible throughout the day
2. Seeing your personality in action
3. Not acting out your impulses

These three elements underlie all the other tools and practices in this book. Whenever we become aware of an aspect of our personality, we can remember to breathe and relax as much as possible while continuing to observe and contain our impulses until something shifts and our state changes. Analyzing what we find is not as important as awareness, relaxing the body, and not acting out.

Even though the Enneagram is not itself a complete spiritual path, it offers immense insight to anyone who is on a spiritual or therapeutic path of any kind. The insights into human nature it provides, particularly when the specificity of the Levels of Development are taken into account, are so "on target" that they cannot help but catalyze our growth.

CHOOSING A PRACTICE

The great religions of the world have provided a multitude of practices for personal transformation; so have modern psychology, the self-help movement, and contemporary spiritual thinkers. No matter what practice we choose—whether it is meditation, prayer, yoga, reading inspirational books, or another—there are three criteria for assessing its helpfulness for transformation.

First, does the practice assist us to become more mindful, awake, and open to our lives—or is it actually supporting our cherished illusions about ourselves, even negative ones? Does it cultivate a sense of Presence and emphasize the importance of being in contact with our life here and now?

Second, does it support us in exploring some of the uncomfortable aspects and limitations of our personality? Many paths offer a kind of "spiritual glamour," reassuring followers that they are somehow separate from and better than the mass of humanity and that they can soon expect to receive grandiose, cosmic powers. While attaining extraordinary powers is always possible, they are more often a distracting sidetrack than a mark of genuine realization. (On the other hand, any path that is continually shaming or judging us is also probably unbalanced.)

Third, does the path encourage us to think for ourselves? Growth comes from the desire to look more deeply into our own natures as well as into the nature of reality. Ready-made answers from gurus or hidebound doctrines of any sort discourage this process. Such "answers" may soothe our personality for a while, covering over our deeper anxieties and wounds, but their limitation is usually exposed when a real crisis comes along.

In fact, *life is our greatest teacher.* Whatever we are doing can be instructive, whether we are at the office, or talking to our spouse, or driving a car on the freeway. If we are present to our experiences, the impressions of our activities will be fresh and alive, and we will always learn something new from them. But if we are not present, every moment will be like every other, and nothing of the preciousness of life will touch us.

No single psychological tool or spiritual practice is right for everyone at all times. Our different states and conditions often require different choices. Sometimes our minds and hearts may be quiet, and we can easily engage in meditation, contemplation, or visualizations. At other times, we will be tired and find that we cannot meditate; at such times perhaps prayer or chanting, or a walking meditation, will be more helpful.

What type we are will also probably influence which practices we

"One of our problems today is that we are not well acquainted with the literature of the spirit. We're interested in the news of the day and the problems of the hour."

JOSEPH CAMPBELL

"Meditation is not a way to enlightenment nor is it a method of achieving anything at all. It is peace and blessedness itself."

DOGEN

will be attracted to. For example, the withdrawn types (Fours, Fives, and Nines), which are out of touch with their bodies, can benefit greatly from walking meditation, yoga, stretching, or even jogging. But because they often prefer more sedentary practices, people of these types might argue that these approaches do not count.

For Threes, Sevens, and Eights—the assertive types—getting in touch with their hearts through loving-kindness meditation and acts of charity may not match their idea of spiritual practice but can be invaluable. Similarly, these action-oriented people may think of meditation as "just sitting around and doing nothing."

Ones, Twos, and Sixes—the compliant types—might not consider going to a silent retreat or getting a massage to be spiritual. To these conscience-driven types, sitting in contemplation seems like the opposite of being dutifully concerned with the welfare of others. And yet anything done with attention can become the basis for a spiritual practice if it grounds us in our body, quiets our mind, and opens our heart. The practices and approaches we describe here help us to come into balance with ourselves.

SEVEN TOOLS FOR TRANSFORMATION

If we want to use the Enneagram on our journey of self-discovery, we are going to need more than interesting information about the nine types. This map of the soul can become useful only when we combine it with some other key ingredients. To this end, we offer seven tools that we have found to be indispensable for the spiritual journey.

1. *Seeking Truth.* If we are interested in transformation, no element is more important than developing a love of truth. Seeking the truth means being curious about what is going on in ourselves and around us, not settling for the automatic answers that our personality feeds us. If we observe ourselves, we will see that many of the stock explanations that we give ourselves for our behavior or for the actions of others are a form of resistance. They are a way of avoiding seeing more deeply into our current state. For example, one stock answer might be "I am really angry at my father," but a deeper truth might be "I really love him and desperately want his love." Both levels of truth might be difficult for our personality to accept. It could take a long time to admit that we are angry with our father—and even longer to acknowledge the love beneath the anger.

As we learn to accept what is real in the present moment, we are more able to accept whatever arises in us, because we know that *it is not the whole of us.* The truth encompasses both our fearful reactions *and* the greater resources of our soul. While our automatic reactions can derail our search for the truth, acknowledging their presence brings us closer to the truth.

"Prayer is not an old woman's idle amusement. Properly understood and applied, it is the most potent instrument of action."

GANDHI

"Inner freedom is not guided by our efforts; it comes from seeing what is true."

BUDDHA

"You will know the truth, and the truth will make you free."

JESUS OF NAZARETH

When we are willing to be with the whole truth—whatever it is—we have more inner resources available to deal with whatever we are facing.

2. *"Not Doing."* The process of transformation sometimes seems paradoxical because we speak of struggle and effort as well as of allowing, accepting, and letting go. The resolution of these apparent opposites lies in the concept of "not doing." Once we understand "not doing," we see that *the real struggle is to relax into greater awareness so that we can see the manifestations of our personality.* By neither acting on our automatic impulses nor suppressing them, we begin to understand what is causing them to arise. (An example can be found in Don's story in the Preface.) Not acting on our impulses creates openings through which we can catch glimpses of what we are really up to. Those glimpses often become some of our most important lessons.

3. *Willing to Be Open.* One of the primary functions of the personality is to separate us from various aspects of our own true nature. It causes us to limit our experience of ourselves by blocking from awareness any parts of ourselves that do not fit our self-image. By relaxing our bodies, quieting the chatter in our minds, and allowing our hearts to be more sensitive to our situation, we open up to the very inner qualities and resources that can help us grow.

Every moment has the possibility of delighting us, nurturing us, supporting us—*if* we are here to see it. Life is a tremendous gift, but most of us are missing it because we are watching a mental movie of our lives instead. As we learn to trust in the moment and to value awareness, we learn how to turn off the internal movie projector and start living a much more interesting life—the one we are actually starring in.

4. *Getting Proper Support.* The more support we have for our Inner Work, the easier our process will be. If we are living or working in dysfunctional environments, Inner Work is not impossible, but it is more difficult. Most of us cannot leave our jobs or our families so easily, even if we are having difficulties with them, although we can seek out others who give us encouragement and act as witnesses to our growth. Beyond this, we can find groups, attend workshops, and put ourselves in situations that foster our real development. Getting support also entails structuring our days in ways that leave room for the practices that nurture our souls.

5. *Learning from Everything.* Once we have involved ourselves in the process of transformation, we understand that whatever is occurring in the present moment is what we need to deal with right now. And whatever is arising in our hearts or minds is the raw material that we can use for our growth. It is an extremely common tendency to flee from what we are actually facing into our imagination, romanticizing or dramatizing our situation, justifying ourselves, or even escaping into "spirituality." Staying with our real experience of ourselves and our situation will teach us exactly what we need to know for growth.

"When Michelangelo was asked how he created a piece of sculpture, he answered that the statue already existed within the marble. . . . Michelangelo's job, as he saw it, was to get rid of the excess marble that surrounded God's creation.

So it is with you. The perfect you isn't something you need to create, because God already created it. . . . Your job is to allow the Holy Spirit to remove the fearful thinking that surrounds your perfect self."

MARIANNE WILLIAMSON

"Each object manifests some power of Allah. His joy or His anger, His love or His magnificence emanates through these objects. That is why we are attracted or repelled. There is no end to these manifestations so long as the process of creation exists."

SHEIKH TOSUN BAYRAK
AL-JERRAHI AL-HALVETI

6. *Cultivating a Real Love of Self.* It has been said many times that we cannot love others if we do not love ourselves. But what does this mean? We usually think that it has something to do with having self-esteem or with giving ourselves emotional goodies to compensate for our feelings of deficiency. Perhaps, but one central aspect of a mature love of ourselves is caring about our growth sufficiently that we do not flee from the discomfort or pain of our actual condition. We must love ourselves enough not to abandon ourselves—and we abandon ourselves to the degree that we are not fully present to our own lives. When we are caught up in worry, fantasy, tension, and anxiety, we become dissociated from our bodies and our feelings—and ultimately from our true nature.

True love of self also entails a profound acceptance of ourselves—returning to Presence and settling into ourselves as we actually are without attempting to change our experience. It is also aided by seeking the company of people who possess some degree of this quality themselves.

7. *Having a Practice.* Most spiritual teachings stress the importance of some kind of practice, be it meditation, prayer, yoga, relaxation, or movement. The important thing is to set aside some time each day to reestablish a deeper connection with our true nature. Regular practice (combined with participation in some kind of teaching or group) serves to remind us over and over again that we are hypnotized by our personality. Spiritual practice interferes with our deeply ingrained habits and gives us opportunities to wake up from our trance more often and for longer periods of time. Eventually we understand that every time we engage in our practice, we learn something new, and every time we neglect our practice, we miss an opportunity to allow our lives to be transformed.

A major obstacle to regular practice is the expectation that we will attain a specific result. Ironically, this obstacle is a problem especially if we have made significant breakthroughs with our practice. The personality seizes on breakthroughs and wants to re-create them on demand. But this is not possible because breakthroughs occur only when we are completely open to the present moment, while anticipating a certain payoff distracts us from such experiences. In this moment, a new gift or insight is available—although most likely not the one that was available last week. Furthermore, the personality may use our breakthroughs as justifications to stop practicing, saying, "Great! You've had a breakthrough! Now you're 'fixed' and you don't need to do this anymore."

Along with our regular daily practice, life presents us with many opportunities to see our personality in action and to allow our essential nature to come forth and transform our personality. But it is not enough merely to think about transformation or talk about it or read books about it. Procrastination is a great defense of the ego. The only time to use the tools of transformation is now.

"At the heart of it, mastery is practice. Mastery is staying on the path."

GEORGE LEONARD

WALKING YOUR WALK

If we are honest about being on a spiritual path, every day we must embody the truths that we understand—indeed, every moment of every day. We must learn to "walk our walk" in every area of our lives. And yet how are we to do this? Like everyone else (particularly at the beginning of our Work), we are riddled with bad habits, old wounds, and unresolved conflicts. Our intention alone to be on a spiritual path will not be enough to make much of a difference.

Because of this problem, spiritual teachers throughout history have given guidelines to their followers. Buddha recommended that people follow what is known as the "Eightfold Path"—Right Understanding, Right Thoughts, Right Speech, Right Action, Right Livelihood, Right Endeavor, Right Mindfulness, and Right Concentration. Moses brought the Ten Commandments to help the Jewish people live according to God's will. Christ upheld the Ten Commandments but also required of his followers that they live his two primary commandments—to "love God with your whole heart, and your neighbor as yourself." Since the Enneagram is nondenominational, no theistic commandments or statutes of ethics are attached to it. However, the question remains: "What do we mean when we say that we are on a spiritual path?"

In your Inner Work Journal, explore what this question means to you. What is your personal "minimum daily requirement" for being authentic about your spiritual work? What are your personal ideals in the matter? What do you sincerely require of yourself? To what are you actually committing yourself when you are "walking the walk" of transformation and human liberation?

Excuses—and More Excuses

A common excuse for people embarking on this journey is that they do not have sufficient energy to run their lives *and* engage in transformational work at the same time. Actually, we are given more than enough energy to transform ourselves every day, but we waste 98 percent of it on tensions, on emotional reactions unrelated to what is actually occurring, and on daydreaming and mental chatter. The fact is, our energy can go to one of two places: it may be poured into maintaining the structures of our personality, or if we disidentify with those structures, it may be liberated for our development and growth. As we begin to experience the truth of this firsthand, we understand the necessity of building our spiritual bank account, learning to keep some life-force in reserve so that transformation can take place.

Another major excuse for postponing inner work is due to the fact that our personality presents us with all sorts of "conditions" and "requirements" that interfere with our regular practice. ("I'll get serious about meditating as soon as I get all the other problems in my life straightened out, when the temperature is exactly right, when there is no noise, and everyone leaves me in peace.")

Conditions and requirements are just a form of spiritual procrastination, and if we listen to this inner voice, we may have a long wait, because the circumstances of our lives will never be perfect. Much as we

"One of the best means for arousing the wish to work on yourself is to realize that you may die at any moment."

GURDJIEFF

"I WILL BECOME PRESENT TO MY LIFE ONLY WHEN . . ."

1	"I have attained complete balance and integrity, make no mistakes, and have everything in my world sensibly organized. When I have achieved perfection, then I'll show up."
2	"I am loved unconditionally by others and feel their love. When others totally appreciate my affection and sacrifices and meet all of my emotional needs, then I'll show up."
3	"I have accomplished enough to feel successful and worthwhile. When I have all the admiration and attention I want and feel completely outstanding, then I'll show up."
4	"I have completely resolved all of my emotional issues and have found my true significance. When I am completely free to express all of my feelings with everyone whenever I want, then I'll show up."
5	"I feel completely confident and capable of dealing with the world. When I have completely understood and mastered everything I might need to know in life, then I'll show up."
6	"I have enough support to feel completely secure and stable. When I have every area of my life handled and nothing can take me by surprise, then I'll show up."
7	"I am totally happy and fulfilled and certain that I've found what I'm supposed to be doing with my life. When I feel completely satisfied, then I'll show up."
8	"I am totally independent and do not have to rely on anyone for anything. When I feel completely in control of everything and my will is never challenged, then I'll show up."
9	"I am completely at peace and without conflicts or problems. When nothing in the world bothers or upsets me, and everyone in my world is happy and at peace, then I'll show up."

Vitality
9
Magnanimity 8   1 Patience
Groundedness 7   2 Self-Respect
Confidence 6   3 Authenticity
Trust 5   4 Inner Calm

THE PAYOFFS OF PRACTICE

would like to, we cannot control all of our external situations. One thing we can do, however, is to show up regularly with Presence and awareness—the very thing that we most resist doing.

As you can probably tell, most of our conditions for Presence are never going to be met, at least not to our satisfaction. The irony is that when we actually do show up, we find the very qualities that we have been looking for. This is because those qualities are part of the world of Essence, not personality, and Essence can be experienced only when we show up in the present moment.

Finally, many of us resist opening more to life because *we are afraid that if we become too healthy, people will not know how much we have been hurt.* If we become healthy, we cannot continue to punish our parents (and other significant figures from our past) for making us suffer. If we are angry at a parent or a spouse, we overeat, or drink too much, or smoke to show them how unhappy we are. If we let these feelings dictate our lives, we have succeeded only in taking over the job of abusing ourselves.

The "Payoffs" of Practice

The qualities listed around the Enneagram are among the important payoffs—so to speak—we get for working on ourselves. The ego does not naturally possess any of these qualities (or "virtues," in more traditional terms). They are, in fact, the *opposite* of the state we are ordinarily in when we are identified with our personality. But when we learn to be present to the *blockages* to our Essence, these qualities start to emerge spontaneously and become available to us as they are needed—our ego does not direct their arising. We need do nothing (and in fact can do nothing) except see what stands in the way.

Facing Addictions

If we are actively abusing medications, alcohol, or controlled substances, the transformational work we are discussing here will not be possible. If we have a substance abuse problem, we need to become "sober" on a regular basis before we can sustain any in-depth inquiry into our true nature. If we are making it difficult for our bodies to function through abuse or neglect, it will be almost impossible to develop the sensitivity and attention necessary to observe ourselves with any clarity.

Fortunately, many resources are available to support us in breaking free of various addictions, including books, workshops, support groups, therapy, and even inpatient care. The Enneagram is not intended to be a substitute for those resources, but combined with

"There are many areas of growth (grief and other unfinished business, communication and maturing of relationships, sexuality and intimacy, career and work issues, certain fears and phobias, early wounds, and more) where good Western therapy is on the whole much quicker and more successful than meditation. These crucial aspects of our being can't be just written off as 'personality stuff.' Freud said he wanted to help people to love and work. If we can't love well and give meaningful work to the Earth, then what is our spiritual practice for? Meditation can help in these areas. But if, after sitting for a while, you discover that you still have work to do, find a good therapist or some other way to effectively address these issues."

JACK KORNFIELD

EATING DISORDERS AND ADDICTIONS OF THE TYPES

1	Excessive use of diets, vitamins, and cleansing techniques (fasts, diet pills, enemas). Undereating for self-control: in extreme cases, anorexia and bulimia. Alcohol to relieve tension.
2	Abusing food and over-the-counter medications. Bingeing, especially on sweets and carbohydrates. Overeating from feeling "love-starved." Hypochondria to look for sympathy.
3	Overstressing the body for recognition. Working out to exhaustion. Starvation diets. Workaholism. Excessive intake of coffee, stimulants, amphetamines, cocaine, or steroids, or excessive surgery for cosmetic improvement.
4	Overindulgence in rich foods and sweets. Use of alcohol to alter mood, to socialize, and for emotional consolation. Lack of physical activity. Bulimia. Depressants. Tobacco, prescription drugs, or heroin for social anxiety. Cosmetic surgery to erase rejected features.
5	Poor eating and sleeping habits due to minimizing needs. Neglect of hygiene and nutrition. Lack of physical activity. Psychotropic drugs for mental stimulation and escape, and narcotics and alcohol for anxiety.
6	Rigidity in diet causes nutritional imbalances. ("I don't like vegetables.") Working excessively. Caffeine and amphetamines for stamina, but also alcohol and depressants to deaden anxiety. Higher susceptibility to alcoholism than many types.
7	The type most prone to addictions: stimulants (caffeine, cocaine, and amphetamines), Ecstasy, psychotropics, narcotics, and alcohol. Tendency to avoid other depressants. Wear body out with effort to stay "up." Excessive cosmetic surgery, painkillers.
8	Ignoring physical needs and problems; avoiding medical visits and checkups. Indulging in rich foods, alcohol, tobacco while pushing self too hard, leading to high stress, stroke, and heart condition. Control issues are central, although alcoholism and narcotic addictions are possible.
9	Overeating or undereating due to lack of self-awareness and repressed anger. Lack of physical activity. Depressants and psychotropics, alcohol, marijuana, narcotics to deaden loneliness and anxiety.

them, it can be extremely helpful in understanding the roots of an addictive pattern.

All nine types can have any kind of addiction, and all nine types can be codependent. We do find some *tendencies* toward certain addictions in the Enneagram types, however, and we offer the following correlations as a beginning guideline. They are not all-inclusive and are not intended to be a complete discussion of this complex problem. (You will also be susceptible to the eating disorders and addictions shown in the box on page 351 for the type in your Direction of Disintegration, or stress, as well.)

WORKING WITH THE SUPEREGO

The superego is the inner voice that is always putting us down for not living up to certain standards or rewarding our ego when we fulfill its demands. When we comply with our superego, it pats us on the back, saying, "Good boy! (or girl!)" That was the right thing to do!" But when we do something that our superego disapproves of, it condemns us—this time in the first person. ("Look at what I've done! I can just imagine what those people must think of me!" "If I try that, I'm bound to fail again.")

If we rephrase these inner criticisms, replacing "I" with "you," we may recognize them as the harsh words that were first directed at us in our childhood. In fact, the superego is the "internalized voice" of our parents and other authority figures, both old and new. Its original function was to make us behave in ways that we believed would keep our parents loving and protecting us. We unconsciously identified with these voices and incorporated them into ourselves so that we would not run the risk of losing our parents' love and support. Rather than have our parents punish us (and therefore have to deal with the suffering that would cause), we learned to punish ourselves instead.

The problem is that even the parts of the superego that may have been useful when we were two years old are probably not very useful to us today. Nonetheless, these voices are just as powerful now as they were then but usually do more harm than good—alienating us again and again from our true nature. In fact, our superego is one of the most powerful agents of the personality: it is the "inner critic" that keeps us restricted to certain limited possibilities for ourselves.

A large part of our initial transformational work centers on becoming more aware of the superego's "voice" in its many guises, both positive and negative. Its voices continually draw us back into identifying with our personality and acting out in self-defeating ways. When we are present, we are able to hear our superego voices without identifying with them; we are able to see the stances and positions of the superego

"The remarkable thing is that we really love our neighbor as ourselves: we do unto others as we do unto ourselves. We hate others when we hate ourselves. We are tolerant toward others when we tolerate ourselves."

ERIC HOFFER

THE "MARCHING ORDERS" OF THE NINE TYPES

	Marching Order	*Contradiction*
1	"You are good or okay if you do what is right."	Sounds reasonable, but how do you know what is "right"? Who says so? Is your set of standards objective or subjective? Where did these ideas come from? Ones struggle to be good, but they are never good enough for their own superegos.
2	"You are good or okay if you are loved by others and close to them."	Why does your value depend on someone loving you, and how do you know if they do? Even if they don't, what has that got to do with you? Twos struggle to get closer to others but still feel unloved.
3	"You are good or okay if you do something valuable."	What makes you think that a particular activity makes you valuable? Why do you have to do something to feel valuable? How much do you have to accomplish to be worthwhile? Threes are often overachievers who feel empty inside.
4	"You are good or okay if you are true to yourself."	What does it mean to be "true to yourself"? What is this self that some other part is being "true" to? Does it mean holding on to old reactions and feelings? Fours try so hard to be unique that they cut off many of life's options.
5	"You are good or okay if you have thoroughly mastered something."	How do you know when you have fully mastered something? When are you finished? How does what you are mastering relate to the real needs in your life? Fives work on a subject or skill for many years and still lack self-confidence.
6	"You are good or okay if you cover all the bases and do what is expected of you."	How can you cover all the bases? Is all your scurrying around and worry really making you feel more secure? Is doing what's expected of you really meaningful to you? Sixes struggle to build up situations they can feel secure in, but they still feel anxious and fearful.
7	"You are good or okay if you feel good and are getting what you want."	Can you distinguish a need from a want? Would you still be okay if a particular need were not met? If so, is it really a need? Sevens pursue the things they believe will bring them satisfaction, but they still feel unsatisfied and frustrated.
8	"You are good or okay as long as you are strong and in control of your situation."	When do you know that you are strong and protected? How much control do you need? Is your drive for control really enhancing your sense of well-being? Eights pursue more and more control but still don't feel safe.
9	"You are good or okay as long as everyone around you is good or okay."	How can you ensure that everyone is really okay? How do you know that they are okay? Why is your well-being dependent on the prior well-being and happiness of others? The impossibility of this task leads Nines to "tune out" problems.

as if they were characters in a play waiting in the wings, ready to jump in and control or attack us once again. When we are present, we hear the superego's voice but do not give it any energy; the "all-powerful" voice then becomes just another aspect of the moment.

However, we must also be on the lookout for the formation of new layers of superego that come from our psychological and spiritual work. We might call these the *spiritual superego* or the *therapy superego*. Instead of berating ourselves with the voices of our parents, we berate ourselves with the voices of Buddha or Jesus or Muhammad or Freud or our therapist! In fact, one of the biggest dangers that we face in using the Enneagram is our superego's tendency to "take over" our work and start criticizing us, for example, for not moving up the Levels of Development or going in the Direction of Integration fast enough. The more we are present, however, the more we will recognize the irrelevance of these voices and successfully resist giving them energy. Eventually, they lose their power, and we can regain the space and quiet we need to be receptive to other, more life-giving forces within us.

The Superego's "Marching Orders"

Before that happens, we need to become aware of the superego's "marching orders." These marching orders, the meat and potatoes of our mental life, dictate most of our ordinary activities. Initially, some of these messages sound quite reasonable. (One of the hallmarks of superego messages is that they will make you feel "normal" but constricted.) However, if we listen more closely, we may see that they are not only arbitrary and subjective but also coercive and damaging. They present us with increasingly impossible standards to live up to, for which we always pay a heavy price. If we feel anxious, depressed, lost, hopeless, fearful, wretched, or weak, we can be sure that our superego is on duty.

Healing Attitudes

Another way we can begin to free ourselves from our superego is by becoming more aware of our automatic reactions to problems or conflicts—and then contemplating a "healing attitude." We have listed some healing attitudes for each of the nine types.

For one week, explore the healing attitude of your own type. See what it brings up for you in your relationships, at work, at home, and so forth. It may be helpful to record your observations in your Inner Work Journal. You may later wish to explore the healing attitudes of the other types.

HEALING ATTITUDES FOR THE TYPES

1	Maybe others are right. Maybe someone else has a better idea. Maybe others will learn for themselves. Maybe I've done all that can be done.
2	Maybe I could let someone else do this. Maybe this person is actually already showing me love in their own way. Maybe I could do something good for myself, too.
3	Maybe I don't have to be the best. Maybe people will accept me just the way I am. Maybe others' opinions of me aren't so important.
4	Maybe there's nothing wrong with me. Maybe others do understand me and are supporting me. Maybe I'm not the only one who feels this way.
5	Maybe I can trust people and let them know what I need. Maybe I can live happily in the world. Maybe my future will be okay.
6	Maybe this will work out fine. Maybe I don't have to foresee every possible problem. Maybe I can trust myself and my own judgments.
7	Maybe what I already have is enough. Maybe there's nowhere else I need to be right now. Maybe I'm not missing out on anything worthwhile.
8	Maybe this person isn't out to take advantage of me. Maybe I can let down my guard a little more. Maybe I could let my heart be touched more deeply.
9	Maybe I can make a difference. Maybe I need to get energized and be involved. Maybe I am more powerful than I realize.

WORKING WITH THE BODY

The body is extremely important for Inner Work, because it is a reliable reality check in ways that our minds and emotions (the other two centers) cannot be. This is because, as we mentioned earlier, *the body is always here,* in the present moment. Our minds or feelings can be anyplace—imagining the future, dwelling on the past, or ruminating on a fantasy—but our body is always here and now. It cannot be anywhere else. Therefore, if we are aware of the sensations of our bodies, it is a solid piece of evidence that we are present.

Eating Consciously

Most people have been exposed to the idea that a good diet and frequent, regular exercise are essential to a healthy life; yet we often forget these simple truths when we talk about psychological or spiritual growth. When we eat sensibly and get sufficient exercise and rest, our emotions are steadier and our minds are clearer, and our transformative processes go much more smoothly.

It is often difficult to be conscious and mindful of our eating habits. In fact, our ways of taking in food are among the most deeply habitual and unconscious aspects of our personality. Yet as we become more aware of how we eat, we often find that our personality leads us to eat much more (or much less) than our body requires. We may eat too quickly without tasting any of our food, or we may dawdle over it. We also may eat many things that actually disagree with us and be attracted to foods that do not serve our physical well-being. While many valuable diet plans and health regimens are available, clearly different kinds of people need to emphasize different things in their diets. For some, vegetarianism or a macrobiotic diet enhances their functioning and sense of well-being. Others require a high-protein diet. As in everything else, awareness can bring an intelligence and sensitivity to our eating patterns.

Relaxation

Perhaps the most important technique for getting in touch with the body and its energies is learning how to relax fully so that we can make deeper contact with each moment. Relaxation is not just something we do in yoga class or during meditation—it is a quality that we can bring to anything that we do. We can do anything in our lives from a place of centeredness and relaxation or from a state of being frantic and having inner tension. Basically, conscious relaxation is a matter of learning how to come back to the here and now again and again, opening up to a deeper and deeper impression of reality.

Many of us confuse numbness with relaxation, when in fact they are polar opposites. We may think that if we do not feel any soreness or tension, we must be relaxed. However, when our muscular tension is severe and long-standing, our body deals with it by numbing the muscles in question. In most of us, our tensions are so long-standing that much of our body has become numb and *we no longer feel our body.* We are literally walking around in painful knots of all kinds, but our numbness covers over the discomfort they cause. But as long as we are not feeling these tensions, they are not going to be released, and they eventually wear down our health and vitality.

Paradoxically, the more relaxed we become, the more we will real-

WORKING WITH THE BODY

There are a number of worthwhile approaches to working with the body, ranging from massage, acupuncture, and yoga to dance, tai chi, and martial arts. Any of these can be useful, but for them to have long-range effectiveness, you need to consider two things.

▶ How does your body respond to this treatment or practice? Do you feel more comfortable in your body? Does it enhance your flexibility? Is it easier for you to be present to yourself and your surroundings?

▶ Is this treatment or practice something that you can commit to doing for a while? Is it something that you will stick with long enough to achieve some lasting benefit?

ize how tense our bodies actually are. This can be confusing, *because our first experiences of relaxation will cause us to feel more uncomfortable.* Our first reaction will therefore be to want to become numb again, but our liberation requires that we stay present to whatever we find—including our tensions. When we do so with persistence, we find that our tensions miraculously begin to dissolve, and our personality becomes lighter and more flexible.

Seeing how easily we numb out, how do we know if we are truly relaxed? The answer is surprisingly simple: *we are relaxed to the degree that we can experience sensations from all parts of our body in the present moment.* To the degree that we do not experience the sensations of our body, we are tense and are not present. To be relaxed is to feel an uninterrupted flow of sensation through the body, from the top of our head to the bottom of our feet. Relaxation entails having full awareness of the self and the environment—to be in the river of Presence and Being. *We fully occupy our body:* we experience both the front and back of it and everything in between. But make no mistake—this kind of freedom, relaxation, and flow are the result of many years of consistent practice.

CULTIVATING THE QUIET MIND

If we become even a little more aware of ourselves, we will notice a constant reality: our minds are always chattering! There is barely a moment in our waking day in which some form of inner dialogue, commentary, or judgment is not going on. But who is talking to whom, and why?

One powerful reason that we talk to ourselves is to figure out what to do next. We talk to ourselves to assess our situation, to rehearse our responses to future events, or to replay events of the past. But with our attention taken up by this nonstop inner chatter, we cannot hear our own inner wisdom. The personality drowns it out. It is a bit like frantically looking around our home for our keys and suddenly realizing that they are in our pocket.

Nonetheless, the idea of quieting the mind initially strikes most of us as strange. We may believe that stopping our stream of mental associations will be boring—that everything will be similar and dull. But once again the opposite is actually true. It is the repetitive quality of our ordinary thinking patterns and of our predictable preoccupations that render the world dull, boring, and apparently lifeless. More importantly, our ongoing mental chatter blocks out the very impressions of life that we need for our growth and realization. For this reason, it is important to distinguish between "monkey mind"—inner chatter, worry, aimless imagination, visualizing future scenarios, or reliving past ones—and quiet mind, the mysterious space from which our knowing arises.

As we become more relaxed and aware, we understand that the "normal" way our mind operates is trancelike, unfocused, and chaotic, whereas the quiet mind has qualities of sobriety, clarity, and steadiness. In short, when our minds become more still and silent, our intelligence becomes aligned with a greater intelligence that understands our situation objectively and sees exactly what we need to do or not do. We are alert and attentive to everything around us. Our senses are sharp, colors and sounds are vivid—everything seems eternally fresh and alive.

Many meditation practices are designed to silence the inner chatter and bring about a more quiet, expansive mind. Centuries ago, Buddhist meditation practitioners identified two kinds of mind-quieting meditation. The first is called *vipassana,* or insight meditation, which develops our ability to be aware of whatever we are experiencing nonjudgmentally and with a simple openness. We allow thoughts and impressions to pass through our awareness without becoming attached to them.

The second branch of meditation is called *samata,* and it develops the capacities of concentration and focus. In these practices, we learn to focus on repeated sounds or syllables (*mantra*) or on an inner visualization or sacred image or diagram (*mandala*). The meditator learns to discipline the mind by concentrating on the sound or image to the exclusion of all other thoughts. Although both of these approaches can be extremely valuable in the cultivation of quiet mind, we feel that *vipassana,* insight meditation, works particularly well in combination with the Enneagram as a way of nonjudgmentally observing our personality at work.

The Art of "Not Knowing"

One of the main tools for entering into the vivid immediacy of quiet mind is "not knowing." Ordinarily, our minds are filled with all kinds of opinions about who we are, what we are doing, what is impor-

"Pay no attention [to your thoughts]. Don't fight them. Just do nothing about them, let them be, whatever they are. Your very fighting them gives them life. Just disregard. Look through. You need not stop thinking. Just cease being interested. Stop your routine of acquisitiveness, your habit of looking for results and the freedom of the universe is yours."

NISARGADATTA

"Good-humored patience is necessary with mischievous children and your own mind."

ROBERT AITKIN ROSHI

A CENTERING MEDITATION

The following is an example of the insight style of mindfulness meditation. It is based on simple guidelines—staying with the impressions and sensations of the moment, following the breath, and staying in contact with the environment while keeping silent. Feel free to experiment and see what works best for you.

Select a place to sit where you can feel relaxed, open, and comfortable. The posture with which you begin makes a difference, because you want to be quietly attentive, and a tense posture will make this difficult. It is often helpful to sit with your feet flat on the floor with your neck and back straight but not tensed. You may want to loosen your shoulders so that your arms hang freely. If you wish, you can close your eyes. You want to sit in a way that honors the long, rich tradition of meditation from all the religious paths of the world and the central place it occupies for all the great souls who have embarked on this journey.

Once you have found a posture that allows you to be open, relaxed, and attentive, you take two or three deep breaths, drawing air deep down into your belly and letting it out slowly. Inhale several times, allowing your chest to fill up with air, then exhale, releasing tension from your body. As you do this, whatever stress and anxiety you feel begins to let go and you begin to become quieter inside.

As you become more quiet and as the voices in your head fade a bit, you may begin to notice different things about yourself and your surroundings. You may become more aware of being here in this place now. You may become aware of the sounds, smells, and temperature around you. You also may begin to be aware of your actual presence as you sit, and that your presence has a particular quality. Simply "check in" with your own experience more deeply. There is no place you are trying to get to, no finish line, no particular way that you are supposed to be, no inspiration or "spiritual feeling" you need to have. Just be aware of yourself as you are. If you are tired, you can be aware of your tiredness. If you are agitated, you can be aware of your agitation.

What impressions and sensations are coming to your body right now? Can you feel yourself sitting in your chair? Are you aware of your feet on the floor? What do they feel like right now? Are they cold or warm, tense or relaxed, tingling or without sensation? What is your presence like right now? Is it fast and revved up? Is it quiet and expansive? Is it thick and heavy or light and flowing?

As you continue to relax, certain tensions that you may be holding in your body begin to reveal themselves, maybe in a certain way you are holding your face, a certain tilt or cocking of the head and the neck. Your shoulders may be scrunched or out of balance with each other. Some parts of your body may feel blocked or numb. As you notice these things, do not react to them or try to change them in any way: simply allow your awareness to enter them more deeply.

Continue to sit silently observing yourself and your thoughts, deepening your ability to settle into yourself, fully inhabiting this moment, fully tasting your presence, and allowing something more profound and more essential in yourself to arise.

If you are new to meditation, begin by practicing for about ten minutes a day, ideally in the morning before your day gets under way. As you become more comfortable with the process, you may wish to extend the length of your meditation. In fact, the more you acquire the habit of daily meditation, the more you will probably want to increase your meditation time, since being in intimate contact with our Essential nature restores us in profound ways while laying the ground for bigger personal breakthroughs. Meditation becomes a respite and an oasis that we *want* to visit rather than something we *have* to do.

tant and not important, what is right and wrong, and how things ought to turn out. Because our mind is full of opinions and old thoughts, it has no internal space for a fresh impression of the real world around us. We learn nothing new. This also prevents us from really seeing other people—especially the people we love. We imagine that we really know people or even what they are thinking. Many of us know from experience, though, that to experience freshly someone we know can instantly transform our state and theirs. In some cases, this can save a relationship.

"Not knowing" involves suspending our opinions and letting our curiosity within the realm of quiet mind take the lead. We begin to trust a deeper wisdom in ourselves—knowing that what we need to know will arise if we remain curious and receptive. We all know what it is like when we are trying to solve a problem and cannot come to a solution by thinking more about it. Eventually, we give up and do something else, and then when we are relaxed and no longer puzzling over it, the answer pops into our head. The same is true for creative inspiration. Where do these insights come from? They come from the quiet mind. When we stop depending on the mental strategies that our egos have adopted for our survival, our "not knowing" becomes an invitation—a magnet that attracts higher knowledge to us in ways that can rapidly transform us.

OPENING THE HEART

Change and transformation do not—and cannot—occur without emotional transformation, without the heart being touched. We feel the call to transformation in our hearts, and only our hearts can answer. What moves us is "E-motion," the movement of our Essence, the movement of love. If our heart is closed, no matter how much spiritual knowledge we have accumulated, we will not be able to respond to the call; nor will our knowledge make any real difference in our lives.

An open heart enables us to participate fully in our experiences and to connect in a real way with the people in our lives. From our hearts, we "taste" our experiences and are able to discern what is true and valuable. In this respect, we might say that it is the heart, not the mind, that knows.

Healing Our Grief

The process of transforming the heart can be difficult because as we open it, we inevitably encounter our own pain and become more aware of the pain of others. In fact, much of our personality is designed to keep us from experiencing this suffering. We close down the sensitivity of our hearts so that we can block our pain and get on with things, but we are never entirely successful in avoiding it. Often, we are aware of our suffering just enough to make ourselves and everyone around us miserable. Carl Jung's famous dictum that "neurosis is the substitute for legitimate suffering" points to this truth. But if we are not willing to experience our own hurt and grief, it can never be healed. Shutting out our real pain also renders us unable to feel joy, compassion, love, or any of the other capacities of the heart.

The point of this is not to wallow in our sorrows. Spiritual work is not designed to make us masochists: the idea is to transform our suffering, not to prolong it. We do not need to take on any additional suffering; rather, we need to explore the roots of the suffering that we already have. We need to look beneath the defenses of our personality and to explore the fears and hurts that are driving us. As we have seen, the more suffering we carry from our past, the more rigid and controlling our personality structures will be, but they are not invincible. And despite what we may believe, our pain, though severe, can be relieved if we are willing to explore it a little at a time.

Fortunately, our Essence supports us in this difficult process of exploring the pain and fear underlying our personality. Whenever we are willing to explore the truth of our immediate experience without conditions or judgments, the Essential quality of *compassion* naturally arises and healing follows.

Compassion is not the same as sentimentality or sympathy or self-pity. Rather, it is an aspect of Divine love that melts all defenses and resistance when anyone's suffering is really seen. There is nothing the personality can do to create compassion, but when we are willing to be completely open and truthful about whatever we are truly feeling, it arises naturally and soothes our hurt. (We could say that truth without compassion is not really truth, and that compassion without truth is not really compassion.)

The Divine love that seeks to express itself in the world through us is a powerful force that can break through all of the old barriers and untruths that have accumulated in us. While we are certainly going to encounter considerable sadness and pain during the process of our Inner Work, it is immeasurably important to remember that *love lies behind it all,* both as the motivating energy and as the end toward which we are drawn.

About Forgiveness

One of the most important elements of spiritual progress is the willingness and ability to let go of the past, and this inevitably means wrestling with the problem of forgiving those who have hurt us in var-

"It seems impossible to love people who hurt and disappoint us. Yet there are no other kinds of people."

FRANK ANDREWS

"Don't you know that the original soul came out of the essence of God, and that every human soul is a part of God? And will you have no mercy on Him, when you see that one of His holy sparks has been lost in a maze, and is almost stifled?"

RABBI SHMELKE OF NIKOLSBURG

AFFIRMATIONS OF FORGIVENESS

I am willing to be willing to forgive myself for my mistakes.
I am willing to forgive myself for my mistakes.
I forgive myself for my mistakes.
I see my mistakes as opportunities for learning discernment and patience.
I thank life for giving me opportunities to become more wise and accepting.

I am willing to be willing to forgive my parents.
I am willing to forgive my parents.
I forgive my parents.
I see my parents as my teachers and my guides.
I thank life for giving me such good teachers for my development.

I am willing to be willing to forgive those who have hurt me.*
I am willing to forgive those who have hurt me.
I forgive those who have hurt me.
I see the hurt I have suffered as an opportunity to learn compassion.
I thank life for giving me a spirit that is forgiving and compassionate.

I am willing to be willing to let go of my pain and suffering.
I am willing to let go of my pain and suffering.
I let go of my pain and suffering.
I see my pain and suffering as places where my heart is open and alive.
I thank life for endowing me with a sensitive, open heart.

I am willing to be willing to let go of the limitations of my past.
I am willing to let go of the limitations of my past.
I let go of the limitations of my past.
I see my past as what needed to happen for me to become me.
I thank life for allowing me to be me through my past.

---

* You may, of course, substitute a specific name in this passage. For instance, "I am willing to be willing to forgive ————." You may also compose your own affirmations in this form, as the need arises. Begin each set of statements with "I am willing to be willing to . . ." Then narrow down the conditional quality of each succeeding statement until, in the third statement, you let go of the thing that has been holding you back. In the fourth statement, indicate a positive quality in the situation, and in the fifth, give thanks for having it happen to you. In the greater scheme of things, it may have been a blessing in disguise, or one of the most important formative experiences of your life.

ious ways. But how can we let go of hurts and resentments that bind us to our old identities and prevent us from moving on with our lives? Again, we cannot simply "decide" to forgive, any more than we can "decide" to be loving. Rather, forgiveness arises from our Essential nature and comes from a deeper understanding of the truth of our situation. It entails recognizing what is happening in ourselves and others at a deeper level than we have previously seen. It requires that we fully experience the depth of our resentment, hatred, and vindictiveness and our desire for revenge—without acting out these impulses. By exploring the background of our feelings about the person with whom we are angry and seeing precisely how these feelings are manifesting in us right now, we begin to loosen the structures that hold our resentments in place. Presence fills us and releases us from our bondage to the past.

> "Love your enemies, bless them that curse you, do good to them that hate you, and pray for them that use and persecute you."
>
> JESUS OF NAZARETH

THE ENNEAGRAM OF LETTING GO

After years of reflection on the transformative process, the two of us began to see that we spontaneously followed a particular sequence whenever we successfully observed and let go of a defensive reaction or limiting pattern. We saw that the letting-go part could not occur simply through our intention to get rid of a troublesome habit. It was not a matter of willpower. Nonetheless, there were many times when particular habits or reactions dropped away spontaneously—or so it seemed—and we wanted to find out what ingredients made it easier to let go of them. Because we knew, thanks to Gurdjieff, that the Enneagram can also be used as *a process model,* we organized our observations around the Enneagram symbol and created what we call *The Enneagram of Letting Go.*

"The Enneagram of Letting Go" is a practice that you can use at any time. It proceeds through nine steps corresponding to the nine points around the circumference of the Enneagram, *although these steps are not directly related to the personality types.* The diagrams at right illustrates the nine-step process. (Notice the first four start with "s," the second four with "r.")

The process always begins with point Nine, to which we have assigned the quality of Presence. Unless we have some degree of Presence, we will not be able to take even the first step. Presence allows us to see that we are in a state of identification in the first place.

Note that we must complete each point before we are able to move on to the next, and that the process is cumulative: we bring the qualities of the previous steps with us as we move to each new stage. With practice, the process of letting go accelerates as we

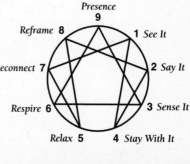

THE ENNEAGRAM OF
LETTING GO

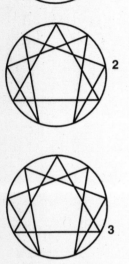

1 *See It*

2 *Say It*

3 *Sense It*

4 *Stay With It*

"The only way out is through."

A SAYING OF THE
TWELVE-STEP PROGRAMS

move through the first few points. Thus, having enough Presence to see that we are identified with some negative or unwanted state allows us to move to point One.

At point One, with the support of Presence, we are able to "See it." We see that we are identified with something—a view, a reaction, the need to be right, a pleasant daydream, a painful feeling, a posture—almost anything. We recognize that we are stuck in some mechanism of our personality and that we have been in a trance. This is the phenomenon that we have previously called *catching ourselves in the act*. It always feels like waking up and "coming to our senses."

At point Two, we consciously name the state we have just recognized. We "Say it"—"I'm angry," "I'm irritable," "I'm hungry," "I'm bored," "I'm fed up with so-and-so," "I don't like this." We simply and honestly name whatever state we are in, without analyzing it or judging it.

At point Three, the process shifts from our minds to our bodies. We "Sense it." Every intense emotional or mental state causes some kind of physical reaction in our body, some kind of tension. A person might notice, for instance, that whenever she becomes angry with her spouse, she clenches her jaw and gets tense in her shoulders. Another person might notice that when he is angry, he experiences a burning sensation in his belly. Yet another might discover that he squints whenever he is talking to himself. Fear might make us feel "electrified" or cause us to curl our toes or hold our breath. At point Three, we *sense* this tension—we do not think about it or visualize it—we simply sense what it feels like right now.

At point Four, we "Stay with it." We stay with the sensation of the tension or energy we have located in our bodies. The temptation at this point is to simply say, "Well, I'm angry and my jaw is clenched. I get the point!" However, if we do not stay with the tension, our state will not be released. Moreover, if we are able to stay with it, underlying feelings of emotional pain or anxiety may begin to arise. If this occurs, we need compassion for ourselves so that we will be able to stay present to these feelings.

It takes some time before we become interested in the simplicity of experiencing ourselves this way. We want the growth process to be more interesting and more dramatic, and we do not want to spend time with the pain of our tensions. Yet without doing so, any extraordinary experiences we have will have little real effect on how we live our lives.

At point Five, if we have gone through the first four steps, we will feel something opening in us and tensions dropping away. We "Relax." We will feel lighter and more awake. We do not force ourselves to relax; rather, by staying with our tensions and our sensations in point Four, we allow the process of relaxation to unfold in us.

Relaxation is not becoming numb or limp. We know we are relaxing when we experience our body and our feelings more vividly and more deeply. As we relax, we may uncover deeper layers in ourselves, and anxiety will often arise. This anxiety may cause us to tense up again, but to the degree that we can allow both relaxation and the sensation of our anxiety, the states that have been gripping us will continue to let go.

Relax **5**

Just as physical tensions dissipate when we sense them, stay with them, and relax, so do whatever emotional patterns that were creating them. *The action of bringing both tensions and emotional patterns into the light of awareness dissolves them.*

At point Six, we remember to breathe. We "Respire." This does not mean huffing and puffing as if we were practicing Lamaze. Rather, it simply means being more aware of our breath. We allow the relaxation from point Five to "touch" our breathing. This is important because *the more we are engaged with the concerns of our personality, the more constricted and shallow our breathing is.* (We might notice, for instance, that when we are in a slightly stressful situation—driving a car or dealing with pressure at work—our breathing becomes shallower.) Breathing grounds us and helps release blocked emotional energy. As our breathing becomes deeper and more relaxed, the pattern of our tensions continues to shift. We do not try to escape from whatever comes up for us emotionally but continue to breathe through it. As we do this, we may begin to feel the sense of ourselves expanding. We may feel more "real," more centered.

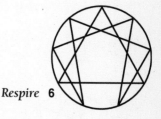

Respire **6**

At point Seven we "Reconnect" with a fuller sense of ourselves and the world around us. We start letting other sensory impressions come into our awareness. We might begin to notice sunlight on a wall, or the temperature and quality of the air. We might notice the texture and color of the clothing that we are wearing.

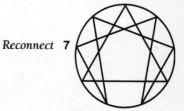

Reconnect **7**

Reconnecting means opening up to whatever part of our experience we were not previously allowing in. We discover that when we really connect with our experience, it does not have our usual associations attached to it. Our habitual goals, agendas, and internal scripts drop away. Suddenly we see and we hear, and we sense, internally and externally, with greater clarity.

If our problem has been with another person, we will not react to them in the ways that our habits have previously compelled us to. When we are entranced by our personality, we believe that we know what the other person is "always like" and what they will do, but when we reconnect with them, we realize how much we do *not* know about them. We appreciate and respect the mystery of their Being because we are more connected with our own Being. Once we allow ourselves to "not know" what the person is going to do or say, or what they are thinking, a much more real and immediate relationship with them becomes possible.

Reframe **8**

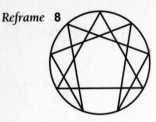

Presence
9

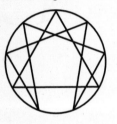

At point Eight, we "Reframe" the situation that we believed was causing our problems. We see our entire situation in a more objective light, and from this place of balance and clarity, we discover a way to handle it more effectively.

If we were angry with someone, for example, we may be able to see the hurt and fear of that person so that we can speak to them with more compassion and acceptance. If we have felt overwhelmed by a problem, reconnecting with something more real in ourselves gives us the ability to see that we actually are up to the task. Or we may see that we have bitten off more than we can chew and that we need to ask for help. In any event, reframing puts ourselves and our problems into a much broader perspective.

Finally, we return to point Nine, where we open to more Presence and, with it, increased awareness. From this increased capacity, it is much easier to go through these nine steps again if we need to.

Once we have started to use "The Enneagram of Letting Go," we may notice that we become stuck at the same place (or "point") in the process over and over again. For instance, we will see something, say it, and then go no further. We may even notice that we are tense, but then get sidetracked before we can stay with the tension long enough to release it. It can be extremely helpful to notice where we abandon the process, and we may want to give some added attention to that point.

As we continue to use this practice, it picks up momentum as we go around the circle, becoming easier and quicker. Also, the further along the sequence we are, the more difficult it becomes to separate the steps sequentially. We may find that we have to struggle more in the first part of the process, but *once we start moving toward Presence, Presence increasingly supports the activity.*

By practicing "The Enneagram of Letting Go," our fundamental experience of ourselves deepens and expands. We are more relaxed, alive, and connected with our own Being and with our surroundings, and more open to grace. We may well be astonished at how differently we experience ourselves compared with the state we were in before we went through this process. We have used the dross of personality and, by cooperating with something beyond ourselves, have turned it into gold.

CHAPTER 17

▼

THE SPIRITUAL JOURNEY—
ALWAYS NOW

▲

AFTER WE HAVE worked with this material for a while, we will no doubt see changes in ourselves, just as others will. We will likely be more at peace with ourselves, more grounded, and more forgiving of ourselves and others. Nonetheless, we may sometimes question the reality of our experiences, wondering whether our progress has mostly been an illusion, the product of self-deception or wishful thinking. There will be times when we will wonder, "Am I really making progress on my path?"

The Levels of Development provide one useful way of answering this question. If we see that we no longer exhibit the behaviors or hold the attitudes that we formerly did and that we are behaving in ways that are consistent with living at a higher Level, then we can be reasonably sure that we are moving in the right direction. For example, if we are a Four, we may have been withdrawn, negatively self-conscious, hypersensitive to criticism, and temperamental (all Level 5 behaviors). If we are now consistently more outgoing and able to not take things so personally while revealing ourselves as we are to others—and if we are also more energetic, creative, and focused outwardly (all Level 3 behaviors)—then we can be reasonably sure that our center of gravity has shifted and we have made some real progress. Likewise, if a Seven can see that she is less scattered and impulsive, that she is more focused and in touch with her own experiences and finds that life is more enjoyable due to being more selective, then some kind of real progress has been made.

But more subtle questions might still remain. We may think we are happier and better able to deal with life's ups and downs—and yet perhaps we are only more adept at dissociating from our surroundings and "spiritualizing" our experience. What is the truth? Are we better off now or not?

The way of love is not
a subtle argument.
The door there
is devastation.
Birds make great sky-circles
of their freedom.
How do they learn it?
They fall, and falling,
they're given wings.

RUMI
(TRANSLATED BY
COLEMAN BARKS)

The answer lies in *seeing our spontaneous reactions in a variety of circumstances,* particularly in those that formerly provoked negative responses from us. If the people and situations that once brought out the worst in us no longer do, then we can be sure that we have made real progress. If we formerly lost our patience or compassion whenever we dealt with a particular person or circumstance and we no longer do, then we can be sure that we have made real progress. If life becomes easier, more expansive and zestful, an unending adventure instead of something we must "get through" until it is over, then we can be sure that we have made real progress. If we find that we are grounded and open-hearted, and are able to bring the full force of our Being to the tasks of the day with the involvement of a curious child and the nonattachment of a disinterested witness—then we can be sure that we have made some real progress.

Moreover, the Enneagram itself points out sure markers of real progress: the high-functioning qualities—actually, the virtues—we find at Level 1 for each type are the keys that open doors on the spiritual path for us. To have any of them is sufficient—but to have access to them all is to have access to Essence at every moment and in all circumstances. Therefore, if we are accepting of our limitations and the limitations of others (from Type One), self-nurturing and unconditionally affirmative of the value of everything (from Type Two), authentically being ourselves with honesty and humility (from Type Three), renewing ourselves and enhancing the quality of life for ourselves and others (from Type Four), seeing the deeper meaning and context of all of our thoughts and actions (from Type Five), solidly grounded in reality and able to courageously handle whatever arises (from Type Six), joyous and grateful in the face of death, loss, and change (from Type Seven), large of heart and forgiving (from Type Eight), and all-embracing and solidly at peace no matter what life holds (from Type Nine)—then we can be sure that we have made progress on our path.

GIVING UP OUR SUFFERING

Gurdjieff said something strange and paradoxical—that the last thing human beings will let go of is their suffering. Could this possibly be correct? If so, why?

First, our suffering is familiar. It is what we know, and it therefore feels safer than some other unknown condition. Perhaps we are afraid that if we give up our own personal brand of suffering, some new and worse form will take its place. The second reason is probably a more important one, and it should not be underestimated. Much of our identity comes from holding on to our suffering, from all the complaints, tensions, conflicts, blaming, drama, rationalizations, projections, justifications, and "energy" that it allows. We could even say that it is the root of our personality. If our suffering—and everything that surrounded it—disappeared, who would we be?

If nothing were wrong with us, we would have to confront the fear of standing alone in the present, and we would have to take responsibility for ourselves. We would have to be willing to make choices and see them through to completion. There would be no more blame, no more stories about the past, no more schemes about the future. We would simply become a living human being facing the vast mystery of existence. In fact, we would simply become what we already are, only now we would fully acknowledge it and live out of that truth.

Until we reach full self-realization, the personality is going to keep shutting us down to some degree. It is important for us to expect this; otherwise we can get discouraged and give up. If we persist and keep showing up, however, even knowing that we are repeatedly going to fall asleep to ourselves, the situation will change. In time, our Essence will arise more frequently. With each awakening, something new is revealed until the whole picture radically shifts. Gurdjieff taught that the process is akin to adding salt to a glass of water: nothing seems to happen for a long while, until suddenly a saturation point is reached and a new crystal grows in the water.

If we refuse to be passive to the mechanisms of our personality, then we open ourselves to the Divine grace that is yearning to be active in us. As our Being gathers force, we become willing to let go of unnecessary suffering and become ever more deeply aware of the astonishing gift of life. In short, the degree to which we release our attachments and their attendant suffering is the degree to which we free our capacity for joy and for life itself.

Once we have entered this state, we understand the great poetry of the mystics—our journey feels less a struggle and more like being in love. Indeed, the Sufis describe the journey as a return to the Beloved. Nothing in life can fulfill us if we have not opened our hearts to our true nature, but if we have opened our hearts, then everything fulfills us. We then experience the world as an expression of infinite love.

Life Supports Us

Generally speaking, 99 percent of the time life is benign and supportive. The ego leads us to fixate on the 1 percent when it is painful, dark, or tragic—although even in these times, it is usually only painful and tragic to us. (Our tragedy might be someone else's good luck.) Although the mind imagines worst-case scenarios—like car crashes—most of our lives are not composed of these kinds of events. If we look

The minute I heard my first love story
   I started searching for you, not knowing
   How blind I was.

Lovers don't finally meet somewhere
   They're in each other all along.

RUMI
(TRANSLATED BY
COLEMAN BARKS)

SUBCONSCIOUS FEARS OF DROPPING THE PERSONALITY

The underlying reason that many of us fear becoming present is because we intuitively understand that doing so entails becoming less attached to our particular ego agendas.

Thus, each of the three Triads has a characteristic false belief about the necessity of continuing its ego projects, along with a subconscious fear of what will happen if these projects stop. These fearful beliefs will show up repeatedly as obstacles to Presence—as "reasons" to not let go of whatever we are identified with. The following are some of the subconscious fears associated with each Triad:

The Instinctive Triad (Types Eight, Nine, and One):

"If I let down my guard and relax into the flow of life, I will disappear. The familiar 'I' will cease to exist. I cannot protect my sense of self if I am truly open. If I really let the world in and allow it to affect me, I will be overwhelmed and lose my freedom and independence. I will be annihilated."

The Feeling Triad (Types Two, Three, and Four):

"If I stop identifying with this image of myself, my worthlessness will be revealed and I will lose the possibility of experiencing love. Deep down, I suspect that I am a horrible, unlovable person, so only by maintaining this ego project do I have any hope of being welcomed into the world or of feeling good about myself."

The Thinking Triad (Types Five, Six, and Seven):

"If I stop this strategy, if I stop figuring out what I need to do, the 'ground' will not be there to support me. The world cannot be trusted—without my mental activity I will be left vulnerable. Everything will fall to pieces—I will fall and be lost. If my mind does not keep 'swimming,' I will sink."

at our lives more objectively, we see that reality is actually highly supportive of us—a miracle, if we could see it for what it is. The universe is much more generous than most of us have ever recognized or acknowledged, and in the face of this overwhelming abundance, it simply makes sense to awaken and open ourselves to this generosity.

The world's great religions all teach that we are not alone and that we are supported in invisible ways and to a depth that we cannot imagine. In much of the Christian tradition, there is belief in the "communion of saints," a teaching that sees the entire community of Heaven constantly interceding on behalf of those still on earth. Hindus see the manifestations of God everywhere, in trees and lakes and mountains—as well as in storms and volcanoes—just as Buddhists see the infinite forms of Buddha-nature. The statues of Christian saints and innumerable bodhisattvas are reminders of this profound spiritual truth: that we are not alone, and that we are supported on our path in an infinite variety of ways.

One of the most famous temples in Japan is the Sanjusangen-do (The Hall of Thirty-Three Bays), dedicated to Kannon, the Buddha of Divine Compassion. What gives this temple its unique impact are the 1,001 gilded statues of Kannon arranged ten rows deep, stretching the length of two football fields inside the temple. It is a quietly overwhelming place, loaded with exquisite delicacy and force, reminding the visitor that the Absolute, God, continuously sends forth countless helpers and wave upon wave of grace to each human being, as well as constant blessings from the limitless depths of Divine compassion. The visitor is overwhelmed by this golden throng of the bearers of grace and goodwill from the world just outside of our ordinary perceptions.

We become aware of this benevolence slowly but inexorably: when we open ourselves to the present moment, everything becomes our teacher because everything in life supports our presence and our growth. The Enneagram shows us how we say no to life, how we turn away from the riches around us all the time. As the 1,001 statues of Kannon remind us, however, what we truly want and are always looking for outside of ourselves is always available here and now.

EXCAVATION AND RECOVERY OF THE TRUE SELF

One evening, on a late-night flight to California to give a training session, we began to reflect on the various stages of growth that we had been going through in our own inner work. Part of our discussion had to do with whether or not we would ever see the proverbial "light at the end of the tunnel," since each of us was constantly going through a fair amount of pain as we uncovered layers of neurotic habits and

"Bidden or not bidden, God is Present."

CARL JUNG

"Ask, and it shall be given to you; seek, and you will find; knock, and it will be opened to you."

JESUS OF NAZARETH

"Those who are awake live in a state of constant amazement."

BUDDHA

"The further you enter into the truth, the deeper it is."

ZEN MASTER BANKEI

unresolved issues from the past. We also wondered if the process of un-peeling the "onion" of our own psyches was unique to us, or if it could be generalized to others. We sat on the plane for several hours, sketch-ing observations and comparing experiences. By the time we landed, we had put together the following model, which we have continued to reflect on and refine over the years.

The answer that we ultimately arrived at that airborne evening was a resounding "Yes!" Our conviction that "excavating our true self" is an accurate description of the process of transformation has become more solid with the passage of time. Even though excavating the various strata of the psyche meant going through layers of pain and negativity, making conscious the old accumulated psychic junk that we had not wished to deal with, it would be worth it. It was possible to uncover our Essential Being, our "core of gold," that not only had been waiting for us but had been urging us on all along.

The work had to proceed layer by layer, as we dug past the outer structures of the personality and into the deeper core qualities of our true nature. As we worked this process ourselves for several years, we identified *nine distinct strata in the process of self-recovery.* These nine strata do not correspond either to the nine personality types or to the nine Levels of Development within each type. Think of them as the different "worlds" that you will encounter as you explore more and more deeply the Essential aspects of your spiritual nature—like nine layers of an onion.

As we reflected further on these strata and taught them for several years, we have not only become convinced of their truth and usefulness but have also seen that parts of them have been discovered by others working in other traditions. This map of the process of transformation brings together insights that everyone faces as they confront the uni-versal barriers to Inner Work.

First Stratum: Our Habitual Self-Image

This first stratum is composed of ideas and images of who we would like to be and how we automatically see ourselves. It usually con-tains a degree of grandiosity and illusion. For example, we may think that we never lie, or that we are never late for appointments, or that we always think first of others, and so forth. We may also have habitually negative views about ourselves: that we are unattractive or unintelligent or lacking in athletic ability. In the trance of personality, we seldom question these deeply held assumptions about ourselves, and we react easily and powerfully when others question or fail to support our (illu-sory) view of ourselves.

At the first stratum, the person is in the average-to-unhealthy range

"The true value of a human being can be found in the degree to which he has attained libera-tion from the self."

ALBERT EINSTEIN

(at Level 4 of the Levels of Development or lower). Unless the person is given some means of waking up (usually from outside of themselves), there is little hope of change, as the person is so deep in the trance of personality identification that they cannot wake up themselves. If we have misidentified our type (and, for example, we are actually a Nine instead of a Five, as we believed ourselves to be), we are automatically operating in the realm of the habitual self-image, *and it is almost impossible to do any meaningful transformational work with the Enneagram.* This is why it is crucial to get our personality type correct and to understand its inner workings clearly.

Second Stratum: Our Actual Behavior

If we enter the path of Inner Work and stay with the process of self-observation, we begin to notice that many of our behaviors are inconsistent with our habitual self-image. This realization allows us to attain the second stratum, in which we begin to "catch ourselves in the act." Our self-image may be that we always tell the truth, but we may begin to notice how often we tell white lies to avoid confrontations or to please people.

Fortunately, all of us have had spontaneous moments of waking up to the truth of our condition and to our greater possibilities. But to expand on these moments, we need to value them enough to seek out ways to stay more awake. This means looking for support for our inner work—through books, practices, friends, or more formal guides such as therapists or teachers. Staying at this stratum, much less moving on to deeper ones, requires that we increasingly cultivate the ability to be present. The deeper we go, the more presence we will need.

Third Stratum: Our Internal Attitudes and Motivations

If we persist on the path, we will begin to notice the attitudes and motives that lie behind our behavior. What is causing us to do the things we do? Are we doing things to get attention? Or because we are mad at our mothers? Or because we want to discharge our own pain or shame? Psychoanalysis and most forms of therapy aim at bringing this layer of the self to consciousness so that our behavior is not automatically governed by unconscious impulses. The more deeply we go into these questions, the more ambiguous the answers become, as it is often not possible to say precisely what "causes" a particular behavior.

At this stratum, we also see the depth of our learned behaviors and habits, and how many of them stretch back for generations within our family and our culture. Our type's motivational core (including and especially our Basic Fear and Basic Desire) is an important element that

> "The most common sort of lie is the one uttered to oneself."
>
> NIETZSCHE

keeps our automatic personality habits and reactions in place. In understanding our motivations, we also begin to glimpse what our soul is truly yearning for. Our motivations reveal what we think we lack and are therefore always seeking in one form or another.

Fourth Stratum: Our Underlying Affects and Tensions

As we become more deeply aware of ourselves in the present moment, we begin to discover what our felt experience is at that moment. For instance, at stratum 2, we might discover that we are pretending to be interested in a conversation at a party. At stratum 3, we might recognize that we actually want to leave the party, and at stratum 4, we might become aware of a feeling of restless agitation in our stomach, or a feeling of tension in our shoulders and neck.

If we are able to develop our ability to observe ourselves sufficiently, we will become aware of subtle layers of muscular and energetic tensions in our body, as well as areas in our body where our energy is blocked or absent. Relaxation and breathing become more important here. Stratum 4 requires considerably more ability to stay present to the sensations in the body than do any of the previous strata.

Fifth Stratum: Our Rage, Shame, and Fear and the Libidinal Energies

"Your resistance to change is likely to reach its peak when significant change is imminent."

GEORGE LEONARD

If we are able to stay with the processes we uncover in stratum 4, we will encounter more primitive—and possibly more disturbing—emotional states as we continue to go deeper. These include the three "master emotions" of the ego: *anger, shame,* and *fear,* which govern the Instinctive, Feeling, and Thinking Triads, respectively.

It is also in this stratum that we encounter the primitive instinctual energies (the basis of the Instinctual Variants) in their raw form—the drive for self-preservation, the drive for social connection with our fellow creatures, and the sexual drive. Primal affects of attachment, frustration, and rejection can also be recognized here. This stratum usually makes us extremely uncomfortable, which is why we need to also practice relaxation techniques and, above all, to be nonjudgmental about what we find in ourselves as we work through the issues that we uncover. Traditional psychotherapy tends to end at this stratum.

Sixth Stratum: Our Grief, Remorse, and Ego Deficiency

This stratum has nothing to do with guilt or the usual feelings of sadness and loss that we experience in our everyday lives. Rather, the heartrending sorrow and natural remorse we encounter here come from the clear perception of how deeply and completely we have been separated from our Essential nature.

This stratum therefore entails a considerable amount of "conscious suffering" that the seeker willingly allows for the sake not only of progress but of truth. The suffering experienced at this stratum is purgative in the purest sense of the word, burning away the last remaining illusions of the ego as they are clearly seen in the light of Essence and truth. There are no good guys and bad guys, and therefore there is no one to blame for one's state. When all is said and done, this stratum is experienced as a profound sorrow for the human condition, felt as an intense burning sensation, especially in the heart. In spiritual traditions, this stratum has been associated with the Dark Night of the Soul.

Seventh Stratum: Emptiness, the Void

This stratum has been described in many of the Eastern religious traditions, especially Buddhism. At this stage, we fully realize that our personality is nothing but a temporary fabrication, a story we have told ourselves for a long time. To leave the familiarity of our ego identity nevertheless feels like stepping into nothing, like walking off the edge of the world. It therefore takes faith of some kind to counteract the terror and despair that usually mark this stratum.

This stratum is experienced by the personality as its end, its death. If we have sufficient support and faith to persevere and make the leap, however, what we find is completely unexpected. Rather than experience the agony that the personality anticipates, what appears to the personality as "nothing" reveals itself as everything, the "shining Void" (called *Sunyata* in Zen) from which everything emanates. Everything that we know to exist arises from this Void; it is completely empty and yet full of potentiality. It is our freedom and the source of our life. There is no longer a distinction between the observer and the observed: experience and experiencer are one.

Eighth Stratum: True Personal Being

Within this state of emptiness, paradoxically, we still experience ourselves as personal beings, functioning effectively in the world, but our identity is centered in Essence and our actions are guided by Divine awareness rather than by the projects and preoccupations of our personalities. There is still a sense of personal, individual awareness, together with a great outpouring of personal love, gratitude, awe, and exaltation from the soul toward Being and its infinite manifestations.

"It is mind-boggling to think that spirituality is dying into yourself. But there is a death in it and people grieve. There is a grief that occurs when who you thought you were starts to disappear."

RAM DASS

"Grace fills empty spaces, but it can only enter where there is a void to receive it, and it is grace itself which makes this void."

SIMONE WEIL

This is the stratum in which we fully embody our personal Essential Being, which in some sacred traditions is referred to as the state of "I am." In Sufism, it is marked by identification with the personal Pearl, the Essential Self, as a personal expression of the Divine. In Christianity, this stratum marks the beginning of the attainment of the Beatific Vision, in which the individual self experiences an ecstatic realization of the Divine.

Ninth Stratum: Nonpersonal, Universal Being.

Little can be said about this state since it cannot be described in words; all phenomena, no matter how subtle or exalted, arise from it. If the seeker has been blessed enough to persist in his or her quest for the Divine, the soul will have finally found its destination in mystical union with God, or what some traditions call the *Supreme* or the *Absolute*. It is the attainment of complete nondual awareness, the total merging of the individual consciousness with God, so that there is only God-consciousness. The individual self and the Divine are one. This state of consciousness is beyond any sense of individual existence and manifests as nonpersonal Essential awareness, the limitless Being from which the manifest universe blossoms.

This is the ultimate destination promised by the great mystical traditions, but to attain this state of consciousness in any lasting way is extremely rare. Only some extraordinary mystics and saints of history have truly lived their lives from this profound state of awareness. But most of us can have at least a taste of it, and often that is enough. To taste this reality even once can change our lives in profound ways. Once we know the unity of existence as a real experience, we can never again regard people, ourselves, or the gift of our lives in the same way.

The Continuum of Consciousness

If we look back at these nine strata, we can see how they form a continuum from the realm of the imaginary, with little connection with reality, to the realm of the purely psychological and into the realm of the spiritual. Strata 1 through 3 are primarily psychological. Strata 4 through 6 include elements that are psychological (especially from depth psychology) but also elements that we would more generally place in the spiritual category. They are *psychospiritual*; our progress through them requires an integrated approach that uses both psychology and spirituality. We can see that strata 7 through 9 are concerned mainly with the realms of the spirit.

The Enneagram can be helpful primarily in strata 1 through 5 and is most powerful in the earlier strata (1 through 3). Strata 1 through 3

> "I sloughed off my self as a snake sloughs off its skin. Then I looked into myself and saw that I am He."
>
> ABU YAZID AL-BISTAMI

> "For the kingdom of God is within you."
>
> JESUS OF NAZARETH

help us move into the healthy range of the Levels of Development. Strata 4 through 6 help us to consolidate a healthy personality and begin the process of transferring our sense of identity from personality to Essence. Strata 7 through 9 involve the realization and maturation of the Essential self and deal with issues at Level 1 (of the Levels of Development) and beyond.

Our journey will take us through some challenging stretches, but we must remember that everything our heart really yearns for awaits us at the end of that journey.

> "The most radical re-mapping or shifting of the [self-] boundary line occurs in experiences of the supreme identity, for here the person expands his self-identity boundary to include the entire universe."
>
> KEN WILBER

BEYOND PERSONALITY

Essence Is Under Our Noses

Although it is true that we need to be patient and persistent during the process of transformation, experiencing our Essence is not as difficult as we usually believe. Indeed, one of the ego's main defenses against doing so is the belief that spirituality is something rarefied, impractical, and very far away. In fact, it is closer than we think, as the mystics assure us; we do not have to go anywhere or accomplish anything. What we must learn is *to stop running away from ourselves.* When we see ourselves as we really are—our truth and our falseness—we begin a process of *unlearning* the habit of abandoning ourselves and of living in illusions, reactions, and defenses.

The good news is that you are already here: your Essence already exists entirely and perfectly. The person who is reading this page does not have to do anything to make himself or herself real or "spiritual." Once we begin to see the reasons why we have abandoned ourselves and have left the moment, we run out of reasons to do so. Understanding our personality type helps us to be aware of these "reasons." When we stop trying to be someone we are not, our true nature emerges: we "observe and let go" and stop interfering with our unfolding; we stop defending a particular self-definition.

We do not need to learn something new or add anything to be our True Nature. Spiritual progress involves seeing what is right under our noses—really, what is right under the layers of our personality. Spiritual work is therefore a matter of subtraction, of letting go, rather than of adding anything to what is already present. From one point of view, this can be extremely challenging because the patterns of our personality have been so deeply ingrained in our Being. But from another perspective, we have the support of the whole universe in this Work. The Divine Consciousness wants us to do the Work and supports us in the process. Inner Work is therefore a continuing mystery and marvel to

> "...Self-realization [is] only the realization of one's true nature. The seeker of liberation realizes, without doubts or misconceptions, his real nature by distinguishing the eternal from the transient, and never swerves from his natural state."
>
> RAMANA MAHARSHI

> "...Where and when God finds you ready, he *must* act and overflow into you, just as when the air is clear and pure, the sun must overflow into it and cannot refrain from doing that."
>
> MEISTER ECKHART

see unfolding in ourselves and others. Always remember, however, that we cannot do it by ourselves, but without us, it cannot be done.

Moments That Live

The Buddhists say, "There are no holy people or holy places, only holy moments"—moments of grace. All of us have experienced such moments. True moments of grace, when we are fully alive and awake, have an entirely different quality, even in our memories, than other events that we might recall. Essential moments are much more vivid and real because they are still with us; they possess immediacy because the impact of life has penetrated the dullness of our consciousness and awakened us. We realize that as we learn to let go of fear, resistance, and self-image, we become more available to these transformative moments and they nourish our spirits. Thus, while we may not yet be able to produce such moments at will, we can create the conditions in ourselves that make it easier for us to have them.

What is most striking about these "moments that live" is that they do not require extraordinary events to trigger them. They occur quietly and often unexpectedly, at the breakfast table, on the commuter train, while walking down the street, or while talking with a friend. We personally have had some of the most fulfilling spiritual experiences while doing nothing more than looking at a doorknob, or really seeing the face of an acquaintance. The beauty of these kinds of experiences is overwhelming and life-changing. It is thus not what we do that makes the difference, but the quality of awareness that we bring to the moment.

Few things in life are more extraordinary than a living moment in which we are face-to-face with another person. To be truly open and present to another human being is awesome and sometimes overwhelming. Being authentically with another person helps to remind us that we are always in the presence of the Divine.

Toward Spiritual Maturity

For many of us, the initial stages of the spiritual journey involve seeking profound and dazzling experiences. We want intimations of the Divine, evidence of all that we have hoped for or have been taught. And if we are sincere in our practice, we achieve many of these experiences. We directly know compassion, joy, inner peace, strength, and will, among other true qualities of the soul. We may come to understand what the Buddhists mean when they speak of emptiness, or what the Sufi poets mean when they write of the Beloved; we may under-

> "The ultimate gift of conscious life is a sense of the mystery that encompasses it."
>
> LEWIS MUMFORD

> "There is nothing more worthwhile and more difficult than the fundamental human task of simply becoming human."
>
> JOHN MACQUARRIE

MOMENTS THAT LIVE

In your Inner Work Journal, write for thirty minutes about the moments of your life that had the most reality for you. What were they like? What were you like at such moments? Were these moments important events or ordinary events? How are they different from your other memories?

stand the mystery of Christ's resurrection in an entirely new and personal way. Yet unless these experiences are integrated as part of our daily lives, they remain little more than vague memories—grist for conversations or, worse, ways to impress our friends with our more "evolved" state.

If we stick with our practice, however, and continue to seek the truth of the situation, we come to realize that these sublime states are not extraordinary; nor do they indicate that we are more "special" than other human beings. Rather, we begin to understand that we are simply glimpsing reality. It is as fundamental as the sky and the sea—inextricable from human life. We realize that our vision is coming into focus and that we are now experiencing reality as it truly is. But because this reality allows us to experience our love, value, wisdom, and strength directly, we see that we no longer have to strive after these things; thus, we are no longer attached to specific possessions or outcomes. We can retire our ego projects with gratitude for bringing us as far as they did. At this stage, we are free to live as mature human beings, acting responsibly and compassionately in the world. This is the true meaning of the expression "to be in the world but not of it."

Not long ago, I, Russ, had a profound realization of this truth while on a spiritual retreat. At the time, we were engaged in a work period, not unlike the one Don described at the beginning of this book, and I had been assigned to wash windows for the afternoon. At this stage, I had been in dozens of such work periods, so the inner reluctance and resistance that once ruled me in such situations was not the main problem anymore. As difficult as it had been, I had learned to enjoy these periods as richly rewarding opportunities to gain insight into myself and to restore a greater inner balance.

I was working on the second floor of a dormitory, slowly and mindfully washing windows. Because this activity had nothing to do with my normal ego agendas, I was free to watch the mechanisms of my personality run wild while I attempted to stay present to my task. Wondering if I was doing a good job, hoping my teacher would notice my efforts, pondering the significance of the moment, and many other thoughts and fantasies played out in my head. Eventually, however, I noticed something more fundamental: I noticed that something in me

"There is no greater mystery than this, that we keep seeking reality though in fact we *are* reality. We think that there is something hiding reality and that this must be destroyed before reality is gained. How ridiculous! A day will dawn when you will laugh at all your past efforts. That which will be on the day you laugh is also here and now."

RAMANA MAHARSHI

"If we could see the miracle of a single flower clearly, our whole life would change."

BUDDHA

felt that it had to "keep track" of everything. I noticed that my mind was busy running the show, recording events, remembering important observations for later use, and at a deeper level, maintaining an orientation to my experience that felt not only familiar but necessary. In fact, I *was* this orientation.

At that moment, something remarkable happened. I saw that I did not really need to maintain that watchful orientation. I could relax and let go, and the windows would still get washed. Some inner tension relaxed, and suddenly my experience became immediate and unmediated by my mental activity. I was simply there as Presence: the window-washing was occurring, my body was moving and breathing, the leaves in the trees moved outside, everything flowed, but there was no sense of separateness. The world, including me, was a single, magnificently beautiful flowering or unfolding that went on and on and on. Yet all of this occurred within a vast, peaceful stillness that was undisturbed by this flowing, transforming play of reality. What I usually took to be the ground of reality—the everyday world—was indeed real but was more like the play of sunlight on the surface of the ocean. I could see the shimmering reflections on the waves but was also aware of the depth of the ocean beneath and knew myself to be at that depth.

As I left my task, the connection with this aspect of reality remained and deepened, such that I was able to interact with other people from this expanded sense of myself. I felt no need to impress others with this "achievement," because I could see that it was not really an achievement but simply an experience of the true nature of the world. Further, I could also see that everyone else was merely an aspect of this same nature, so whom would I be impressing?

What was most striking about this experience was that I saw that it was entirely possible to be aware of myself as a profound depth of Being, but also to function quite normally in the world—eating, conversing, working, and resting. Respecting and loving others came quite naturally because I actually experienced the true nature of the situation. In other words, realizing our true nature liberates us from the cravings and illusions of our personality, so that we are able to interact from moment to moment with simplicity, grace, and unshakable inner peace. We know who and what we are, and that endless inner restlessness ceases. We are free to accept the greatest and most precious gift of all: the unfathomable mystery of our Being, our very existence.

The Heroism of the Work

One of the most astonishing things we discover in exploring our habits, reactions, and inner voices is how many of them are inherited from our parents. Although many of us would like to see ourselves as

> "The unfolding of Essence becomes the process of living. Life is no longer a string of disconnected experiences of pleasure and pain but a flow, a stream of aliveness."
>
> A. H. ALMAAS

being totally different from our mother and father, the more closely we examine our attitudes and behavior, the more we see how many of their psychological issues and "solutions" have been passed down to us. Our parents, too, carried many of the issues and reactions of their parents— and so on back for generations.

From this perspective, we can see that when we bring awareness to our habitual personality, we are healing not just our own problems but also the destructive patterns that have been taking their toll for many generations, possibly for centuries, within our bloodline. Working on ourselves therefore redeems not only our own sufferings and struggles, but the sufferings and struggles of all our ancestors, which led to producing people who could be free of them. It is the same as when people became free after generations of slavery and realized that their freedom gave meaning and dignity to the struggles of all the generations that preceded them.

A further, perhaps even more compelling reason to do this Work is *to prevent destructive patterns from being passed on to the next generation.* For instance, we are becoming aware that many of our unconscious habits and attitudes about the environment or racism have reached a critical point. Consequently, many young parents are doing their best to embody new socially and environmentally aware values so that their children will not continue in the same destructive ways. From a personal as well as a generational perspective, therefore, working on ourselves is a noble act and parenting a child is a call to awaken—to see, to respond, and to give wholeheartedly. Raising a child is as close as most people get to being in a spiritual school, because parenting is bound to bring up all of one's own childhood issues. Often these issues are passed on either by repeating them or by reacting to them—*unless* we use the opportunity to work on ourselves, to overcome our issues and redeem our past.

Indeed, the work of releasing the habits of the past is a heroic endeavor. It requires tremendous courage to face our hurts, losses, anger, and frustrations; it takes real compassion to not flee from our suffering. Moreover, seeing the generational nature of our personality patterns makes it abundantly clear that our personal transformation has far-reaching consequences that we cannot always anticipate. In a very real way, when we work on ourselves we are taking part in the evolution of human consciousness.

Everyone is aware that something momentous is happening in the world today. While these intimations may be no more than reactions to the millennium, many of us feel that they reflect something more fundamental—the awakening of our collective consciousness. We know that we cannot, as a species, continue to live as we have and survive much longer. The time for rampant egoism, heedless

". . . Spiritual opening is not a withdrawal to some imagined realm or safe cave. It is not a pulling away, but a touching of all the experience of life with wisdom and with a heart of kindness, without any separation."

JACK KORNFIELD

"Our greatest need is to con-secrate life through being faithful to a deeper reality in ourselves. Can we see now that our prayer is for our birthright, lost and long forgotten, although not totally, for the memory of its taste is there, calling me, reminding me."

CHRISTOPHER FREEMANTLE

consumption, and grasping individuality is over. They have run their course, and we see the damaging results on a global scale. It may be that the Enneagram has been given to mankind in our era as a tool for accelerating the transformation of the individual ego self. Spiritual teachers around the world are speaking about the need for a shift in consciousness on the planet, and the two may be linked.

It may not be possible just yet to know where humanity is going, but if the Enneagram accelerates our awakening, then it will have pro-found and far-reaching effects. If even a few hundred individuals awak-ened and began to live fully conscious lives, the history of the world undoubtedly would change.

Transformation happens when our ordinary perspective shifts and we attain a new understanding of who we really are. We must remem-ber, however, that awareness of who we really are happens—as do all moments of grace—only *always now*. When all is said and done, this is the wisdom of the Enneagram.

►► *THE STAGES OF THE WORK*

*If we were to really observe ourselves,
we would become aware of our tensions and habits.*

*If we were to become aware of our tensions and habits,
we would let go and relax.*

*If we were to let go and relax,
we would be aware of sensations.*

*If we were to be aware of sensations,
we would receive impressions.*

*If we were to receive impressions,
we would awaken to the moment.*

*If we were to awaken to the moment,
we would experience reality.*

*If we were to experience reality,
we would see that we are not our personality.*

*If we were to see that we are not our personality,
we would remember ourselves.*

*If we were to remember ourselves,
we would let go of our fear and attachments.*

*If we were to let go of our fear and attachments,
we would be touched by God.*

*If we were touched by God,
we would seek union with God.*

*If we were to seek union with God,
we would will what God wills.*

*If we were to will what God wills,
we would be transformed.*

*If we were transformed,
the world would be transformed.*

*If the world were transformed,
all would return to God.* ◄ ◄

ACKNOWLEDGMENTS

Even teachers have teachers, and we are no exception. Some are not well known, some are known to everyone. It would be impossible to write any set of acknowledgments without remembering the Great Teachers who have most influenced us—Buddha, Christ, and Muhammad—as well as more contemporary teachers—Gurdjieff, Krishnamurti, Dogen, Jellaludin Rumi, Sri Aurobindo, and Sri Nisargadatta Maharaj. It is their spirit that has inspired this book and that, we hope, echoes through these pages.

We would also like to acknowledge and thank our personal teachers in the Great Work of human transformation—Jerry Brewster, Alia Johnson, and Hameed Ali (writing under the name of A. H. Almaas) for their guidance of us over the years. Their personal integrity, wisdom, and humor have been an inspiration and a great blessing. Above all, their humanity and the depth of their genuine spirituality have been a constant example of how to be "in the world, but not of it."

Through their ongoing questions, needs, and suggestions, our students and friends have been direct contributors to this project. Over the last three years of writing, we asked many of them to send us accounts of their experiences so that the book could resonate with the voices of real people. We would like to thank the following for their generous response: Brenda Abdilla, Sarah Aschenbach, Annie Baehr, Barbara Bennett, Ann-Lynn Best, Bryann Bethune, Nancy Boddeker, Marion Booth, Jane Bronson, Katherine Chernick, Mona Coates, Les Cole, Kate Corbin, Martha Crampton, Ginny Cusack, Jack DeSantis, Alice Downs, Robin Dulaney, Arlene Einwalter, Diane Ellsworth, David Fauvre, Rod Ferris, Peg Fischer, Cathie Flanigan, Lisa Gainer, Belinda Gore, Brian Grodner, Joe Hall, Anita Hamm, Paul Hanneman, Robert Harnish, Helen Hecken, Jane Hollister, John Howe, Andrea Isaacs, Ed Jacobs, Jim Jennings, Joan Jennings, Dan Johnston, Michelle

Jurika, George Kawash, Ann Kirby, Ken Kucin, Tomar Levine, Lori Mauro, Doris McCarthy, Gil McCrary, Colleen McDonald, Damon Miller, Maurice Monette, Leslie Moss, Tal Parsons, Connie Pate, James Peck, Gillette Piper, Marie-Anne Quenneville, Joyce Rawlings-Davies, Richard Reese, Joan Rhoades, John Richards, Sylvia Roeloffs, Tony Schwartz, Marin Shealy, Cynthia Smith, Dan Stryk, Lois and Bob Tallon, Vanessa Thornton, Kathleen Tomich, Terri Waite, and Gloria White. Their stories are true, but we have changed their names (and occasionally some details) to protect their privacy. We also thank members of the Japan Enneagram Association, especially Mr. Hayashi—as well as Tim McLean and Yoshiko Takaoka. Also our special thanks and acknowledgments go to our student and colleague Carl Dyer, who inspired our development of QUEST.

We would also like to acknowledge the tireless efforts of Dan Napolitano, the director of operations here at The Enneagram Institute, and of Brian Taylor, general counsel, for their support during the years that it has taken us to write this book. There were many days when we could not attend to the business of the Institute, and Dan and Brian filled in patiently, taking a great burden off our minds. Thanks also to Ampara Molina, Karl Goodman, M.D., and Rocky Knutsen, who each in their own way have helped to sustain our health and well-being.

Brian Taylor and Nusa Maal have also been tremendously supportive of both of us, as well as reliable sounding boards for advice at every turn. In a similar vein, we want to acknowledge the support of our agent, Susan Lescher, and our consulting editor, Linda Kahn, for her superb help in structuring the manuscript. We would also like to thank Toni Burbank, our editor at Bantam Books, for sharing our vision of bringing the Enneagram to the world through a practical book that would help people transform their lives.

Russ would also like to thank his parents, Al and Honey Hudson, as well as his sisters, Lorraine Mauro and her family, as well as Meredith Van Withrow and her family. I offer heartfelt gratitude to my friends Laura Lau Kentis, Russell Maynor, Steve Varnum, Molly MacMillan, Karen Miller, Maggi Cullen, Stacey Ivey, Tucker Baldwin, Peter and Jamie Faust, Mark Nicolson, Joan Clark, Richard Porter, Janet Levine, Nancy Lunney, Julia Connors, Lisa Morphopoulos, Butch and Wendy Taylor, Jerry and Vivian Birdsall, Paula Phillips, Randy Nickerson, Tony Schwartz, Deborah Pines, Lee and the staff at Mana Restaurant, Mark Kudlo, David Santiago, Alan and Kathy Fors, Franc D'Ambrosio, D.C. Walton, and Mindi McAlister. I also want to acknowledge my gratitude for the compassionate guidance I have received from Jeanne Hay, Scott Layton, Rennie Moran, Morton Letofsky, and Michael Gruber. Great thanks go to my friends in the Ridhwan School, for the countless moments we have shared on the Way. Thanks go also to my friends at La Rosita Restaurant for allowing me to take up tables with manuscripts day after day. I would also like to thank my grandmother, Meredith Eaton, who named me and welcomed me into this world. She passed on during the writing of this book, but her kind, gentle ways will long be remembered by all of us who knew her.

Last, I especially want to acknowledge the extraordinary blessing of my friendship with Don, who has consistently shown up in my life with unwavering support and love. Almost daily I am struck by Don's brilliance, eloquence, and humor and am deeply moved by his generosity of spirit and dedication to this Work.

Don would like to thank all of his students, family, and friends for their ongoing love and support. Since they have been mentioned in my previous books, I will not rename them here. They know who they are. (Many of them have also already been mentioned above as contributors of their personal experiences to this book.) Nevertheless, I would like to remember Ruben St. Germain, Geoff Edholm, Charles Aalto, Rick Horton, and Anthony Cassis in particular.

Last, although I have also thanked Russ in previous books for his friendship, I would once again like to acknowledge the blessings of that friendship, and to say that I am convinced that not only would my life be profoundly different were it not for Russ, but so would the future of the Enneagram. I believe that he is an extraordinary spirit who has been sent not merely to me but to the world as a significant spiritual teacher.

Above all, we both want to acknowledge the Divine Spirit who has, we believe, been the sustaining Presence throughout the years of effort that it took to write this book. For the support and guidance that we have received, we give thanks, and we rededicate ourselves, our work, and our lives to the Great Work of human liberation and transformation.

Don Richard Riso
Russ Hudson
August 1998

BIBLIOGRAPHY

Almaas, A. H. *Diamond Heart*. Vols. 1–4. Berkeley, CA: Diamond Books, 1987–1997.

———. *Essence*. York Beach, ME: Samuel Weiser, 1986.

———. *The Pearl Beyond Price*. Berkeley, CA: Diamond Books, 1988.

———. *The Point of Existence*. Berkeley, CA: Diamond Books, 1996.

———. *The Void*. Berkeley, CA: Diamond Books, 1986.

Andrews, Frank. *The Art and Practice of Loving*. New York: Jeremy P. Tarcher/Putnam, 1991.

Barks, Coleman, et al. *The Essential Rumi*. San Francisco: HarperSanFrancisco, 1995.

Beck, Charlotte. *Nothing Special*. San Francisco: HarperSanFrancisco, 1993.

Bennett, J. G. *Enneagram Studies*. York Beach, ME: Samuel Weiser, 1983.

Bradshaw, John. *Bradshaw On the Family*. Deerfield Beach, FL: Health Communications, 1988.

———. *Homecoming*. New York: Bantam Books, 1990.

Cameron, Julia, and Mark Bryan. *The Artist's Way*. New York: Jeremy P. Tarcher/Putnam, 1992.

DeMello, Anthony. *Awareness*. New York: Doubleday, 1990.

———. *The Way to Love*. New York: Doubleday, 1991.

Diagnostic and Statistical Manual of Mental Disorders, 4th ed. Washington, DC: American Psychiatric Association, 1994.

Epstein, Mark. *Thoughts Without a Thinker*. New York: Basic Books, 1995.

Epstein, Perle. *Kabbalah, The Way of the Jewish Mystic*. Boston: Shambhala, 1988.

Fremantle, Christopher. *On Attention*. Denville, NJ: Indication Press, 1993.

Goleman, Daniel. *Emotional Intelligence*. New York: Bantam Books, 1995.

Greenberg, J., and Stephen Mitchell. *Object Relations in Psychoanalytic Theory*. Cambridge, MA: Harvard University Press, 1983.

Guntrip, Harry. *Schizoid Phenomena, Object Relations, and the Self*. Madison, CT: International Universities Press, 1995.

Gurdjieff, G. I. *Beelzebub's Tales to His Grandson*. New York: Viking Arkana, 1992.

———. *Views from the Real World*. New York: Dutton, 1975.

Hales, Dianne, and Robert Hales. *Caring for the Mind*. New York: Bantam Books, 1995.

Halevi, Z'ev Ben Shimon. *The Way of Kabbalah*. York Beach, ME: Samuel Weiser, 1976.

Hanh, Thich Nhat. *The Miracle of Mindfulness*. Boston: Beacon Press, 1975.

Hinsie, Leland, and Robert Campbell. *Psychiatric Dictionary*, 4th ed. New York: Oxford University Press, 1970.

Horney, Karen. *Neurosis and Human Growth*. New York: W. W. Norton, 1950.

———. *Our Inner Conflicts*. New York: W. W. Norton, 1945.

Ichazo, Oscar. *Between Metaphysics and Protoanalysis*. New York: Arica Institute Press, 1982.

———. *Interviews with Oscar Ichazo*. New York: Arica Institute Press, 1982.

Isaacs, Andrea and Jack Labanauskas, "Interview with Oscar Ichago," Parts 1–3, *Enneagram Monthly*, Vol. 2, Numbers 11 and 12, 1996 and Vol. 3, Number 1, 1997.

Johnson, Stephen. *Character Styles*. New York: W. W. Norton, 1994.

Jung, C. G. *Psychological Types*. Princeton, NJ: Princeton University Press, 1974.

Kasulis, T. P. *Zen Action, Zen Person*. Honolulu: University of Hawaii Press, 1981.

Kernberg, Otto. *Borderline Conditions and Borderline Narcissism*. New York: Jason Aronson, 1975.

Knaster, Mirka. *Discovering the Body's Wisdom*. New York: Bantam Books, 1996.

Kornfield, Jack. *A Path with Heart*. New York: Bantam Books, 1993.

Krishnamurti, J. *The Flame of Attention*. San Francisco: HarperSanFrancisco, 1984.

Leonard, George, and Michael Murphy. *The Life We Are Given*. New York: Jeremy P. Tarcher/Putnam, 1995.

Lowen, Alexander. *Narcissism*. New York: Macmillan, 1983.

Mahler, Margaret S., Fred Pine, and Anni Bergman. *The Psychological Birth of the Human Infant*. New York: Basic Books, 1975.

Maslow, Abraham. *The Farther Reaches of Human Nature*. New York: Esalen Books, 1971.

Matt, Daniel. *The Essential Kabbalah*. San Francisco: HarperSanFrancisco, 1994.

Millon, Theodore. *Disorders of Personality*. New York: John Wiley & Sons, 1981.

Moore, James. *Gurdjieff: The Anatomy of a Myth*. Rockport, MA: Element, 1991.

Mouravieff, Boris. *Gnosis*. Vols. 1–3. Newbury, MA: Praxis Institute Press, 1989. Original French edition, 1961.

Napier, Nancy J. *Sacred Practices for Conscious Living*. New York: W. W. Norton, 1997.

Naranjo, Claudio. *Character and Neurosis*. Nevada City, CA: Gateways/IDHHB, 1994.

Nicoll, Maurice. *Psychological Commentaries on the Teaching of Gurdjieff and Ouspensky*. Vols. 1–5. Boston: Shambhala, 1955, 1980.

Nisargadatta, Maharaj. *I Am That*. Translated by Maurice Frydman. Durham, NC: Acorn Press, 1973, 1982.

Nott, C. S. *Teachings of Gurdjieff*. London: Arkana, 1961, 1990.

Oldham, John, and Lois Morris. *The Personality Self-Portrait*. New York: Bantam Books, 1990.

Olsen, Andrea, with Caryn McHose. *Body Stories*. Barrytown, NY: Station Hill Press, 1991.

Ornstein, Robert. *The Roots of the Self*. San Francisco: HarperSanFrancisco, 1993.

Ouspensky, P. D. *In Search of the Miraculous*. New York: Harcourt, Brace & World, 1949.

———. *The Fourth Way*. New York: Vintage Books, 1957, 1971.

Plotinus. *The Enneads*. New York: Penguin Books, 1991.

Powell, Robert. *The Wisdom of Sri Nisargadatta Maharaj*. New York: Globe Press Books, 1992.

Riso, Don Richard. *Discovering Your Personality Type*. Boston: Houghton Mifflin, 1992, 1995.

———. *Enneagram Transformations*. Boston: Houghton Mifflin, 1993.

———. *Understanding the Enneagram*. Boston: Houghton Mifflin, 1990.

Riso, Don Richard, with Russ Hudson. *Personality Types*. Boston: Houghton Mifflin, 1987, 1996.

Rudolph, Kurt. *Gnosis: The Nature and History of Gnosticism*. San Francisco: HarperSanFrancisco, 1987.

Rumi, Mevlana Jellaludin. *Jewels of Remembrance*. Translated by Camille and Kabir Helminski. Putney, VT: Threshold Books, 1996.

Satir, Virginia. *The New Peoplemaking*. Mountain View, CA: Science and Behavior Books, 1988.

Schimmel, Annemarie. *The Mystery of Numbers*. New York: Oxford University Press, 1993.

Schimmel, Solomon. *The Seven Deadly Sins*. New York: Free Press, 1992.

Scholem, Gershom. *Origins of the Kabbalah*. Princeton, NJ: Jewish Publication Society, Princeton University Press, 1962.

Shah, Idries. *Caravan of Dreams*. London: Octagon Press, 1968.

———. *Learning How to Learn*. London: Octagon Press, 1978.

———. *Tales of the Dervishes*. New York: Arkana/Penguin, 1967.

Shapiro, David. *Neurotic Styles*. New York: Basic Books, 1965.

Smith, Huston. *Forgotten Truth*. San Francisco: HarperSanFrancisco, 1985.

Speeth, Kathleen Riordan. *The Gurdjieff Work*. Berkeley, CA: And/Or Press, 1976.

Tart, Charles, ed. *Transpersonal Psychologies*. New York: Harper & Row, 1975.

———. *Waking Up*. Boston: Shambhala, 1986.

Taylor, Thomas. *The Theoretical Arithmetic of the Pythagoreans*. York Beach, ME: Samuel Weiser, 1983.

Tracol, Henri. *The Taste for Things That Are True*. Rockport, MA: Element, 1994.

Trungpa, Chogyam. *Cutting Through Spiritual Materialism*. Boston: Shambhala, 1973.

Walsh, Roger, and Frances Vaughn. *Paths Beyond Ego*. Los Angeles: Jeremy P. Tarcher/Perigee, 1993.

Wegscheider-Cruse, Sharon. *Another Chance*. Palo Alto, CA: Science and Behavior Books, 1981.

Wilber, Ken. *The Eye of Spirit*. Boston: Shambhala, 1997.

———. *Sex, Ecology, Spirituality*. Boston: Shambhala, 1995.

———. *The Spectrum of Consciousness*. Wheaton, IL: Quest Books, 1977, 1993.

A NOTE ON ENNEAGRAM BOOKS

Numerous books on the Enneagram are currently available. Readers have become confused, however, by the inconsistencies and contradictions among them. We feel strongly that Enneagram books about relationships, business, spirituality—or any other topic, for that matter—will be of little use if they are based on distorted notions of the types or of the Enneagram as a whole.

For better or worse, there is no such thing as "the Enneagram"—only different interpretations of it by different authors. Those interested in this system are therefore urged to read all Enneagram books (including our own) critically, to think for themselves, and always to judge everything by their own experience.

FOR MORE
INFORMATION

Your local bookstore can provide you with copies of Don Richard Riso's other books: *Personality Types* (1996, rev. ed. with Russ Hudson), *Understanding the Enneagram* (1990), *Discovering Your Personality Type: The New Enneagram Questionnaire* (1995, containing the *Riso-Hudson Enneagram Type Indicator,* RHETI questionnaire), and *Enneagram Transformations* (1993). To order the self-scoring offprint of the RHETI, or to have the RHETI interpreted by an Enneagram teacher trained and certified by Don Riso and Russ Hudson, please contact The Enneagram Institute at the address below for a free referral to a teacher in your area.

Don Richard Riso and Russ Hudson offer a comprehensive, three-part Enneagram Professional Training Program. The training is designed to equip serious students of the Enneagram to teach the system and to apply it in areas as diverse as personal growth, education, therapy, counseling, spirituality, business, and relationships. Please contact The Enneagram Institute for more information.

To contact Don Richard Riso and Russ Hudson for information about their Enneagram workshops, business seminars, new publications, and audiotapes, or to have your name added to their mailing list for workshops in your area, please contact:

The Enneagram Institute[SM]
222 Riverside Drive, Suite 10
New York, NY 10025
Telephone: (212) 932-3306
Fax: (212) 865-0962
E-mail: ennpertype@aol.com
Web site: www.EnneagramInstitute.com

© RUSSELL MAYNOR

DON RICHARD RISO, M.A., is one of the foremost writers and developers of the Enneagram in the world today. The most-published and bestselling author in the field, he is president of Enneagram Personality Types, Inc., and co-founder of The Enneagram Institute. He has been teaching the Enneagram for over twenty years and is a founding director of the International Enneagram Association. His four bestselling books are available in British, German, Italian, Japanese, Chinese, Korean, and Spanish editions. He was a Jesuit for thirteen years, holds degrees in English and philosophy, was elected to the Jesuit honor society, Alpha Sigma Nu, and was a Ford Foundation Fellow at Stanford in communication (social psychology).

© RUSSELL MAYNOR

RUSS HUDSON is one of the principal scholars and innovative thinkers in the Enneagram world today. He is executive director of Enneagram Personality Types, Inc., and co-founder of The Enneagram Institute. He has been co-teaching the Enneagram Professional Training Programs since 1991 and is a founding director and former vice-president of the International Enneagram Association. He assisted Don Riso in writing *Discovering Your Personality Type* and *Enneagram Transformations.* He is also the co-author of *Personality Types* (Revised Edition), *The Power of the Enneagram,* and of their forthcoming book, *Personality Types at Work.* He holds a degree in East Asian studies from Columbia University in New York, from which he graduated Phi Beta Kappa.